The Septuagint's Translation of the
Hebrew Verbal System in Chronicles

Supplements

to

Vetus Testamentum

Edited by the Board of the Quarterly

VOLUME 136

The Septuagint's Translation of the Hebrew Verbal System in Chronicles

By

Roger Good

BRILL

LEIDEN • BOSTON
2010

This book is printed on acid-free paper.

Library of Congress Cataloging-in-Publication Data

Good, Roger.
  The Septuagint's translation of the Hebrew verbal system in Chronicles / by Roger Good.
    p. cm. — (Supplements to Vetus Testamentum ; 136)
  Includes bibliographical references and index.
  ISBN 978-90-04-15158-1 (hardback : alk. paper) 1. Bible. O.T. Chronicles. Greek—
Versions—Septuagint.
  2. Bible. O.T. Chronicles—Translating. 3. Bible. O.T. Chronicles—Criticism, Textual.
  4. Greek language—Verb. 5. Hebrew language—Verb. I. Title.

  BS1344.G7G66 2009
  222'.6048—dc22

                                                                        2009043284

ISSN 0083-5889
ISBN 978 90 04 15158 1

Copyright 2010 by Koninklijke Brill NV, Leiden, The Netherlands.
Koninklijke Brill NV incorporates the imprints Brill, Hotei Publishing,
IDC Publishers, Martinus Nijhoff Publishers and VSP.

PRINTED IN THE NETHERLANDS

לֹא לָנוּ יְהוָה לֹא לָנוּ כִּי־לְשִׁמְךָ תֵּן כָּבוֹד

μὴ ἡμῖν κύριε μὴ ἡμῖν ἀλλ' ἢ τῷ ὀνόματί σου δὸς δόξαν

NON NOBIS DOMINE, NON NOBIS, SED NOMINE TUO DA GLORIAM.

Ps 115:1

TABLE OF CONTENTS

LIST OF TABLES

FOREWORD

This book deals with the Septuagint's (Old Greek's) translation of the verbs of Chronicles. It begins by investigating the cultural context of the Septuagint translators in terms of their background, task, and achievement, including a rationale for the translation's close following of the Hebrew. Due to a desire to educate the Jewish community in Alexandria and to mitigate the impact of Hellenization on the Jewish community, they followed a translation principle of bringing the reader to the source text as opposed to bringing the source to the reader. As a result, the Hebrew text with its word order and idioms was privileged over considerations of Greek style.

The book continues by looking at the Hebrew and Greek verbal systems and considers the historical linguistic context, particularly of the Hebrew language in terms of two registers, a written register that contains archaic verbal forms, such as the consecutive forms, and a spoken register that corresponds to the Hebrew that the translator would have spoken at the time of translation. It also mentions the text-linguistic features of both languages and their effect on verb choice.

The bulk of the book identifies and analyzes Greek equivalents chosen for the 4168 non-volitive Hebrew verb forms in Chronicles. These forms are distinguished in their use in main clause narrative, main clause reported speech, and subordinate clauses. By looking at the way Hebrew verbal forms were translated, we can get some insight into the Hebrew of the time of the translator, which was the primary influence on his understanding of the Hebrew verbs. In addition to this, he recognized, through the reading tradition and through his study, archaic meanings to certain verb forms (e.g., consecutive *wayyiqtol* forms that he translated as aorists). He also realized that the text-linguistic context dictated, or strongly suggested, the use of certain Greek verb forms (e.g., imperfects and perfects) that did not directly correspond to a particular Hebrew form. Occasionally he translated archaic Hebrew forms by Greek verbs that reflect an understanding that corresponds more closely to Hebrew of his time (e.g., translating *qotel* forms as present indicatives, especially in reported speech).

The penultimate chapter reworks the data, investigating the rationale for the choice of indicative Greek verb forms (including participles but not infinitives) to render the various Hebrew verb forms. One striking characteristic of his verb choice is the avoidance of circumstantial participles and historic presents to translate consecutive forms. The translator endeavored to be more literal than his predecessors in the translation of the Pentateuch and Samuel/Kings (who employed both forms), yet without going to the extreme of using the same common equivalent for each distinct Hebrew verb form, which would have resulted in a nonsensical translation. He was sensitive enough to use non-standard Greek forms where the context dictated or suggested them, and minor anomalies (minuses, pluses, and changes in word order, text types, and structure) reflect improvements or variations within a basically literal approach.

In conclusion, the translation of Chronicles (*Paraleipomenon*) slices through two diachronic developments: the development of the Hebrew verbal system and the trend toward a more literal translation of the Bible. Firstly, in the translation of Chronicles we can see the development of the Hebrew verbal system in the Hellenistic period (approx. 150 BCE) as part of the continuum in the development of the Hebrew verbal system from classical biblical Hebrew to rabbinic or Mishnaic Hebrew. Secondly, the translation of the book of Chronicles is part of a trend in the process of the translation of the Bible from the freer (but still literal) translation of the Pentateuch and Samuel/Kings to the slavishly literal translation of Aquila. This was motivated by the desire to bring the reader to the source text and an increasing reverence for the holy writings.

ACKNOWLEDGEMENTS

There are many that I would like to acknowledge in the completion of this book, a revision of my UCLA Ph.D. dissertation. Firstly, I would like to acknowledge my professors, especially the chair of my committee, William Schniedewind for his continual encouragement and direction. His suggestions were always helpful, and without them this book would have lacked clarity and would have been of less interest to the reader. I would also like to thank the other members of my committee: especially Professors Peter Cowe and James Barr, for their numerous helpful suggestions. I would also like to thank the faculty, staff, and students of the Department of Near-eastern Languages and Cultures for their help and encouragement over the years.

I would also like to thank my colleagues at Living Stream Ministry for their encouragement and support over the years, particularly Kerry Robichaux for his help and his inspiration and example in the field of linguistics and biblical languages, and for his scholarly integrity. Thanks also to Martha Ball for a careful proofreading of the manuscript and to Jerry Reimer for his reading and comments.

I would also like to thank the staff at Brill, Mattie Kuipers, Machiel Kleemans, Camila Werner, Liesbeth Hugenholtz, Saskia van der Knaap, and particularly Professor André Lemaire for his careful reading, help, and encouragement in preparing this book. Professor Hans Barstad also contributed some advice.

Thanks also to Professors Anneli Aejmelaeus, Trevor Evans, Robert Hiebert, Peter Gentry, James Aitken, and Anssi Voitila for their advice and helpful comments.

Last, but not least, I would like to express heartfelt thanks to the members of my family, my dear wife, Julie who endured this project with long-suffering and joy and my three children, John, Sarah, and Anna, who also bore me during various stages of this project.

Roger Good
Anaheim, California
July 2009

CHAPTER ONE

INTRODUCTION

This book investigates the translation of Hebrew verbs in Chronicles. The translation was influenced by two main factors: the translator's "philosophy" of translation derived from the cultural context and the translator's understanding of the Hebrew verbal system derived from the historical linguistic context. His "philosophy" of translation was influenced by his background, probably that of the Jewish community in Alexandria, and by precedents or examples of translation within that community.[1] The Septuagint translator's understanding of the Hebrew verbs of Chronicles was based upon the use of verbs in his own times (i.e., in spoken Hebrew) and upon his traditional understanding of the way archaic forms operated in the register of written biblical Hebrew. In addition, he realized that from the text linguistic context, he could derive finer distinctions of meaning (contextual meanings or implicatures) and convey these in the inventory of verbs of the target language.

I. THE PLAN OF THIS STUDY

In order to investigate the translator of Chronicles' understanding of the Hebrew verbal system, we first briefly survey other studies on the translation of Hebrew verbs into Greek in the Septuagint, comparing them with the approach of this study. Then we consider his background and "philosophy" of translation, the Greek and Hebrew verb systems, how the Hebrew forms were rendered into Greek, the rationale for choosing particular Greek forms, and how the resulting translation demonstrates the translator's understanding of the Hebrew verb system and reflects his philosophy of translation.

---

[1] The translator's "philosophy" of translation is not to be considered in the same way as in modern translation theory. Strictly speaking, the translator probably accomplished his task not governed by a "philosophy" but rather influenced by concerns of the community and translation precedents.

It seems that the philosophy of translation was to bring the reader to the source text, to preserve the nuances of the original as much as possible. It also appears that the translator wanted to make Chronicles closer to its source than prior translations of other books into Greek; in particular, the Pentateuch (using conjoined aorists rather than circumstantial participles used on occasion by the Pentateuch translators) and the sections of Samuel-Kings parallel to Chronicles (replacing historic presents with aorists). Chapter 2 deals with the Septuagint translators (in general) and their background, and how this influenced them in the carrying out of their task (including their philosophy of translation), and their achievement.

In translating from Hebrew into Greek, the translator realized that the languages do not have identical verb systems. It is not possible to find exact equivalents for each verbal form, and forcing the verbs into exact equivalents would produce a nonsensical translation. While the Hebrew verb system, as preserved in the text of the Bible, functions as an integrated system, there are actually two categories of verb forms—archaic and contemporary.[2] Archaic forms (as preserved in the written text of the Bible) such as the consecutive forms, probably no longer operated in the same way in the spoken Hebrew contemporary with

---

[2] This has also been noted by Joosten, that Hebrew writers of the late Persian and Hellenistic ages were "not dealing with one system of language, but with two: classical Hebrew as they knew it from the study of texts, and post-classical Hebrew, which was their natural medium of communication," Jan Joosten, "Pseudo-Classicisms in Late Biblical Hebrew, in Ben Sira, and in Qumran Hebrew," in *Sirach, Scrolls and Sages* (ed. T. Muraoka and J. F. Elwolde; Studies on the Texts of the Desert of Judah 33; Leiden: Brill, 1999), 149. We also believe that translator's understanding of the Hebrew verb system was also informed by the way that Hebrew verbs operated in these two systems. Similarly, Smith notes regarding the use of the *waw*-consecutive in Qumran literature, "two usages of tenses co-existed from the period of the monarchy down to Qumran: one was more formal and literary, and the other approximated more closely the spoken language. The use of tenses in speech eventually may have superseded the formal use of converted forms," Mark S. Smith, *The Origins and Development of the Waw-Consecutive: Northwest Semitic Evidence from Ugarit to Qumran* (Atlanta: Scholars Press, 1991), 63. It seems that a situation of diglossia (with an archaic written dialect and a colloquial spoken dialect) existed at the time of translation and perhaps extended back to classical Hebrew times. The written dialect corresponded more closely to the classical Hebrew preserved in the Bible, and the spoken dialect corresponded to Mishnaic Hebrew and was closer to what is preserved in reported speech sections of the Hebrew Bible (see chapter 4, note 150). We don't know whether the translators of the LXX/OG were speakers of Hebrew or not, and it is perhaps difficult to prove. It seems they would have had some exposure to spoken Hebrew through contacts with the Palestinian Jewish community, at least to be made aware of major features such as the different functions of verbal forms.

the translator. Other forms, such as the *yiqtol* future, function a similar way in ancient Hebrew as in spoken Hebrew contemporary with the translator. Chapter 3 deals with the two verbal systems. It looks at the inventory of verb forms in both languages and scholars' understanding on how they operate. It also briefly mentions how the verb forms operate in three different clause or text types: narrative main clauses, reported speech main clauses, and subordinate clauses (covered in more detail in chapters 4 and 5).[3] Chapter 3 also introduces the concepts of tense, aspect, *Aktionsart*, sentence topic and focus, discourse contexts, and clause types, indicating how they might influence the translator's verb choice.

Where possible the translator uses a common equivalent for each Hebrew form. He recognized the two categories of verb forms. Based upon his understanding of the current Hebrew spoken at the time of translation, he translated *qatal* forms with aorists (simple past), *qotel* forms with presents (in reported speech and subordinate clauses), *yiqtol* forms with futures, and periphrastic forms with periphrastic forms. Based upon the traditional understanding of archaic forms, he translated וַיְהִי with καὶ ἐγένετο, *yiqtol* duratives and preterites with imperfects and aorists respectively, and consecutive *wayyiqtol* and *weqatal* forms with καί + aorists and καί + futures, respectively. In addition, following the aforementioned translation principle, the translator mostly preserves the Hebrew word order, the distinction between paratactic and hypotactic structures, clause distinctions, and the time frame of actions. Chapter 4 looks at how each Hebrew indicative form, participle, and infinitive were translated into Greek. It briefly considers what the rationale might have been for each translation equivalent.

The resulting translation differs in verb use from the Greek texts contemporary with the translation mostly in the relative frequency of

---

[3] There is some variation in the literature as to what to call narrative, reported speech, and subordinate clauses. Niccacci calls narrative and reported speech "genres," Alviero Niccacci, "Analysis of Biblical Narrative," in *Biblical Hebrew and Discourse Linguistics* (ed. Robert D. Bergen; Dallas: Summer Institute of Linguistics, 1994), 175-98. Longacre calls narrative, hortatory, procedural, and instructional discourses "text types (genres)," Robert E. Longacre, "*Weqatal* Forms in Biblical Hebrew Prose," in *Biblical Hebrew and Discourse Linguistics* (ed. Robert D. Bergen; Dallas: Summer Institute of Linguistics, 1994), 50-98. Mostly, I use the terms *text types* or *clause types* rather than *genres* to refer to these three types of clause, so as not to confuse with the more common use of the word *genre* to distinguish literary genres, such as poetry and prose.

certain verb forms and structures. Greek verb forms and structures that occur more frequently in translation include aorist forms and structures such as καὶ ἐγένετο, paratactic clauses, and noun sentences. They occur because they are common equivalents or a result of closely following the Hebrew syntax due to the philosophy of translation.

Other verb forms and structures that occur less frequently are imperfects, perfects, pluperfects, and historic presents, circumstantial participles, and hypotactic clauses. However, these Greek verb forms are still used in translation because the translator recognized that Hebrew forms could have finer nuances in meaning in different contexts. Verb forms are sometimes constrained by the situation aspect or *Aktionsart* (the interrelationship between the meaning of the verbal root and its context) toward a particular form of the verb (e.g., εἰμί or certain stative roots only have imperfect past tense forms). The syntactic-pragmatic context may dictate or allow the translator to use rare or more marked verb forms to strengthen the topicalization or focusing of elements in the text. The discourse-pragmatic context may prompt the translator to highlight events (i.e., the foregrounding or backgrounding of certain events). Also the verb forms operate differently in three text or clause types (narrative, reported speech, and subordinate clauses). Occasionally the translator was an innovator or an improver of his original source, though he may not consider himself as such, (or perhaps the innovation is a reflection of his *Vorlage* compared with the Masoretic text—it is not always easy to distinguish the cause of the variant).[4] Chapter 5 goes through all the Greek indicative verb forms and participles, looking at how they function in three clause types and considering the rationale for their use by the translator according to these contextual gauges mentioned above.

Although he was driven by the translation philosophy of bringing the reader to the source (by using common equivalents and following Hebrew word order), he was flexible enough to produce a text that, for

---

[4] Occasionally the translator makes changes in word order, changes the paratactic structure to hypotactic or vice versa (e.g., relatives translated by attributive participles), and changes the genre and time sequences (reinterpreting archaic forms according to their use current to the time of translation). Sometimes he even adds or subtracts verb forms (including translating verbal with non-verbal forms and vice versa). Sometimes actions are foregrounded when they are not in Hebrew, (e.g., the translator moves the event line on more rapidly in his use of καί + aorist or καί + future for non-sequential, non-event line Hebrew forms) or vice versa.

the most part, was lucid and readable. His translation demonstrates that he understood the Hebrew verbs according to the Hebrew language spoken at his time, while having a traditional understanding of the archaic use of certain forms (derived from the reading tradition and study of the Hebrew text). By his use of non-standard equivalent Greek forms, he also displays an understanding of the range of meanings of the Hebrew forms dictated by the context. He not only made the source text available in Greek; he was an innovator, and even a storyteller, in that in a measured sense, he gave it a life of its own. The fact that the Greek translation endured attests that the translators handled the verbs appropriately and did not produce a nonsensical translation. Chapter 6 deals with the translation as a whole. It deals with the translator's understanding of the Hebrew verbal system according to his historical linguistic context, textual linguistic context, and cultural context.

II. PREVIOUS STUDIES

Until recently most of the previous work on the translation of the Hebrew verb in the Septuagint consisted of generalized surveys as part of a larger work, either of a grammar or of a study of translation technique that encompassed more than the verb.[5] In the past thirty years there have been a number of studies, mostly dissertations but also some important articles, on the translation of the Hebrew verb by the Septuagint (or Old Greek) translators.[6] The studies can be divided

---

[5] Such as Frederick C. Conybeare and St. George Stock, *A Grammar of Septuagint Greek: With Selected Readings from the Septuagint according to the Text of Swete* (Boston, New York: Ginn and Company, 1905), 68-80; Leslie C. Allen, *The Greek Chronicles: The Relation of the Septuagint of I and II Chronicles to the Massoretic Text: Part 1: The Translator's Craft* (SVT 25; Leiden: Brill, 1974), 41-43; and John W. Wevers, *Notes on the Greek Text of Exodus* (SBLSCS 30; Atlanta: Scholars Press, 1990), x-xiii, cf. the overview of previous studies in John H. Sailhamer, *The Translation Technique of the Greek Septuagint for the Hebrew Verbs and Participles in Psalms 3-41* (New York: Peter Lang, 1991), 10-16. In addition to these studies, there is the specific treatment of a particular verbal form, such as the study by Ilmari Soisalon-Soininen, *Die Infinitive in der Septuaginta* (AASF; Helsinki: Suomalainen Tiedeakatemia, 1965).

[6] The term *Septuagint* (abbreviated LXX) has been used in both its *original* sense to refer to the translation of the Pentateuch by seventy(-two) translators (cf. the *Letter of Aristeas*) and in its *enlarged* sense to refer to the entire translation of the Hebrew Scriptures into Greek (including apocryphal books). In this book, the term *Septuagint* is used mostly in its enlarged sense. The term *Old Greek* (OG) is used by many scholars to indicate the first translation of a book into Greek. See Jennifer M. Dines, *The Septuagint*

into two kinds: either the study focuses more on the translation from the perspective of the Hebrew verb and how it was translated, or it focuses on the translation from the perspective of the syntax and use of the verb tenses in translation Greek.[7] Three larger studies and a few important articles focus on the Hebrew verb forms and translation technique used to render them into Greek, while three other studies focus on the Greek verb forms and which Hebrew verb forms they translated. Interestingly, most of the studies that focus on the Hebrew verb looked at poetry and most of the studies focusing on the Greek verb looked at prose. A recent study by Beck (2000) also deals with the translation of verb forms, although his interest is more on the literary dimension of the translation.

The main task of a study of the translation of verbs is to identify the most common form or common equivalent used to render a particular Hebrew verb form (i.e., accounting for more than half of the forms), to identify other forms used to render the Hebrew verb form, and to indicate unusual or unexpected use of tense forms.[8] Most of the time a

---

(London: T&T Clark, 2004), 1-3, for a succinct treatment on the use of the terms *Septuagint* and *Old Greek*.

[7] This distinction of focusing on how the Greek represents the supposed Hebrew source or on how the Greek text reads in the target language (albeit with Hebrew interference) is similar to the recent distinction noted by Pietersma and others. Pietersma distinguishes between "the Septuagint *as produced*" which emphasizes "the process by which the target text was derived from its source" or "vertical dimension" and "the Septuagint *as received*" which emphasizes "its horizontal dimension…discourse analysis (or text linguistics)…analyzing its linguistic makeup," Albert Pietersma, "LXX and DTS: A New Archimedean Point for Septuagint Studies?" *BIOSCS* 39 (2006): 1-11 [3-6]. In terms of the framework of Descriptive Translation Studies (DTS) this distinction can be described as translation technique ("process") and textual linguistic makeup ("product"), together with the prospective slot ("function") of the text within its recipient culture (11). For an overview of DTS as it impacts the Septuagint see also the article by Gideon Toury, "A Handful of Methodological Issues in DTS: Are They Applicable to the Study of the Septuagint as an Assumed Translation? *BIOSCS* 39 (2006): 13-25. Also see Benjamin G. Wright, "The *Letter of Aristeas* and the Reception History of the Septuagint." *BIOSCS* 39 (2006): 47-67, who diagrams Toury's relations among function (position), product, and process (49), and applies Toury's scheme to the intended function of the Septuagint as portrayed in the *Letter of Aristeas* with the Greek text-linguistic makeup (product) (see chapter 2, especially note 14).

[8] Cf. Sailhamer who used the terms common equivalents, dynamic equivalence, and formal equivalence (borrowing the terminology of dynamic equivalence and formal equivalence from translation theory as outlined in Eugene A. Nida, in *Towards a Science of Translating*, (Leiden: Brill, 1964), chapter 2), and gave these terms a specific and nuanced definition in terms of translating the verbs, Sailhamer, *Translation Technique*, 21ff. Evans uses the term "matches", Trevor V. Evans, *Verbal Syntax in the*

common equivalent is the appropriate choice in the contexts that it occurs. However, in certain contexts the translators also employed other verb forms that were considered more appropriate.[9] When the verb tense form chosen by the translator (either a common equivalent or another verb form) fits the context (and is not an "obligatory equivalent"), it can be considered a case of "dynamic equivalence." When the translation seems awkward in the context, sometimes the translator "defaults" to the common equivalent, perhaps because of difficulty in understanding the Hebrew text or due to insufficient attention to the larger context, it can be called formal equivalence, which perhaps reflects a literalizing tendency.

Of the studies that focus on the Hebrew verb and translation technique, the main one was conducted by Sailhamer (in his 1981 dissertation published in 1991) who looked at the translation of the Hebrew verbs and participles in Psalms 3-41. He deals with problems with the *Vorlage*, the translator's exegesis, common equivalents, and specific rules that influenced the translator (such as obligatory equivalents, temporal markers, the influence of the Pentateuch, the influence of Aramaic, the use of an attributive participle to render a relative clause when the relative is the subject, the use of circumstantial participles, changing from parataxis to hypotaxis, formal equivalents—especially when there is uncertainty as to the meaning of the text, and verb forms not reflecting Hebrew verb forms or without any equivalent). He concluded that the translation was

---

Greek Pentateuch: Natural Greek Usage and Hebrew Interference (Oxford: Oxford University Press, 2001) xff., and Schehr the term "correspondences" along with the term "equivalents." Schehr labeled as formal correspondence certain structures that were uncommon or barely tolerable in Greek syntax, such as, καὶ ἐγένετο to introduce temporal clauses, λέγων to introduce direct discourse, προστίθημι used with an infinitive, participles (and nouns) from the same cognate stem with a finite verb, and the use of the participle ἀναστάς (rather than φέρε etc.) before an imperative, Timothy P. Schehr, "Syntax of the Moods and Tenses of the Greek Verb in Septuagint Genesis 1-15" (Ph.D. diss., Hebrew Union College, 1990), 73-74.

[9] Sometimes the equivalent is "obligatory." The translators were constrained by the target language to use a certain form because another form is lacking, for example, there is no aorist form of the verb εἰμί "to be," so an imperfect is used to indicate past time. This greatly increases the number of imperfect forms in the translation. Similarly, there is no present or aorist of the verb οἶδα "to know." Instead, Greek uses a perfect and pluperfect form in present and past time frames respectively. This also increases the number of perfect and pluperfect forms in the translation, but not nearly as significantly as εἰμί does to the imperfect forms. See section I.A in chapter 3.

literal but makes sense following the principle of dynamic equivalence.[10] Three additional studies that deal with the translation of verbs, although not exclusively, are Busto Sáiz (1978) Zuber (1986) and Gentry (1995). Busto Sáiz deals with Symmachus's translation of the Psalms. He looks at many aspects of the translation but includes a large section on the translation of all the verbal forms.[11] Zuber examined prefix and suffix forms of the verb in a varied and somewhat random corpus of the Bible in Hebrew and Aramaic and their translation in the Septuagint and Vulgate, using these ancient versions as the closest he could get to living informants for his theory of the Hebrew verb.[12] Gentry looks at the translation technique for various parts of speech, including a large section devoted to the translation of 402 finite verb forms, in the corpus of the revised Greek text (R or Theodotion) of Job. In comparing other studies, he observed a slightly higher percentage of *qatal* forms translated by aorists (86.1% or 87/101) and *yiqtol* forms by futures (74.6% or 176/236) and a slightly lower percentage of *wayyiqtol* forms translated by aorists (73% or 19/26) and only 33.3% or 2/6 *w*ᵉ*qatal* forms translated as futures (but 50% or 3/6 of them translated by aorists). He concludes that these results indicate, "the perspective of R towards the system of the verb appears to be that of Late Biblical Hebrew," with the breakdown of the system *qtl—wayyqtl* and *yqtl—wqtl*, especially "where *qtl* is mainly a past tense" (207).[13]

In addition to these four studies that deal with the translation of the Hebrew verb, there have been a few articles that deal with the

---

[10] Sailhamer, *Translation Technique*, 208-10.

[11] José Ramón Busto Sáiz, *La traducción de Símaco en el libro de los Salmos* (Madrid: CSIC, 1978). While Busto Sáiz does not deal with the Septuagint translation directly, the results of his study are interesting to compare with Sailhamer's (cf. note 24 below). He also compares Symmachus's translation of verbs with Aquila's, noting that there was very little difference between them in the way they handled the Hebrew verb forms (332).

[12] Beat Zuber, *Das Tempussystem des biblischen Hebräisch. Eine Untersuchung am Text* (BZAW 164; Berlin: Walter de Gruyter, 1986). Zuber's theory of the Hebrew verb returns to the traditional view of the *waw* conversive. However, he breaks with tradition in seeing the opposition between the suffix and prefix forms as indicative versus modal (future) rather than aspectual or just temporal. He considers that the ancient versions confirm his theory, although there are a number of anomalies, notably the use of the Greek present and imperfect to translate Hebrew verb forms.

[13] Peter Gentry, *The Asterisked Materials in the Greek Job* (SBLSCS 38; Atlanta: Scholars Press, 1995), 207. See note 24 below for the percentages in other studies. His observation agrees with my own, although it would be more significant if there were a larger number of *w*ᵉ*qatal* forms.

translation of verb forms in difficult or semantically ambiguous contexts. James Barr's article focused on the Psalms, particularly on Psalm 18 paralleled to 2 Samuel 22, comparing the Septuagint with Aquila, Symmachus, and Jerome in the same contexts. He noted the "normal" and "abnormal" ways to translate particular Hebrew verb forms, particularly Hebrew imperfects in past contexts and *waw* consecutive imperfects considered as future. He concluded that, while the translators displayed some consistency in literalism in translation, when it came to verb tenses, this was not always followed. The translators generally handled the tenses well, translating them according to the context, producing a translation that was readable, usable, and accepted.[14] Voitila, in contrast to Barr, in his first article uses examples of *qatal*, *wayyiqtol*, and *yiqtol* forms in the Pentateuch where the translators used a form that did not fit in the context but was in accordance with the normal equivalent of the Hebrew verb. He minimizes the influence of context on the way the translators handled tense forms and considers that the translators translated small segments at a time and sometimes seemed not to pay attention to the surrounding context.[15] In contrast to Voitila, Evans argues in another article that confused verbal renderings, due to paying insufficient attention to the context, are isolated phenomena and that when the Greek verbal context is considered many readings make sense.[16]

Three dissertations that focused more on the Greek verb forms and syntax all examined the Pentateuch. Schehr produced a syntax of moods and tenses of the Greek verb in the Septuagint of Genesis 1-15, first looking at how the Hebrew verb forms were rendered into Greek. He identifies true Hebraisms, idiomatic Greek structures (although

---

[14] James Barr, "Translators' Handling of Verb Tense in Semantically Ambiguous Contexts," in *LXX VI Congress of the International Organization for Septuagint and Cognate Studies, Jerusalem 1986* (ed. Claude Cox; SCS 23; Atlanta: Scholars Press, 1986), 381-403. The context includes the superscription for the Psalms which probably influenced Symmachus in his use of tenses, cf. Alison G. Salvesen, review of Claude E. Cox, ed., *LXX VI Congress of the International Organization for Septuagint and Cognate Studies, Jerusalem 1986*, *JSS* 34 (1989): 203-5, which includes comments on Barr's article.

[15] Anssi Voitila, "What the Translation of Tenses Tells About the Septuagint Translators," *SJOT* 10 (1996): 183-96, so also "La technique de traduction du *yiqtol* (l'imparfait hébreu) dans l'histoire du Joseph grecque (Gen 37, 39-50)," in *LXX VII Congress of the International Organization for Septuagint and Cognate Studies, Leuven 1989* (ed. Claude E. Cox; SCS 31; Atlanta: Scholars Press, 1989), 223-37.

[16] Trevor V. Evans, "Some Alleged Confusions in Translation from Hebrew to Greek," *Bib* 83 (2002): 238-48.

with different frequencies), and structures that are compatible with classical, Hellenistic, and New Testament Greek. The translation contains many formal correspondences (conforming to Hebrew syntax), which were balanced by dynamic equivalents according with Greek idiom.[17] Schehr concluded that the Greek of the Pentateuch exhibits characteristics of Hellenistic Greek with Hebrew influences (especially in frequencies of structures), which are a result of the translation process.[18] Evans's study covers a much larger corpus than Schehr's—the verbal syntax of the entire Greek Pentateuch and deals with the question of Hebrew interference. He also deals with the debate between Fanning and Porter over Greek verbal aspect, arriving at his own theory (see chapter 3, notes 46-47). He focuses on Greek verb forms that do not have exact correspondences to Hebrew, e.g., the Greek perfect system, the optative mood, the relative frequencies of aorist and imperfect forms, and periphrastic tense forms. Evans's conclusion was similar to Schehr's: namely, the Greek Pentateuch represents idiomatic Greek with Hebrew interference, particularly in word order and frequencies of occurrence.[19] Voitila focused on the use of the present and imperfect indicative in a select corpus of the Pentateuch to render Hebrew verb forms, distinguishing between narrative and direct speech. He brings insights from recent linguistic studies on verbal aspect, tense, and *Aktionsart* and discourse functions in terms of background in discourse, topic, and focus. Voitila's

---

[17] Examples of Hebraisms are noted by Schehr (as mentioned in note 8 above). In addition, there are the impersonal use of ἔσται followed by a substantive clause without an introductory conjunction and the use of a conditional clause as a complement of a verb of swearing. Examples of syntactical features that occur in translation Greek compared with standard Greek are: a larger number of nominal clauses, independent clauses linked by a coordinating conjunction, futures with imperatival force, infinitives to express purpose, λέγων introducing direct speech, predicative participles cognate to the main verb, and aorists in narrative. In contrast, there are a diminished number of imperfect and perfect indicatives in narrative. Examples of structures that reflect idiomatic Greek and are not reflections of Hebrew are: the use of the different Greek aspects with infinitives, participles, imperatives, and subjunctives; and the use of the subjunctive mood following various Greek particles such as οὐ μή for emphatic negation, ἐάν in conditional clauses, ἵνα and ὅπως in purpose clauses, and with ἄν in indefinite relative clauses, Schehr, "Syntax of the Moods and Tenses," 267-71.

[18] Schehr, "Syntax of the Moods and Tenses," 279-80.

[19] In addition to the examples of Hebrew interference noted by Schehr, above, Evans also noted the combination of a finite verb plus an infinitive to render Piel and Hiphil forms and increased frequencies of the volitive optative (reflecting the jussive of wish), Evans, *Verbal Syntax*, 260-61.

conclusions were also similar to those of Schehr and Evans although specific to the present and imperfect. He concluded that the translators had mastered all the uses of the present and imperfect in Koine Greek in their use of these forms in translation. However, the Hebrew original influenced the translation in two ways: it has an increased use of the present, reflecting the translation of Hebrew nominal clauses (particularly those containing a predicative participle)—the most common equivalent, and a reduction in the numbers of historic presents and imperfects—forms without direct Hebrew equivalents.[20]

Sang-Hyuk Woo's recent dissertation on the study of the verbal system in the Septuagint of Job also focuses on which Greek verbs were used to render the Hebrew verbs in translation. He distinguishes between the different use of verbs in narrative (past) and the moment of speech distinguishing between temporality, aspect, and modality (especially deontic and epistemic modality) embodied in the various verb forms. He is particularly interested in the translator's use of different Greek verb forms in close proximity to render Hebrew forms (micro-systems of neutralization—different forms with the same meaning, opposition—different forms carrying opposite meaning, and complementation—different forms complementing each other). He also considers, from the point of translation technique, how two of the same Hebrew verbs were rendered by different Greek verbs (dissimilation) and where different Hebrew verbs were rendered by the same Greek verbs (assimilation). He considered what this tells us about the translator's understanding of the Hebrew verb system and the extent to which the translator's own "freer" style is manifest in his translation of the verbs independent of constraints of the source and target languages.[21]

In Beck's study of Septuagint translation technique, the translation of verb is one of a number of features he investigates, with his main interest in how the translators reworked the Hebrew story to produce their own story in translation. He looks at the percentages of Greek verb forms for the Hebrew verb forms in independent clauses as well as the preservation of parataxis in the translation for selected texts drawn from the three sections of the Hebrew Bible: the Pentateuch

---

[20] Anssi Voitila, *Présent et imparfait de l'indicatif dans le Pentateuque grec: une étude sur la syntaxe de traduction* (Göttingen: Vandenhoeck & Ruprecht, 2001), 261.

[21] Sang-Hyuk Woo, "Études sur le système verbal dans la Septante de Job" (Ph.D. diss., Université Strasbourg II—Marc Bloch Faculte de Theologie Protestante, 2006).

(Gen 22, 34, Exod 13-14, Num 13), the Prophets (Judg 4, 1 Sam 31, 2 Sam 6, Jonah 1, 3-4), and the Writings (Job 1-2, Ruth 1-2, 1 Chr 10, 13). He is particularly interested in how the translation reads in terms of foregrounding and backgrounding as well as changes in prospective and retrospective action through the use of the different Greek tense forms. He also notes the use of circumstantial participles to break up strings of coordinated paratactic verbs. In his analysis of multiple features, the most variation in percentage of literalness occurs in the translation of the verb.[22] Here the translators display their greatest literary sensitivity in terms of the translation of linguistic forms. The translation is literal (indicated by an average of 90% literalness for all of the texts, with Job the least literal text with an average of 81% literalness and 1 Chronicles 10 the most with 94%). He concedes that while a linguistic study serves textual criticism well, there are limited literary insights to be gained from this approach alone and that there is need to resort to narrative criticism to gain further insights.[23] After his literary and geographical analysis, he concludes that the Septuagint translators were storytellers in their own right and not just translating mechanically. However, the story they related was mostly a reflection of the Hebrew story.

Although these previous studies differ in their focus, the results are similar.[24] All acknowledge that the Septuagint translators had some

---

[22] As James Barr states, "literalism, which was so potent a force acting upon the lexical usage of the translators and upon their syntactical habits, was unable to make a real conquest of the question of the use of tenses," Barr, "Translators' Handling of Verb Tense," 400.

[23] John A. Beck, *Translators as Storytellers: A Study in Septuagint Translation Technique* (New York: Peter Lang, 2000), 51-53.

[24] The studies (mentioned above) came up with the following common equivalents for Hebrew forms with approximate percentages: 70-80% of *qatal* forms and 80-90% of *wayyiqtol* forms are translated by aorist indicatives. 45-63% of *yiqtol* forms are translated by Greek futures (with about 6-20% by aorist subjunctives), and 80-85% of *wᵉqatal* forms are rendered into a Greek future. Most variation occurs in the studies on verb forms in poetry. The percentages of the above mentioned common equivalents were lowest for Symmachus's translation of the Psalms (only 326 of 492 or 66.3% of *qatal* forms and 49 of 95 or 51.6% of *wayyiqtol* forms were translated by aorist indicatives; and 310 of 714 or 43.4% of *yiqtol* forms and 10 of 16 or 62.5% of *wᵉqatal* forms were translated by future indicatives, Busto Sáiz, *La traducción de Símaco*, 123, 136, 132, 126). Also 16 of 25 (64%) *wᵉqatal* forms and 80 of 363 (22%) *yiqtol* forms were translated by aorist indicatives in Sailhamer's selection of the Psalms (*Translation Technique*, 50, 55). The reason for the lower percentages are due to the fact that the use of verb forms is more variable in poetry. (See chapter 3 on the significance and meaning of these verb forms in Hebrew and Greek).

facility in their use of the Greek verbal forms. By virtue of the fact that the translation survived indicates that the use of Greek tense forms mostly made sense, although some elements of Greek verbal syntax differed in frequency compared with other classical or Hellenistic Greek documents.[25] The previous studies also recognize that the reason for this was due to the influence of the Hebrew original, especially on the relative frequencies of certain Greek forms to the detriment of others.

III. This Study Compared with Previous Studies

This book focuses particularly on the translation of verbs in the book of Chronicles, a study that has yet to be done, at least in such detail.[26] It attempts to ascertain what was the Septuagint translator of Chronicles' understanding of the Hebrew verbal system as well as comment on how he handled the verb forms. It is the contention of this book that the translator was informed by contemporary spoken Hebrew, by a traditional understanding of the archaic use of certain verb forms in written Hebrew (derived from the study of the text and reading traditions), and by the realization that the context may bring additional meanings to the verb forms. The Chronicles text is unique for a diachronic study both of the function of verb forms and their translation. Firstly, it is particularly interesting since it contains archaic verb forms but also displays changes in verb use that would have been manifested in the spoken register at the time of its writing. A study of the translation of Chronicles enables us to see how the translator handled the variations in meaning between these two kinds of verb forms and hence say something about the translator's understanding of these forms. Secondly, a study of the translation of Chronicles (which followed the translation of the Pentateuch and Samuel-Kings, with passages parallel to Chronicles) enables us to look at how the Chronicles' translator handled verb forms compared to the other translators. This also enables us to say something about the translation

---

[25] Indeed, the function of the translation and the community that employed it were also outside the norm of "typical" Greek society and culture.

[26] It focuses on indicative verb forms and participles (as opposed to volitive forms) as these forms constitute the main part of the verbal system and are more problematic in terms of understanding their function.

technique and whether there was a change in the philosophy of
translation over time.

This study resembles the first group of studies mentioned above in
that it begins with the analysis of the translation of the Hebrew verb
forms into Greek. It is similar to the second group of studies in that it
looks at verbs in predominantly prose text. This study differs from
some of the previous studies in that it is more concerned with how the
resulting Greek translation reads and reflects the Hebrew source text
in terms of how the verb forms operate in three text or clause types:[27]
main clause narrative, main clause reported speech, and subordinate
clauses, especially from the point of view of the three contextual
factors: *Aktionsart*, sentence topic and focus, and the discourse as a
whole. (The studies mentioned above, apart from Voitila's and Woo's,
pay little attention to the different clause types, lumping all the verbal
forms together. Apart from Voitila's and Beck's studies, they also do
not much consider the use of the verb forms from the larger
perspective of the discourse).

The book is divided into five main sections that correspond to the
areas mentioned in the first section. In the next chapter we look at the
"philosophy" of translation, the background of the translators, and

---

[27] Other scholars have also considered the need to distinguish among clause types
in analyzing the Hebrew verb. Longacre distinguishes four main text types according
to parameters "agent and temporal succession": *narrative* (+ agent, + past temporal
succession), *predictive* (+ agent, + future temporal succession), *procedural/instructional* (−
agent, + temporal succession), *hortatory* (+ agent, − temporal succession—Robert E.
Longacre, "Discourse Perspective on the Hebrew Verb: Affirmation and
Restatement," in *Linguistics and Biblical Hebrew* (ed. Walter Bodine; Winona Lake:
Eisenbrauns, 1992), 177-89). Niccacci simplifies Longacre's hortatory, procedural,
predictive discourse types to direct speech and distinguishes just two different text
types—narrative and direct speech (Alviero Niccacci, "Basic Facts and Theory of the
Biblical Hebrew Verb System in Prose," in *Narrative Syntax and the Hebrew Bible: Papers of
the Tilburg Conference 1996* (ed. Ellen van Wolde; Leiden: Brill, 1997), 167-202). Endo
also distinguishes between verbs in direct discourse and narrative but treats verbs in
volitive and subordinate clauses separately, Yoshinobu Endo, *The Verbal System of
Classical Hebrew in the Joseph Story: An Approach from Discourse Analysis* (SSN 32; Assen:
Van Gorcum, 1996), 30-31. Endo's rationale for distinguishing subordinate clauses
from main clauses is that "the verbal form in the subordinate clause is chosen not
from the viewpoint of the deictic center of the narrator, but from that of the
immediate participant in the main clause," (299). Verheij's study also takes into
account different uses of verb forms in narrative and reported speech in Chronicles
(but not on their translation into Greek), Arian J. C. Verheij, *Verbs and Numbers: A Study
of the Frequencies of the Hebrew Verbal Tense Forms in the Books of Samuel, Kings, and Chronicles*
(SSN 28; Assen/Maastricht: Van Gorcum, 1990). See chapter 4, note 11 for his
breakdown according to verb forms.

their task and achievement; the third chapter deals with the nature of
the Hebrew and Greek verbal systems. These two chapters lay a
foundation for the following three chapters, which deal with the
translation of Hebrew verb forms, the function of the Greek verb
forms, and how the translation of the verbs reflects the translator's
understanding of the Hebrew verbal system and his philosophy of
translation.

CHAPTER TWO

THE TRANSLATORS, THEIR TASK AND ACHIEVEMENT

The Septuagint[1] is the earliest recorded known written translation of the Bible. Three main reasons are postulated for the translation: literary, educational, and liturgical. Firstly, literary, so that a translation of the Hebrew writings could be added to Ptolemy's library, then educational and liturgical, both to meet the needs of the Alexandrian Jewish community, which, for the most part, had a limited facility in reading and understanding Hebrew. Most of the books of the Septuagint were translated by Jewish scholars during the Ptolemaic era (304-30 BCE).

Due to their view of the text and the main reason for the translation (which was probably to educate the Jewish community) the translators, for the most part, privileged the source text over the target language and set about their task to bring the reader of the translation to the original text (introducing to him or her the particular or peculiar nuances of the original—to cast this in modern theoretical terms, formal equivalence). This is in contrast to the more recent concern (as expressed by translation theorists such as Nida[2]) to bring the original text to the reader (conveying as best as possible the message of the original in the target language—in modern theoretical terms, dynamic equivalence).[3] It seems, at least in the eyes of the Alexandrian Jewish community, they achieved their task, if the favorable reception of the translation by them is anything to judge by. Only later did the translation come under increasing criticism and revision, and retranslating was deemed necessary.[4]

---

[1] See note 6 in the previous chapter on the expanded use of the term *Septuagint* to refer to the translation of the Hebrew Scriptures into Greek.

[2] As formulated in Eugene A. Nida, *Towards a Science of Translating* (Leiden: Brill, 1964), ch. 2.

[3] See Sebastian P. Brock, "The Phenomenon of the Septuagint," *OtSt* 17 (1972): 11-36, and note 46 below.

[4] We could say that the revising process began while the books of the Hebrew Bible were being translated. For example, in the translation of verb forms, the translator of Chronicles avoided the use of circumstantial participles (which were common in the Pentateuch) and historic presents (which were common in Samuel) to translate

This chapter investigates the background of the Greek translation of the Bible in general (paying particular attention to the book of Chronicles where specific information is available),[5] how social/cultural factors influenced the translators and the way they approached their task of translating Hebrew (particularly the verbs), and what they produced in accomplishing such a task.

I. THE TRANSLATORS AND THEIR BACKGROUND

We actually know very little about the external conditions in which the work of translation was done. It seems plausible that the translation was done to meet the needs of the Jewish community in Alexandria in the Ptolemaic era and, perhaps, under the sponsorship of the Ptolemies. But who the translators were, what their education was, when, where, and how it was carried out—these and many other important questions remain unanswered. In order to find out more about the translators, it is necessary first to consider the Alexandrian Jewish community and factors such as the language environment, which created the need for the translation of the Hebrew Bible into Greek, and the religious/cultural situation, which permitted the translation of the Scriptures[6] into another language and even

---

wayyiqtol forms (see note 61). Perhaps this was because he felt that circumstantial participles and historic presents were not as close to the meaning of *wayyiqtol* as the standard equivalent, καί and the aorist.

[5] The book of Chronicles (Gk. *Paraleipomenōn*) contains narrative history with many parallel passages in Samuel-Kings (Gk. *Basileiōn* "Reigns"). This gives us an opportunity to compare the translation of Hebrew verbs by the Samuel-Kings translators with those of Chronicles and consider if differences reflect a change in the method or philosophy of translation or in understanding of the Hebrew verb. A study of Chronicles also enables us to see if the Greek translators paid any attention to the development of the Hebrew language from classical biblical Hebrew to late biblical Hebrew as recorded in Chronicles.

[6] There is some debate as to what constitutes and what determines "Scriptures." Although it is anachronistic to talk about a fixed canon, there may have been some recognition among the Jewish community that certain writings or books (e.g., the Torah) were more authoritative or of more value. As Nickelsburg and Kraft asked, "At what point and under what circumstances did Jews…consider certain writings to have special authority, beyond that of other writings? Did those who perpetuated the apocalyptic materials have the same attitude to the authority of fixed biblical texts as Philo?" George W. E. Nickelsburg with Robert A. Kraft, "Introduction: The Modern Study of Early Judaism," in *Early Judaism and Its Modern Interpreters* (ed. Robert A. Kraft and George W. E. Nickelsburg; vol. 2 of *The Bible and Its Modern Interpreters*, ed. Douglas A. Knight; Atlanta: Scholars Press, 1986), 16. At least there was a body of sacred

considered the translation acceptable for use in worship in the synagogue.

A. The Alexandrian Jewish Community—Its Language and Culture

Jews may have been present in the area of Alexandria (or at least in the Nile Delta region) as early as the sixth century BCE. Since the Babylonian capture of Jerusalem, Egypt was a destination of Judean refugees (cf. Jer. 44:1), and Jews were present in a military garrison in Elephantine in the fifth century. The city of Alexandria itself was founded in 331 BCE by Alexander the Great, and after his death it came under the jurisdiction of his general Ptolemy, son of Lagos, who became Ptolemy I, king of Egypt in 304 BCE. Greek culture developed and flourished in the area under Ptolemy I and his descendants. At the same time migration from Judea was encouraged (at times even forced), especially when Judea was under the Ptolemies' rule (301-198 BCE), and by the reign of Ptolemy II Philadelphus (285-246 BCE), there was a large and thriving Jewish community in Alexandria.

Greek was the predominant language used by the community, although new immigrants would have kept Aramaic and perhaps Hebrew alive.[7] Hebrew was probably used mostly as a scholarly language by those studying the Bible or by those Jews who had recently arrived from Palestine, while Aramaic would have been used in daily life for communication within the community.[8] Greek would have been the language of communication with those outside the community and increasingly rivaled Aramaic as the language within the community. Eventually, as Hebrew and Aramaic became less and less understood, the use of Greek became acceptable, and indeed it was felt necessary to have a translation of the Hebrew Bible into

---

Hebrew and Aramaic literature that was recognized by the Jewish community as worthwhile to translate into Greek.

[7] It is interesting to note that almost 99% of the inscriptions found in Egypt are in Greek with only 1% in Aramaic or Hebrew. See Steve Weitzman, "Why did the Qumran Community Write in Hebrew?," *JAOS* 119 (1999): 39.

[8] A number of loan words transliterated into Greek follow the Aramaic language rather than the Hebrew, especially technical and cultural terms. They are marked as Aramaic by a final -α. For example, γειώρας "sojourner, proselyte" for Aramaic גיורא cf. Hebrew הגר, πάσχα "passover" for פסחא cf. Hebrew פסח so also σάββατα, μάννα, musical instruments νάβλα and κινύρα both "lyre," and σίκερα "strong drink," cf. John P. Brown "The Septuagint as a Source of the Greek Loan-Words in the Targums," *Bib* 70 (1989): 194-216 (especially pp. 200-1).

Greek.[9] The translation was one of the first works among a rich and diverse Greek literature produced by the Jewish community. Apart from many Greek papyri, which largely deal with mundane affairs such as business correspondence, there are also literary works of history (Demetrius), philosophy (Aristobulus and Philo), poetry (the *Sibylline Oracles*), tragedy (Ezekiel), and romance (*Joseph and Asenath*). The Greek written by the members of the Jewish community displays varying degrees of competence. Overall, the authors of the literary works mentioned here demonstrate a good grasp of the Greek language, while the Septuagint has its own Greek style, giving prominence to particular structures that mirror the Hebrew source.[10] The Greek found in the papyri is of varying standards and reflects the Greek of the majority of the Jewish community, not a Jewish-Greek dialect, as some scholars have maintained, but it reflected an uneven and imperfect mastery of the Greek vernacular by a large percentage of the populace.

This use of the Greek language by the Jewish community raises the issue of the extent of Hellenization among the Jewish community. There is some debate about Hellenization and the attitudes toward it among the Jews of the Diaspora in general and in Alexandria in particular. Barclay distinguishes three levels of integration into

---

[9] This was in contrast to the situation in Palestine, which was probably trilingual, with Greek more prevalent in some areas, Aramaic being most prevalent, and Aramaic and Hebrew preferred in religious contexts (e.g., by the Qumran community). There were various attempts to revive the use of Hebrew, especially in conjunction with phases of religious nationalism such as the Maccabean and Bar Kochba revolts. After the destruction of the temple in 70 CE, there was a tendency of many Jews to begin to distance themselves from Greek. The rabbis gave more preeminence to the Hebrew original, considering it—God's language—as superior. The initial stages of this reaction can also be seen in the translation attempts of Aquila and Theodotion, which reflect further attempts to bring the Greek Bible closer to its Hebrew source.

Both Robert H. Gundry, "The Language Milieu of First-Century Palestine: Its Bearing on the Authenticity of the Gospel Tradition," *JBL* 83:4 (1964): 404-408, and R. Steven Notley, "Non-Septuagintal Hebraisms in the Third Gospel" (paper presented at the annual meeting of the SBL, Boston, Mass., 22 November 2008) argue for a trilingual (Greek, Hebrew, Aramaic) linguistic environment in Palestine around the time of the New Testament. Randall Buth "Hebrew Poetic Tenses and the Magnificat," *JSNT* 21 (1984): 67-83, also believes that the use of Hebrew was much more widespread than previously considered, pointing out that the tense switching of Luke 1-46-47 seems to indicate that the poem was originally constructed in Hebrew, rather than Aramaic and Greek. He believes that this "fits the linguistic background of the time" (67).

[10] For further comment on the Greek of the Septuagint, see section on the achievement of the translators below.

Hellenistic society: assimilation (social integration), acculturation (in language and education), and accommodation (to what use acculturation is put—cultural convergence).[11] He also acknowledges resistance to these pressures (cultural antagonism) among certain elements among Diaspora Jews, particularly from those trying to preserve the distinctiveness of the Jewish population living in the midst of a largely Gentile populace. However, in spite of the increasing and widespread use of the Greek language among the majority of the members of the Alexandrian community to the detriment of Aramaic and Hebrew, in general, the community was able to preserve its distinctiveness. The Jews were able to absorb and internalize certain Greek influences without compromising unique aspects of their culture. On the whole, Judaism was not radically transformed among Hellenistic Jews.[12] It seems that the Alexandrian Jewish community, just like Jewish communities in the Diaspora up to the present day, managed to maintain a semi-permeable membrane allowing certain elements of the surrounding culture to penetrate it, while resisting other influences, particularly in the area of religion. There was still the ethnic bond of ancestry and custom, the conducting of activities such as festivals and fasts, maintaining of links with Jerusalem and other Diaspora communities; there was still the veneration of the Torah and the rest of the Hebrew Scriptures, and for Moses the lawgiver, philosopher, and ideal; there were also the continued practice of

---

[11] For a clear distinction and the definition of these terms, see John M. G. Barclay, *Jews in the Mediterranean Diaspora* (Edinburgh: T & T Clark, 1996), 92-98.

[12] For discussion of the debate as to how much Hellenization influenced Judaism, see Lee I. Levine, *Judaism and Hellenism in Antiquity: Conflict or Confluence?* (Peabody: Hendrickson, 1999), 6-32. The "most positive estimate of the Greeks and Greek culture and of the possibility for peaceful and productive coexistence between Jews and Greeks" in all the Jewish literature up to the Mishnah is seen in the *Letter of Aristeas*, cf. George W. E. Nickelsburg, *Jewish Literature between the Bible and the Mishnah* (Minneapolis: Fortress Press, 2005), 196. Honigman also focuses on a positive view of things Hellenic among the Jews, following a trend in the field of Judaeo-Hellenistic literature to "get the Jews out of the imaginary cultural and religious ghetto in which scholars of the nineteenth and early twentieth centuries tended to enclose them, and to underline their integration into their Hellenistic environment," Sylvie Honigman, *The Septuagint and Homeric Scholarship in Alexandria: A Study in the Narrative of the Letter of Aristeas* (New York: Routledge, 2003), 6. She considers that there was "complete cultural integration of the Jews into their surrounding world," as is demonstrated by the *Letter of Aristeas*. It is not a matter of whether an author is polemical against Greek culture or whether he advocates Hellenization...but that "Hellenization *is* there" (*Septuagint and Homeric Scholarship*, 7).

dietary laws, male circumcision, and refusal to work on the Sabbath.[13] This is not to diminish the effect that Hellenism had on certain elements of the community, with some individuals giving up virtually all features that designated them Jewish in order to advance in Hellenistic society. No doubt, this accommodation and acculturation, especially by leading and upper-class elements of the community, impacted the community and was perhaps a cause of concern to those who wished to preserve the distinctiveness of the Jewish community.

B. The Reason(s) for the Translation

The Hebrew Scriptures played an important role in Jewish life. They contained their unique history, laws, and customs. Through the decreasing knowledge of Hebrew and even of Aramaic, the Scriptures became less accessible to the community. One way to educate the Jewish community and preserve its distinctiveness was to translate the Hebrew Scriptures into the language of most of the community, Greek. However, there is some controversy as to whether this was the only reason.

As was mentioned above, the three main reasons cited for the translation are: literary, educational, and liturgical. Perhaps all three contributed to the production of the translation.[14]

The quasi-historical *Letter of Aristeas*, written perhaps 150 years after the events it purports to relate, sets forth the literary reason, the Pentateuch was translated by royal decree for the library of Ptolemy II Philadelphus (285-246 BCE) to enhance his collection of books.[15] This

---

[13] This is also reflected in the Semitic coloring of the Greek translation of the Bible. This is due to the desire to preserve the distinctive character of the Hebrew Bible as much as possible in translation.

[14] In addition, Dominique Barthélemy proposes that it was translated for the political purpose of Hellenizing the Jews, providing the Jewish community of Egypt with a code of law, "Pourquoi la Torah a-t-elle été traduite en grec?" in *On Language, Culture, and Religion: In Honor of Eugene A. Nida* (ed. M. Black and W. A. Smalley; The Hague: Mouton, 1974), 31. Also Mélèze-Modrzejewski argues that Jewish legal texts in Greek were needed by the Ptolemies for administrative purposes, however the Pentateuch contains more than just a law code. See Marguerite Harl, Gilles Dorival, and Olivier Munnich, *La Bible grecque des Septante: Du judaïsme hellénistique au christianisme ancien.* (Paris: Cerf, 1988), 73-76.

[15] Although widely accepted in antiquity, scholars since Humphrey Hody, "Contra Historiam Aristeae de LXX Interpretibus Dissertatio," in *De Bibliorum Textibus* (Oxford: Oxford University Press, 1705), 1-89 challenged and for the most part rejected this reason for the translation of the Septuagint. While scholars do not agree

on the actual date of the composition of the *Letter of Aristeas*, "linguistic and other considerations point to the last third of the second century B.C.E., specifically during the reign of Ptolemy VIII Euergetes, probably between 138 and 130," Nickelsburg, *Jewish Literature*, 198.

Two recent books, Nina L. Collins, *The Library in Alexandria and the Bible in Greek* (SVT 82; Leiden: Brill, 2000), and Sylvie Honigman, *Septuagint and Homeric Scholarship*, (see note 12 above) argue that the motivation for the translation accords more with that expressed in the *Letter of Aristeas*. Collins considers that the Pentateuch was translated in 281 BCE for Ptolemy II by a team of translators working for Demetrius of Phalerum, the librarian of the great library of Alexandria, and that the translation was made "through the energy of the Greeks, and in the face of sophisticated opposition from the Jews...composed by Jewish translators working reluctantly in Alexandria...for the benefit of the Greeks rather than the Jews" (180). She considers the resulting translation was a product of deeply religious Jewish translators reluctantly producing a literal translation of the Hebrew Pentateuch into Greek. She also believes that the translation was not intended for religious or liturgical use initially, indicated by Demetrius' role in the ceremony at Pharos commemorating the completion of the text as indicated in the *Letter of Aristeas*, 308-310 (119-120, 122). Cf. a scathing review, David J. Wasserstein, review of Nina Collins, *The Library in Alexandria and the Bible in Greek*, *Scripta Classica Israelica* 22 (2003): 318-20.

Honigman also accepts Aristeas's account regarding the origins of the LXX with a few adjustments. "Aristeas" is a learned Alexandrian Jew adopting the persona of a Ptolemaic court official. The "letter" is considered a "charter myth" for a standardized authorized revision of the Pentateuch against carelessly transcribed copies that were circulating since the time of its initial translation. The Ptolemaic court initiated the translation (and revision) to benefit the Jews, whom Ptolemy wanted to favor, rather than the Jewish community itself, and whether the translation was ordered for the royal library in Alexandria is questionable. (*Septuagint and Homeric Scholarship*, 130-139).

However, the view of many scholars including Armin Lange, "'Considerable Proficiency' (*Letter of Aristeas* 121): The relationship of the *Letter of Aristeas* to the Prologue of Ecclesiasticus" (paper presented at the annual meeting of the SBL, San Diego, California, 19 November 2007) that the *Letter of Aristeas* was written to defend the third century Old Greek texts against first century recensions attempting to revise the Old Greek to the proto-MT seems more plausible. The *Letter of Aristeas* emphasizes the inspiration or divine intervention in the original translation. Sebastian Brock, "To Revise or Not to Revise: Attitudes to Jewish Biblical Translation," in *Septuagint, Scrolls, and Cognate Writings* (ed. George J. Brooke and Barnabas Lindars; SCS 33; Atlanta: Society of Biblical Literature, 1992), 301-338 mentions two conflicting attitudes current at round the turn of the common era, the attitude of Philo, to place the translation "on a par with the original [and hence no need to revise]...polemicizing against those who sought to revise and correct the Septuagint," represented by the Greek XII prophets fragments, 8HevXIIgr, (304-305). He traces these attitudes back in time to the late second century BCE contrasting the *Letter of Aristeas* (representing the former attitude of no need to revise) with the preface of Ben Sira's grandson, apologizing for the inadequacy of his translation compared to the Hebrew (representing the need to revise) (305-306). Benjamin G. Wright, "The *Letter of Aristeas* and the Reception History of the Septuagint." *BIOSCS* 39 (2006): 47-67, notes the disparity between the intended function of the Septuagint as presented in the *Letter of Aristeas* (to be a stand alone text, having prestige among Greek literature and holding a status equal to the Hebrew Law) with the actual text-linguistic makeup of the Greek text (which at best gives "'special prominence...to certain correct, though unidiomatic, modes of speech because they happen to coincide with Hebrew idioms'" reason, postulated for the translation of the Pentateuch, is difficult to verify. It seems more probable that the Pentateuch along with the remaining books, including *Reigns* (Samuel-Kings) and *Paraleipomenon* (Chronicles) were translated because of the needs of the Jewish community rather than by royal decree, although the translation work may have received royal funding.[16]

The needs of the community for a translation were probably two-fold—educational (producing texts for study) and liturgical (producing texts for worship). The former need was probably primary and the liturgical need was secondary and was met later.

Pietersma argues that the translation was made initially to meet educational needs over liturgical needs.

> Liturgical use does not tend to produce continuous translations of whole books, but tends to be selective....Liturgy has to do primarily with performance instead of comprehension...and tends to be more tolerant of a text in a foreign medium than is education.[17]

He believes that "the translation arose in a school environment before it was put to other uses, including liturgical use" (358). He concurs with Brock (1978, 29) and Barthélemy that the movement to correct the Greek to the Hebrew was the product of a school but also proposes including the schoolroom as the originating environment for the translation as well.

(62, quoting Albert Pietersma, "A New Paradigm for Addressing Old Questions: The Relevance of the Interlinear Model for the Study of the Septuagint," in *Bible and Computer: The Stellenbosch AIBI-6 Conference. Proceedings of the Association Internationale Bible et Informatique "From Alpha to Byte". University of Stellenbosch 17-21 July, 2000.* (ed. Johann Cook; Leiden: Brill, 2002), 337-64 [343], who in turn cites H. St. J. Thackeray). Wright considers that the *Letter of Aristeas* is part of the reception history of the Septuagint and marks a change in its function, losing its dependence on the Hebrew, and becoming "an independent free-standing replacement for the Hebrew" with "*Aristeas* offering a foundational myth of origins for the LXX's transformed function/position as an independent, scriptural authority" (66-67).

[16] The extent to which the Ptolemies were involved is somewhat a moot point. Perhaps they sponsored the entire translation endeavor. Certainly, for the most part, the community enjoyed good relations with the Ptolemies during the early Ptolemaic period (323-180 BCE). This period corresponded roughly to the time of the translation of much of the Bible (cf. Barclay, *Jews in the Mediterranean Diaspora*, 32). It seems that the Ptolemies had minimal effect on the translation philosophy, given that the translation was quite different from the literary norm. However, perhaps the translators took care not to offend the ruling family (cf. note 52). The translation seemed to meet the need of the community, judging by its enthusiastic reception by the community.

[17] Pietersma, "New Paradigm," 358. See also Dines, *The Septuagint*, ch. 3, for a brief presentation of the two needs of the community.

After the community warmly received the translation of the Pentateuch (see the final section of this chapter) other books of the Bible were translated. Therefore, the book of Chronicles was translated as part of the process of completing the translation of the books considered sacred to, or of some value in, the community. The purpose of Chronicles "to exhort the post-exilic community to seek the LORD and to support the temple" from the perspective of Israel's (Judah's) history[18] could also have been considered relevant to the Jewish community at the time of its translation. Its message could have inspired the community to stand firm in times of trial, and it reinforced the importance of the temple in contemporary Jewish thought.[19]

C. The Translators

Although difficult to verify, and perhaps written to link the translation efforts more to Jerusalem and defend the credentials of the Pentateuch translators, the *Letter of Aristeas* indicates they came from Palestine. We do not know who the translators of the remaining books were and where they came from. Perhaps they mostly came from among the Alexandrian community.[20] Although some of the translators may have

---

[18] Cf. William M. Schniedewind, *The Word of God in Transition: From Prophet to Exegete in the Second Temple Period* (JSOTSup 197; Sheffield: Sheffield Academic Press, 1995), 12.

[19] Such as the trials caused by struggles between the Ptolemies and the Seleucids (200-167 BCE), and the struggles for Jewish nationalism at the time of the rise of the Maccabees (167-141 BCE). The importance of the temple is also stressed in the *Letter of Aristeas*, especially 83-120.

[20] Pietersma considers the provenance of the Greek Psalter as either Egypt or Palestine but concludes that, "the cumulative weight of the various pieces...confirms what we once presupposed...that the Greek Psalter originated in Egypt, in "The Place of Origin of the Old Greek Psalter," in *The World of the Aramaeans I. Biblical Studies in Honour of Paul-Eugène Dion* (ed. P. M. Michèle Daviau, John Wevers and Michael Weigl; JSOTSup 324; Sheffield Academic Press, 2001), 252-274 [273]. In contrast, Cook proposes a Palestinian origin for the translation of Proverbs based on its "pro-Jewish and strong anti-Hellenistic attitude" (29) and similarities between Proverbs and Ben Sira, Johann Cook, "The Septuagint as Contextual Bible Translation—Alexandria or Jerusalem as Context for Proverbs?" *JNSL* XIX (1993): 25-39. Sidney Jellicoe, "Some Reflections on the ΚΑΙΓΕ Recension," *VT* 23 (1973): 15-24, also questions, "supposing that translational activity was confined to [Alexandria]." He points to the "extensive use of Greek in Palestine...and the presence of large communities of Greek speaking Jews in Western Asia Minor" as well as literary activity associated with the extensive library at Pergamum that could also have provided a venue for some translation work (23).

recently migrated to Alexandria, the Greek used in translation betrays a particular Alexandrian flavor (see note 23 for specific examples from Chronicles). As far as their education was concerned, we can assume that they received some amount of education in Greek.[21] Perhaps we could also surmise that they were stronger in Greek than Hebrew, since most translators translate from their weaker into their stronger language, but there is some debate as to their facility in Greek.[22]

D. *The Place and Time of Translation*

The Pentateuch and most of the remaining books of the Old Testament were probably translated in Alexandria. The Chronicles translation probably stems from Alexandria. Allen identifies geographical, cultural, and technical terms (both religious and political) in the translation of Chronicles that occur in Ptolemaic Egypt, although the linking of some terms conclusively to second century Alexandria is tenuous.[23] Alternatively, it may have been

---

[21] Cf. Chaim Rabin "The Translation Process and the Character of the Septuagint," *Text* 6 (1968): 1-26 who states, "As early as the third century BCE, Jews would certainly not have had access to the schools which catered to the upper-class citizenry, and thus had no practice in writing educated Greek.... [However,] being literate, they acquired practical experience through reading legal documents, and perhaps fiction. An important part of their linguistic education was played no doubt by listening to the effusions of political and forensic orators" (21-22).

[22] Ibid., 7. Van der Kooij argues that the translators were scribe-translators who were familiar with the reading tradition(s), Arie van der Kooij, "Perspectives on the Study of the Septuagint: Who Are the Translators?" in *Perspectives in the Study of the Old Testament and Early Judaism: A Symposium in Honour of Adam S. Van Der Woude on the Occasion of His 70th Birthday.* (ed. Florentino Garcia Martinez and Ed Noort; SVT 73; Leiden: Brill, 1998), 214-229.

[23] Allen argues for "a strong cumulative effect" of the terms to indicate "*Par[aleipomenon]* is a pre-Christian Egyptian creation, probably of second century origin" (*Greek Chronicles*, 23). He follows Gillis Gerleman, *Studies in the Septuagint II. Chronicles* (LUA 43/3; Lund: Gleerup, 1946), citing terms used by the translator of Chronicles that indicate an Alexandrian provenance for his work (*Greek Chronicles*, 21-23). For example, the translator uses specific terminology to describe the temple in Jerusalem, such as a rare word παστοφόριον for the priests' chambers (1 Chr 9:26; 23:28; 26:16; 28:12; 2 Chr 31:11) and κώδωνας "bells" for pomegranates (2 Chr 4:13), also used to describe the Serapeum, the temple of the Greco-Egyptian god Sarapis in Alexandria. Allen also cites political terminology such as the translation of the term "friend of the king" (1 Chr 27:33) ὁ πρῶτος φίλος, which was a parallel term current among the court of the Ptolemies. The term "friend of the king" in 2 Samuel 16:16-17, is translated ἑταῖρος,, which was an earlier official title in the court of the Ptolemies superseded by the title φίλος (22-23). Gerleman considers that this may also indicate the translation of Samuel preceded Chronicles (*Studies*, 18). However, Sarah Pearce, "Contextualising Greek Chronicles," in *Zutot* 2001 (eds. S.

translated in Palestine as part of the process of revising the Greek translation to make it closer to the Hebrew text (cf. the *kaige* recension in Palestine).[24] Perhaps the way the translator of Chronicles translated *wayyiqtol* forms avoiding historic presents (compared with the translation of Samuel-Kings) and circumstantial participles (compared with the translation of the Pentateuch) was part of this revising process (see notes 4 and 61).

Chronicles was probably translated in the mid-second century (c. 150 BCE) following the translation of the Pentateuch (c. 282 BCE) and Samuel-Kings (beginning of the second century).[25] Two dates that indicate a *terminus ad quem* for the translation are given by the testimony of the grandson of Ben Sira (who knew the translation of the books of the prophets and the writings—dated from 132 to 116 BCE) and by quotations of the Greek Chronicles in the works of the Jewish historian Eupolemus (mid-second century BCE).[26]

Berger, M. Brocke, and I. Zwiep; Dordrecht/Boston: Kluwer Academic Publishers, 2002), 22-27 cautions against Gerleman's use of this kind of vocabulary to date Greek Chronicles. She argues that the terminology such as διάδοχος "successor, deputy," while used by the Ptolemies, is not unique to them. She cites examples of the same terminology used in other times and at other geographical locations.

[24] Cf. Dominique Barthélemy, *Les Devanciers d'Aquila* (SVT 10; Leiden: Brill, 1963), 271. However, there are also papyri containing portions of the Pentateuch such as P.Ryl. III 458 dated to around the mid-second century BCE and P. inv. Fouad 266 dated to the mid-first century BCE with textual variants that may indicate that the revising process toward the Hebrew occurred even in Alexandria (Honigman, *Septuagint and Homeric Scholarship*, 123).

[25] Cf. Harl, Dorival, and Munnich, *La Bible grecque des Septante*, 96-97, who propose a time frame for the translation of all of the books of the Old Testament into Greek. James Donald Shenkel, "A Comparative Study of the Synoptic Parallels in I Paraleipomena and I-II Reigns," *HTR* 62 (1969): 63-85, considers that "the Greek translation of Samuel and Kings undoubtedly preceded that of Chronicles" and that at least "[I] P[araleipomenon] in chapters 17-18 is based upon [II] R[eigns], with a large part of P being simply copied from R verbatim" (63, 65). The translator of Chronicles used the Greek Samuel-Kings parallels as his base even in the few cases where the underlying Hebrew (MT) is different (e.g., 1 Chr 11:2 // 2 Sam 5:2 where P = R ἦσθα but C Ø ≠ S הָיִיתָ). Martha Wade, "Which Is More Literal? A Comparative Analysis of Translation Techniques and Discourse Features of 1 Kgs 11:43-12:24 and 2 Chr 9:31-11:4 in the Old Greek" (paper presented at the annual meeting of the SBL, Boston, Mass., 24 November 2008), also considers that the translation of Chronicles followed Kings, stating, "the high percentage of identical translation choices would indicate probable dependence on or at least knowledge of one of the texts by the translator of the other text. The more polished nature of OG 2 Chr 9:31-11:4 would seem to indicate that the translator of this passage had access to a translation of 1 Kgs 11:43-12:24 and improved upon it" (1).

[26] Cf. Emanuel Tov, "The Septuagint," in *Mikra: Text, Translation, Reading and Interpretation of the Hebrew Bible in Ancient Judaism and Early Christianity* (ed. Martin Jan Mulder and Harry Sysling; Philadelphia: Fortress, 1988), 162. There is some

II. THEIR TASK AND ACHIEVEMENT

Having established some information about the background of the translators, there are a number of things we need to consider related to the task. Translation is essentially recoding a message. The translator simultaneously receives in the source language and transmits into the target language the same message. The success of the translation depends on the ability of the translator to understand the source and perform in the target language.[27] In addition to the translators' facility in source and target languages, other factors also influenced the translation, such as, their view of the source text (i.e., whether it is inspired and invested with authority), the relative prestige they give the source and target languages, and examples of translation in the social/cultural environment, including the translation of the Pentateuch, which also provided an example for the translation of the remaining books of the Bible and other sacred writings. This section looks at these factors before dealing with the method and kind of translation that was produced, which was governed by the translators' view of the source text and source and target languages, along with examples and precedents, combined with the translators' ability. Finally, the resulting translation experienced varying receptions over time and in the different communities who used it.

A. The Source Text and the Prestige of the Source and Target Languages

It seems likely that the translators of the Septuagint considered their source text inspired. They believed that not only its meaning but even its detail was inspired by God.[28] At least this was the view of later writers and writings such as Aristobulus (3rd to 2nd century BCE), the

---

uncertainty as to whether the writings referred to by Ben Sira's grandson refer to the "Writings," which conclude with Chronicles, or are just other works. The quotations of Eupolemus can be found in *Fragmenta Historicorum Graecorum* (ed. Carolus Müller; vol. 3. Frankfurt/Main: Minerva, 1975), 225-28. An English translation can be found in F. Fallon, "Eupolemus," in *The Old Testament Pseudepigrapha* (ed. James H. Charlesworth; vol. 2. Garden City: Doubleday, 1983), 861-72. See chapter 4, section I on the production and translation of the book of Chronicles.

[27] Rabin, "Translation Process," 3.

[28] Cf. James Barr, *The Typology of Literalism in Ancient Bible Translations* (MSU 15; Göttingen: Vandenhoeck & Ruprecht, 1979), 50.

Letter of Aristeas, and Philo (c. 20 BCE to c. 50 CE) who wrote about the translators and the translation.[29]

Not only was the source text considered inspired but the Hebrew language itself had a certain prestige as the language of sacred Scripture, the language of the Jerusalem temple and its cult, and some even considered it the language of creation.[30] The Hebrew of the Bible contains many archaic words, expressions, and some syntactic structures that would have seemed strange and unfamiliar to the translators, predating the time of translation by as much as 800 years. While the scribes who transmitted the text updated the language to a certain degree, the text mostly contains archaic and classical Hebrew vocabulary and syntax that differed from the Hebrew used in Palestine at the time of the translation of the Septuagint. Perhaps this archaic language enhanced the sacredness of the text and language, conveying divine utterances as well as the utterances of ancestors going back to ancient times.[31]

However, the Greek language also had certain prestige among the community.[32] It was the language of the dominant culture, of the educated, the language of commerce and administration, and it increasingly replaced Aramaic as the first language of the people of the Jewish community. The translation could have afforded the translators an opportunity to demonstrate their ability to grasp the finer nuances of the Greek language, to demonstrate a certain facility in the

---

[29] For the development of the view of the inspiration of the translation itself, see the section on the reception of the Septuagint at the end of this chapter.

[30] Cf. *Jub.* 12:26-27. "26 And I opened his mouth, and his ears and his lips, and I began to speak with him in Hebrew in the tongue of the creation. 27 And he took the books of his fathers, and these were written in Hebrew, and he transcribed them, and he began from henceforth to study them, and I made known to him that which he could not (understand), and he studied them during the six rainy months." Translation by R. H. Charles, *The Apocrypha and Pseudepigrapha of the Old Testament in English* (Oxford: Clarendon Press, 1913).

[31] The view of the verbal inspiration of the text became increasingly rigid after the translation of the Septuagint. This view created the desire to correct or emend the Septuagint translation so that it corresponded more closely to the Hebrew. This can be seen in the so-called *kaige* recension of Samuel-Kings, in the translation of Chronicles compared to (especially the Old Greek of) Samuel-Kings, and it culminates in completely new and slavishly literal Greek translations by Theodotion and Aquila.

[32] This can be seen among the elite of the community, especially those who desired social advancement. Many better-off Jewish families began to use Greek names (Barclay, *Jews in the Mediterranean Diaspora*, 25). In addition, the prestige of Greek can be seen in the abandonment of one of the most important cultural legacies of ancient Israel, the national language of Hebrew (ibid., 31).

language corresponding to their education. This can be seen on occasion in the use of the Greek tenses to indicate finer discourse features reflecting not only the Hebrew source text but also considering the Greek text in its own right. However, it seems that among the translators and among those who would be recipients of the translation, these considerations were secondary.[33]

The privileging of Hebrew relative to Greek may also confirm an educational origin of the translation, since for education "the source text is the object of study *and* the receptor language is the tool in that study."[34]

B. Model(s) for and Precedents of Translation

Although the written translation of the Bible into Greek was probably a pioneering effort, the translators did have some translation precedents already existing in the culture that they could use as models for translation. They had models both in the secular and religious realms. In the secular realm, there were two distinct kinds of texts, legal and commercial texts, and literary texts. Legal and commercial texts were most familiar to members of the community and most frequently translated. Literary texts were mostly the domain of the educated and very little translation of literary texts was done into Greek.[35] Translators of legal and commercial texts followed a more literal, word for word, method of translation. Another feature of the translation of legal or commercial texts, which seems to contradict the desire for literalness was the condensing and omitting of phraseology and stylistic ornamentation of the source, so as to transmit the message as clearly and precisely as possible.[36] This is a feature of oral translation but also occurs in written texts. In contrast, the translation of literary texts into other languages (e.g., from Greek into Latin) tended to follow a freer, sense for sense, method of translation. The art

---

[33] Cf. a recent article by James K. Aitken, "Rhetoric and Poetry in Greek Ecclesiastes," *BIOSCS* 38 (2005): 55-77, in which he discusses the problem of source-oriented and target-oriented translation, noting Greek literary effects in the translation of Ecclesiastes, which is usually considered to be very literal.

[34] Pietersma, "New Paradigm," 359; see the next section.

[35] In fact, Greek literature was considered the literature par excellence and the literary standard of Homer and Plato, etc., worthy of imitation.

[36] Rabin, "Translation Process," 23.

of producing a literary, dynamic equivalent translation tended to be a later Roman achievement.[37]

In the realm of religion, oral translations accompanying the reading of the Hebrew Scriptures in the synagogue were made into Aramaic and probably into Greek. These translations also tended to be literal, but in places could be much freer, interspersing the translation with exposition and explanation.[38]

Pietersma proposes an "interlinear" model for the translation of the Septuagint according to the method of the Greek education system from the third century BCE to the third century CE. He cites an example of this approach used in teaching Homer (MSS PSI 12.1276) in which a colloquial Greek translation is arranged underneath the *Iliad* ii 617-38, 639-70.[39] Although Pietersma concedes that the translators probably did not produce interlinear Hebrew-Greek texts, he considers that the initial translation used Greek as a crib to study the Hebrew text. He feels that this approach to translation best explains the following features:

> The Greek [of the LXX]…is colloquial rather than literary, regularly literal and often hackneyed rather than dynamic and flowing, but there are a great many items that are unintelligible, including most of the transliterations. On the reasonable assumption that, especially if he is deemed to be translating a sacred text, the translator would surely have done his best, [there are] essentially two explanatory options…: (a) the translator lacked basic linguistic competence, since he did not have

[37] Elias J. Bickerman, "The Septuagint as a Translation," in *Studies in Jewish and Christian History*. Vol. 1. (ed. Elias J. Bickerman; Leiden: Brill, 1976), 177-79.

[38] According to van der Kooij, the scribe-translators, who were familiar with a reading tradition of the unpointed Hebrew text, approached the text "on a clause-and sentence-level" rather than translators as dragomen, who proceeded "on a *word-by-word* basis," van der Kooij, "Perspectives," 225. In terms of the Aramaic Targums that we have preserved, it is interesting to note that the supposedly earlier Targum Onkelos (approximately 1st to 2nd centuries CE) is a more literal translation compared with the later and more expansive Neofiti and Pseudo-Jonathan.

[39] Pietersma, "New Paradigm," 348-349. See Jan Joosten's recent critique of Pietersma in "Reflections on the 'Interlinear Paradigm' in Septuagintal Studies" in *Scripture in Transition: Essays on Septuagint, Hebrew Bible, and Dead Sea Scrolls in Honour of Raija Sollamo* (ed. Anssi Voitila and Jutta Jokiranta; JSJSup 126; Leiden: Brill, 2008), 163-178. Joosten questions the use of the interlinear paradigm to explain the origin of the Septuagint, as an "'interlinear' crib intended to assist Jewish pupils in the study of the Hebrew text" (164-165). He argues that the translation was originally intended as a "freestanding, independent text" (178). However, see Pietersma's objections to its being used as a theory for Septuagint origins rather than "as a metaphor…as a heuristic tool [for describing]…the linguistic relationship of the Septuagint to its source text" (16), in "Beyond Literalism: Interlinearity Revisited" (paper presented at the annual meeting of the SBL, Boston, Mass., 24 November 2008).

native fluency or failed a basic course in Greek, or (b) the Greek he came up with is, on reflection, not as bad as it seems on first reading.[40]

He considers the second option preferable and that the "interlinear paradigm...can account for anything from literary beauty to errant nonsense."[41]

Once the process of translation from Hebrew to Greek began, prior translations impacted later ones. The translation of the Pentateuch had a great influence on the choice of words and phrases, and on the grammar and syntax of later books.[42] A characteristic feature of the translation was the lack of variation, the translator frequently choosing the same equivalent for the same Hebrew words. As a result the Pentateuch provided a translation vocabulary of Hebrew-Greek equivalents, and perhaps served as a lexicon for later translators when they encountered "difficult" Hebrew words.[43] Quotations and allusions to the Pentateuch were phrased in the same manner in later books. Certain books were more "Pentateuchal" than other books, for example the translator of Chronicles paid more attention to the

---

[40] Pietersma, "New Paradigm," 356-357.

[41] Ibid, 357.

[42] There may even have been some earlier (carelessly made) written translations preceding the Pentateuch if the testimony of Aristobulus and the *Letter of Aristeas* (para. 30) are to be believed. (However, Aristobulus may have mentioned early translations (Fragment 3, Eusebius *Praep. Ev.* 13.12.1-2) because he wanted to demonstrate the antiquity of the Bible translated into Greek and hence to be accessible to and able to influence Greek philosophy and culture, Naomi Janowitz, "The Rhetoric of Translation: Three Early Perspectives on Translating Torah," *HTR* 84 (1991): 129-40. It is more likely that this is referring to oral translation into Greek (cf. Harl, Dorival, and Munnich, *La Bible grecque des Septante*, 54), or perhaps carelessly prepared Hebrew manuscripts, cf. George Howard, "The Septuagint: A Review of Recent Studies," *ResQ* 13 (1970): 158. See also James Barr, "Did the Greek Pentateuch Really Serve as a Dictionary for the Translators of the Later Books?" in *Hamlet on a Hill: Semitic and Greek Studies Presented to Professor T. Muraoka on the Occasion of His Sixty-Fifth Birthday* (ed. M. F. J. Baasten and W. Th. van Peursen; OLA 118; Louvain: Peeters, 2003), 523-43, who hypothesizes that the translation of the Torah may have been preceded by the translation of more marginal writings such as Job (cf. the discovery of a Targum of Job at Qumran). Since the Torah was central to the Jewish religion and continually read, people would have been able to follow it, even if their Hebrew was weak. The translation of less central books with more difficult language, such as Job, Isaiah, and the other prophetic books such as the Twelve Prophets, Ezekiel, and Jeremiah, which underwent later revision, may have actually preceded the translation of the Pentateuch (539-40).

[43] Cf. Barr, who argues that the Pentateuch was not a "dictionary" for "difficult" words, as "a source that defined standard equivalents," but a "great bag of diverse resources from which material could be gathered up and used," "Pentateuch as Dictionary?," 540.

vocabulary of the Pentateuch than the Samuel and Kings translators did.[44]

It seems all of these models of translation in the cultural/religious environment combined to influence the method of translation. The literal approach to translation along with condensing the message (as in legal and commercial texts from the secular realm) together with expansions for exposition and explanation (as in the oral targums of the religious sphere) were combined in the translation of the Septuagint. Therefore, a translation of the Bible that was literal but contained elements of condensing and expansion was familiar and acceptable to the Alexandrian Jewish community.[45]

C. The Method of Translation

While the translators were probably not conscious of following a particular technique in their translation work (such as formal equivalence vs. dynamic equivalence), their view of the source and the models and precedents mentioned above, no doubt, influenced the way they went about the task of translation. Governed by a desire to bring the readers to the source, they set about their task to produce a literal translation that was as faithful to the original as they could.[46]

---

[44] Cf. Gerleman cited in Emanuel Tov, "The Impact of the LXX Translation of the Pentateuch on the Translation of Other Books," in *Mélanges Dominique Barthélemy: Études bibliques offertes à l'occasion de son 60e anniversaire* (ed. P. Casetti O. Keel, A. Schenker; Göttingen: Vandenhoeck & Ruprecht, 1981), 577-92, (579).

[45] The Pentateuch, which contains both legal and literary sections, has been considered a compromise between a literal approach (especially in legal sections) and a freer approach of translation (especially in literary sections), cf. Brock, "Phenomenon of the Septuagint," 20. However, although the translators had as precedents condensed and expanded translations, we cannot always attribute differences between the Masoretic text and the Septuagint translation to the translators. Perhaps the differences were in the source text (that lay before them, the *Vorlage*). While we do not have the source text used by the translators, we do have examples of condensed (e.g., from Jeremiah, 4QJer[b, d]) and expanded (e.g., from Samuel, 4QSam[a]) Hebrew texts preserved from the Dead Sea Scrolls that are probably closer to the Septuagint *Vorlage* than the MT, cf. Emanuel Tov, *Textual Criticism of the Hebrew Bible* (Minneapolis: Fortress, 1992), 115. For further discussion, see note 49 below.

[46] Sebastian P. Brock, "Translating the Old Testament," in *It is Written: Scripture Citing Scripture: Essays in Honour of Barnabas Lindars* (ed. D. A. Carson and Hugh G. M. Williamson; Cambridge: Cambridge University Press, 1988), 91. Brock also states, "The literal type translation receives short shrift to-day at the hands of modern translation theorists, such as Nida, since their primary concern is with translation as a means of communication. But one should understand why the fashion for literal

In order to produce a literal translation bringing the reader to the source, the translators, for the most part, characteristically aspired after 1) internal consistency (stereotyped renderings consistently rendering elements a particular way irrespective of the context), 2) to represent each constituent, 3) to follow the original word order, and 4) to produce a quantitative 1:1 representation of elements of the original.[47]

Of all the criteria mentioned above, closely adhering to the original word order is perhaps the most striking feature of literalness observed in the translation of most of the Bible, especially in relation to rendering verbal forms into Greek. The translators were particularly careful to preserve the characteristic Hebrew VSO (Verb-Subject-Object) word order. This is not the usual Greek word order, which is more commonly SVO, although Greek word order is much more flexible and varied than Hebrew. (See chapter 3, section I.B. on the significance of variations in word order).

In the translation of Hebrew verb forms the translators tended toward internal consistency using standard equivalents for each verb form. However, the same standard equivalent, the aorist, was typically used to render the two most common Hebrew verb forms in narrative, the *wayyiqtol* and X-*qatal* (perfect) forms. Also the future was frequently employed for both the *w^eqatal* and X-*yiqtol* (imperfect) in sections of speech.[48] The translators did not always follow these standard or common equivalents in their translation, especially if the context demanded the use of a different verb tense (cf. departures from the

---

translation was adopted and not simply condemn it." Modern translators tend to regard the Bible as a piece of literature rather than a hieratic text and see their task as one of bringing the original to the reader (Brock, "Phenomenon of the Septuagint," 28).

[47] Cf. Emanuel Tov, *The Text-Critical Use of the Septuagint in Biblical Research* (JBS 3; Jerusalem: Simor, 1997), 20-24. Tov lists five criteria for literalness within translation units, the first four mentioned here can be expressed statistically. His fifth criterion is the linguistic adequacy of lexical choices in the context.

[48] Woo classifies this phenomenon "assimilation" or the rendering of different verbal constructions by the same verbal form ("Études," 189). As far as the convention of classifying Hebrew verbal form goes, we follow many Hebrew grammars in distinguishing these forms by the pattern of consonants and vowels which occurs when a triconsonantal verbal root (*q-t-l* "to kill" is frequently used) interdigitates with vowels and the consonants of the verbal patterns. The simplest form is adopted (e.g., for the indicative the third person masculine singular form) as a label for the entire paradigm. In this study the four indicative forms are mostly referred to as *qatal, yiqtol, wayyiqtol,* and *w^eqatal* using this convention; cf. the first section of chapter 3 for a full account of the Hebrew verbal system using this convention. In the expressions X-*qatal* and X-*yiqtol,* X- refers to an element other than *waw* preceding the verbal form.

standard equivalents in the translation of verbs as dealt with in chapter 4 and especially in chapter 5). Sometimes departing from standard or common equivalents was also driven by limitations in the inventory of the Greek language.

For the most part the translators endeavored to represent each Hebrew constituent with a Greek equivalent and produce a quantitative 1:1 representation of the original. However, the translators were willing at times to add, to omit, or to substitute certain phrases (or, perhaps in the case of the book of Jeremiah, even larger sections of text—although there could also have been two editions) in their work of translation. It is often difficult to know whether these so called pluses and minuses reflect a different Hebrew *Vorlage* or the translators' license to be a little free in places.[49] Sometimes they were motivated by a need to make sense of a difficult text or to harmonize with a parallel or a similar text. Some additions were glosses, expansions, and interpretations, such as those seen in the targums.[50] Some of the omissions could have been motivated by a desire to simplify and make the translation more forceful, as in the legal and commercial translations mentioned above.[51] Perhaps words or phrases

---

[49] It is often difficult to know what to attribute the differences between the Hebrew text (e.g., the Masoretic text (MT) as it is available electronically in a program such as *GRAMCORD*) and the Greek text of the Septuagint (e.g., Rahlfs's as in *GRAMCORD*). Are the differences due to the translators, or are they due to the editors and scribes responsible for the Hebrew text (i.e., the MT or the *Vorlage* that was before the translators)? For a discussion of two different approaches to the problem: that of J. W. Wevers, who attributes the differences more to the creative work of the translators than to differences between the translators' Hebrew *Vorlage* and the MT, and that of A. Aejmelaeus, who attributes the differences more to different Hebrew texts rather than the creativity of the translators (who on the whole imitated the *Vorlage* as much as possible), cf. Karen H. Jobes and Moisés Silva, *Invitation to the Septuagint* (Grand Rapids: Baker, 2000), 149 ff., who outline the two positions, while favoring the approach of Wevers, and James Barr, review of Karen H. Jobes and Moisés Silva, *Invitation to the Septuagint, RBL* (10/2002): online at http://www.bookreviews.org/bookdetail.asp?TitleID=1341 (5 Nov. 2002), who critiques their approach in favor of one more in line with that of Aejmeleaus. For problems of the difference between the *Vorlage* and the MT, particularly as it relates to the book of Chronicles, see the first section of chapter 4. Also see note 51 below.

[50] As Brock points out, "the interpretational element is either necessarily imposed on him [the translator] by the ambiguity of the original Hebrew, or when the introduction of this element is optional, it features only sporadically and in a limited way, perhaps often at a subconscious level; whereas in the case of the *expositor* the interpretational element is deliberately and usually consistently introduced" (Brock, "Translating the Old Testament," 96).

[51] This may be the explanation for the shorter version of the book of Jeremiah in the Septuagint, which due to omissions is "simpler, more natural, and more forcible." There are also more omissions than additions in the Pentateuch (Rabin, "Translation

were substituted for theological or social/cultural reasons, or even to
update the text.[52] While the addition to or omission of parts of the text
seems strange in a translation that is, for the most part, literal, this is
not out of keeping with the examples from the culture mentioned
above.

In fact, in places where there is a departure from this literal
approach, especially from using common equivalents, the Septuagint
translators display a fairly sophisticated understanding of the Hebrew
verbal system.[53]

Process," 23). However, Tov considers that the translator of Jeremiah, who translated
quite literally, used a Hebrew manuscript that was considerably shorter than the MT.
This seems to be confirmed by the discovery of 4QJer[b, d] which resembles the textual
tradition that lies at the base of the Septuagint (Tov, *Text-Critical Use*, 19). Two cases
of the omission of larger sections of text comparing *Paraleipomenon* with the MT of
Chronicles occur in the shortening of Ham's genealogy omitting 1 Chronicles 1:11-16
and 18-23. Cases of addition occur in 2 Chronicles 35:19 (4 verses), 36:2 (3 verses),
36:4 (1 verse) and 5 (4 verses), where sections are added that closely correspond to
additional verses in parallel passages in 2 Kings 23:24-27, 31b-33; and 24:1-4
respectively. See also chapter 5 sec. II on anomalies in the translation of verbs in
Chronicles including minuses and pluses, word order variation, structure and clause
type variation, and tense variation.

[52] For example, the Hebrew word צוּר "rock" is translated θεός "God" or βοηθός
"help" when it refers to God (e.g., in Deut 32; and most places in the book of Psalms).
When צוּר is not employed as a divine name, a standard Greek equivalent πέτρα
"rock" is mostly used (Staffan Olofsson, *The LXX Version: A Guide to the Translation
Technique of the Septuagint* (ConBOT 30; Stockholm: Almqvist & Wiksell, 1990), 44-45).
The translators were also sensitive to the cultural environment, for example, avoiding
the use of the word λαγῶς for "hare" (an unclean animal—Lev 11:6) due to the fact
that it was the name of one of the Ptolemies (Barclay, *Jews in the Mediterranean Diaspora*,
126; see also Collins, *Library in Alexandria*, 11-12). However, as Sarah Pearce indicates
in her paper, "Hairy Feet or Just Plane Hares: Monarchy in the Greek Pentateuch"
(paper presented at an International Colloquium of the AHRB Greek Bible Project,
Oxford, 24 March 2003), the "translation choices in order to show respect to the
Ptolemaic monarchy rests on rather uncertain foundations" (19). The translators also
corrected and updated the biblical geography of Egypt.

[53] The Hebrew verb system as preserved in the biblical text has two kinds of verb
forms. Some verb forms functioned in a way that corresponded to Mishnaic or
rabbinic Hebrew (and probably the Hebrew spoken at the time of translation). Other
verb forms functioned in a way that did not correspond to rabbinic Hebrew use (i.e.,
they are archaic in their function). The translator chose appropriate equivalents for
these two kinds of verb forms, as well as recognizing that the context allowed for or
dictated the use of other non-standard Greek equivalents (see chapter 3, section II.E,
chapter 4, section III.D, and chapter 5 for summaries of the different verb forms and
how the translator handled them).

D. The Achievement of the Translators—What Was Produced, and Their Ability

As a result of following a literal approach to translation, the translation of the Septuagint is for the most part subservient to Semitic syntax. The translators of most books, including the translator of Chronicles, closely followed Hebrew word order, formal correspondence, particles, compounds, and lexical features. Certain Semitic features are almost always followed. Words do not come between an article and a noun, the adjective follows its substantive, the genitive immediately follows its construct, a direct personal pronominal object always follows its governing verb, a demonstrative adjective follows its noun, the VSO word order is almost always respected, and post-positive conjunctions rarely occur.[54]

As a result, Septuagint Greek reads quite differently from classical Greek texts, and, indeed, more contemporary Hellenistic Greek texts, such as the *Letter of Aristeas* and the writings of Josephus (see chapter 3, note 53). This has caused scholars to question the ability of the translators to produce proper idiomatic Hellenistic Greek, some even considering that they produced instead a special dialect of biblical Greek (cf. Turner),[55] and even question whether they had a good grasp of the Hebrew original.

While the translators gave a lot of prestige to the Hebrew original, they also displayed a certain amount of sensitivity to the Greek target language. On the whole, the translators demonstrate a good knowledge of the rules of Greek syntax, and in certain books, such as the Pentateuch, constructions that have no place in Hebrew but are considered good idiomatic Greek style, such as the genitive absolute, frequently occur. The translators also distinguished exactly between the tenses of the indicative in if-clauses, used the subjunctive to represent the Hebrew imperfect in conditional sentences, and alternated the tenses of the subjunctive in order to express different shades of Hebrew meaning.[56] Translators used surface Hellenizations giving Greek case endings to Semitic words such as personal names. They also utilized a richer Greek vocabulary to make lexical distinctions that were not present in Hebrew, for example, in some

---

[54] J. Merle Rife, "The Mechanics of Translation Greek," *JBL* 52 (1933): 244-52.

[55] Nigel Turner, "Biblical Greek—the Peculiar Language of a Peculiar People," in *Studia Evangelica Vol. 7. International Congress on Biblical Studies Papers 1973* (ed. Elizabeth A. Livingstone; Berlin: Akademie Verlag, 1982), 512.

[56] Bickerman, "Septuagint as Translation," 177.

sections, two Greek words were used for the Hebrew word מִזְבֵּחַ "altar" to distinguish between a pagan altar (βωμός) and an altar used in the worship of the God of Israel (θυσιαστήριον).[57]

The Greek of the translation mostly agrees with the common speech of the contemporary Greeks. In orthography and morphological inflection, some vocabulary, and in the relaxation of syntax, the translation is vernacular.[58] Certain structures, while present in Greek, are given much more prominence due to the frequency of their equivalents in Hebrew, for example, the coordination of sentences with καί (translating וְ *and*—reflecting the paratactic nature of Hebrew syntax), and the occurrence of ἰδού (*behold*—reflecting the common occurrence of the presentative particle הִנֵּה in Hebrew). As a result of the excess prominence of structures such as these, the Septuagint translation offends the literary standard of Greek, in that the language is foreign and clumsy, following the original slavishly as to wording, syntax, and style. However, due to the kind of document (i.e., considered as an archaic and inspired text), this is in some ways acceptable. It is a unique document. In it the God of Israel spoke to a new world in the Greek language. The awe due to divine utterances imposed the literalness of translation.[59]

There is quite a bit of variation among and within translation units as to how closely the translators followed standard equivalents and how much they were willing to depart from these. Therefore, we could say that the Greek translation of the Bible is characterized by

---

[57] Cf. Allen Wikgren, *Hellenistic Greek Texts* (Chicago: University of Chicago Press, 1947), xxi. The distinction was also made to contrast altars used for true or false worship (e.g., Josh 22:19; 1 Macc 1:59), see Robert Hanhart, "Earlier Tradition and Subsequent Influences," in *Septuagint, Scrolls, and Cognate Writings* (ed. George J. Brooke and Barnabas Lindars; SCS 33; Atlanta: Society of Biblical Literature, 1992), 339-379 (346-347). In some places in the Minor Prophets, Isaiah, and Jeremiah, βωμός is also used to translate the similar sounding Hebrew word בָּמָה "high place," referring to a heathen place of worship. In 2 Chronicles 14:5<4>, θυσιαστήριον is even used to translate בָּמָה.

[58] Cf. Bickerman, "Septuagint as Translation," 176. See also Evans's discussion of Hebrew interference (features such as the paratactic clausal structure, low frequencies of the imperfect to aorist) and natural Greek usage, *Verbal Syntax*, 259-263. He characterizes "verbal syntax in the Greek Pentateuch...generally as typical of early Koine vernacular usage" (262). In contrast, Turner believes that the Greek Old Testament is only superficially part of the contemporary Koine, but rather it has the distinction of being the peculiar language of a peculiar people, and is barely intelligible, except to someone familiar with the contents and concepts of the Old Testament (Turner, "Biblical Greek," 512).

[59] Bickerman, "Septuagint as Translation," 198-99.

variations within a literal approach.[60] The units of translation have been classified according to various criteria into groups reflecting their literalness. The freer sections of translation are mostly in books of poetry such as Proverbs, Job, and Isaiah. The books also seem to become more literal over time; for example, the Pentateuch is less literal than the Old Greek of Samuel-Kings, which in turn is less literal than Chronicles.[61]

Chronicles can be viewed as part of a broader trajectory of increasing literalness in translation, driven by a desire to get closer to the original Hebrew text. This can be seen even more clearly with the translation of other ancient versions, e.g., the Armenian and Georgian versions of the Bible.[62] Paradoxically, the most sacred portion of the

---

[60] Cf. Barr, *Typology of Literalism*, 7. Cf. also Anneli Aejmelaeus, *On the Trail of the Septuagint Translators: Collected Essays* (Kampen: Kok Pharos Publishing House, 1993), 1.

[61] For example, Tov, in *Text-Critical Use*, 20-24, 27, classifies Chronicles and the *kaige*-Th sections of Samuel-Kings, (2 Sam 10:1—1 Kgs 2:11; 1 Kgs 22—2 Kgs 25) as literal according to his criteria. Other literal units are: Judges (B text), Psalms, Ezra, Nehemiah, Ruth, Song of Songs, Lamentations. His free and even paraphrastic units are: Isaiah, Job, Proverbs, Esther, and Daniel. So also Raija Sollamo, "The Letter of Aristeas and the Origin of the Septuagint," in *X Congress of the International Organization for Septuagint and Cognate Studies, Oslo, 1998* (ed. Bernard Taylor; SCS 51; Atlanta: Society of Biblical Literature Publications, 2001), 329-342, "the overwhelming majority of the books were rendered much more literally than the Pentateuch (340-341). She considers that the *Letter of Aristeas*, probably written after and around the time other books were translated and which "defends the original, third century translation against those who desired to correct it and bring it closer in line with the Hebrew," could neither "prevent the Septuagint translation of the Pentateuch from being corrected or revised in Egypt according to the Masoretic text nor prevent the other books of Scripture from being originally translated in a very slavish way." (341-342). Both Sollamo, *Renderings of Hebrew Semiprepositions in the Septuagint* (AASF, Diss. hum. litt., 19), Helsinki, Suomalainen Tiedeakatemia, 1979, 280-289 and Soisalon-Soininen, *Die Infinitive*, 176-196 compare the translation techniques of the different books.

In terms of the translation of the verbs, the translator wanted to make Chronicles closer to its source than the Pentateuch (where he used conjoined aorists rather than circumstantial participles—see chapter 3, note 53, chapter 4, note 35, and chapter 5, notes 2 and 34) and the sections of Samuel-Kings parallel to Chronicles (replacing historic presents with aorists—see chapter 5, note 27). Also in the translation of וַיְהִי introducing temporal clauses the translator of Chronicles is more consistent and closer to the Hebrew (mostly using καὶ ἐγένετο) than the translators of the Pentateuch (see chapter 4, note 24). While the Pentateuch translators frequently rendered וַיְהִי καὶ ἐγένετο, they also rendered it a variety of other ways, including ἐγένετο δὲ, καὶ ἐγενήθη, ἐγενήθη δὲ, ὡς δὲ + indicative verb, ἡνίκα δὲ and καὶ ἡνίκα, none of which the Chronicles' translator employed (perhaps considering their work too free, see note 68 below).

[62] Sebastian P. Brock, "The Phenomenon of Biblical Translation in Antiquity," in *Studies in the Septuagint: Origins, Recensions, and Interpretations: Selected Essays* (ed. Sidney Jellicoe; New York: Ktav, 1974), 541-71.

Hebrew Bible, the Pentateuch, was translated early and hence more freely.

E. The Reception of the Septuagint

The local Alexandrian community received the translation of the Pentateuch enthusiastically. They celebrated its completion annually by holding a festival on the site of the translation, the island of Pharos.[63] This indicates that they felt that the translation was appropriate for its need.

However, the translation of the Septuagint did not always enjoy such an enthusiastic reception. Later, it came under attack as not being literal enough. As was mentioned above, later books (such as Chronicles) were translated more literally than those translated earlier (e.g., Samuel-Kings), and certain books, such as Judges and portions of Samuel-Kings were revised. Later, the Septuagint was largely abandoned by some groups (particularly among the Jewish community in Palestine), and slavishly literal later translations, most notably Aquila and Theodotion, were made.[64] Some examples of the literalism employed in these versions are the translation of גַּם by καί γε (giving the name to the so called *kaige* recension of Samuel-Kings) and Aquila's translation of the direct object marker אֵת by the preposition σύν "with" followed by an object in the accusative case. This results in an ungrammatical structure in Greek, as σύν governs an object in the dative case.[65]

---

[63] Philo, *Vit. Mos.* 2.41-43, quoted in Barclay, *Jews in the Mediterranean Diaspora*, 424.

[64] Geza Vermes, review of Dominique Barthélemy, *Les Devanciers d'Aquila*, *JSS* 11 (1966): 264, proposes that this slavishly literal approach may have been to produce a translation to help Greek-speaking Jews with a rudimentary knowledge of Hebrew to understand the sacred text of the Old Testament, rather than due to anti-Christian polemics or the need to adapt the Greek text to Palestinian *halakah* (cf. Barthélemy).

[65] In Hebrew אֵת has two meanings, a direct object marker, which is usually not translated, and a preposition meaning *with*. Due to his desire to represent each Hebrew morpheme with a corresponding Greek one, Aquila frequently translated the direct object marker by σύν (using the ambiguity in the meaning of אֵת). However, as Jellicoe points out, this was "not his universal practice," but he usually represents אֵת followed by a definite article or a detached pronoun, Sydney Jellicoe, *The Septuagint and Modern Study* (Oxford: Oxford University Press, 1968), 81. Barthélemy considers that maybe Aquila's use of σύν with the accusative case can be understood as σύν functioning as an adverb rather than a preposition, as it does sometimes in Homer, (*Devanciers*, 16).

However, as revisions were made, a defense of the translation of the Septuagint was also mounted. This can be seen in attitudes to the translation. There was a progression in the view of the text that can be seen in comparing three accounts of its translation. Aristobulus considered that the text was inspired,[66] Aristeas implied that the translators carried out their work with divine sanction (compared to previous failed attempts, which were prevented by divine intervention),[67] and Philo went as far as to consider that the translators were also inspired, and that the phrases chosen by the translators correspond 'literally' with the Hebrew. "If any individual knew both languages and read both texts, he would find that they are 'one and the same.'"[68] Philo's view was expressed at a time when major revisions were probably being made in Greek texts to bring the translation closer to the Hebrew and make it more literal.

After the beginning of the Christian era, the Rabbis became more hostile to the Septuagint as it was adopted by the Christian church and even compared the time of its translation with that of the making of the golden calf—a dark time in Israel's history.[69] However, its reception by the church insured its spread and its lasting legacy, particularly among the Greek-speaking eastern branch of the church and its descendants.[70]

---

[66] Frag. 4, Eusebius, *Praep. Ev.* 13.12.3, quoted in Janowitz, "Rhetoric of Translation," 131.

[67] *Ep. Arist.* 312-16, quoted in Janowitz, "Rhetoric of Translation," 134. The *Letter of Aristeas* may have been written to defend the original Greek translation against the later recensions that were being made about the time of its writing (i.e, 150 BCE. The translation of Chronicles around the same time as the writing of the *Letter of Aristeas* could have been part of this trend to make the Greek translations closer to the Hebrew (see note 15 above).

[68] Philo, *Vit. Mos.* 2.40, quoted in Janowitz, "Rhetoric of Translation," 138-39. It seems unlikely that the translators of later books would have considered their predecessors' work as inspired. Although the translator of Chronicles was indebted to the Pentateuch translators for providing a source of vocabulary for his work, it seems that he did not follow all of the translation decisions the Pentateuch translators made. At least, as far as the translation of the verbs is concerned, he preferred to avoid using a conjunctive circumstantial participle to render a *wayyiqtol* form (see note 61 above).

[69] *Massekhet Soferim* 1.7, quoted in Joseph Mélèze-Modrzejewski, "How to Be a Greek and Yet a Jew in Hellenistic Alexandria," in *Diasporas in Antiquity* (ed. Shaye J. D. Cohen and Ernest S. Frerichs; BJS 288; Atlanta: Scholars Press, 1993), 80.

[70] Note however continued Jewish translation of the Bible into Greek in the diaspora, as mentioned by Natalio Fernández Marcos, *The Septuagint in Context: Introduction to the Greek Version of the Bible* (trans. Wilfred G. E. Watson; Leiden: Brill, 2000) in his chapter "Jewish Versions into Medieval and Modern Greek," 174-187.

Having looked at the background of the translators and their task and achievement in this chapter, the following chapter deals with the nature of the Hebrew and Greek verbal systems. These two chapters lay a foundation for the chapters that follow dealing with the collecting of data, its analysis, and its comparison. Finally, we consider the translation of the verbs in Chronicles related to some of the principles outlined in this chapter.

CHAPTER THREE

THE HEBREW AND GREEK VERB SYSTEMS

Before we analyze the translation of Hebrew verbal forms of Chronicles into Greek, it is necessary to consider the inventory of verb forms of each language, their meaning (e.g., aspect, tense, and *Aktionsart*), and how they function in the textual-linguistic context. In addition, we will mention historical-linguistic developments in the use of verb forms, particularly within the Hebrew verbal system to account for changes in the use and meaning of Hebrew verb forms in their textual-linguistic contexts. The book of Chronicles is particularly interesting since it contains classical biblical Hebrew (as preserved in parallel texts in Samuel-Kings) and late biblical Hebrew (especially in sections unique to Chronicles). It is our contention that the translator understood the Hebrew verbal system according to two different registers of Hebrew, spoken and written Hebrew. He understood some verb forms according to the Hebrew spoken at the time he translated Chronicles, and others according to the traditional understanding of archaic biblical Hebrew forms as preserved in written Hebrew texts.

In analyzing the verb systems of the two languages, the verbs are divided into indicatives, participles, infinitives, and volitives. Then the way these verbs function in three types of clauses—main clauses in narration, main clauses in reported speech, and subordinate clauses— are presented for each of the languages. The analysis concludes with a brief comparison of the languages, their similarities and differences, and the appropriateness of certain Greek verb forms for rendering Hebrew forms. We begin with an excursus on verbal features, focusing particularly on *Aktionsart* (*lexis* and the textual-linguistic context) and its impact on verb choice.[1]

---

[1] This excursus deals with the impact of *Aktionsart* and the text-linguistic context on Hebrew and Greek verb forms in more detail. Tense and aspect, since they are grammatically coded into certain verb forms, and clause types are dealt with in the treatment of the verb forms according to the two languages.

I. EXCURSUS: VERBAL FEATURES: *AKTIONSART—LEXIS* AND THE TEXTUAL-LINGUISTIC CONTEXT

Recent studies of the Hebrew and Greek verbal systems, such as Goldfajn, Binnick, and Fanning, have stressed the need to distinguish between *tense, aspect,* and *Aktionsart.*[2] *Tense* is the "grammaticalised expression of location in time."[3] *Aspect* is the speaker or writer's grammaticalized portrayal of the situation (portraying the action as a complete whole—perfective, or portraying the action in progress without indicating its completion—imperfective). *Aktionsart* (kind of action)[4] is a description of the action features ascribed to the verbal referent as to the way it happens or exists according to the verb's lexical meaning (or *lexis,* e.g., divided into stative and fientive verbs, or verbs of state, activity, accomplishment, achievement)[5] combined with

---

[2] Tal Goldfajn, *Word Order and Time in Biblical Hebrew Narrative* (Oxford: Clarendon Press, 1998), 60-64, R. I. Binnick, *Time and the Verb: A Guide to Tense and Aspect* (Oxford: Oxford University Press, 1991), 452-61, B. M. Fanning, *Verbal Aspect in New Testament Greek* (Oxford: Clarendon Press, 1990), 8-85, and Stanley E. Porter, *Verbal Aspect in the Greek of the New Testament, with reference to Tense and Mood* (Studies in Biblical Greek 1; New York: Peter Lang, 1993), 17-65.

[3] B. Comrie, *Tense* (Cambridge: Cambridge University Press, 1985), 9. Many languages use grammatical, morphological categories to express location in time. This is usually expressed in the verbal system, either by inflection or by periphrasis. Although tense is an important indicator of time in many languages, it is seldom (if ever) the only factor involved in expressing temporal location. It is argued by most Hebrew scholars and a few Greek scholars that neither Hebrew nor Greek verb forms grammaticalize tense but only aspect. Temporal location is indicated by other contextual factors such as temporal adverbs and verb sequence.

[4] Also called "situation aspect" as opposed to "viewpoint aspect" (which distinguishes perfective versus imperfective aspects), cf. Fanning, *Verbal Aspect,* 40-41. See also the discussion of F. W. Dobbs-Allsopp, "Biblical Hebrew Statives and Situation Aspect," *JSS* 45 (2000): 21-53, who uses the terms 'viewpoint aspect' (i.e., grammatical aspect: perfective and imperfective) and 'situation aspect' ("'the intrinsic temporal qualities' of the situation itself," i.e., *Aktionsart*) to distinguish between the two (25). He also distinguishes a third kind of aspect, phasal aspect, which looks at the phases of a procedure (beginning, middle, and end). It is regrettable that older Greek grammar books (such as Blass and Debrunner, Robertson, and Moulton) use the German word *Aktionsart* in a way that is very similar to more recent treatises' use of the word *aspect,* (F. Blass and A. Debrunner, *A Greek Grammar of the New Testament and Other Early Christian Literature* (trans. R. W. Funk; Chicago: University of Chicago Press, 1961), A. T. Robertson, *A Grammar of the Greek New Testament in the Light of Historical Research* (Nashville: Broadman Press, 1934), and J. H. Moulton, *A Grammar of New Testament Greek I. Prolegomena* (Edinburgh: T and T Clark, 1908).

[5] Cf. Z. Vendler, "Verbs and Times," *Philosophical Review* 66 (1957): 43-60. A verb's lexical meaning can be simplified into two main types, stative and fientive (active or dynamic), as it is mostly in this study, or can be expanded to include as many as seven or eight different verb types. However, the multiplying of categories with over-fine and idiosyncratic differences hinder the usefulness of such distinctions. *Aktionsart* is not

other contextual features.[6] Campbell treats *Aktionsart* as a pragmatic value describing "how an action actually takes place" that combines the semantic values encoded in the verbal form (aspect, proximity) with the lexeme (transitive [+/- punctiliar], intransitive [+/- stative]) and the context.[7]

A. Lexical Meaning (Lexis)

The effect of a verb's lexical meaning on the choice of the Hebrew verb form is minimal. The main distinction in choice of form occurs between stative and fientive roots. Stative verbs function differently to fientive verbs in terms of which forms they prefer and the meanings the forms carry.[8] For example, the suffix or *qatal* forms of stative verbs

---

only derived from the meaning of the verb's lexical form (*lexis*). Other grammatical and contextual factors such as adjuncts (especially temporal adverbials), and the number and role of participants (e.g., subject[s], object[s]) also affect the temporal/aspectual force of an expression. Cf. Randall Garr, "Affectedness, Aspect, and Biblical Hebrew *'et*," *ZAH* 2 (1991): 119-34, in which he argues that the particle *'et*, especially with verbs of motion, marks a dynamic situation as perfective or completed, or as telic (i.e., attaining a goal). Consequently, the term *situation aspect* is preferred by some to the term *Aktionsart* (see note 4 above).

[6] Another verbal feature is *modality*, which also has some bearing on temporal and aspectual issues. Modality reflects the writer or speaker's attitude (cognitive or epistemic—to do with knowledge, emotive, volitive or deontic—what ought to be) and mostly is realized in independent clauses. In addition to "attitudinal" modality, Binnick distinguishes "functional" modality, which occurs mostly in subordinate clauses as a function of the grammar or syntax (e.g., subjunctives in purpose clauses in Greek). Binnick also distinguishes between *mood* (morphological marking of the verb or by use of a modal auxiliary—such as may, can, must, ought [to], will, and shall in English) and *modality* (meaning categorization), *Time and Verb*, 70-73. Woo divides *modality* into *marked modality* (reflecting the participation of the will or the opinion of the speaker in a statement mostly expressed by the subjunctive, the optative, the imperative, and the future indicative moods in Greek, but also by other indicative moods) and *unmarked modality* (mostly expressed by the non-future indicative mood in the past time or at the moment of speech), "Études," 71-73.

[7] Constantine C. Campbell, *Basics of Verbal Aspect in Biblical Greek*, (Grand Rapids: Zondervan, 2008), 23-25, 62-63. Campbell considers the traditional categories of ingressive or gnomic (aorist), and iterative, progressive, or conative (imperfect) as a function of *Aktionsart* (verbal semantics + lexeme + context).

[8] There is some difference in opinion as to what constitutes a stative verb. Creason classes a stative verb as having the truth value able to be evaluated at a[ny] point of time and not involving a change of state, e.g., "to be impure." Verbs such as "to live" and "to stand" he classifies as unchanging activity verbs. He classifies verbs that indicate a change in state as telic achievements, e.g., "the land *became ritually unacceptable*" or accomplishments, e.g., "the river *dried up*," Stuart Alan Creason, "Semantic Classes of Hebrew Verbs: A Study of *Aktionsart* in the Hebrew Verbal System" (Ph.D. diss., University of Chicago, 1996), 71-74. Dobbs-Allsopp, "Biblical

sometimes have present meaning,[9] especially in speech,[10] and imperfective or prefix forms (including *wayyiqtol* forms) frequently indicate a change in state or an inception into a state.[11]

Lexical meaning has a greater influence on the choice of the Greek verb form. Some verbs such as the verb εἰμί "to be" only have imperfective forms (therefore it is considered by Porter as aspectually vague). Other verbs such as ἔχω "to have" prefer imperfective forms over perfective forms. In contrast to Hebrew, a perfective form (e.g., the aorist) is mostly used when stative verbs indicate a change in state or inception into a state.[12] Other verbs such as οἶδα "to know" only occur as perfects or pluperfects with stative (perfect) aspect.[13] This

---

Hebrew Statives and Situation Aspect," 2000, establishes criteria for dynamic and change-of-state readings of stative verbs based on non-standard associations in the pragmatic context (for dynamic readings, such as syntactic collocations of *hlk, hyh*, effected objects, control frames, and participle forms) and in narrative sequence and punctiliar frames (for change of state readings).

[9] The fact that a *qatal* form can have static/durative meaning appears unusual at first glance, since the *qatal* form is a perfective form. However, if we understand the notion of perfectivity to refer to viewing the action or state as a complete whole (rather than a complet*ed* whole), it is logical. The *qatal* form of stative verbs was historically a conjugated adjective, cf. the Akkadian permansive or verbal adjective.

[10] For example in Chronicles, יָדַעְתִּי "*I know* that God has determined," translated by a Greek present γινώσκω (2 Chr 25:16; so also 6:30). Also יָדַעְתָּ "*You know* your servant," is translated by the perfect (with present meaning) οἶδας (1 Chr 17:18). Interestingly, יָדַעְתִּי "*I know*, my God, that you search the heart," is translated by an aorist ἔγνων (1 Chr 29:17). This also illustrates some degree of sensitivity to the context and flexibility on behalf of the translator in rendering almost identical Hebrew verb forms.

[11] Hebrew stative verbs may refer to three different situations, dependent on the context in which they occur. For example, "If a clause which contains a stative verb occurs as a part of the foreground of a narrative, then it will be interpreted as a change of state or as a remain-in-state situation. If such a clause occurs in the background of a narrative, then it will simply be interpreted as a state," Creason, "Semantic Classes of Hebrew Verbs," 403. In the former context the stative verb is likely to be a *wayyiqtol* form, whereas in the latter context it is likely to be a *qatal* form. Stative verbs occurring with a momentary adverbial expression and verbs occurring in narrative sequence should be interpreted as changes of states (ibid, 75). Therefore, *wayyiqtol* "stative" forms in narrative sequence tend to have inceptive meaning, e.g., וַיִּגְדַּל "thus King Solomon excelled [lit., *became greater than*] all the kings of the earth" translated ἐμεγαλύνθη (2 Chr 9:22), וַיִּזְקַן "But Jehoiada grew old" translated ἐγήρασεν (24:15), and (וַיֵּדַע) "*then* Manasseh *knew*" translated ἔγνω (33:13). All of the translated forms are aorists (i.e., the so-called inceptive aorist).

[12] Fanning, *Verbal Aspect*, 137-38.

[13] A few verbs occur frequently as perfects with particular nuances, for example, the perfect of ἵστημι, ἕστηκα "I stand," occurs 138 out of 771 times in the perfect in the LXX (15/55 times in Chronicles) and the perfect of πείθω "I persuade" πέποιθα/πέπεισμαι with the notion of "I have confidence, I trust" occurs 156/187 times (6/6 times in Chronicles). Occurring less commonly are ἀνέῳγα "I open" which occurs 16/181 times (3/6 times in Chronicles), μέμνημαι "I remember" 16/272

aspect describes an existing state or the result of the entrance into a state.

B. Context: Clause Types and Discourse Pragmatics

The textual-linguistic context includes clause types, arguments in the clause (including word order), and influences on the text (and verb choice) beyond the immediate context of the sentence.

Clause types can be divided into three different types of clauses: main clauses in narration, main clauses in reported speech, and subordinate clauses in both narration and reported speech. These clauses have different temporal frames or reference times. In past narration the reference time precedes that of narration time, in reported speech the reference time is relative to and overlaps with the time of speaking, and in subordinate clauses the reference time is relative to the time of the main clause. The verb forms operate differently, and different verb forms predominate in these three types of clauses.[14]

Another influence on verb forms is the impact of topic and focus on word order. Topic relates to the subject about which something is said, and focus refers to an element that the writer or speaker is drawing special attention to.[15] Word order variation, such as the fronting of a constituent to indicate topic shift or focus, may bring about a change in the verb forms (especially in Hebrew). Biblical Hebrew has an unmarked constituent order V-S-O and V-O.[16] The extraposition of a

---

times, τέθνηκα "I am dead" 84/92 times (1/1 time in Chronicles), cf. 0/595 times for ἀποθνῄσκω "I die," and [ἐπι-]κέκλημαι "I am called" 41/696 times (2/24). They have present force and stative meaning, with very little distinction between the act and its results.

[14] Goldfajn (following Hans Reichenbach, *Elements of Symbolic Logic*, (New York: Macmillan, 1947)) distinguishes between past narration (R<Tn—in which a reference time "R" precedes time of narration "Tn") and reported speech (R/Ts—in which a reference time "R" overlaps the time of speaking "Ts"), Goldfajn, *Word Order*, 78ff., 116-22. See sections II.D and III.D below for a fuller treatment on how the verb forms function in each of these clause types.

[15] Cf. Michael Rosenbaum, *Word-Order Variation in Isaiah 40-55: A Functional Perspective* (Assen: Van Gorcum, 1997), 26, 62ff.

[16] Barry L. Bandstra, "Word Order and Emphasis in Biblical Hebrew Narrative," in *Linguistics and Biblical Hebrew* (ed. Walter Bodine; Winona Lake, Indiana: Eisenbrauns, 1992), 109-123, (123). Holmstedt, who postulates that biblical Hebrew exhibits SV basic word order, has recently disputed this. He proposes that SV order inverts to VS in modal clauses, negative clauses, and when a function word (which is also used to explain *wayyiqtol* clauses) or a fronted phrase occurs at the beginning of

constituent, for example, to produce the word order X-V (where X is another element) is employed for: 1. Focus marking, 2. A new topic, a comparative topic, or an action discontinuity (simultaneous or previous action)—indicating background information or unit boundaries and 3. Dramatic pause (peak).[17] The extraposition of a constituent in a sequence of sequential verb forms constrains the Hebrew language to switch from a sequential to a non-sequential (marked) verb form. The reason for this is that another constituent cannot occur between Hebrew sequential forms (with order *waw*-V[S][O]) and the conjunction *waw* "and." Therefore, changes in word order for topicalization or focus influence the Hebrew verb form. However, changes in word order do not specify exactly which verb form should be used, only that a non-sequential form be used (e.g., in past contexts a *qatal* form, a rare *yiqtol* form, or a non-verbal *qotel* form or a noun sentence). Other factors such as the temporal situation of the discourse determine which of these non-sequential forms would be appropriate.

Traditionally, scholars have considered that Greek has an unmarked constituent order S-V-O and V-O.[18] However, due to case markings on substantives (which indicate the subject, object, etc.) word order in Greek is much more flexible than in Hebrew.

---

the clause, Robert Holmstedt, "The Relative Clause in Biblical Hebrew: A Linguistic Analysis" (Ph.D. diss., University of Wisconsin, Madison, 2002), 198. He considers that the remaining word order variation found in the Hebrew Bible is influenced by pragmatics, i.e., Theme [Topic], Rheme [Comment], and Kontrast [Focus].

[17] Christo H. J. van der Merwe, "Discourse Linguistics and Biblical Hebrew Grammar," in *Biblical Hebrew and Discourse Linguistics* (ed. Robert D. Bergen; Dallas: Summer Institute of Linguistics, 1994), 13-49, (33). Creason, in a study of 1781 relative clauses in Genesis through 2 Kings found that they are almost exclusively verb-initial, with the order VSO pp adv (with only 35 exceptions or 2%), Stewart Creason, "Word Order in Relative Clauses" (paper presented at the annual meeting of the SBL, Washington, D.C., November 1993). According to William M. Schniedewind, review of Ziony Zevit, *The Anterior Construction in Classical Hebrew*, *BASOR* 318 (2000): 79-81, topic or focus is more salient than action discontinuity in Hebrew narrative, in which he argues that "narrative is not ordered linearly, but rather topically...The syntax marks a change in topic and the temporal relationship is at best ancillary to topic...Backgrounding [is] related to characterization which is also marked disjunctively," cf. Zevit who emphasizes the temporal dimension.

[18] Joseph Greenberg, "Some Universals of Grammar with Particular Reference to the Order of Meaningful Elements," in *Universals of Language* (ed. J. Greenberg; Cambridge: MIT Press, 1966), 73-113 Cited 23 January 2008. Online: http://angli02.kgw.tu-berlin.de/Korean/Artikel02/; cf. Helma Dik, *Word Order in Ancient Greek: A Pragmatic Account of Word Order Variation in Herodotus* (Amsterdam: J. C. Gieben, 1995), 6, who cites recent scholarship debating the question of Greek word order.

In addition to considerations of topic and focus (which impact word order and the choice between a sequential and a non-sequential form in Hebrew), temporal succession-temporal discontinuity (overlay) and foreground-background (salience) in discourse structure also influence verb choice.

Temporal succession refers to the connecting of clauses together according to the sequence in which they occurred in real time. If the order of clauses matches the chronological unfolding of events in the world described by the narrative, the sequence is temporally iconic. This is the unmarked order of events in narrative. Changes and disruptions to the default iconic order of events (anachronies or dischronologizations—temporal discontinuity or overlay) occur when simultaneous events, prior events (flashback, retrospection, analepsis), or future events (flashforward, foreshadowing, anticipation, prolepsis) are related.[19]

While foreground and background have been considered as equivalent to temporal succession and temporal discontinuity by scholars, they can also be considered broader terms to indicate relative salience or prominence and not just indicate temporal concerns. Some linguists such as Hopper and Longacre, and Hebrew scholars such as Niccacci and Buth use the term *foreground* to describe the main or event line (e.g., of narrative, expressed by unmarked verb forms), and the term *background* to refer to the out-of-line or off-line events and states (expressed by marked forms).[20]

---

[19] Cf. Jean-Marc Heimerdinger, *Topic, Focus, and Foreground* (JSOTSup 295; Sheffield: Sheffield Academic Press, 1999), 48-51.

[20] Cf. John A. Cook, "The Semantics of Verbal Pragmatics" (paper presented at the annual meeting of SBL, Toronto, Canada, 25 November 2002) in which he discusses *wayyiqtol* and *weqatal* verb forms in terms of temporal succession and foreground-background. He proves that *wayyiqtol* and *weqatal* forms do not necessarily indicate temporal succession, but considers that *wayyiqtol* is marked for foreground. He distinguishes between temporal succession (considering it a semantic feature) and foreground (a psycholinguistic feature). Paul J. Hopper, "Aspect and Foregrounding in Discourse," in *Discourse and Syntax* (Syntax and Semantics 12; ed. Talmy Givón; New York: Academic, 1979), 213-42, Alviero Niccacci, "On the Hebrew Verbal System," in *Biblical Hebrew and Discourse Linguistics* (ed. Robert D. Bergen; Dallas: Summer Institute of Linguistics, 1994), 117-37, and Randall Buth, "Functional Grammar, Hebrew and Aramaic: An Integrated Textlinguistic Approach to Syntax." *Discourse Analysis of Biblical Literature: What It Is and What It Offers.* (ed. Walter R. Bodine. SBLSS; Atlanta: Scholars Press, 1995), 77-102. Regrettably, the terms *foreground* and *background* have been used in diametrically opposite ways by other scholars, such as Heimerdinger and Rosenbaum (for Hebrew), and Porter and Bakker (for Greek), Heimerdinger, *Topic, Focus, and Foreground*, 221-60; Rosenbaum, *Word-Order Variation*, 149-228; Porter, *Verbal Aspect*, 91-93; and Egbert J. Bakker, "Foregrounding and

In summary, the choice of marked or less common verb forms may be governed by the lexical meaning of the verb in its context (its *Aktionsart*), the introduction of new topic or focusing on new information (both of which influence the word order and especially Hebrew verb choice), or to indicate discourse prominence (temporal overlay or background). No one of these is unique in influencing verb choice to the exclusion of the others. Sometimes all three factors may combine to influence verb choice, and it may not be possible to determine which factor is more prevalent. For example, a verb may have a plural argument or iterative adverbials (situation aspect), a different subject compared to the other verbs in the context (topicalization), and indicate a break in the story line representing simultaneous action (discourse structure).[21]

II. THE HEBREW VERB SYSTEM

There are eleven major verb forms in Hebrew, which can be divided into three groups: four indicative forms, four "verbals" (two infinitives and two participles), and three volitive forms. The four indicative forms are the *qatal* (also called the perfect or suffix) form, the *yiqtol* (also called the imperfect or prefix) form, and two sequential or consecutive (or conversive) forms, the *wayyiqtol* and the *wᵉqatal*

Indirect Discourse: Temporal Subclauses in a Herodotean Short Story," *Journal of Pragmatics* 16 (1991): 225-47. The term *foreground* (Porter also uses an additional term *frontground*) is used to indicate marked structures that highlight what the writer or speaker considers significant or worthy of attention (e.g., to indicate a change of subject), *Idioms of the Greek New Testament* (Biblical Languages: Greek 2; Sheffield: Sheffield Academic Press, 1999), 23. Conversely, *background* is used for everything that is familiar and not much can be said about. It is expressed by unmarked structures. It is unfortunate that there is this confusion among scholars in terms of the terminology used to indicate this feature of discourse prominence.

[21] In individual languages, one factor may predominate more than others. In Greek, Fanning considers that the procedural characteristics of verbs and actions (*Aktionsart*) are more significant in determining verb choice. He considers the use of verbal aspects for foreground and background and to show temporal sequence in narrative only secondary, Fanning, *Verbal Aspect*, 72-77, 126. He does concede, however, "secondary distinctions do at times supersede in the writer's choice of the form" (82). In Hebrew, it is not *Aktionsart* but word order variations due to topic and focus, which seem to be more significant than discourse prominence (foregrounding and backgrounding), as far as determining whether a sequential rather than a non-sequential form is used. However, as was pointed out above, these word order variations do not specify which non-sequential form is appropriate. The discourse context is more important in determining this.

(*weqaltî*) forms. There are two participles, an active *qotel* and a passive *qatul* (also known as *qal* passive participle), two infinitives (an infinitive absolute *qatol* and an infinitive construct *qetol*), and three volitive forms (an imperative *qetol,* a first person cohortative *'eqtelah,* and a third person jussive *yiqtol* form).[22]

A. Indicative Forms

Before we indicate the function and meaning of the indicative forms, let us consider how they have been considered (and labeled) historically, paying particular attention to how they operate together in the Hebrew verbal system. The Hebrew verbal system is one of the most enigmatic features of the Hebrew language. One of the most debated features of Hebrew is whether the four indicative verb forms grammatically code aspect and/or tense. As van der Merwe stresses, any theory of the Hebrew verbal system has to account for "the semantic value of the oppositions...*qatal-yiqtol* and...*wayyiqtol-weqatal.*"[23] The earliest Hebrew grammars considered this opposition as one of tense (past-future, converted past-converted future). The addition of the conjunction "*waw*" somehow "converted" the future *yiqtol* form to a past and the past *qatal* form to future giving rise to the name "*waw* conversive" for the *wayyiqtol-weqatal* forms.

This framework changed to an aspectual approach following the work of Ewald (1827), who introduced the terms "perfect" and "imperfect," and S. R. Driver (1892). As a result, many scholars have favored an aspectual interpretation to the opposition *qatal-yiqtol* (complete(d)—perfective vs. nascent/incipient—imperfective, and the notion that the *wayyiqtol-weqatal* forms indicate consecutive action, which gave rise to the name "*waw* consecutive." While a few scholars

---

[22] *GRAMCORD* includes the cohortative and jussive forms under the *yiqtol* imperfect forms. Many times they are formally identical with the *yiqtol* form and can be distinguished only by use in the context.

[23] C. H. J. van der Merwe, "An Overview of Hebrew Narrative Syntax," in *Narrative Syntax and the Hebrew Bible: Papers of the Tilburg Conference 1996* (ed. Ellen van Wolde; Leiden: Brill, 1997) 1-20, 6. Useful summaries of various approaches are found in Leslie McFall, *The Enigma of the Hebrew Verbal System* (Sheffield: Almond Press, 1982), who summarizes most major work from the earliest medieval Jewish grammarians to T. W. Thacker (1954), and Endo, *Verbal System of Classical Hebrew,* (1996), who reviews most of the recent work done after McFall. See also a most recent summary by John A. Cook, "The Hebrew Verb: A Grammaticalization Approach," *ZAH* 14 (2001): 117-143.

still prefer a modified view of the older tense system, the aspectual view has mostly been accepted with some modifications.[24] We mostly follow this aspectual approach in our analysis. See the presentation of Waltke and O'Connor, which looks at the Hebrew verbal system from the perspective of theories based on tense, on aspect, and comparative-historical approaches.[25]

The *qatal* (suffix or perfect) form expresses perfective aspect and probably had its origin in the stative verbs.[26] These verbs, indicating states such as *to be heavy, to love, to hate, to be great, to be small, to hope, to wait, to trust,* and *to know,* are usually understood to occur simultaneously with the time they are located in and are frequently translated by a present tense in reported speech. Active (fientive) *qatal* forms occur in the past, present, and future, omni-temporal, and timeless time frames, although most frequently in the past time. They occur in the past when a sequence of *wayyiqtol* forms is broken and another element (e.g., a fronted subject or a negative particle) comes between the conjunction and the verb, either because of topicalization or focusing another element. Eventually *qatal* forms replace *wayyiqtol* forms as the standard past time event line verb.[27] Sometimes *qatal* forms occur with past perfect meaning, especially when they are used to indicate an action antecedent to the narrative event line.[28] In the

---

[24] Scholars have employed a comparative-historical approach to account for certain archaic verb forms. A short prefix **yaqtul* form (preserved in the *wayyiqtol* form) is understood as a preterite (cf. Akkadian, Amarna Canaanite, and Ugaritic) which developed into a narrative consecutive form. By analogy the *wᵉqatal* form developed into a consecutive future modal form. An example of an approach which combines aspect and tense is Peter Gentry, "The System of the Finite Verb in Classical Biblical Hebrew," *HS* 39 (1998): 7-39. He believes that "base forms are primarily aspectual, with temporal deixis a function of aspectual default and discourse setting," 7.

[25] Bruce K. Waltke and Michael O'Connor, *Biblical Hebrew Syntax* (Winona Lake: Eisenbrauns, 1990), 455-78. See also Evans, *Verbal Syntax,* 57-66 for a succinct analysis of the Hebrew verbal system, which accounts for various theories that have been proposed.

[26] For a fuller treatment of the Hebrew verb forms see Paul Joüon and Takamitsu Muraoka, *A Grammar of Biblical Hebrew* (2 Vols.; Rome: Pontifical Biblical Institute, 1991), 359 ff.

[27] For example, 32% of the *qatal* forms in Chronicles occur in 1 Chronicles 1—9. This text is unique to Chronicles and perhaps reflects late biblical Hebrew. However, it is more likely a reflection on the type of text. This section consists mostly of genealogies. In genealogies the subject is changing a lot. The use of the *qatal* form is due to the topicalization of the subject in SVO word order particularly in the expression "X begot Y."

[28] E.g., וַיֵּדַע דָּוִיד כִּי־הֱכִינוֹ יְהוָה לְמֶלֶךְ "Then David perceived that the LORD *had established* him as king" translated καὶ ἔγνω Δαυιδ ὅτι ἡτοίμησεν (aorist) αὐτὸν κύριος (1 Chr 14:2).

present time, they sometimes occur as performatives, especially with verbs of saying and in the first person. They occur in omni-temporal or timeless contexts (e.g., for general truths) and are generally translated by an English present tense. In the future *qatal* forms may be used to express action prior to another future event. Sometimes a *qatal* form occurs as a rhetorical device to present events in the future, as if they have already happened (prophetic perfect).

The *yiqtol* (prefix or imperfect) form expresses imperfective aspect and occurs in the past, present, and future, although most frequently in the future time. In the future, it is used for predictions and promises, as well as with a modal or volitive sense. The *yiqtol* form also occurs in omni-temporal or timeless contexts (and is generally translated by a present tense in English). In the past, the *yiqtol* form has a durative sense, although some may have punctual sense equivalent to the preterite *wayyiqtol*, especially after the adverbs אָז and the conjunctions טֶרֶם and עַד. These past time uses of the *yiqtol* form were probably only used in archaic written Hebrew (reflecting a preterite), rather than spoken Hebrew at the time of the writing of Chronicles. It is difficult to distinguish a *yiqtol* form from a cohortative or jussive volitive form. In II weak root consonants, *hiphil*, and III weak second and third person singular verb forms *yiqtol* indicative forms can be unambiguously formally distinguished from volitives. This has implications for determining the force of the coordinated form *wᵉyiqtol*, which is used in a distinctive way compared to the consecutive *wᵉqatal* form in its continuing another *yiqtol* form (see below and note 149 in chapter 4). Baden identifies eleven unambiguous cases of the coordinated form *wᵉyiqtol* (i.e., morphologically distinguishable from jussives and cohortatives in II-weak, hiphil, and III-weak verbs) in Genesis through 2 Kings (with two parallels in 1 Kings 12:9 // 2 Chronicles 10:9 and 1 Kings 15:19 // 2 Chronicles 16:3) to determine the force of these forms and concludes that in both volitive and indicative contexts they should <u>all</u> be understood "as connoting purpose or result."[29]

The *wayyiqtol* form is formed by the addition of the conjunction *waw* to what is probably a frozen preterite *yiqtol* form, similar to the free standing preterite found in Akkadian and in archaic Hebrew poetry. The *wayyiqtol* form has perfective aspect and mostly indicates a

---

[29] Joel S. Baden, "The *wᵉyiqtol* and the Volitive Sequence," *VT* 58 (2008): 150. See also chapter 4, notes 77 and 91.

sequential event following a preceding action (usually another *wayyiqtol* form or a *qatal* form). (The succession is logical as well as mostly temporal).[30] It is the most common verb form in Hebrew narrative. It rarely occurs in present and even more rarely in future time frames. Most of the *wayyiqtol* forms in the present time (the time of narration) involve stative verbs or continue a participle.

*We*qatal* is formed by the addition of the conjunction *waw* to the *qatal* form. There are two kinds of *w*qatal*: a simple coordinated form and a consecutive form, and these forms are perhaps only rarely formally

---

[30] Occasionally the *wayyiqtol* form occurs when there does not seem to be any sequentiality or succession. It may be used either for introducing (especially the *wayyiqtol* form of הָיָה "be, become" וַיְהִי "and it came to pass," e.g., 1 Chr 10:8; 19:1) or concluding and summing up a series of actions, or it may even occur for simultaneous or even anterior events. Cf. Randall Buth, "Methodological Collision Between Source Criticism and Discourse Analysis: The Problem of 'Unmarked Temporal Overlay' and the Pluperfect/Nonsequential *Wayyiqtol*," in *Biblical Hebrew and Discourse Linguistics* (ed. R. D. Bergen; Dallas: Summer School of Linguistics, 1994), 138-54, and C. John Collins, "The *Wayyiqtol* As 'Pluperfect': When and Why," *TynBul* 46.1 (1995): 117-40, contra Z. Zevit, *The Anterior Construction in Classical Hebrew* (SBLMS 50; Atlanta: Scholars Press, 1998). See also W. J. Martin, "'Dischronologized' Narrative in the Old Testament," *Congress Volume: Rome 1968* (VTSup 17; Leiden: Brill, 1969), 179-86, in which he cites examples from 2 Kgs 24:7; 2 Sam 12:26; 1 Kgs 2:7ff.; 2 Sam 4:4; 1 Kgs 1:5; 11:14-22; 18:1-7. So also M. Sternberg, "Temporal Discontinuity, Narrative Interest, and the Emergence of Meaning," M. Sternberg, *The Poetics of Biblical Narrative: Ideological Literature and the Drama of Reading* (Bloomington: Indiana University, 1985), 264-320. In addition, see John A. Cook, "Semantics of Verbal Pragmatics" in which he argues that foreground rather than temporal succession can be assigned as a discourse-pragmatic marking on the narrative verb *wayyiqtol*.

Rarely in Chronicles does a *wayyiqtol* form appear when there is a dischronologization. The death of Saul is mentioned twice using a *wayyiqtol* form וַיָּמָת "So Saul died" (1 Chr 10:6, 13 as a conclusion), after his death was clearly implied or mentioned in vv. 4-5. It functions as a resumption to the narrative rather than moving the story on from the preceding event. In the itemization of Solomon's building of the parts of the temple *wayyiqtol* forms are employed (2 Chr 4). However, the sequence is not necessarily temporal as some of the building probably went on simultaneously and was completed in various stages. Other examples of the same verb being repeated in a *wayyiqtol* sequence to indicate a resumption of the sequence (perhaps with additional temporal information) are: וַיָּחֶל שְׁלֹמֹה לִבְנוֹת "And Solomon began to build..." וַיָּחֶל לִבְנוֹת...בַּשֵּׁנִי "So he began to build on the second day..." (3:1-2), and וַיִּקָּבְצוּ...בַּחֹדֶשׁ הַשְּׁלִישִׁי וַיִּקְבֹּץ אֶת־כָּל־יְהוּדָה "And He gathered all Judah..." "So they were gathered in the third month..." (15:9-10). Repeated *wayyiqtol* forms also occur in statements summarizing the building achievements of Solomon in the verses preceding: וַיַּעַשׂ שְׁלֹמֹה כָּל־הַכֵּלִים הָאֵלֶּה "And Solomon made all these utensils..." וַיַּעַשׂ שְׁלֹמֹה אֵת כָּל־הַכֵּלִים "So Solomon made all the utensils..." (4:18-19). So also the same *qatal* verb is repeated by a *wayyiqtol* form that resumes the narrative עָלָה שִׁישַׁק מֶלֶךְ־מִצְרַיִם עַל־יְרוּשָׁלָם "King Shishak of Egypt *came up* against Jerusalem" וַיַּעַל שִׁישַׁק מֶלֶךְ־מִצְרַיִם עַל־יְרוּשָׁלַם "So King Shishak of Egypt *came up* against Jerusalem" (12:2, 9). (It is interesting to note that in all of these examples the *wayyiqtol* forms are translated into Greek by καί and an aorist).

differentiated from each other by a shift in accent. For example, *w^eqatálti* means "and I killed" and *w^eqataltí* "and I will kill."[31] Since most of the time there is no way to distinguish the two forms, the context is necessary to determine the sense of the form. Sometimes there is controversy as to how a form is to be understood. The coordinated form has the same sense as the *qatal* form.

The consecutive *w^eqatal* is the sequential equivalent of the *yiqtol* (prefix or imperfect) form and expresses imperfective aspect. It is used to indicate succession (logical and often temporal succession) and occurs in the past, present, and future, although most frequently in the future time. It most commonly continues a *yiqtol* form, but also frequently follows a volitive form. When it follows a volitive form, it continues the sense of the volitive form. It also can continue infinitive forms and participles, especially if they have future meaning. It is fairly rare in the present or omni-temporal and timeless contexts when it continues a *yiqtol* form with present meaning or noun sentence without a verb or with a participle or an infinitive. In the past the consecutive *w^eqatal* form is used to continue a *yiqtol* form or a participle with a durative sense and carries the same sense as the preceding verb.[32]

B. Participles and Infinitives

1. Participles

The Hebrew participle is a verbal adjective that can function both as a verb (predicate) and as an adjective (or a noun, which is in origin a substantival use of the adjective).[33] The participle was originally

---

[31] Cf. two articles by Revell, who argues that this stress difference is determined by the phonological environment rather than by formal considerations, E. J. Revell, "Stress and the *Waw* 'Consecutive' in Biblical Hebrew," *JAOS* 104.3 (1984): 437-44 and "The Conditioning of Stress Position in *Waw* Consecutive Perfect Forms in Biblical Hebrew," *HAR* 9 (1985): 277-300.

[32] However, as with the *wayyiqtol* form, the consecutive *w^eqatal* sometimes occurs when there does not seem to be any succession, e.g., when it is used for two simultaneous events. Also sometimes, the distinction in meaning between a consecutive *w^eqatal* and coordinated *w^eyiqtol* form is not that clear.

[33] As a verb it can govern objects, and it derives its aspectual and temporal sense from a finite verb in the context. Porter, *Verbal Aspect*, 158, and Peter Nash, "The Hebrew Qal Active Participle: A Non-Aspectual Narrative Backgrounding Element" (Ph.D. diss., University of Chicago, 1992) argue for the non-aspectual value of the participle. Its occasional sense to indicate ongoing action simultaneous to the event line verb(s) is a function of discourse context rather than inherent aspect. Nash considers participles on a "continuum of fuzzy sets from time stable agents...to

atemporal, but it came to have a temporal function, especially when used <u>predicatively</u>, equivalent to a main clause or a circumstantial clause (as opposed to <u>attributively</u>, when it is mostly preceded by a definite article, has suffixes, or is in construct state, and it retains its atemporal force). The participle occurs in all three time frames—the past, the present, and the future—and when used as a predicate expresses *action as a state*.[34] It lends itself most readily to the present time frame and eventually becomes the form of the present tense in rabbinic and modern Hebrew (when Hebrew verb forms mark tense). In a past context, sometimes the participle with הָיָה as a periphrastic form (especially in late biblical Hebrew) can indicate action simultaneous with another verb form. In a future context, it often carries the notion of imminent future action or of action in progress and may occur as a periphrastic form accompanied by a *yiqtol* form of הָיָה.

The Hebrew participle has two forms, an active *qotel* and a passive *qatul* form. The *qotel* form occurs much more frequently than the *qatul* form.[35] The *qatul* passive participle is used either to indicate a state resulting from a process (cf. the process itself, the action in process, which would be represented by a *niphal* participle)[36] or a completed action or state. In its verbal use, it does not always carry a passive notion, occurring with intransitive verbs (especially verbs of movement) as well as transitive verbs. The *qatul* form frequently carries the notion more of a present state resulting from a prior action than a purely passive form, e.g., אָחוּז (*having been seized*, hence, *held*).

2. Infinitives

The Hebrew infinitives are verbal nouns, and, as such, they function both as nouns, e.g., as subjects and objects of clauses, as well as verbal

---

predicates...noun-adjective-participle-infinitive-stative verb-active verb" (81), and in certain environments its nominal-adjectival function predominates, and in others its verbal predicative function predominates (see also chapter 4, note 105). For example, as an adjective or substantive the participle declines as a noun, has absolute and construct forms, mostly takes nominal suffixes (e.g., the first person singular יִ - rather than the verbal suffix נִי-), and can be modified by a definite article.

[34] See note 33 above. For the classification of and distinction between the kinds of participles see chapter 4, note 105.

[35] The participles of the Hebrew *binyanim* or verbal stems such as *niphal, piel, pual, hiphil, hophal* and *hitpael* are included under *qotel*, although *niphal, pual* and *hophal* participles are passive in meaning.

[36] cf. Joüon and Muraoka, *Grammar of Biblical Hebrew*, 418.

forms, equivalent to finite verb forms. They are atemporal and neutral as regards aspect; the sense of time and aspect is to be derived from other verbs in the context.

The q^etol or infinitive construct is the more common of the two infinitive forms. It is most commonly preceded by the preposition לְ and occurs as the object (complement) of certain verbs such as "begin," "continue," "cease," "be able to," and "wish;" objects of verbs such as "remember" and "know;" and as objects of verbs of saying, speaking, and commanding, indicating indirect speech. As objects of prepositions, infinitive constructs mostly function as equivalent to subordinate clauses, equivalent to a subordinate conjunction followed by a finite verb. The most common of which are purpose clauses preceded by the preposition לְ. They also commonly function as equivalent to temporal clauses preceded by prepositions such as בְּ "in," כְּ "as," אַחֲרֵי "after," and עַד "until," or causal clauses following עַל "upon," יַעַן "because," or מִן "from." Sometimes the infinitive construct functions like a gerund explaining the preceding action or indicating the manner in which it was carried out. In its verbal function, an infinitive construct can have subjects, objects, verbal suffixes, and adverbial modification, as well as functioning rarely as a finite verb.

The $qatol$ or infinitive absolute rarely functions in a temporal sense. It mostly functions adverbially with the adverbial force (e.g., affirmation or doubt) derived from the context. In this adverbial use, the infinitive usually derives from the same root as the main verb (the internal or cognate accusative), although certain infinitive absolute forms such as הַרְבֵּה "much, a lot" function as adverbs in their own right and occur with many different verbs. Less frequently the infinitive absolute is equivalent to another finite verb form, especially an imperative, a $yiqtol$ form (especially with injunctive force), or equivalent to the preceding verbal form. Sometimes two infinitive absolutes occur in sequence with the second verb reflecting (quasi-) simultaneous action.

C. Volitive Forms

There are also three volitive forms distinguished according to person, a second person form (imperative q^etol), a third person form (jussive '*let him* ...'), and a first person form (cohortative, '*let us* ..., *may I*

..., *I want* ...'). In addition, the jussive with אַל functions as a second person prohibition (instead of the imperative). These volitive forms are mostly used to elicit immediate action. For stronger, less immediate or timeless (e.g., legal) injunctions the *yiqtol* form functions as both an injunctive ('*you shall*') and a prohibition with לֹא (also called the vetitive '*you shall not*').[37] When the volitive forms are preceded by a *waw* they frequently have the force of a subordinate purpose clause or indicate consequence, particularly if a volitive form of a <u>different</u> person follows the first volitive form, e.g., "give (imperative) me your vineyard *so that it may become* (jussive) my garden" (1 Kgs 21:2)[38]. This use of the volitive forms occurs especially where the execution of the order is beyond the control of the addressee.

D. Clause Types

1. *Narrative Main Clauses*

In narrated (past) main clauses, the *wayyiqtol* form predominates. It is the standard unmarked form for sequential past actions with perfective aspect.[39] The presence of a *qatal* form (also with perfective aspect) or another non-*wayyiqtol* form may mark a break in the narrative sequence (perhaps for topicalizing or focusing another element—see above). Occasionally *yiqtol* and *weqatal* (consecutive) forms with imperfective aspect indicate past durative action. The sequential form of the verb הָיָה "to be, become" וַיְהִי is frequently employed to indicate setting. Another sequential form may or may not follow it. Existentials and noun clauses (lacking a verb) also indicate setting.

---

[37] Many times the first and third person volitive forms are formally identical to the prefix *yiqtol* form. In order to distinguish them the reader is reliant on the context and the presence of particles such as אַל (not) or נָא (particle of entreaty 'please') or word order to distinguish them.

[38] Cf. Baden's article, referenced in note 29 above, showing how rare coordinated *yiqtol* indicative forms (distinguished from coordinated volitives) should be considered as purpose or result clauses.

[39] For exceptions where *wayyiqtol* is used for non-sequential action, see note 30 above.

2. *Reported Speech Main Clauses*

The verb forms in reported speech are much more varied than narrated past, since the speech may refer to action prior to, simultaneous with, or future to the time implied by the verb of speaking. As a result, in action prior to the verb of speaking the same verb forms for narrated past occur (i.e., *qatal* and *wayyiqtol* forms); in action in a present time frame, simultaneous with the verb of speaking, noun sentences (lacking a verbal form), existentials, and participles occur; and for action future to the verb of speaking *yiqtol* and *w^eqatal* forms predominate. Volitive forms occur solely in reported speech.

The diachronic changes to the verb system mentioned above are more likely to be observed in reported speech clauses, since they reflect more closely the Hebrew spoken of the time of writing.

3. *Subordinate Clauses*

While the majority of Hebrew clauses are main clauses linked together by the conjunction *waw*, Hebrew texts also have a number of subordinate clauses. The verb forms in these subordinate clauses are also more varied than narrative main clauses. Just like reported speech clauses, they also occur in a variety of time frames. Subordinate clauses take the time frame of the main clause or the clause of speech as their reference time. Consequently, the action can be prior to, simultaneous with, and future to the time of the main verb. Action prior to the main verb will be expressed by a *qatal* form (which may be continued by a *wayyiqtol* form), action simultaneous with the main verb will be expressed by noun sentences (lacking a verbal form) and participles, and action future to the time of the main verb tends to be expressed by *yiqtol* forms (which may be continued by a *w^eqatal* form).

The most common subordinating conjunctions or particles in Hebrew are אֲשֶׁר and כִּי. They can have a variety of meanings and even sometimes do not indicate subordination. אֲשֶׁר functions most commonly as a relative pronoun and less frequently as the marker of an object clause. כִּי functions most commonly as a marker of cause or reason, or as a marker of an object clause. It can also occur in the protasis of a condition, as a marker for a temporal clause or as an adversative or emphatic marker in a main clause. Other subordinating conjunctions are אִם "if" which is mostly used to mark the protasis of a

condition, יַעַן which marks a causal clause, לְמַעַן which marks a
purpose clause, and פֶּן "lest" which marks a negative purpose clause.

Infinitives also function as equivalents to subordinate clauses,
especially when they are preceded by prepositions. The most common
prepositions preceding infinitives are לְ to indicate purpose; עַד, לִפְנֵי
to indicate antecedent action in temporal clauses, בְּ and כְּ used to
indicate (mostly) simultaneous action in temporal clauses, and אַחַר or
אַחֲרֵי to indicate subsequent (following) action in temporal clauses.

Participles are also equivalent to subordinate clauses both as
circumstantial participles (equivalent to adverbial clauses) and as
attributive participles (equivalent to relative adjectival clauses).

E. Changes in the Hebrew Verbal System

Certain verb forms in the biblical text are used in a way that was no
longer current in the Hebrew spoken at the time of the translation of
Chronicles.[40] The consecutive (or conversive) *wayyiqtol* and *wᵉqatal*
forms no longer functioned as sequential past and future forms. They
were replaced by *wᵉqatal* and *wᵉyiqtol* forms as coordinated (and
sequential) past and future forms respectively. וַיְהִי followed by a
temporal adverbial no longer introduced temporal clauses. The
temporal adverbial alone sufficed. Infinitive constructs following the
prepositions בְּ and כְּ were increasingly replaced by indicative forms.
Yiqtol forms no longer have punctual or durative past sense. *Qatal*
forms replace the punctual sense of *yiqtol* (e.g., with אָז), and a
periphrastic form composed of הָיָה "to be" and a participle took the
place of the durative *yiqtol*.[41] The *qotel* participle becomes increasingly a

---

[40] While we do not have a record of the register of Hebrew spoken at the time of
the translation of Chronicles, we can infer what it was like by developments in the
Hebrew verb system from classical to Mishnaic or rabbinic Hebrew. These changes in
the use of verbs probably took place in the spoken register first, whereas the written
register preserved the archaic use of verb forms. However, by the time of the writing
of Chronicles late biblical Hebrew is beginning to show some of these changes in the
written register, especially in reported speech sections.

[41] A possible reason for the decline in the use of the prefix *yiqtol* form is the
reduction of the introductory וַיְהִי and the resultant change of sentence structure (cf.
Robert Polzin, *Late Biblical Hebrew: Toward an Historical Typology of Biblical Hebrew Prose*
(HSM 12; Missoula: Scholars Press, 1976), 56-58; so also A. Hurvitz, *Bein Lashon
Lelashon* English Title: *Biblical Hebrew in Transition—A Study in Post-Exilic Hebrew and its
Implications for the Dating of the Psalms* (Jerusalem, Bialik Institute, 1972) and Ursula
Schattner-Rieser, "L'hébreu post-exilique," in *La Palestine à l'époque perse*, (ed. E.-M.
Laperrousaz and A. Lemaire; Paris: Cerf, 1994), 189-224). The pattern וַיְהִי +

present tense form. Infinitive absolutes are no longer used except as frozen adverbial forms.[42] Some of these developments can be observed in Chronicles (especially when the relative frequency of verb forms and their use is compared to classical Hebrew texts in Samuel-Kings). Infinitive absolutes are sometimes used as finite verbs, although less so in Chronicles in comparison with other later texts.[43]

These changes in verb use affect the structure of Hebrew syntax. With the loss of וַיְהִי the paratactic sequence of consecutive forms is replaced by subordinate clauses preceding the main verb. Infinitives also replace following consecutive forms, as can be observed when comparing parallel passages in the classical biblical Hebrew of Samuel with the late biblical Hebrew of Chronicles (2 Sam 6:6 // 1 Chr 13:9; 2 Sam 6:12 // 1 Chr 15:25). These changes also impact Hebrew word order. The verb is less frequently in initial position with other elements preceding. Participles, which increasingly function as a present tense, mostly have an expressed subject that precedes the participle producing an SV[O] word order. Sometimes a verb even occurs in final position, perhaps imitating Aramaic (cf. 2 Sam 2:10 [SVO] // 1 Chr 19:13 [SOV]; 2 Sam 7:20 [SVO] // 1 Chr 17:18 [SOV]).

---

adverbial element + *wayyiqtol* is replaced by the pattern adverbial element + *qatal* (see chapter 4, notes 21 and 24 for specific examples from Chronicles). This apparently precipitates the development that led to the disappearance of *wayyiqtol* and the use of *(wᵉ)qatal* in its place as a narrative sequential form (Mats Eskhult, *Studies in Verbal Aspect and Narrative Technique in Biblical Hebrew Prose* (Studia Semitica Upsaliensis 12; Uppsala: Acta Universitatis Upsaliensis, 1990), 120).

These changes in the use of verbal forms are matched by corresponding changes on the sentence level. Clauses of the kind *subject—qatal* begin to show up in the event line of narrative. Sentences become longer and the verb sometimes occurs toward the end. This is perhaps due to the influence of Official Aramaic especially Eastern Aramaic where the order subject—verb is preferred. An interesting case of Aramaic influence can be seen in 2 Chronicles 35:21 where not only does the verb occur toward the end of the clause but even an Aramaic verb form אָתָה is used.

[42] For a brief summary of the change in the use of the verb tenses in Hebrew in the Second Temple period and rabbinic Hebrew, see Angel Sáenz-Badillos, *A History of the Hebrew Language* (Cambridge: Cambridge University Press, 1993), 144-45, 193.

[43] See Polzin, *Late Biblical Hebrew*, 43-44 (who cites 1 Chr 5:20; 2 Chr 7:3; 31:10 in non-parallel texts), and Arno Kropat, *Die Syntax des Autors der Chronik verglichen mit der seiner Quellen* (BZAW 16; Gießen: Verlag von Alfred Töpelmann, 1909), 23-24. It is however, more common in Esther, Jeremiah, and Ecclesiastes. See A. Rubinstein, "A Finite Verb Continued by an Infinitive Absolute in Biblical Hebrew," *VT* 2:4 (1952): 362-367, who gives three examples in Chronicles (1 Chr 5:20; 16:36; and 2 Chr 28:19), and John Huesman, "Finite Uses of the Infinitive Absolute," *Bib* 37 (1956): 271-295.

F. Summary

Biblical Hebrew contains four indicative forms. The *wayyiqtol* and *qatal* forms mostly occur in narrative as sequential and non-sequential forms respectively. The *yiqtol* and *wᵉqatal* (consecutive) forms mostly occur in reported speech as non-sequential and sequential forms respectively. Participles function circumstantially (sometimes as a main verb, especially in late biblical Hebrew, with and without הָיָה), or attributively (equivalent to adjectival relative clauses). Infinitives are mostly equivalent to subordinate clauses in their function. The *qatal* and *yiqtol* forms also occur in subordinate clauses. Verbless noun sentences also occur quite frequently in all three types of genres.

III. THE GREEK VERB SYSTEM

The Greek verbal system of Hellenistic or Koine Greek used in the translation of the Septuagint is basically a modified form of the classical Attic Greek verbal system of the fifth and fourth centuries BCE. Hellenistic Greek has six indicative verb forms, participles, infinitives, and three other moods, which include volitive forms.[44] The Greek verbal system underwent a major restructuring in the Koine vernacular roughly during the period 300 BCE to 600 CE. For example, middle and passive voices combine, the optative mood disappears (apart from a few fossilized forms), the perfect merges with the aorist, and periphrastic tense formations increase.[45] However, at the time of the Septuagint translation, these changes were only in their infancy, and Attic Greek usage was, for the most part, still in place.

As with Hebrew, aspect is more significant in Greek than tense, and there is even debate whether Greek actually marks tense

---

[44] A seventh future perfect form also existed in Attic Greek but has mostly disappeared (apart from as periphrastic tenses) in Hellenistic or Koine Greek.

[45] For more details concerning the changes between Attic and later Greek, see Robert Browning, *Medieval and Modern Greek* (Cambridge: Cambridge University Press, 1983), 29-36. See also the discussion in Evans, *Verbal Syntax*, 163-166, in which he argues against Schehr's observation of perfects with an aoristic sense in the translation of the Pentateuch. Evans also points out that "the perfect indicative is not found in pure narrative in early Koine Greek for the simple reason that it is not functionally appropriate to such linguistic contexts, so long as its classical meaning persists" (165). On the use of the perfect in reported speech and subordinate clauses see chapter 5, section I.A.3.

grammatically.[46] For the most part, a traditional approach to the Greek verb system is followed in this book, understanding three aspects: perfective (portraying action externally, as a complete whole, also called *punctual* frequently in this book), imperfective (portraying action internally, as incomplete, also called *durative* frequently in this book), and perfective-imperfective or stative (perhaps combining the two aspects, frequently expressing a resultant state of a prior action, also labeled perfective in some grammars).[47] In the indicative mood the aorist, present, and perfect indicate perfective, imperfective, and perfective-imperfective or stative aspects respectively, while the imperfect and pluperfect forms are used to indicate remote (i.e., past) imperfective and stative aspect respectively. The future form grammaticalizes the feature of expectation (i.e., future action) and is aspectually vague in the sense that it does not exhibit the contrasting aspectual oppositions of the other tense forms. Traditionally, scholars have considered that these six tense forms of the indicative mood

---

[46] Porter has recently raised this question in his book *Verbal Aspect*. See the following note. For a succinct summary of the more recent debates on the Greek verbal system see chapter 2 of Evans, *Verbal Syntax*.

[47] Cf. Robertson, *Grammar of the Greek New Testament*, 824-25, who calls them punctiliar, durative and perfected state and Porter (*Verbal Aspect*, 90), who calls them perfective, imperfective, and stative. There is a lot of variation in the terminology used in recent grammars to describe these aspects, for example: Rijksbaron refers to them as completed - resulting state, not-completed, and completed + resulting state, A. Rijksbaron, *The Syntax and Semantics of the Verb in Classical Greek: An Introduction* (Amsterdam: J. C. Gieben, 1994), 5. McKay refers to the three aspects as aorist, imperfective, and perfect, K. L. McKay, *A New Syntax of the Verb in New Testament Greek: An Aspectual Approach* (Studies in Biblical Greek 5; New York: Peter Lang, 1994), 7. Fanning refers to them as aorist, and present aspects, and perfect (with perfective aspect) forms (*Verbal Aspect in New Testament Greek*, 86-125). Wallace is even more nuanced referring to them as external (summary), internal (progressive), and perfective-stative, Daniel B. Wallace, *Greek Grammar beyond the Basics: An Exegetical Syntax of the New Testament with Scripture, Subject, and Greek Word Indexes* (Grand Rapids: Zondervan, 1996), 501. Evans refers to the first two aspects as perfective and imperfective, and he treats the perfect as a special type of imperfective aspect expressing stativity (*Verbal Syntax*, 32). He considers that the prior-occurrence reference of traditional definitions of the perfect should be ascribed to the lexical semantics of verbs that express actions (145). Finally, Campbell also uses the terminology of perfective and imperfective for the two aspects. He treats the perfect as an imperfective aspect form with a heightened spatial proximity (in comparison with the present) and the pluperfect as heightened spatial remoteness (in comparison with the imperfect), Constantine C. Campbell, *Verbal Aspect, the Indicative Mood, and Narrative: Soundings in the Greek of the New Testament* (Studies in Biblical Greek 13; New York: Peter Lang, 2007), 195-199, 228-231 and *Verbal Aspect and Non-Indicative Verbs: Further Soundings in the Greek of the New Testament* (Studies in Biblical Greek 15; New York: Peter Lang, 2008), 11.

indicate time in addition to aspect.[48] With non-indicative moods, participles, and infinitives, aspect only and not time is indicated.[49] The aorist, present, and perfect non-indicative forms indicate the three aspects mentioned above respectively.

A. Indicative Mood

1. Non-analytic Tenses

The aorist tense is used to indicate perfective aspect and generally occurs in past narrative, although it can occur in three time frames: past, present, and future, as well as omni-temporal and timeless contexts. The aorist is used in omni-temporal or timeless contexts for general truth statements (the "gnomic" aorist) in a similar way to the Hebrew perfect. The imperfect indicates imperfective aspect in past contexts, although it can also occur in non-past contexts.

The perfect tense indicates perfective-imperfective or stative aspect. It also occurs in three time frames: past, present, and future (rare), as well as omni-temporal and timeless contexts, although it occurs most readily in the past and present time. It frequently has the sense of the resultant state of an action that has occurred prior to and still exists up to the time of speaking.

The pluperfect tense also indicates perfective-imperfective or stative aspect. It occurs mostly in past contexts. It frequently has the sense of the resultant state of an action that has occurred prior to and still exists up to the time of another past time verb.

The present tense indicates imperfective aspect. It also occurs in three time frames: past, present, and future, as well as in omni-

---

[48] Porter, who believes that in the indicative mood aspect alone is indicated, has recently disputed this. He gives numerous examples where indicative verb forms occur in all time frames: past, present, future, timeless, and omni-temporal contexts. The distinction between the present and imperfect forms (which both indicate imperfective or durative aspect) and the perfect and pluperfect forms (which both indicate stative aspect) is one of remoteness. The imperfect and pluperfect are more remote than the present and perfect (*Verbal Aspect*, 188-208). Evans considers that the exceptional patterns of verbal usage that provide the basis for Porter's theory to be "better taken as fossilized survivals of an older, purely aspectual structure overlaid by the growing importance of temporal reference" (*Verbal Syntax*, 51).

[49] Greek participles and infinitives may also indicate relative time in addition to aspect with the aorist and perfect indicating antecedent time, the present indicating simultaneous time, and the future indicating subsequent time, all relative to the time of the main verb.

temporal and timeless contexts, although it occurs most readily in the present time. When a present occurs in past time frames (the so called historic present) it indicates past imperfective aspect. It is considered by many as a colloquial use of the form, although it does occur fairly frequently in classical, Hellenistic, and New Testament Greek. In future contexts, the present most frequently occurs with verbs of motion. It also draws attention to an action and may have the force of imminent future action.

The future form "grammaticalizes the semantic feature of expectation" and most commonly occurs in future but also in omni-temporal or timeless contexts.[50] It can also have modal use, being used for command, deliberation, or intention.

2. Analytic (Periphrastic) Tenses

In addition to these uses of the indicative forms in Greek, there are the so-called analytic or periphrastic tenses. These usually consist of a form of the verb εἰμί "to be" (which grammaticalizes mood, tense, person, and number) and a participle (which grammaticalizes aspect and voice). Periphrastic tenses are an alternate way of indicating actions or states in Greek especially with imperfective or stative aspects. When periphrastic forms occur with present participles (the most frequent), they indicate imperfective or durative aspect and when they occur with perfect participles, they indicate perfective-imperfective or stative aspect. They occur in past, present, or future contexts and are equivalent to regular indicative forms.

B. Participles and Infinitives

1. Participles

Greek participles as verbal adjectives can be divided into three main categories of use: attributive, circumstantial and supplementary.

---

[50] Stanley E. Porter, *Idioms of the Greek New Testament* (Biblical Languages: Greek 2; Sheffield: Sheffield Academic Press, 1999), 44. Fanning views the future being a non-aspectual tense as opposed to the traditional view of it as having future tense and punctiliar aspect (*Verbal Aspect*, 120, 123). McKay considers that the future expresses intention and consequently simple futurity (*New Syntax*, 34), and Evans concurs with the traditional view that the future conveys temporal reference with non-aspectual force (*Verbal Syntax*, 50-51).

Attributive participles suggest the adjectival function of the participle. They modify nouns and most frequently follow a definite article. Circumstantial or adverbial participles imply the verbal function of the participle. They have a broad range of nuances, equivalent to subordinate clauses with a variety of relationships with the main verb such as temporal, means, manner, cause, concession, condition, attendant circumstances, and purpose. Supplementary participles, as their name suggests, supplement the idea of the main verb. They occur with verbs such as "begin" and "cease." The periphrastic tenses (mentioned above) can be categorized as a supplementary use of the participle.

2. Infinitives

Infinitives are verbal nouns that bear characteristics of both nouns and verbs. They can function as substantives and be both subjects (fairly rare) and objects in clauses. Infinitives function as objects or complements with several verbs, such as δύναμαι "to be able to," θέλω "to want to," μέλλω "to be going to," δεῖ "it is necessary to." An infinitive can be used as an object of a verb such as speaking or thinking to convey indirect speech. Infinitives also function adverbially to indicate purpose or result. Infinitives combine with certain prepositions (especially in translation Greek, translating Hebrew infinitive constructs preceded by a preposition) and can indicate cause (e.g., with δία) or have temporal force (e.g., with πρό "before," ἕως "until," ἐν "when, at the time," and μετά "after").

C. Volitive Forms

Greek employs three non-indicative moods to indicate volitivity. The imperative is used for second and third person commands, the subjunctive mood is used for first person deliberation and exhortation, with the aorist subjunctive mostly used for second person prohibitions with perfective aspect (instead of the aorist imperative). The rarer optative mood is used mostly for wishes.

D. Clause Types

1. Narrative Main Clauses

In main narrated (past) clauses, the aorist with its perfective aspect is the usual verb form to indicate simple sequential action of the unmarked event line (especially the aorist indicative and postposed aorist participles). Other verb forms such as (preposed) participles, and forms with imperfective aspect (such as historic presents, imperfects), "be" verbs, verbless clauses and forms with perfective-imperfective or stative aspect (such as perfects and pluperfects) are "marked" (e.g., for background, circumstance, etc.).[51]

2. Reported Speech Main Clauses

As with Hebrew, a much greater variety of verb forms occurs in reported speech. In action prior to the verb of speaking the same verb forms for narrated past occur (i.e., perfective and imperfective and perfective-imperfective or stative forms); in action in a present time frame, simultaneous with the verb of speaking, present tense forms, noun sentences (lacking a verbal form), and participles occur; in reported speech in future contexts, future or volitive forms (e.g., imperatives) are usually the unmarked form. Greek also frequently reports speech indirectly as opposed to directly. In indirect speech, the verb is frequently reported in the infinitive. Alternatively, the conjunctions ὅτι or εἰ may introduce indirect speech, and the verb remains in the indicative, with the person and tense perhaps altered to fit in with the verb of speech.

3. Subordinate Clauses

Greek has a variety of subordinate conjunctions and is more precise than Hebrew (with two main subordinating conjunctions אֲשֶׁר and כִּי) in marking the different types of subordinate clauses. Relative pronouns (declined for case, gender, and number) indicate relative clauses. Attributive participles also occur frequently and are equivalent

---

[51] Cf. R. E. Longacre, "Mark 5.1-43: Generating the Complexity of a Narrative from Its Most Basic Elements," in *Discourse Analysis and the New Testament: Approaches and Results* (ed. Stanley Porter and Jeffrey T. Reed; JSNTSup 170; Sheffield: Sheffield Academic Press, 1999), 169-96.

in function to relative clauses. Ὅτι occurs frequently as a conjunction to mark causal clauses as well as object clauses (especially clauses as objects of verbs of speaking). Ὅτε (ὅταν) and ὡς usually mark temporal clauses; ὡς also marks comparative clauses, and sometimes result (especially combined with τε as ὥστε) and purpose clauses (especially as ὅπως with the subjunctive mood). Ἵνα with the subjunctive mood is the most frequent subordinating conjunction used to mark purpose clauses. Conditional clauses are indicated by εἰ and various moods, or ἔαν and the subjunctive mood. Infinitives are also used quite frequently to indicate purpose and result clauses. They also occur with prepositions such as δία (with the genitive case) to indicate causal clauses; and πρό, πρίν, and ἔως, to indicate antecedent action in temporal clauses, ἐν to indicate simultaneous action, and μετά to indicate subsequent (following) action in temporal clauses.

In addition, participles and infinitives with adverbial or circumstantial force frequently occur as equivalents to subordinate clauses. Circumstantial participles correspond to almost all of the different kinds of subordinate clauses, (e.g., temporal, causal, condition, concession, and purpose), as well as indicating the manner and means by which the action of the main verb is accomplished. Infinitives mostly function as equivalent to purpose clauses.

E. Summary

The six indicative forms operate primarily in main clauses. The aorist mostly occurs in narrative as the main event line verb interspersed with aspectually marked imperfect, perfect, pluperfect, and present forms. All of the indicative forms occur in reported speech, along with volitive forms. Participles occur circumstantially or attributively (equivalent to adjectival relative clauses). Infinitives are mostly equivalent to subordinate clauses in their function. Non-indicative moods are most frequently found in subordinate clauses. Verbless noun sentences occur in all clause types but not as frequently as in Hebrew.

IV. COMPARISON AND CONCLUSION

As can be seen from this brief overview of the Greek and Hebrew verbal systems, Greek has a richer variety of forms than Hebrew, with Hebrew having four indicative forms (including two sequential forms), while Greek has six. Both languages use periphrastic forms, although they are much more common in classical and Hellenistic/Koine Greek than in biblical Hebrew (but they become increasingly common in rabbinic Hebrew).[52] In both Hebrew and Greek verbal aspect is more significance than tense. Both languages have perfective and imperfective aspects, while Greek has an additional perfective-imperfective (stative) aspect. In Greek, aspect also is important in the non-indicative forms, while in Hebrew these forms (apart from perhaps the participle) are aspectually neutral.

In terms of syntax, Greek tends to be much more hypotactic (from the term *hypotaxis*, arranging clauses *under* or *subordinate to* the main clause) than Hebrew, especially in its use of the circumstantial participle. Hebrew prefers to coordinate clauses of sequential forms on the same level, classified as paratactic (from the term *parataxis*, arranging main clauses *parallel to* or *on* the same level linked by a coordinating conjunction) with fewer subordinate clauses and even less circumstantial participles than Greek.[53] In narrative clauses, the

---

[52] For a succinct analysis of the Hebrew verbal system (including seven stems) compared to Greek see John W. Wevers, "The Use of Versions for Text Criticism The Septuagint," in *La Septuaginta en la Investigación Contemporánea: 5th Congress of the International Organization for Septuagint and Cognate Studies 1983: Salamanca, Spain* (ed. Natalio Fernández Marcos; Madrid: Instituto "Arias Montano," C.S.I.C., 1985), 15-24 (especially 16-18). To demonstrate the richer inventory in Greek as opposed to Hebrew he calculates that "a complete generation of possible inflections for a verbal root in Greek would produce 973 forms over against a potential 204 in Hebrew" (16).

[53] For example, if we compare the Hebrew narrative of 1 Chronicles 10:1-12 with the Greek of Josephus' *Antiquities of the Jews*, book 6.368-73 (which both contain an account of the death of Saul), the Chronicles section has 36 main clause verb forms (32 *wayyiqtol* forms and 4 *qatal* forms—translated by 35 aorists, 1 imperfect), and no circumstantial participles. The Josephus section has 21 main clause forms (7 aorists, 11 historic presents, 3 imperfects) and 26 circumstantial participles (19 aorist and 7 present participles). However, when comparing subordinate clauses the difference is not nearly as distinct. The main difference is that Josephus favors infinitives to the indicative forms favored by *Paraleipomenon*. *1 Paraleipomenon* 10:1-12 has seven subordinate clauses: three object clauses following the verb *to see*, one causal clause, and one relative clause (with four aorist indicatives and one imperfect indicative to translate *qatal* forms) and two infinitives of purpose. Josephus has seven subordinate clauses: one purpose clause (ὡς + infinitive), two object clauses (ὡς + infinitive, ὡς + indicative), and one result clause (ὡς + infinitive), one temporal clause (πρίν +

sequential *wayyiqtol* form predominates in Hebrew, while the aorist predominates in Greek. Both languages use a greater variety of verbal forms in both reported speech and subordinate clauses.

In the following chapter, we will investigate the way the translator of Chronicles used these Greek verb forms to render the Hebrew verbs, and how much the distinction between the languages was preserved in their translation. The focus of this study is Hebrew indicative forms (*wayyiqtol*, *qatal*, *wᵉqatal*, *yiqtol*, and *wᵉyiqtol* forms) as well as the *qotel* participles (especially where they are beginning to be used as a tense form in late biblical Hebrew). The study also investigates infinitive constructs that function as temporal clauses, especially when they are translated by Greek indicative forms.

---

infinitive), one causal clause (διά + τό + infinitive), and one relative clause (ὁποίαν + present indicative).

CHAPTER FOUR

THE TRANSLATION OF HEBREW VERBS IN CHRONICLES

This chapter first deals briefly with the production and translation of the book of Chronicles and then gives an overview of the Hebrew verb forms found in the book of Chronicles. The Greek equivalents chosen by the translator for each Hebrew verb form are tabulated, in total and according to three clause types, and discussed in detail. At the end of the chapter, brief mention is made of how each Hebrew verb form functions in three clause types: main clause narrative, main clause reported speech,[1] and subordinate clauses, including the historical-linguistic changes that have occurred in the Hebrew verb system.

I. THE PRODUCTION AND TRANSLATION OF CHRONICLES

The book of Chronicles is a narrative history produced during post-exilic times. There has been some debate among scholars as to the exact dating of the book of Chronicles. It must have been produced between the time of the rise of the Persian Empire 539 BCE (2 Chr 36:20) and the citation of the Greek translation of Chronicles in Eupolemus ca. 150 BCE (which would imply the completion and recognition of the Hebrew text of Chronicles by no later than 200 BCE). It was completed sometime in the Persian period, perhaps in the early Persian period (539-460 BCE), with the genealogical material completed no earlier than 400 BCE (cf. 1 Chr 3:19-24).[2] The book of

---

[1] Reported speech includes both direct and indirect speech, except when an infinitive is used to indicate indirect speech. Then the clause is included under subordinate clauses (as narrative). Sometimes indirect speech in Hebrew is translated as direct speech, e.g., אָז אָמַר דָּוִיד לֹא לָשֵׂאת אֶת־אֲרוֹן הָאֱלֹהִים "Then David said that no one was to carry the ark of God" τότε εἶπεν Δαυιδ οὐκ ἔστιν ἆραι τὴν κιβωτὸν τοῦ θεοῦ "Then David said, 'no one is to take the ark of God' (1 Chr 15:2). In cases like this, we classify the clauses according to the Hebrew structure.

[2] Cf. W. M. Schniedewind, *Society and the Promise to David: The Reception History of 2 Samuel 7:1-17* (Oxford: Oxford University Press, 1999), 125-28, who argues for an early Persian date based on its emphasis on David and his descendants. Cross (1975) proposes three stages in its production (in conjunction with the books of Ezra and Nehemiah), the first edition (1 Chr 10—2 Chr 34) produced between 520-515 BCE,

Chronicles consists of material taken from canonical sources, of which Samuel-Kings is the most frequent source, some non-canonical sources (e.g., the story of the prophet Iddo—cf. 2 Chr 13:2-22, about Abijah; and the records of the seers—cf. 2 Chr 33:11-19, about Manasseh), and work originating from the Chronicler himself. The Chronicler has selectively drawn from the canonical material, and in places the canonical material has been rewritten, rearranged, and even reinterpreted.

The language of Chronicles contains both classical biblical Hebrew and late biblical Hebrew. In synoptic passages, where text that is almost verbatim that of its source (e.g., 1 Chr 10:1-14), classical biblical Hebrew predominates. In text that is heavily based on parallel passages but has redactional changes and editorial comments (e.g., 1 Chr 14-16), there is a mixture of classical and late biblical Hebrew. The source is classical biblical Hebrew. The editorial changes, while influenced by the classical Hebrew of the surrounding text, sometimes reflect a modernization to late biblical Hebrew forms and uses. In the writings of the Chronicler himself, observed in the material unique to Chronicles (e.g., 2 Chr 26), late biblical Hebrew forms occur more frequently, but the classical biblical Hebrew style still exerts a strong influence. Modernization of the language can be observed in the forms and uses of verbs in each of these three types of text.[3]

---

the second edition produced after Ezra's mission in 450 BCE, and the final edition dated to around 400 BCE incorporating the genealogies of 1 Chronicles 1—9. Japhet supposes one author for Chronicles (distinct from the author(s) of Ezra-Nehemiah) and argues for a date at the end of the fourth century, as late as this due to the genealogy of Jehoiachin (1 Chr 3:17-24), and as early as this due to the absence of Greek influence, cf. Sara Japhet, *I & II Chronicles: A Commentary* (OTL; Louisville: Westminster, John Knox Press, 1993), 4-7, 23-28. Williamson postulates a slightly later date than Japhet for the writing of Chronicles, perhaps following the disappointment after the Persian suppression of a revolt for independence led by the Sidonian Tennes in 351-348 BCE, cf. H. G. M. Williamson, *New Century Bible Commentary: 1 and 2 Chronicles* (Grand Rapids: Eerdmans, 1982), 16. For a summary of recent literature on the date and authorship of Chronicles, see Yigal Levin, "Who Was the Chronicler's Audience? A Hint from His Genealogies," *JBL* 122 (2003): 229-30, 243-45 and especially his notes 3 and 4.

[3] Some of the changes to the verb system that occurred in late biblical Hebrew can be observed in the book of Chronicles. For example, the *qatal* suffix conjugation is increasingly becoming a past preterite form (Verheij notes an increase in the percentage of *qatal* forms (from 14% to 26.1%) and a decline in the percentage of *wayyiqtol* forms (from 64% to 40.3%) in narrative when comparing Samuel, Kings, and the non-synoptic portions of Chronicles, *Verbs and Numbers*, 97). See chapter 3, section II.E for a comparison between archaic and contemporary verb use as found in biblical Hebrew texts. See also the comments on and examples of the translation profile of the Greek (although not pertaining specifically to the verb) in S. Peter Cowe, "To the

Since only four verses are preserved in the Hebrew manuscripts of the Dead Sea Scrolls, the primary witnesses to the book of Chronicles are the Masoretic text (MT) and two Greek translations.[4] The first Greek translation, 1 Esdras, which contains only chapters 35-36 of 2 Chronicles, was written in Egypt in the second century BCE. The second, *Paraleipomenon* is a translation of the entire book of Chronicles that was probably made also in the second century BCE in Egypt.[5] This translation is best preserved in the G family of texts (Vaticanus [= B], Sinaiticus [= ℵ], and miniscule c2), of which L, R, and O families are revisions.[6] According to Allen, G itself has been extensively revised, so its fairly close approximation to the MT may stem from the recensional process.[7] This book uses the BHS Hebrew text (which largely preserves the MT) and Rahlfs's Greek text (critical text based on B, cf. Brooke and McLean's diplomatic text which reproduces B).[8] Wherever a variant is considered significant, reference is made to parallel texts of Samuel-Kings or Qumran MSS (of Samuel-Kings) for Hebrew variants, and parallel texts of Rahlfs's Septuagint of Samuel-Kings or other extant Greek MSS for alternative treatment of the verb in translation.

Reader of 1 and 2 Supplements" *A New English Translation of the Septuagint* (ed. Albert Pietersma and Benjamin G. Wright; New York: Oxford University Press, 2007), 342-348.

[4] 4QChr (4Q118) contains 2 Chronicles 28:27; 29:1-3, cf. J. Trebolle Barrera, "Édition préliminaire de 4QChroniques," *RevQ* 15 (1992): 523-28.

[5] *Paraleipomenon,* meaning *of the things remaining, left behind,* or *left over,* is the name for the book of Chronicles in the Septuagint. Perhaps this reflects the concept of the Septuagint translator that it contained events left out of earlier biblical history. On the significance of the name, see Gary N. Knoppers and Paul B. Harvey "Omitted and Remaining Matters: On the Names Given to the Book of Chronicles in Antiquity," *JBL* 121 (2002): 227-43. For the dates of *Paraleipomenon,* see chapter 2, especially notes 23 and 24. In addition, see also R. Klein, "Chronicles, Book of 1-2," *ABD* 1:992-1002 [995].

[6] L. C. Allen, *Greek Chronicles,* 65-108.

[7] Ibid., 142-74.

[8] These two texts are available electronically through the GRAMCORD Institute and Oak Tree Software (*Accordance*). The version of *GRAMCORD for Windows* used in this book was that contained in Bible Companion 1.6.4. It uses the Groves-Wheeler Westminster Hebrew Morphology of the Masoretic Text, version 3.1, copyright 1999, Westminster Theological Seminary, and the CCAT Septuagint Morphological Database, copyright 1999, Center for Computer Analysis of Texts, University of Pennsylvania. It uses *Hebpar* and *Greek Parse* Hebrew and Greek fonts. The English translations of the verses quoted in this book for the most part come from the New Revised Standard Version (NRSV), copyright 1989, the Division of Christian Education of the National Council of the Churches of Christ in the United States of America.

In synoptic passages, *Paraleipomenon* often agrees with Samuel-Kings (either conforming to the Hebrew text of Samuel-Kings and/or the Greek translation of Samuel-Kings) against the MT of Chronicles.[9] It seems that the *Vorlage* of *Paraleipomenon* and even *Paraleipomenon* have assimilated to the Samuel-Kings text, thus removing the changes made by the Chronicler. On the other hand, the MT of Chronicles may also be corrupt. The study of the translation of the verbs of the Chronicles MT into Greek will take into account possible differences in the *Vorlage* underlying the translation of *Paraleipomenon* and places where *Paraleipomenon* conforms to the Greek of Samuel-Kings or the MT of Samuel-Kings, so far as they affect the understanding of the verb form.[10]

II. VERB FORMS IN CHRONICLES ACCORDING TO TEXT TYPES

There are 4331 Hebrew verbal forms in Chronicles. Almost 70% of the verbal forms are indicative forms (which are the focus of this book). There are 1449 *wayyiqtol* forms, 1163 *qatal* forms (including 128 *wᵉqatal* forms), 351 *yiqtol* forms, 495 *qotel* active participle forms, 73 *qatul* passive participle forms, 612 *qᵉtol* infinitive construct forms, 25 *qatol* infinitive absolute forms, and 163 *qᵉtol* imperative forms.[11]

---

[9] The Samuel-Kings text used by the Chronicler was probably the Palestinian text of Samuel-Kings attested to by Qumran MSS (especially 4QSam[a]), the Old Greek and proto-Lucianic recensions of LXX, and Josephus; as opposed to the Babylonian (proto-MT) and Egyptian texts (Klein, "Book of Chronicles 1-2," 995), cf. chapter 2, note 45 on the differences between the MT and the LXX either due to the free translating of the translator or of a Hebrew editor producing differences between the *Vorlage* and the MT.

[10] As listed in M. Rehm, *Textkritische Untersuchungen zu den Parallelstellen der Samuel-Königsbücher und der Chronik* (ATA 13/3; Münster: Aschendorff, 1937), 53ff. for the former and 63ff. for the latter. Gerleman, *Studies in the Septuagint*, Allen, *Greek Chronicles*, 175ff, and E. Talstra and A. J. C. Verheij, "Comparing Samuel/Kings and Chronicles: The Computer Assisted Production of an Analytical Synoptic Database," *Text* 14 (1988): 41-60 also comment on the textual variants in the Greek translation of Chronicles as they impact verbal forms. See Trevor Evans, *Verbal Syntax*, 76-79, who discusses questions concerning the Hebrew text regarding the use of the MT as approximating the LXX *Vorlage* concluding, "the evidence of those Hebrew variants which are germane to the issue would not have a major impact on the statistics" (79).

[11] Verheij counts 1034 *qatal*, 128 *wᵉqatal*, 298 *yiqtol*, 51 *wᵉyiqtol*, and 1453 *wayyiqtol* forms in Chronicles. These can be divided into 284 *qatal*, 108 *wᵉqatal*, 261 *yiqtol*, 48 *wᵉyiqtol*, and 77 *wayyiqtol* forms in direct speech and 750 *qatal*, 20 *wᵉqatal*, 37 *yiqtol*, 3 *wᵉyiqtol*, and 1376 *wayyiqtol* forms in narrative (*Verbs and Numbers*, 96-99). Our count agrees with *GRAMCORD*, however, *GRAMCORD* has 1450 *wayyiqtol* and 1164 *qatal* forms, which should add up to 4333 forms. The difference between the three results is

As can be seen in the following table, the majority of verbal forms in Chronicles occur in narrative main clauses. This is not surprising given that Chronicles is a book of narrative history. *Wayyiqtol* forms are the most common forms in narrative followed by *qatal* forms. There are also significant numbers of predicate participles. Within this body of narrative history, there are sections of reported speech and numerous subordinate clauses. A greater variety of forms occur in reported speech. Most *yiqtol, weqatal,* and imperative forms occur in reported speech; *qatal* and *wayyiqtol* forms also occur. In subordinate clauses infinitive constructs are the most common form followed by *qatal* forms.

TABLE 1: VERB FORMS IN CHRONICLES

	Narrative Main Clauses	Reported Speech Main Clauses	Subordinate Clauses	TOTAL
WAYYIQTOL	1375	74	—	1449
QATAL	515 (19 *weqatal*)	240 (109 *weqatal*)	408	1163[12]
YIQTOL	27 (3 *weyiqtol*)	239 (51 *weyiqtol*)	85	351
QOTEL	340 (98 pred.)	110 (45 pred.)	45 (21 pred.)	495 (165 pred.)
QATUL	54 (23 pred.)	11 (9 pred.)	8 (7 pred.)	73 (39 pred.)
QᵉTOL (Inf. Cstr.)	—	—	612	612
QATOL	11	11	3	25
QᵉTOL (Impv.)	—	162	1	163
TOTAL	2322	847	1162	4331

III. THE HEBREW VERB FORMS WITH THEIR GREEK EQUIVALENTS

We look at the translation of indicative forms in the following order: *wayyiqtol* forms, *qatal* forms (including *weqatal* forms which are also

---

due to slight variations in the coding of the two databases used (cf. notes 12 and 85 below, for a couple of examples).

[12] *GRAMCORD* arrives at a figure of 1164 *qatal* forms. This includes one *Ketiv* (written) *qatal* form יִשְׁבוּ whose *qere* (read) form יֹשְׁבֵי (a *qotel* form) is also counted (1 Chr 2:55) by *GRAMCORD*. The verb is translated by a present participle in Greek. However, in our analysis the *qere* form is counted as the underlying Hebrew form in the analysis of the Greek verb forms (see note 59 and table 6 in this chapter, and the section on Greek present participles in chapter 5).

treated separately), and *yiqtol* forms (including *wᵉyiqtol* forms which are indicated in parentheses), followed by the non-indicative *qotel*, and *qatul* forms, and the infinitives construct and absolute. We briefly comment on the imperative but do not include it in the analysis. We analyze each verb form, given in the order above, in the following way. Each form is introduced, making brief mention of the text types it occurs in. If the form is a coordinated verb form, the form that precedes it is taken into account to see if the context aids in distinguishing formally identical forms in their archaic and contemporary uses (i.e., distinguish *wayyiqtol* from *wᵉyiqtol*, which were mostly formally identical in the unpointed text of the *Vorlage*, and the consecutive and coordinated *wᵉqatal* forms). We also mention different archaic and contemporary uses of the verb form that may influence the translator in his choice of equivalent. We briefly mention the main Greek equivalents (firstly establishing the most common Greek form or common equivalent that each Hebrew form is rendered into and then mentioning the other equivalents) used to translate the Hebrew form.[13] This is followed by the results presented in tabular form. Then verse references are given for the Greek forms used to translate the Hebrew form according to three clause types (main clause narrative, main clause reported speech, and subordinate clauses).

Then a detailed account is given of all the equivalents chosen for each Hebrew form. We investigate the significance of each Greek form used in translating the Hebrew form. We comment on the different clause types where there is significant variation. At the end of each Hebrew verb form, we make further comment on the equivalents chosen. We also note where the translation switches from paratactic structure to hypotactic and vice versa. Finally, we conclude each section by commenting on the rationale for using a particular Greek form and the adequacy of the translation of the particular form.

---

[13] The Greek forms are categorized according to the order indicative, participle, infinitive, volitive, adjective, adverb, noun forms, and minuses (if the form is not translated, or if two Hebrew forms are translated by one Greek form).

A. Indicative Forms

1. Wayyiqtol

As can be seen from the table below, most of the *wayyiqtol* forms occur in narrative main clauses. The few *wayyiqtol* forms in reported speech occur mostly in reported narrative within reported speech. They are interspersed with *qatal* forms, which occur twice as often as *wayyiqtol* forms as a perfective form in past contexts in reported speech (see table 3 below). (Perhaps this is due to the lack of longer sections of contiguous narrative in reported speech, but it could also be due to the decline in the use of *wayyiqtol* in spoken Hebrew at the time of the production of Chronicles). Most of the *wayyiqtol* forms follow other *wayyiqtol* forms, but *qatal*, and *w^eqatal* (coordinated, not sequential) forms, and noun sentences, and occasionally *qotel* and *yiqtol* forms with past durative force precede them. In this way the translator was able to distinguish the archaic *wayyiqtol* form from the formally identical *w^eyiqtol* form in unvocalized text. The common equivalent for *wayyiqtol* forms is the aorist indicative preceded by καί. This common equivalent has the highest percentage of all common equivalents for any Hebrew verb form. Other equivalents include imperfects and a few presents, futures, imperatives, circumstantial participles, and infinitives. Sometimes one of the verbs is omitted.

Table 2 shows how the *wayyiqtol* forms were translated into Greek. The most significant percentages of the verb in each clause type are given in parentheses ( ) under each clause type (e.g., 5.4% of *wayyiqtol* forms in reported speech main clauses were translated as futures).

TABLE 2: THE TRANSLATION OF *WAYYIQTOL* FORMS

WAYYIQTOL	TOTAL	Percentage	Narrative Main Clauses (Clause %)	Reported Speech Main Clauses	Subordinate Clauses
Aorist Indicative	1330	91.79	1261 (91.7)	69 (93.2)	
Imperfect Indicative	76	5.24	76 (5.5)		
Present Indicative	2	0.14	2		
Future Indicative	6	0.41	2	4 (5.4)	
Aorist Participle	2	0.14	2		
Present Participle	3	0.21	3		
Aorist Infinitive	4	0.28	4		

Aorist Imperative	3	0.21	3		
Adjective	1	0.07	1		
Adverb	1	0.07	1		
Noun	1	0.07	1		
Minus	20	1.38	19 (1.4)	1 (1.4)	
Total	1449	100	1375	74	

Total 1449

Aorist Indicative (1330 = 91.79%)[14]

Narrative Main Clauses (1261)[15]

Wayyiqtol + *wayyiqtol* > *Aorist Indicative* (934)

1 Chr 1:44, 45 (2), 46 (2), 47 (2), 48 (2), 49 (2), 50 (2), 51; 2:3, 19 (2), 23, 35; 4:10, 40, 41 (4), 43; 5:20 (2), 22, 25, 26 (2); 6:32<17>,[16]

---

[14] Including six forms interpreted by *GRAMCORD* as aorist participles κατίσχυσαν (1 Chr 5:20; 2 Chr 11:17 (2)); ἐνίσχυσαν (24:13); ἐσκύλευσαν; (25:13); συνεπίσχυσαν (32:3) and one form interpreted by *GRAMCORD* as an aorist optative καθεῖλαν (30:14), but all of them are better taken as aorist indicatives (see all the coding differences in Appendix 1).

[15] In counting verbs preceding the *wayyiqtol* forms, intervening verb forms in reported speech and subordinate clauses are ignored unless the *wayyiqtol* form continues on from verbs in those clauses (examples are given in note 18 below). In addition, clauses with elided verbs, where the verb is understood from the context [indicated in brackets], are not counted as the form preceding the *wayyiqtol* form. For example, "So the king did not listen [*qatal*]...And all Israel [saw] that the king would not listen to them, and the people *answered* [*wayyiqtol*]" (2 Chr 10:16; so also 25:24; 29:32) is analyzed as *qatal* + *wayyiqtol*. Introductory temporal clauses without *wayhi* forms and/or infinitive constructs are treated as noun sentences and analyzed as noun sentence + *wayyiqtol*, e.g., בִּשְׁנַת שְׁמוֹנֶה עֶשְׂרֵה לַמֶּלֶךְ יָרָבְעָם וַיִּמְלֹךְ אֲבִיָּה "[And it came to pass] in the eighteenth year of King Jeroboam, that Abijah began to reign" translated ἐν τῷ ὀκτωκαιδεκάτῳ ἔτει τῆς βασιλείας Ιεροβοαμ ἐβασίλευσεν (13:1. The Greek does not translate the *waw* of the *wayyiqtol* with καί, cf. 25:27 and 28:22, both of which do translate καί). Sometimes a subject or object is fronted and comes between two verb forms e.g., with a fronted subject (underlined): וְאַחַר מוֹת (infin. const.) חֶצְרוֹן בְּכָלֵב אֶפְרָתָה וְאֵשֶׁת חֶצְרוֹן אֲבִיָּה וַתֵּלֶד לוֹ "And after the death of Hezron, in Caleb-ephrathah, Abijah wife of Hezron bore him..." translated καὶ μετὰ τὸ ἀποθανεῖν Εσερων ἦλθεν (Greek plus) Χαλεβ εἰς Εφραθα καὶ ἡ γυνὴ Εσερων Αβια καὶ ἔτεκεν αὐτῷ (1 Chr 2:24; so also 2 Chr 25:13). This is analyzed infinitive construct + *wayyiqtol*. For examples of a fronted object coming between two verb forms see 2 Chronicles 10:17 and 8:8.

[16] In citing the verses in which verb forms are found, we follow the following conventions. The standard English and Septuagint verse references are given first with the Hebrew verse where it differs in brackets < >. There are four sections of text where the versification differs between the English and Hebrew, ranging from 1 Chronicles 6:1<5:27> until 6:81<66>, from 12:5<6> until 12:40<41>, from 2 Chronicles 2:1<1:18> until 2:18<17>, and from 14:1<13:23> until 14:15<14>. The differences are due to the different chapter divisions in the Masoretic text in comparison with the English (and Greek). There are four verse sections in which the

65<50>, 66<51>, 67<52>; 7:16 (2), 22, 23 (4); 10:1, 2 (2), 3 (3), 4 (2),
5 (3), 6, 7 (4), 8 (3), 9 (3), 10, 12 (5), 13, 14; 11:1, 3 (3), 4, 5, 6 (3), 7, 14
(3), 15, 17, 18 (4), 19, 23 (2); 12:16<17>, 17<18> (2), 18<19>; 13:2,
4, 5, 6, 7, 9, 10 (3), 11 (2), 12, 14 (2); 14:1, 2, 3 (2), 8 (3), 10 (2), 11 (3),
12, 13 (2), 14 (2), 16 (2), 17; 15:1 (2), 4, 11, 12, 14, 15, 16, 17, 26 (2),
29; 16:1 (3), 2 (2), 3, 4, 37, 43 (2); 17:1 (2), 2, 3 (2), 16 (2); 18:1 (4), 2, 3,
4 (3), 5 (2), 6, 7 (2), 10 (2), 14; 19:1 (2), 2 (3), 3, 4 (4), 5 (3), 6 (2), 7 (3), 8
(2), 9, 10 (2), 12, 14 (2), 15 (2), 16 (3), 17 (6), 18 (2), 19 (2); 20:1 (5), 2
(2), 4 (2), 5 (2), 6, 7; 21:1 (2), 2, 3, 4 (2), 5, 7, 8, 9, 11 (2), 13, 14 (2), 15
(2), 16 (2), 17, 20 (2), 21 (2), 22, 23, 24, 25, 26 (4), 27 (2); 22:2 (2), 5, 6
(2), 7, 17; 23:2, 3 (2), 6; 24:3, 4 (2), 5, 6; 25:1 (2), 8, 9; 26:14; 28:2 (2),
11, 20; 29:1, 6, 7, 20 (3), 21 (2), 22 (4), 23 (3), 25, 28; 2 Chr 1:1, 2, 3, 6
(2), 8, 11, 13 (2), 14 (3), 15; 2:2 <1>, 11<10> (2), 12<11>, 17<16>
(2), 18<17>; 3:1, 2, 5, 6, 10, 14, 15, 16 (4), 17 (2); 4:1, 2, 6, 7, 8 (3), 9,
11, 19; 5:1, 4 (2), 5; 6:3, 12 (2), 13 (3), 14; 7:3, 5, 8, 9, 12; 8:1, 3 (2), 4,
5, 8, 18 (2); 9:1 (2), 2, 3, 9, 17 (2), 25, 27, 31 (3); 10:1, 2 (2), 3 (3), 5 (2),
6, 7, 8 (2), 9, 10, 12, 13 (2), 14, 16, 17, 18 (3); 11:1 (2), 2, 4 (2), 5 (2), 6,
11 (2), 12, 17, 18, 19, 21, 22, 23 (3); 12:1, 4, 6 (2), 9 (2), 10, 13, 16 (2);
13:4, 14, 15, 16, 17 (2), 18 (2), 19 (2), 20, 21 (3); 14:1 <13:23> (2),
3<2> (3), 4<3>, 5<4> (2), 7<6>, 8<7>, 9<8>, 10<9> (2), 11<10>
(2), 12<11> (2), 13<12> (3), 14<13> (2), 15<14>; 15:2, 8, 9, 10, 11,
12, 14, 15 (2), 16; 16:2 (2), 4 (3), 5 (3), 6, 10 (3), 13, 14 (3); 17:1 (2), 2
(2), 3, 5 (2), 6, 10, 12; 18:1, 2 (2), 3 (2), 4, 5 (3), 6, 7 (2), 8 (2), 10, 14 (3),
15, 16, 17, 18, 23 (3), 24, 25, 27, 28 , 29 (3), 31 (2), 32 (2), 33, 34; 19:1,
2 (2), 4 (3), 5, 6, 9; 20:2 (2), 3 (3), 4, 6, 20 (2), 21 (2), 23, 25 (3), 28, 29,
30 (2), 31, 36, 37 (2); 21:1 (2), 4 (2), 6 (2), 9, 10, 11, 12, 17 (2), 20; 22:1
(2), 5, 6, 8 (2), 9 (3), 10, 11 (4); 23:2 (3), 3 (2), 8 (2), 9, 10, 11 (5), 12 (2),
13 (3), 14 (2), 15 (3), 16, 17 (2), 19, 20 (4), 21; 24:3 (2), 4, 5 (2), 6, 8, 10,
11, 12, 13 (3), 15 (2), 16, 18, 19 (2), 20, 21 (2), 22, 23, 25 (2); 25:3, 5
(3), 6, 9, 10 (3), 11 (2), 13 (2), 14 (3), 15 (2), 16 (4), 17 (2), 18, 21, 22 (2),
23, 24, 25, 27 (3), 28 (2); 26:1 (2), 4, 6 (3), 7, 8, 9 (2), 10 (2), 11, 15 (2),
16, 17, 18 (2), 19, 23 (2); 27:9 (2); 28:5 (4), 6, 7, 8, 9 (2), 12, 13, 14, 15
(7), 17, 18, 20, 23, 24 (3), 27 (2); 29:2, 4 (2), 5, 12, 15 (2), 16 (3), 17, 18,
20 (3), 21 (2), 22 (4), 23 (2), 24 (2), 25, 26, 27, 30 (3), 31 (3), 32, 36;
30:1, 4, 5, 6, 14 (2), 15 (2), 16, 20, 21, 22, 23, 25, 26, 27 (3); 31:1 (3), 2,

---

Greek contains a total of twelve additional verses in comparison with the English (and
Hebrew). The additional verses follow four verses in 2 Chronicles and are numbered
accordingly: 35:19 (4 verses—19a, b, c, d), 36:2 (3 verses—2a, b, c;), 36:4 (1 verse—
4a) and 5 (4 verses—5a, b, c, d).

8 (3), 10 (2), 11 (2), 12, 20; 32:1 (2), 2, 3 (2), 4 (2), 5 (4), 6 (3), 8, 19, 20 (2), 21 (4), 22, 24, 26, 30, 33; 33:3 (6), 9, 10, 11 (3), 13 (5), 14, 15, 16 (3), 20 (2), 24, 25 (2); 34:2, 7, 9, 10 (2), 11, 15 (2), 16 (2), 18 (2), 19 (2), 20, 22, 23, 28, 29 (2), 30 (2), 31 (2), 32 (2), 33 (2); 35:1, 2 (2), 3, 7, 10, 11 (2), 13, 17, 21, 23 (2), 24 (5), 25 (2); 36:1, 3, 4 (2), 10, 13, 15, 17, 19

Qatal + wayyiqtol > Aorist Indicative (216)

1 Chr 2:49; 3:4; 4:6, 10, 28, 39; 5:10; 6:11<5:37>, 64<49>; 8:9; 10:1, 4, 7, 11, 14; 11:8, 14, 18, 25; 12:18<19>; 14:9, 12; 15:1, 3, 29; 17:16; 18:9, 13; 19:7, 11, 15, 19; 20:1, 3, 4, 7, 8; 21:4, 7, 15, 19, 21; 22:1, 5; 23:1, 11, 22; 24:2; 26:10, 14, 31; 27:24; 29:9, 10, 25, 28; 2 Chr 1:7; 2:1 <1:18>; 3:5, 10; 4:6, 11, 18; 6:3, 13; 7:1, 11, 12; 8:2, 14, 16, 18; 9:1, 5, 11, 12; 10:16, 19; 11:14, 15, 17, 20, 21; 12:2, 5, 9, 13; 13:3, 4, 13, 16, 20; 14:2<1>, 15<14>; 15:2, 8, 15, 16, 18; 16:1, 6, 7, 13; 17:5; 18:13, 31 (2), 33; 20:5, 15, 19, 20, 22, 24, 27; 21:1, 4, 8, 9, 11, 19 (2), 20; 22:4, 5, 8, 10; 23:1, 18, 24:6, 11, 14, 17, 18, 20, 23 (2), 25; 25:3, 5, 9, 11, 13, 21, 23; 26:2, 6, 16, 20, 23; 27:5, 6, 9; 28:2, 5, 8, 15, 17, 18, 20, 21, 24, 25; 29:3, 17, 18, 29, 34; 30:2, 11, 13, 14, 15, 20; 31:1, 6; 32:1, 18, 22, 24, 25, 27, 30, 33; 33:2, 7, 11, 12, 22 (2), 24; 34:2, 4, 5, 7, 9, 15; 35:1, 10, 13, 16, 20, 22; 36:3, 4, 5, 6, 7, 9, 10, 12, 13, 14, 19, 20, 22

Wᵉqatal + wayyiqtol > Aorist Indicative (6)

1 Chr 7:22; 2 Chr 3:8; 12:11; 33:5, 14; 34:4

Noun Sentence + *wayyiqtol > Aorist Indicative* (63)

1 Chr 1:34, 44; 2:19, 21, 29, 30, 32, 35; 4:17, 43; 5:25; 6:55<40>; 7:15, 24; 8:6; 11:5, 17, 23; 14:8; 19:1, 10; 23:13, 22; 24:2, 31; 25:5, 7; 26:13, 32; 28:1; 2 Chr 1:1, 5; 2:3<2>; 3:4, 7, 8, 14; 4:7; 5:1, 11, 13; 12:4, 14, 16; 13:1, 14; 14:7<6>, 9<8>; 17:9; 18:1; 20:25, 32; 21:3; 24:2; 25:2, 27; 27:2; 28:22; 29:35; 30:27; 31:4, 20; 36:17

Infinitive Construct + *wayyiqtol > Aorist Indicative* (2)

1 Chr 2:24; 21:28

Infinitive Absolute + *wayyiqtol > Aorist Indicative* (1)

1 Chr 5:21

Yiqtol + wayyiqtol > Aorist Indicative (5)

1 Chr 20:3; 2 Chr 5:3; 9:16, 22; 25:15

Qotel[17] + *wayyiqtol > Aorist Indicative* (24)

1 Chr 12:15<16>; 13:1, 9; 15:29; 20:1; 21:16; 2 Chr 5:7; 6:4; 7:3, 5, 7; 9:15; 13:15; 18:10, 34; 22:9; 26:20; 30:10, 22, 23; 32:23; 34:22; 35:12, 25

---

[17] Including two periphrastic *qotel* forms (2 Chr 18:34; 30:10).

Qatul + wayyiqtol > Aorist Indicative (10)

1 Chr 24:7; 2 Chr 9:30; 14:1 <13:23>; 16:12; 24:27; 28:27; 32:33; 33:20; 36:1, 8

Reported Speech Main Clauses (69)

Wayyiqtol + wayyiqtol > Aorist Indicative (34)

1 Chr 17:8, 17; 28:6; 2 Chr 6:6, 7, 8, 10 (4), 11; 7:22 (2); 13:6, 7 (2); 18:19, 20 (4), 21 (2); 20:8 (2); 21:13; 25:18; 29:6 (2), 8; 34:17, 27 (3)[18]

Qatal + wayyiqtol > Aorist Indicative (28)

1 Chr 16:17, 21; 17:17, 22; 22:8; 23:25; 28:4, 5; 2 Chr 1:11; 2:3<2>; 6:6, 15; 7:22; 9:6, 8; 13:9; 14:7<6>; 18:16, 19; 20:7; 21:13; 25:18; 28:9; 29:7, 8; 30:7; 32:12; 34:25

W^eqatal + wayyiqtol > Aorist Indicative (1)

2 Chr 29:6

Noun Sentence + *wayyiqtol > Aorist Indicative* (4)

1 Chr 11:2; 17:26; 2 Chr 13:6; 34:27

Qotel + wayyiqtol > Aorist Indicative (1)

2 Chr 34:17

Infinitive Construct + *wayyiqtol > Aorist Indicative* (1)

1 Chr 16:20

Imperfect Indicative (76 = 5.24%)[19]

Narrative Main Clauses (76)

Wayyiqtol + wayyiqtol > Imperfect Indicative (46)

1 Chr 1:51; 2:25, 26, 28; 5:26; 15:25; 18:2, 6 (2), 13 (2), 14; 20:6; 21:5; 2 Chr 1:17; 5:8 (2), 9 (2); 8:18; 9:13, 26; 11:12; 17:9; 18:2; 21:9, 16, 17; 24:10 (2), 13, 18; 25:12; 26:5, 8, 21; 27:5; 28:4; 29:22 (3); 29:30; 30:10; 31:9; 36:16, 20

---

[18] As in narrative, so also in reported speech, there are intervening verb forms between the two *wayyiqtol* forms, and these are not counted. This is particularly true in dialogue when the intervening verb forms are contained in additional reported speech (e.g., *"and he said, 'I will entice him' and the LORD said to him 'How?' and he said, 'I will go out…'' then the Lord said 'You are…'"* (2 Chr 18:20 (2), 21 (2); so also 6:10; 18:19). Sometimes an intervening subordinate clause contains a verb form that the *wayyiqtol* form is not directly joined to, e.g., *"you humbled yourself* before God <u>when you heard</u>…*and you humbled yourself* before Me…" (34:27; so also 6:10 (2) *"Now the* LORD *has fulfilled* his promise, <u>which He spoke</u>, *and I have succeeded*…<u>as He promised</u>, *and have built*…").

[19] Including three verbs with identical aorist and imperfect forms interpreted as imperfects by *GRAMCORD* ἐπήγειρεν (1 Chr 5:26; 2 Chr 21:16) and ἐξέκλινεν (1 Chr 13:13); and including two wrongly coded forms κατεκρήμνιζον (2 Chr 25:12) coded as an aorist V3PAAI and ὕμνουν (29:30) coded as a present V3PPAI that should both be coded imperfect V3PIAI (see Appendix 1).

Qatal + *wayyiqtol* > *Imperfect Indicative* (12)
1 Chr 2:3, 22, 52; 4:9; 7:19; 8:3; 11:13; 13:13; 2 Chr 22:12; 25:12; 26:21; 28:3
Noun sentence + *wayyiqtol* > *Imperfect Indicative* (12)
1 Chr 2:27; 5:16, 19; 6:32<17>; 8:40; 12:21<22>, 39<40>; 20:2; 23:11, 17; 2 Chr 17:9; 26:14
Qotel + *wayyiqtol* > *Imperfect Indicative* (3)
1 Chr 11:21; 2 Chr 9:25; 17:12
Yiqtol + *wayyiqtol* > *Imperfect Indicative* (3)
1 Chr 11:9; 2 Chr 1:17; 5:9

Present Indicative (2 = 0.14%)

Narrative Main Clauses (2)
Wayyiqtol + *wayyiqtol* > *Present Indicative (2)*
1 Chr 19:9, 17

Future Indicative (6 = 0.41%)[20]

Narrative Main Clauses (2)
Noun Sentence + *wayyiqtol* > *Future Indicative (2)*
1 Chr 16:36; 2 Chr 28:23 (reported speech in Greek)
Reported Speech Main Clauses (4)
W^{e}qatal + *wayyiqtol* > *Future Indicative (1)*
1 Chr 17:10
Noun sentence + *wayyiqtol* > *Future Indicative (1)*
2 Chr 15:4
Wayyiqtol + *wayyiqtol* > *Future Indicative (1)*
2 Chr 15:4
Qatal + *wayyiqtol* > *Future Indicative (1)*
2 Chr 24:20

Aorist Participle (2 = 0.14%)

Narrative Main Clauses (2)
Wayyiqtol + *wayyiqtol* > *Aorist Participle (2)*
1 Chr 29:20; 2 Chr 20:18

Present Participle (3 = 0.21%)

Narrative Main Clauses (3)
Wayyiqtol + *wayyiqtol* > *Present Participle (2)*
1 Chr 5:10; 29:10
Qatal + *wayyiqtol* > *Present Participle (1)*
2 Chr 19:8

---

[20] Including one verb αὐξήσω (1 Chr 17:10) wrongly coded as an aorist subjunctive (see Appendix 1).

Aorist Infinitive (4 = 0.27%)

Narrative Main Clauses (4)

Wayyiqtol + wayyiqtol > Aorist Infinitive (4)
1 Chr 14:12; 19:5; 2 Chr 22:9; 28:15

Aorist Imperative (3 = 0.21%)

Narrative Main Clauses (3)

Wayyiqtol + wayyiqtol > Aorist Imperative (3)
2 Chr 24:8 (2), 9

Adjective (1 = 0.07%)

Narrative Main Clauses (1)

Wayyiqtol + wayyiqtol > Adjective (3)
2 Chr 24:15

Adverb (1 = 0.07%)

Narrative Main Clauses (1)

Wayyiqtol + wayyiqtol > Adverb (1)
2 Chr 19:4

Noun (1 = 0.07%)

Narrative Main Clauses (1)

Qatal + wayyiqtol > Noun
2 Chr 30:24

Minus (20 = 1.38%)

Narrative Main Clauses (19)

Wayyiqtol + wayyiqtol > Minus (18)
1 Chr 12:17<18>; 21:21 (2); 2 Chr 9:12; 10:3; 11:23; 14:6<5>, 7<6>;
15:16; 18:27; 20:1; 24:12, 14; 28:4, 15; 29:15; 32:5; 33:15
Qatal + wayyiqtol > Minus (1)
2 Chr 20:36

Reported Speech Main Clauses (1)

Wayyiqtol + wayyiqtol > Minus (1)
2 Chr 15:4

a. Wayyiqtol > Aorist Indicative (1330 = 91.79%)

This equivalent is by far the greatest equivalent among all verbal
forms, with about 92% of all *wayyiqtol* forms translated by aorists. This
is understandable since the *wayyiqtol* form has perfective aspect and is
used to indicate succession in narrative. The aorist also has perfective
aspect and is the most common tense form used in Greek narrative.
Although the coordinated prefix form *wyqtl* had future significance in
the Hebrew spoken at the time of translation, the translator recognized

from his study and from the traditional reading of the text that in biblical Hebrew narrative these forms had past perfective significance. He really did not have much choice except to use an aorist in his translation. Most of these forms are translated literally by καί and an aorist, following the Hebrew word order. Only in a few places is this word order changed. Καί is omitted in a few places (e.g., 1 Chr 16:17; 19:1; 28:5; 29:20; 2 Chr 13:1; 16:5; 26:2).[21] Other element(s) come between καί and an aorist in a few places, changing the word order (e.g., 1 Chr 12:17<18>; 21:7, 21; 2 Chr 36:13).[22]

Most of the *wayyiqtol* forms translated by an aorist are preceded by another *wayyiqtol* form (and most of these are also translated by an aorist). In narrative, about 75% of the *wayyiqtol* forms are preceded by another *wayyiqtol*; whereas in reported speech, the percentage is only about 50%. A much higher percentage of *qatal* forms precede the *wayyiqtol* forms in reported speech than in narrative (41% as opposed to 17%—including conjunctive *wᵉqatal* forms). This is due to the fact that *qatal* forms occur more frequently in reported speech and that most reported speech sections are introduced by non-*wayyiqtol* forms. Also there are shorter sections of narrative and hence shorter *wayyiqtol* strings in reported speech.

The *wayyiqtol* form of הָיָה has two meanings: a static sense of "to be" and an inceptive sense of "to become, to enter into a state of being."[23] When it means "become," it is mostly translated by the aorist

---

[21] One time a preceding *wayyiqtol* form is translated by a conjunctive circumstantial participle (1 Chr 29:20), thereby removing the need for the conjunction καί before the aorist indicative. One *wayyiqtol* form is translated by an aorist followed by the post-positive conjunction δὲ, εἶπαν δὲ (1 Chr 11:5). Twice the *wayyiqtol* form translated by an aorist with καί omitted is preceded by וַיְהִי (1 Chr 19:1; 2 Chr 16:5), and one time the *wayyiqtol* form translated by an aorist with καί omitted is preceded by an adverbial phrase without וַיְהִי (26:2). See note 24 below, which deals with וַיְהִי and the different ways that it is translated in Chronicles.

[22] For example, the subject is fronted: וַיֵּצֵא דָוִיד "and David went out" translated καὶ Δαυιδ ἐξῆλθεν (1 Chr 12:17<18>), making the Greek more emphatic, "and [it was] David [himself who] went out"; or the object is fronted: וַיְאַמֵּץ אֶת־לְבָבוֹ "and he hardened his heart" translated καὶ τὴν καρδίαν αὐτοῦ κατίσχυσεν "and [it was] his heart he hardened" (2 Chr 36:13).

[23] The two meanings of הָיָה develop diachronically. The meaning of הָיָה "to become" decreases in rabbinic Hebrew with the disappearance of וַיְהִי. Conversely, the static sense of הָיָה as "to be" increases in rabbinic Hebrew with the replacement of classical Hebrew stative verbs with adjectives. For example, classical Hebrew גָּדַל with the meaning "he was great" is replaced in rabbinic Hebrew by גָדוֹל (adjective) with הָיָה (marking the tense of the adjective). גָּדַל in rabbinic Hebrew only has the meaning "he became great, he grew," cf. Miguel Pérez Fernández, *An Introductory Grammar of Rabbinic Hebrew* (trans. John Elwolde; Leiden: Brill, 1997), 98.

of γίνομαι. When it means "be" it is translated by the imperfect of εἰμί (see next section). Almost 60% of the *wayyiqtol* forms of הָיָה are translated by γίνομαι and the rest by εἰμί. It functions in a particular way when the third person singular וַיְהִי is used to introduce temporal clauses, usually at the start of a section of narrative, and it is consistently translated καὶ ἐγένετο "and it came to pass, and it happened." וַיְהִי introduces temporal clauses thirty times in Chronicles.[24]

Outside of the temporal structure indicated above, *wayyiqtol* forms of הָיָה with the meaning "become" are also translated by the aorist of γίνομαι, e.g., "he *became* a ruler" (1 Chr 11:6; so also 23:11), coming, e.g., "the word of God *came*" (1 Chr 17:3; so also 22:8; 27:24; 2 Chr

---

[24] וַיְהִי occurs eighteen times in the structure וַיְהִי + temporal adverbial + *wayyiqtol*, which is usually translated by the structure καὶ ἐγένετο + adverbial + καὶ + aorist, e.g., וַיְהִי מִמָּחֳרָת וַיָּבֹאוּ "The next day when the Philistines came, lit., *and it came to pass* on the next day that the Philistines came" translated καὶ ἐγένετο τῇ ἐχομένῃ καὶ ἦλθον (1 Chr 10:8; so also 1 Chr 15:26; 17:1, 3; 18:1; 20:1, 4; 2 Chr 5:11; 10:2; 18:32; 22:8; 24:11; 25:3, 14, 16; 34:19; twice translated without καί—1 Chr 19:1; 2 Chr 16:5, see note 21 above).

When an element in the second clause (underlined) is fronted, the structure is slightly altered to וַיְהִי + temporal adverbial + wᵉ-noun + *qatal*. This occurs three times in Chronicles, e.g., וַיְהִי בְּהָרִיעַ אִישׁ יְהוּדָה וְהָאֱלֹהִים נָגַף אֶת־יָרָבְעָם "And when the people of Judah shouted, <u>God</u> defeated Jeroboam" translated ἐν τῷ βοᾶν ἄνδρας Ιουδα καὶ κύριος ἐπάταξεν τὸν Ιεροβοαμ (2 Chr 13:15; so also 8:1; 18:31). In late biblical Hebrew (i.e., the time of the writing of Chronicles and the time of its translation into Greek) this structure is "modernized" with the omission of the second *waw* or by the omission of the introductory וַיְהִי, or both (cf. note 3 above).

The second *waw* is omitted, with the structure וַיְהִי + adverbial, + asyndetic *qatal* occurring nine times, e.g., וַיְהִי כְּהָכִין מַלְכוּת רְחַבְעָם וּכְחֶזְקָתוֹ עָזַב אֶת־תּוֹרַת "When the rule of Rehoboam was established and when he grew strong, he abandoned the law" translated καὶ ἐγένετο ὡς ἡτοιμάσθη ἡ βασιλεία Ροβοαμ καὶ ὡς κατεκρατήθη ἐγκατέλιπεν τὰς ἐντολὰς (2 Chr 12:1, so also 1 Chr 15:29; 2 Chr 12:2, 11; 20:1; 21:9, 19; 24:4, 23). It is interesting to note in three of these cases, the translation inserts the conjunction καὶ before the second verb (1 Chr 15:29; 2 Chr 21:9; 24:4). Perhaps this is because of familiarity with the more standard way of expressing these temporal clauses in translation Greek (καὶ ἐγένετο + adverbial + καὶ + aorist), or perhaps because the *Vorlage* had a *waw*, which seems unlikely because the verb form would then be changed from *qatal* to *wayyiqtol*.

Introductory temporal clauses without וַיְהִי (i.e., those with a preposition and an infinitive construct, a temporal noun, or a temporal preposition) occur 42 times in Chronicles, especially in passages unique to Chronicles (e.g., 1 Chr 2:24; and 29 other places, compared to only 13 places in parallel passages). This is reflected when the introductory וַיְהִי in Kings is omitted in parallel passages in Chronicles (1 Kgs 8:54 // 2 Chr 7:1; 1 Kgs 9:1 // 2 Chr 7:11; 2 Kgs 22:3 // 2 Chr 34:8). One time the translator of Chronicles also omitted to translate it (or the *Vorlage* lacked it, 2 Chr 20:1, see the minus section (*l.*) below). Conversely, three times καὶ ἐγένετο occurs when the Masoretic text lacks וַיְהִי (2 Chr 20:26 [in Gk. MS B; but MSS A, y, N, L, g lack it]; 24:17; 29:3 [in which it perhaps translates the pronoun הוּא]).

5:13; 11:2; 17:10; 20:29; 24:18; 32:25), being (or for a setting clause),
e.g., "there *was* still war" (1 Chr 20:5, 6; so also 6:66<51>; 23:3; 25:1,
7; 2 Chr 6:7; 13:13; 14:8<7>; 17:3; 20:25; 29:32; 30:10, 26) including
the notions of having in expressions like "Asa *had* an army, lit., there
was to Asa an army" (2 Chr 14:8<7>; so also 1:14; 17:5; 18:1; 26:11;
32:27).

b. Wayyiqtol > Imperfect Indicative (76 = 5.24%)

Almost 60% (40) of the imperfect forms are translations of a *wayyiqtol*
form of הָיָה with the sense of "to be" into the past form of the verb
εἰμί "to be."[25] In these cases, the use of the imperfect form is due to a
constraint of the target language since εἰμί only has imperfect forms in
the past.[26] It occurs with a predicate nominative, e.g., "the sons of
Jerahmeel *were…*" (1 Chr 2:25; so also 1:51; 2:27, 28; 7:19; 8:40;
11:13; 12:21<22>; 18:2, 6, 13; 20:6; 21:5; 23:11, 17; 2 Chr 9:13). It
also occurs with a predicate adjective e.g., "Er *was wicked*" (1 Chr 2:3;
so also 4:9; 2 Chr 26:21), or with an adverb "they *were there* with
David" (1 Chr 12:39<40>; 20:2; 2 Chr 5:9). Sometimes the *wayyiqtol*
form of הָיָה occurs with a participle and is translated by the imperfect
of εἰμί and a present participle, emphasizing the past imperfective or
durative nature of the action, e.g., "they *were ministering*" (1 Chr
6:32<17>; so also 15:25; 18:14[27]; 2 Chr 9:26; 17:12; 30:10; 36:16).[28]
Occasionally הָיָה and a participle are translated by the imperfect of
εἰμί and a perfect participle, e.g., וַיִּהְיוּ הַכְּרוּבִים פֹּרְשִׂים כְּנָפַיִם "and

---

[25] 1 Chr 1:51; 2:3, 22, 25, 26, 27, 28, 52; 4:9; 6:17; 7:19; 8:3, 40; 11:13, 21;
12:21<22>, 39<40>; 15:25; 18:2, 6, 13, 14; 20:2, 6; 21:5; 23:11, 17; 2 Chr 5:8, 9;
9:13, 25, 26; 11:12; 17:12; 22:12; 26:5, 21; 30:10; 36:16, 20. One time the verb הָלַךְ
"to go" in the clause "and his name *was spread* (lit., *went*)" is translated by ἦν "and his
name *was*" (2 Chr 26:8). The use of εἰμί to translate הָיָה may also be influenced by
the diachronic development of the meaning of הָיָה from "to become, happen" to "to
be" as is found in rabbinic Hebrew (see note 23 above).

[26] See chapter 3, section I on *Aktionsart*. The use of the verb οἴχομαι "go, depart,"
which occurs twice in the imperfect (2 Chr 8:18, 21:9), could also be considered as
constrained by the target language, as it only occurs in the imperfect and perfect
tenses in the past in classical Greek, not being used in the aorist. However, there are
many other verbs indicating motion that have aorist forms that could have been used
by the translator instead of οἴχομαι.

[27] In 18:14 the Chronicler emphasizes the periphrastic, perhaps by eliminating the
word between הָיָה and the participle, i.e., וַיְהִי עֹשֶׂה מִשְׁפָּט, cf. the parallel passage,
וַיְהִי דָוִד עֹשֶׂה מִשְׁפָּט (2 Sam 8:15).

[28] One time הָיָה and an infinitive is translated by εἰμί and a present participle (2
Chr 26:5).

the cherubim *spread out* their wings" καὶ ἦν τὰ χερουβιν διαπεπετακότα τὰς πτέρυγας αὐτῶν "and the cherubim *had* their wings *spread out*" (2 Chr 5:8; so also 22:12), emphasizing the past stative nature of the action.

הָיָה also indicates possession, equivalent to the verb "to have" which is lacking in Hebrew, e.g., "he had twenty-three towns, lit., *there were* to him…" (1 Chr 2:22; so also 2:26, 52; 8:3; 2 Chr 9:25; 11:12). Most of the time when הָיָה has the notion of "to become" it is translated by the aorist ἐγένετο "and it came to pass" or "and he became" (see above). Occasionally הָיָה with this notion (especially followed by the preposition לְ and indicating a change of state) is translated by εἰμί and the preposition εἰς, e.g., καὶ ἦν αὐτοῖς εἰς ἄρχοντα "and he *became* their commander; lit., and he *was* to them *unto/for* a commander" (1 Chr 11:21; so also 2 Chr 36:20).

In certain contexts, the imperfect is chosen by the translator when a past durative form is more appropriate than an aorist, for example, to indicate habitual or customary actions in the past, e.g., the description of the cherubim *covering* the ark and its poles, the ends of which *extended* and *could be seen* (2 Chr 5:8, 9 (2)); so also "and the Lord *delivered* David wherever he went" (ἔσῳζεν—1 Chr 18:6, 13).[29] Imperfects are used to describe the levitical priests *teaching* throughout the cities of Judah (17:9 ἐδίδασκον (2)), the people *bringing* their offering and *casting* it into the treasury (2 Chr 24:10), for the people *serving* Astarte and idols (24:18), for Ahaz *causing* his children *to pass* through the fire and his *sacrificing* on the high places (28:3-4), for the children of Ammon annually *giving* Uzziah tribute (27:5), and for certain actions of Hezekiah and the people such as the *pouring out* (προσέχεον (2), περιέχεον) and *singing* of hymns after they purified the temple (29:22 (3), 30).[30] Perhaps the translator understood some of these *wayyiqtol* forms as *wᵊyiqtol* forms with past durative force. One time an imperfect is used to indicate a conative imperfect, "Ahab *tried to induce* Jehoshaphat to go" (ἠπάτα—18:2), although eventually Jehoshaphat did actually go with him.[31]

About half of the *wayyiqtol* forms translated by imperfects other than εἰμί (i.e., they are not constrained by the grammar to be imperfects) are preceded by a verb that was translated by an imperfect (e.g.,

---

[29] Some MSS (S, h, j, p, q, t, z) read an aorist ἔσωσε in 8:6.

[30] Some MSS (N, a, c, n) read an aorist προσέχεαν (2) for the first two imperfects.

[31] Some MSS (B, A) read the stative verb ἠγάπα "and he desired greatly" (lit., loved) here.

wayyiqtol 1 Chr 18:6, 13; 2 Chr 5:8, 9 (2); 17:9; 24:10, 13; 25:12; 28:4;
qatal 2 Chr 28:3), or are preceded by a noun sentence (which translates
a Hebrew noun sentence in 1 Chronicles 5:16, 19; and 2 Chronicles
26:14). The imperfects often occur together in strings. It seems that the
context and the way the preceding form was translated may have
influenced the translator in favor of an imperfect.

Other times there does not seem to be any apparent reason for the
imperfects in terms of the semantics of the verb. For example, in 1
Chronicles 5:16 and 19 the verbs "dwell" κατῴκουν and "make
[war]" ἐποίουν occur. However, the same verbs are used in the aorist
in v. 11 and v. 10 to translate *qatal* forms in almost identical contexts.[32]
Perhaps these verbs are translated by imperfects as a background to
the events following in verses 17 and 20 (see chapter 5, section I.A.2).

c. Wayyiqtol > Present Indicative (2 = 0.14%)

The two present indicatives are examples of the so-called historic
present, which occurs only rarely in Chronicles. They both occur with
the same verb παρατάσσω and both are in a sequence of *wayyiqtol*
forms that include the same verb, which is translated by an aorist. In
the first example, "The Ammonites came out and *drew up in battle array*
(וַיַּעַרְכוּ translated παρατάσσονται—present)" (1 Chr 19:9), "and he
[Joab] arrayed them against the Arameans (וַיַּעֲרֹךְ translated
παρετάξαντο—aorist) (v. 10) the historic present is followed by an
aorist of the same verb. In the second example "and he [David] drew
up his forces (וַיַּעֲרֹךְ translated παρετάξατο—aorist) against them.
When David *set the battle in array* (וַיַּעֲרֹךְ translated παρατάσσονται—
present)...they fought with him" (v. 17), the historic present is preceded
by an aorist of the same verb. Perhaps the translators wanted to
contrast the two verbs by giving them a different tense. In the first
example, the subject is different; in the second example, the same
thought is repeated but the subject of the verb following is different.
Perhaps the present tense is used to indicate simultaneous
circumstances with both sides drawing up their forces at the same
time.

---

[32] The verb ἐποίουν in verse 19 is preceded by a number of participles describing
the Reubenites, the Gadites, and the half-tribe of Manasseh, and perhaps this
influenced the imperfect verb.

d. Wayyiqtol > Future Indicative (6 = 0.41%)

Four of the *wayyiqtol* forms translated as futures occur in reported speech in Hebrew but are interpreted as having future time significance rather than past time by the translator. Perhaps the translator read them as coordinated *wᵉyiqtol* forms. In the first example a *wᵉqatal* form (usually translated "*and I will subdue* all your enemies") translated by an aorist "*I subdued*" is followed by a *wayyiqtol* וָאַגִּד לְךָ "Moreover *I declare* to you," which is translated into a Greek future αὐξήσω σε "*I will increase* you" (1 Chr 17:10).[33] 2 Chronicles 15:4-6 is interpreted as future prophecy as opposed to past narrative by the translator. The two *wayyiqtol* forms usually translated "but when in their distress *they turned* to the LORD... *he was found* by them" are translated as Greek futures "And *He shall turn* [them] to the Lord their God, and *He will be found* by them." In 2 Chronicles 24:20 a *wayyiqtol* form is interpreted as a future promise as opposed to a past event, "Because you have forsaken the LORD, he *has* also *forsaken* [Gk. *will forsake*] you." This is another example of interpretative translation.

The other two examples of *wayyiqtol* forms translated as futures in narrative are actually interpreted as reported speech by the translator. The first is at the end of a section of poetry at the end of the song "then all the people *said*, Amen!" and is translated as an injunction "and all the people *shall say*, Amen!" (1 Chr 16:36). It follows a noun sentence at the end of the song that has an implied injunctive, "Blessed *be* the LORD." In the second example, the Greek text varies from the Hebrew with an aorist verb of speaking inserted in the preceding verse, direct speech following, and the verb changed from *sacrifice* to *seek*. Instead of the Hebrew text usually translated "this same King Ahaz. For *he sacrificed* to the gods of Damascus," the Greek translation reads, "the king said, *I will seek* the gods of Damascus." Rather than report Ahaz actually sacrificing to foreign gods (something that may have offended the translator's religious sentiments) the translation has

---

[33] Interestingly the translator translated the *wᵉqatal* form preceding as an aorist. It seems that the translator read the *wayyiqtol* form וָאַגִּד לְךָ "*I declare* to you" as וָאַגְדִלְךָ (from the *hiphil* of גדל "to make big or increase") and translated it as one word. This is a very theologically loaded text, referring to the promise to David, which has already undergone reworking in the hands of the Chronicler compared to 2 Samuel 7, see Schniedewind, *Society and the Promise to David*, 128-34. In his retelling of history, the Chronicler is interested in legitimizing the Davidic dynasty, see D. N. Freedman, "The Chronicler's Purpose," *CBQ* 23 (1961): 436-42. Perhaps this tendency was also noted by the translator and influenced him in the way he read and translated the verb here to further enhance David.

Ahaz merely *seeking* them (2 Chr 28:23).[34] However, the change is perhaps not motivated by theological reasons but by a desire to make the text more logical. The end of the preceding verse is awkward, and the verb *sacrifice* is repeated in the following section "and he said, 'Because the gods of the kings of Aram helped them, *I will sacrifice* to them so that they may help me.'"

e. Wayyiqtol > Aorist Participle (2 = 0.14%)

The two *wayyiqtol* forms translated by aorist participles are rare examples of circumstantial (hypotactic) participles being used for the typical paratactic string of *wayyiqtol* forms, וַיִּקְּדוּ וַיִּשְׁתַּחֲווּ "and *they bowed their heads* and *prostrated themselves*" becomes καὶ κάμψαντες...προσεκύνησαν "and *bowing their heads*...they prostrated themselves" (1 Chr 29:20). The second example is similar, "and Jehoshaphat *bowed down* (וַיִּקֹּד—translated καὶ κύψας "and bowing down") with his face to the ground, and all Judah and the inhabitants of Jerusalem[, they] fell down...to worship" (2 Chr 20:18). In both examples, the verbs are semantically close and frequently associated together.[35]

---

[34] Cf. V. M. Rogers, "The Old Greek Version of Chronicles: A Comparative Study of the LXX with the Hebrew Text from a Theological Approach" (Ph.D. diss., Princeton Theological Seminary, 1954), 83-84, who cites two examples, 2 Chronicles 28:4 and 28:25 in which the translator makes changes that involve Ahaz which indicate a respect for royalty. He does not include this case in his examples. See also the criteria set out by Anneli Aejmelaeus for theologically motivated translation in her article "What We Talk about When We Talk about Translation Technique" in *X Congress of the International Organization for Septuagint and Cognate Studies, Oslo 1998.* (ed. Bernard A. Taylor; SCS 51; Atlanta: Scholars Press, 2001). She states that, "only in those cases in which the translator deviates form the normal procedure of linguistic representation of the original...is it justified to talk about interpretation in the sense of intended alteration of the wording for theological (or other) motives" (548). She questions whether a deviation was "deliberate or dictated by the translator's inability to understand some details of the *Vorlage*...if the latter was the case...was he guided by the...context of the text...a parallel passage...or did he guess? If...difficulties in the Hebrew cannot explain the case," did the translator have difficulty "expressing the content of the *Vorlage* in Greek" or was he guided by his theology? (549).

[35] According to Anneli Aejmelaeus, the combination of the two verbs קדד and השתחוה is always rendered with the conjunctive (circumstantial) participle (a participle preceded by καί usually translating a coordinated Hebrew form) and a finite verb in all of its occurrences in the Pentateuch (*Parataxis in the Septuagint: A Study of the Renderings of the Hebrew Coordinate Clauses in the Greek Pentateuch* (Helsinki: Suomalainen Tiedeakatemia, 1982), 94). In Chronicles, the combination only occurs three times. Twice the conjunctive participle is used in translating these verbs (as indicated in this section), and one time both verbs are translated by καί and an aorist (2 Chr 29:30). Aejmelaeus also deals with the rendering of a coordinate clause by a circumstantial

f. Wayyiqtol > Present Participle (3 = 0.21%)

Three *wayyiqtol* forms are translated by present participles. In the first example the participle κατοικοῦντες translates וַיֵּשְׁבוּ from יָשַׁב "to dwell" and modifies the preceding *wayyiqtol* form (1 Chr 5:10). In the second example וַיָּשֻׁבוּ (pointed by the Masoretes as the verb שׁוּב "return," but understood by the translator as the verb יָשַׁב) is translated as an attributive participle object of the preceding infinitive "to judge *those dwelling* in Jerusalem" (2 Chr 19:8). The third participle is a translation of וַיֹּאמֶר by the participle λέγων, which usually corresponds to the Hebrew infinitive לֵאמֹר used to introduce reported speech (1 Chr 29:10). The verb וַיֹּאמֶר is preceded by the *wayyiqtol* form of another verb of speaking, "and he blessed...*and said.*"

g. Wayyiqtol > Aorist Infinitive (4 = 0.28%)

Three of the *wayyiqtol* forms translated by aorist infinitives are closely tied to the three *wayyiqtol* forms preceding them. The first example is understood as an infinitive of indirect speech in Greek "and David said *to burn* [them] with fire" (1 Chr 14:12).[36] The second aorist infinitive functions as an infinitive of purpose "and [some] came *to announce* to David" (19:5). The third aorist infinitive is part of an expanded translation of two *hiphil* forms in the expression וַיַּאֲכִלוּם וַיַּשְׁקוּם וַיְסַכּוּם "He caused them to eat and caused them to drink, and they anointed them" which is translated in Greek ἔδωκαν

(conjunctive) participle in two articles: "*Participium Coniunctum* as a Criterion of Translation Technique" in *On the Trail of the Septuagint Translators: Collected Essays* (Kampen: Kok Pharos Publishing House, 1993), 7-16 (especially 11-16), and "The Septuagint of 1 Samuel" published in the same book (131-49). The latter is also in *VIII Congress of the International Organization for Septuagint and Cognate Studies, Paris 1992* (ed. Leonard Greenspoon and Olivier Munnich; Atlanta: Scholars Press, 1995). In it she compares the number of conjunctive circumstantial participles used to render coordinate clauses in the text of 1 Samuel (9 times, or 16 times in the Lucianic text) with the Pentateuch (ranging from 200 times in Genesis to 21 times in Leviticus), 118-19. See also Frank H. Polak, "Context Sensitive Translation and Parataxis in Biblical Narrative" in *Emanuel: Studies in Hebrew Bible, Septuagint and Dead Sea Scrolls in Honor of Emanuel Tov* (ed. Shalom M. Paul, Robert A. Kraft, Weston W. Fields; VTSup 94; Leiden, Brill, 2003), 525-539, who also deals with the translation of paratactic Hebrew structures by participles and the particle δέ especially to indicate staging in a discourse in the translation of Genesis and Exodus.

[36] This is also a theologically sensitive text. In the parallel passage, David and his men carry the idols [abandoned by the Philistines] (2 Sam 5:21). The account in Chronicles changes the verb from "carry" to "said," omits "and his men," and adds "and they *burned* [them] with fire."

φαγεῖν καὶ ἀλείψασθαι "He gave them to eat and *to be anointed*" (2 Chr 28:15).[37] One time a *wayyiqtol* form וַיְבַקֵּשׁ אֶת־אֲחַזְיָהוּ "*and he searched* for Ahaziah," is translated by the addition of an aorist verb of saying followed by an infinitive καὶ εἶπεν τοῦ ζητῆσαι "and he said *to seek for*" as an indirect command (2 Chr 22:9). The translation of these *wayyiqtol* forms by infinitives may reflect a late biblical Hebrew trend to replace or omit *wayyiqtols* when they occur together in strings in close proximity.[38]

h. Wayyiqtol > Aorist Imperative (3 = 0.21%)

The clauses in which the three *wayyiqtol* forms are translated as aorist imperatives are understood as reported speech clauses following וַיֹּאמֶר, "and the king gave command, *and they made* a chest, *and set* it...[and] a proclamation *was made*" (2 Chr 24:8-9) is translated into Greek by three third person imperatives: "*let* a chest *be made*, and *let it be placed*...and *let them proclaim*." The translator probably interpreted them as *wyiqtol* jussive forms following the verb of speaking.

i. Wayyiqtol > Adjective (1 = 0.07%)

A stative *wayyiqtol* verb וַיִּשְׂבַּע following another *wayyiqtol* stative form וַיִּזְקַן in the expression "and he became old and *full* of days" is translated by adjective πλήρης "full" in Greek (2 Chr 24:15). Perhaps

---

[37] The first hiphil causative is translated by δίδωμι and an infinitive, and δίδωμι also governs the third *wayyiqtol* form, which is translated by an aorist infinitive. The second *wayyiqtol* form is not translated (see minus below). Cf. Emanuel Tov, "The Representation of the Causative Aspects of the *Hiph'il* in the Septuagint—A Study in Translation Technique," *Bib* 63 (1982): 417-24, in which he cites only one example of a *hiphil* translated by δίδωμι and an infinitive (Jer. 36[43]:20).

[38] This can be seen in a couple of places where a *wayyiqtol* form in 2 Samuel is replaced by an infinitive in the parallel passage in Chronicles. Second Samuel 6:6 reads, וַיִּשְׁלַח עֻזָּא אֶל־אֲרוֹן הָאֱלֹהִים וַיֹּאחֶז בּוֹ "And Uzzah put [his hand] to the ark of God *and took hold* of it." In the parallel passage וַיֹּאחֶז is replaced by the infinitive לֶאֱחֹז "*to hold*" (1 Chr 13:9). So also 2 Samuel 7:12, כִּי יִמְלְאוּ יָמֶיךָ וְשָׁכַבְתָּ אֶת־אֲבֹתֶיךָ "When your days are fulfilled *and you lie down* with your ancestors," the parallel has וְהָיָה כִּי־מָלְאוּ יָמֶיךָ לָלֶכֶת "When your days are fulfilled *to go* to be" (1 Chr 17:11). The first example is theologically charged. The Chronicler may have used an infinitive to indicate intention, and thus remove the offense of Uzzah actually touching the ark. Perhaps Uzzah only attempted to touch it (although v. 10, שָׁלַח יָדוֹ עַל־הָאָרוֹן "he put [lit., sent] his hand upon [or, over] the ark," indicates that he probably did), and that was sufficient to bring about God's wrath.

this is indicative of the trend in rabbinic Hebrew to replace stative verbs with adjectives (see note 23)?

j. Wayyiqtol > Adverb (1 = 0.07%)

The first *wayyiqtol* verb in the expression "and he returned and went out" (וַיָּשָׁב וַיֵּצֵא) is translated by the adverb πάλιν "and he went out *again*" (2 Chr 19:4). The use of the adjective (above) and the adverb (here) may reflect late biblical Hebrew style to break up *wayyiqtol* strings found either in the *Vorlage* or as an influence on the translator of Chronicles.

k. Wayyiqtol > Noun (1 = 0.07%)

The *wayyiqtol* form וַיַּקְדִּשׁוּ is translated into a noun object τὰ ἅγια "holy things" of the preceding *qatal* verb "set apart" in Greek (2 Chr 30:24).

l. Wayyiqtol > Minus (20 = 1.38%)

Many times a *wayyiqtol* form is omitted (indicated by italics in the English translation) when there are two verbs (mostly two *wayyiqtol* forms) in close proximity with the same or similar meaning, e.g., verbs of speaking, "and he *answered* and said," (1 Chr 12:17<18>), "and they *spoke* to Rehoboam, saying," (2 Chr 10:3; also 18:27).[39] So also a verb of motion is omitted "they gathered their brothers…*and went*…to cleanse the house" (29:15). Other examples are, "and *they sought Him*, and He was found" (15:4), "and he sacrificed (וַיִּזְבַּח) and made offerings (וַיְקַטֵּר)" translated ἐθυμία "he sacrificed" or "he burned incense" (28:4).[40] One time the same verb "and he joined" that occurs in the previous verse is omitted (20:36). This also could be a case of

---

[39] For a more detailed discussion and examples regarding the omission or condensation of various elements that the translator considered superfluous, see Emanuel Tov, *Text-Critical Use*, 47–48. He also distinguishes between minuses and omissions, stating that, "Many of the elements of the MT are not represented in the LXX, due to a shortening either introduced by the translator or already existing in his *Vorlage*. The neutral term 'minus' refers to both possibilities. The term 'omission' seemingly refers only to the translator's omissions, but many scholars use it also with reference to a shorter Hebrew *Vorlage*, *Ibid*, 130, (see also chapter 2, note 51).

[40] Cf. Rogers, "Old Greek Chronicles," 83, who cites this as an example of the translator making changes, which indicate a respect for royalty. He tones down "the offensiveness of Ahaz's deed" by deleting one of the verbs (see note 34 above).

parablepsis by homoioteleuton where a section of text that ends with
the same expression is omitted. Sometimes the meaning of two verbs is
combined in translation "And she turned and went" becomes "and she
returned" (9:12). Sometimes two verbs are translated by one of
different meaning e.g., וַיָּבֶן וַיִּפְרֹץ "And he dealt wisely, and
distributed" becomes "he grew" ηὐξήθη (11:23). Sometimes the
omission does little to change the sense, e.g., "Asa cut down her
image, *crushed it*, and burned it" (15:16) or "he built up the entire
wall...and *raised* towers" (32:5). Sometimes the omission changes the
sense, e.g., "He took away the foreign gods and the idol from the
house of the LORD, and all the altars that he had built on the
mountain of the house of the LORD and in Jerusalem, and *he threw
them* out [side] of the city" (33:15) reads in translation "... that he built
in Jerusalem and outside the city." A narrative section becomes
reported speech in Greek and a verb is omitted "'he has given us peace
on every side.' *So they built* and prospered" becomes "'he has given us
peace on every side and prospered us'" (14:7<6>). These omissions of
wayyiqtol forms also reflect the tendency in Chronicles to reduce the
number of *wayyiqtol* forms in strings as seen in comparison with
Samuel-Kings.

As we mentioned in note 24 above, one time a pleonastic וַיְהִי
"and it came to pass" is omitted (20:1). Perhaps the *Vorlage* also
omitted it. This is one of the features of classical biblical Hebrew (e.g.,
as preserved in Kings) that is sometimes lacking in the late biblical
Hebrew in Chronicles. וַיְהִי in Kings is omitted in four parallel
passages (2 Chr 7:1, 11; 12:9; 34:8). Twice a periphrastic וַיְהִי and a
participle is translated just by one indicative form corresponding to the
meaning of the Hebrew participle (and analyzed as such—2 Chr
24:12, 14).

m. Summary

As was mentioned above, the *wayyiqtol* forms are mostly rendered by
the common equivalent, aorist indicatives immediately preceded by
καί, imitating Hebrew word order. Only rarely is the καί omitted or
another element comes between καί and the aorist. Imperfects are
used mostly when the constraints of the target language dictate the
verb form. However, there are a few occasions when the translator
consciously chose a form different to the common equivalent apart

from the constraints of the language. Some imperfects and historic presents may have been chosen when the translator wanted to make a contrast between two actions (perhaps simultaneous). Future forms and imperative forms may have been used because of graphic confusion of *wayyiqtol* forms with *wᵉyiqtol* forms, especially in reported speech. Although there may be some theological motivations behind understanding a future (prospective) rather than a past time (retrospective) form, the translated text still makes sense with a future reading. Participles and infinitives (or even adverbs) rarely break up the paratactic strings of *wayyiqtols* translated by καί and an aorist. Only four times circumstantial participles (three present, two aorist) translate *wayyiqtol* forms. Three times infinitives break up a paratactic string by modifying the preceding verbs, either indicating purpose or indirect speech. Sometimes two *wayyiqtol* forms are translated by only one form in Greek. These breaking up or omission of *wayyiqtol* forms reflects the trend in late biblical Hebrew to reduce the number of *wayyiqtol* forms in strings (as found in Chronicles compared to Samuel-Kings). The Septuagint translation was continuing the same trend that was underway in late biblical Hebrew.

Because the forms preceding the *wayyiqtol* forms (either other *wayyiqtol* forms, or *qatal*, and *wᵉqatal* forms) are mostly translated by aorists, the Greek text contains long strings of aorists, and the reader of the translation is struck by the ubiquity of this form. There is little variation to the paratactic string of verbs by using a participle or infinitive, or by omitting καί or by changing the word order. Therefore, the reader can easily approximate the underlying Hebrew verbal form from the word order. Perhaps this was one of the reasons why the word order was so closely followed, so that the different Hebrew verb forms could be approximated. It also seems that sometimes the translation of the preceding verb influences the verb choice (e.g., about half of the imperfects not constrained by Greek grammar follow other imperfects or noun sentences).

2. Qatal

In this section, we mostly focus on *qatal* forms apart from *wᵉqatal* forms (dealt with in the following section). *Qatal* forms occur in all text types. They are the most common perfective forms in past contexts in both reported speech and subordinate clauses. The *qatal* forms were most commonly translated into aorist indicatives, with almost 80% of the *qatal* forms being translated this way (if *weqatal* forms are excluded). This is understandable as they both express perfective aspect, and both occur most frequently in past time frames. Other equivalents include imperfects (especially in narrative and subordinate clauses), perfects (in reported speech main clauses and subordinate clauses), present indicatives (in reported speech main clauses), and participles (especially in subordinate clauses). A number of *qatal* forms are also omitted.

The following table gives the breakdown on how the *qatal* forms in Chronicles were translated into Greek. The top figure is the number of *qatal* forms excluding *weqatal* forms and the bottom figure is the total of all *qatal* forms.

TABLE 3: THE TRANSLATION OF *QATAL* FORMS

QATAL	TOTAL	Percentage	Narrative Main Clauses (Clause %)	Reported Speech Main Clauses	Subordinate Clauses
Aorist Indicative	817 -*weqatal* 840 *all qatal*	78.94 72.23	418 (84.3) 429 (83.3)	87 (66.4) 99 (41.3)	312 (76.5) 312 (76.5)
Imperfect Indicative	76 81	7.34 6.97	45 (9.1) 49 (9.5)	3 (2.3) 4 (1.7)	28 (6.9) 28 (6.9)
Perfect Indicative	33 35	3.19 3.01		19 (14.5) 21 (8.8)	14 (3.4) 14 (3.4)
Present Indicative	16 17	1.55 1.46		13 (9.9) 14 (5.8)	3 (0.7) 3 (0.7)
Future Indicative	1 62	0.10 5.33		1 62 (25.8)	
Aorist Participle	24 24	2.32 2.06	2 2	2 2	20 (4.9) 20 (4.9)
Present Participle	5 7	0.48 0.60	1 3	2 2	2 2
Perfect Participle	3 3	0.29 0.26	2 2		1 1
Aorist Infinitive	7 7	0.68 0.6	5 5		2 2
Present Infinitive	1 1	0.10 0.09			1 1
Perfect Infinitive	2 2	0.19 0.17	1 1	1 1	
Aorist Subjunctive	2 28	0.19 2.41	1	1 27 (11.3)	1 1

Present Subjunctive	0			0	
	2	0.17		2	
Aorist Imperative	0			0	
	4	0.34		4	
Adjective	7	0.68	2	1	4
	8	0.69	3	1	4
Adverb	1	0.10	1		
	2	0.17	2		
Noun	5	0.48	4		1
	5	0.43	4		1
Minus	35	3.38	15 (3.0)	1	19 (4.7)
	35	3.01	15 (2.9)	1	19 (4.7)
Total	1035	100	496	131	408
	1163	100	515	240	408

Total 1163
Aorist Indicative (840 = 72.23%)[41]
Narrative Main Clauses (429)

1 Chr 1:10 (2), 32; 2:3, 4, 10 (2), 11 (2), 12 (2), 13, 17, 18, 20 (2), 21 (2), 22, 36 (2), 37 (2), 38 (2), 39 (2), 40 (2), 41 (2), 44 (2), 46 (2), 48, 53; 3:4 (2), 5; 4:2 (2), 8, 9, 11, 12, 14 (2), 18, 23, 27, 38, 42; 5:1, 9, 10, 11, 23 (2), 6:4<5:30> (2), 5<5:31> (2), 6<5:32> (2), 7<5:33> (2), 8<5:34> (2), 9<5:35> (2), 10<5:36>, 11<5:37>, 12<5:38> (2), 13<5:39>, 14<5:40> (2), 15<5:41>; 6:54<39>, 56<41>, 57<42>; 7:14, 15, 18, 21, 29, 32; 8:1, 7, 8, 11, 12, 13, 28, 29, 32 (2), 33 (3), 34, 36 (3), 37; 9:3, 22, 34, 35, 38 (2), 39 (3), 40, 42 (3), 43; 10:1, 6, 10, 14; 11:7, 11, 13 (2), 18, 19, 20, 22 (3), 23, 24; 12:8<9>, 18<19>, 19<20> (2), 20<21>, 21<22>, 38<39>; 13:13; 14:9, 11 (2), 17; 15:2, 29, 16:7; 17:15; 18:8 (2), 11, 12; 19:7, 11, 15, 18, 19; 20:2, 3, 4, 8; 21:4, 6, 15, 18; 22:3, 14 (2), 18 (2); 23:11, 17; 26:6, 14, 27, 31; 27:23, 24 (3); 29:8, 9, 24, 26; 2 Chr 1:4 (2), 7; 3:5, 7, 9; 4:10, 14 (2), 16, 17; 5:1, 13; 6:1, 7:1 (2), 10, 11; 8:2, 11, 12, 15; 9:1, 2, 4, 11, 12, 19; 10:15, 18; 11:13, 16, 20; 12:1, 2, 5, 7, 9, 10, 12, 13; 13:2, 3, 7, 13, 15, 20; 14:1<13:23>, 15<14>; 15:1, 8, 11, 15, 16, 17 (2); 16:1, 6, 7, 12; 17:3, 4, 6, 7, 13; 18:12, 30, 31 (2), 33; 19:8; 20:1, 4, 14, 18, 20, 22, 23, 24, 26 (2) 31, 33, 35 (2), 37; 21:3, 5, 8, 9, 11, 17, 18, 19 (2), 20, 22:2, 3, 5, 6, 7 (2), 10,

---

[41] Including two verbs with identical aorist and imperfect forms interpreted as aorists by *GRAMCORD:* ἐσκλήρυνεν (2 Chr 10:4) and κατεύθυνεν (20:33), and one form εὐλόγησας (1 Chr 17:27) coded by *GRAMCORD* as an aorist participle (which would be accented εὐλογήσας) and one form ἀνήγαγον (2 Chr 6:5) coded imperfect by *GRAMCORD* but should be taken as an aorist indicative (see Appendix 1).

11; 23:1, 17 (2), 21 (2), 24:1, 4, 5, 7, 11, 14, 17 (2), 19, 20, 22 (2), 23 (2), 24 (2), 25 (2); 25:1 (2), 4, 7, 11, 12, 15, 20, 23; 26:2, 3, 5, 16, 19, 20; 27:1, 2, 3 (2), 4, 5; 28:1 (2), 2, 5, 8, 15, 16, 17, 18, 23, 25; 29:1 (2), 3, 17 (2), 27, 29; 30:1, 3, 11, 12, 14, 15, 24; 31:1, 5 (2), 6, 7 (2), 21 (2), 32:1, 9, 16, 17, 21, 24 (2), 25, 26, 27, 29, 30, 31, 33, 33:1, 4, 6 (2), 10, 12, 14, 19, 21; 34:1, 3 (2), 4 (3), 5, 7 (2), 8, 14; 35:8 (2), 9, 13, 14, 15, 18 (2), 20, 22 (2); 36:2, 4, 5, 6, 7, 9, 10, 11, 12, 14, 17 (2), 18, 19, 21

Reported Speech Main Clauses (99)

1 Chr 15:12, 13; 16:15, 21, 26, 17:4, 6, 7, 8, 10, 17, 19, 25, 27; 19:3; 21:17 (3); 22:7, 8 (2); 23:25; 28:2, 3 (2), 4, 19; 29:17 (3); 2 Chr 1:8 (2), 11 (2); 2:11<10>; 6:1, 4, 5 (2), 8, 15, 37 (3); 7:12 (2), 16, 21, 22; 9:6 (3); 10:4, 11 (2), 14; 12:5 (2), 7; 13:9, 10, 11; 14:7<6>; 16:7, 8; 18:7, 16, 17, 18, 22 (2), 23, 26, 27; 19:3 (2); 20:10, 37; 21:13; 24:6; 25:16, 18, 19 (2); 28:9; 29:6, 7 (3), 18, 31; 32:12, 13; 34:18, 23, 27; 35:21; 36:23 (2)

Subordinate Clauses (312)

1 Chr 2:7, 9; 4:9, 10, 18, 22, 41; 5:6, 20 (2), 22, 25, 6:10<5:36> (2), 6:13<5:39>; 6:31<16>, 49<34>, 7:4, 14, 21, 23; 10:5, 7 (2), 11, 13 (2); 11:19, 12:18<19>, 19<20>, 31<32>, 39<40>; 13:3, 6, 11, 14:2 (2), 8, 15, 16; 15:2, 3, 13, 15, 16:1, 12, 16, 40; 17:1, 5 (2), 6, 8, 10, 13, 16, 20, 21 (2), 23, 25, 27; 18:9, 10, 11; 19:2, 3, 6, 15, 16; 21:6, 8 (2), 19, 28, 29, 30; 22:8, 11, 13, 18; 23:5, 25; 24:19; 26:5, 26; 27:23; 28:5; 29:9, 25, 30; 2 Chr 1:3, 5, 9, 11 (2), 12; 2:3<2>, 7<6>, 12<11> (2), 15<14>, 17<16>; 3:1 (2); 4:11, 18; 5:1, 5, 10 (2), 11, 14; 6:4, 5, 8 (2), 10 (2), 11, 13, 15 (2), 16 (2), 17, 18, 20, 25, 27, 31, 33, 34 (2), 37, 38 (3); 7:2, 7 (2), 9, 10, 17, 18, 19, 20 (2), 22; 8:1, 2, 4, 6, 8, 9, 11 (3), 12; 9:2, 3, 5, 6 (2), 8, 9, 12 (2), 23; 10:2, 4, 8, 9 (2), 12, 15, 16; 11:4, 14 (2), 15, 17; 12:2, 7, 9, 13, 14; 13:5, 8, 18; 14:6<5> (2), 7<6>, 11<10>, 13<12>, 14<13> (2); 15:6, 8, 9, 15; 16:6, 14 (2); 17:2, 3, 4, 19; 18:33; 19:3; 20:10 (2), 11, 26, 27, 29, 34; 21:6, 7 (2), 10, 12; 22:1, 6, 9 (2); 23:3, 8 (2), 14, 18; 24:7, 16, 20, 22, 24 (2); 25:3, 4, 9, 13, 15, 16, 20, 27; 26:4, 8, 15 (2), 18, 20, 21, 23; 27:2, 6; 28:3, 11, 15, 19, 21, 27; 29:2, 6, 19, 24, 32, 36; 30:3 (2), 5, 7, 8, 17, 18 (3), 24; 31:10, 19, 21; 32:14, 17, 25, 29, 31; 33:2, 3, 4, 7 (3), 8 (2), 9, 15, 19, 22 (2), 23; 34:9, 11, 15, 21, 25, 26, 27; 35:3, 18, 22, 23; 36:8, 13

Imperfect Indicative (81 = 6.97%)[42]

Narrative Main Clauses (49)

---

[42] Including eight verbs with identical aorist and imperfect forms interpreted as imperfects by *GRAMCORD* ἐξέκλινεν (1 Chr 13:9; 2 Chr 20:32; 34:2, 33), ἐβάρυνεν (10:10), ἐπλήθυνεν (33:6, 23), and ἐξήγειρεν (36:22), and one verb ἐφέροσαν (1 Chr 22:4) incorrectly coded aorist (see Appendix 1).

1 Chr 2:33, 34, 50; 3:1; 4:5; 9:20, 26; 10:4; 11:13, 19, 20, 21, 25;
21:30; 23:17, 22; 24:2, 28; 2 Chr 5:14; 7:2; 8:17; 9:9; 12:11, 12; 13:2,
7; 15:19; 17:10; 18:34; 20:32, 33; 21:7, 20; 24:11; 25:12; 27:5; 28:3, 9;
29:34 (2); 33:6 (4), 22, 23; 34:2, 33; 36:22

Reported Speech Main Clauses (4)
2 Chr 10:10; 13:9; 16:8; 32:13
Subordinate Clauses (28)
1 Chr 4:14; 10:4; 13:9; 14:4; 18:6, 7, 10, 13; 19:5; 22:4; 24:5; 26:10;
28:12; 2 Chr 1:3; 7:7; 8:6; 9:10; 10:1, 15; 11:21; 18:32; 21:6; 22:3, 4;
25:16; 26:10 (2); 32:14

Perfect Indicative (35 = 3.01%)[43]
Reported Speech Main Clauses (21)
1 Chr 17:6, 18; 21:8; 21:23 (2); 29:1, 2, 3 (2), 14; 2 Chr 2:10<9>,
13<12>; 6:2; 7:16; 16:3, 9; 25:16; 28:9; 29:9, 19 (2)
Subordinate Clauses (14)
1 Chr 12:17<18>; 19:10, 19; 28:4, 6, 10; 29:16; 2 Chr 2:8<7>; 6:33;
7:14; 14:11<10>; 22:10; 29:11; 34:21

Present Indicative (17 = 1.46%)
Reported Speech Main Clauses (14)
1 Chr 17:7; 21:10, 11; 2 Chr 11:4; 18:10; 20:15; 21:12; 24:20; 25:16,
19; 32:10; 34:24, 26; 36:23
Subordinate Clauses (3)
1 Chr 22:14; 2 Chr 6:30; 32:2

Future Indicative (62 = 5.33%)
Reported Speech Main Clauses (62)
1 Chr 4:10; 14:10 (2), 14; 15:12; 17:9 (3), 11 (3), 12, 14; 19:12 (2);
22:9, 10, 11 (2); 23:32; 28:7; 2 Chr 6:21 (3), 23 (2), 25 (2), 26 (2), 27 (2),
30 (2), 33, 35 (2), 36 (3), 39 (3); 7:16, 18, 20, 21, 22; 10:7; 12:5, 7; 15:6;
18:11, 12, 21, 26; 19:10 (2); 20:16; 23:7; 25:19; 34:28

Aorist Participle (24 = 2.06%)
Narrative Main Clauses (2)
1 Chr 9:1; 12:23<24>
Reported Speech Main Clauses (2)
1 Chr 29:17; 2 Chr 20:7
Subordinate Clauses (20)
1 Chr 3:1; 12:15<16>; 19:9; 21:17; 2 Chr 6:38; 6:39; 7:22; 8:8; 9:13;
10:8, 10 (2); 12:3, 5; 18:12; 25:10; 29:16; 34:16, 21, 23

---

[43] Including one form ἥκατε (1 Chr 12:17<18>) wrongly coded by *GRAMCORD*
as a present indicative, one form ᾠκοδομήκατε (17:6) wrongly coded as a pluperfect,
and ᾑρέτικεν (2 Chr 29:11) wrongly coded as an aorist indicative (see Appendix 1).

Present Participle (7 = 0.6%)[44]
Narrative Main Clauses (3)
1 Chr 21:20; 2 Chr 12:11 (2)
Reported Speech Main Clauses (2)
1 Chr 16:31; 2 Chr 30:19
Subordinate Clauses (2)
1 Chr 17:13; 36:15

Perfect Participle (3 = 0.26%)
Narrative Main Clauses (2)
2 Chr 4:9; 26:22
Subordinate Clauses (1)
2 Chr 34:24

Aorist Infinitive (7 = 0.6%)
Narrative Main Clauses (5)
2 Chr 20:22; 29:27; 35:14; 36:13, 21
Subordinate Clauses (2)
1 Chr 13:10; 2 Chr 24:25

Present Infinitive (1 = 0.09%)
Subordinate Clauses (1)
2 Chr 15:16

Perfect Infinitive (2 = 0.17%)
Narrative Main Clauses (1)
2 Chr 29:36
Reported Speech Main Clauses (1)
2 Chr 16:7

Aorist Subjunctive (28 = 2.41%)
Reported Speech Main Clauses (27)
1 Chr 10:4; 28:8; 2 Chr 6:19, 22 (3), 24 (4), 29, 32 (3), 34, 37 (3), 38 (2); 7:19 (4); 10:7 (2); 32:4
Subordinate Clauses (1)
1 Chr 17:11

Present Subjunctive (2 = 0.17%)
Reported Speech Main Clauses (2)
1 Chr 4:10 (2)

Aorist Imperative (4 = 0.34%)
Reported Speech Main Clauses (4)
1 Chr 17:4; 19:5; 21:10; 2 Chr 18:33

---

[44] Including one form κατευθυνούσης (2 Chr 30:19) coded by *GRAMCORD* as an aorist participle but which is identical with the present participle and is taken as such (see Appendix 1).

Adjective (8 = 0.69%)
Narrative Main Clauses (3)
1 Chr 20:6; 23:1 (2)
Reported Speech Main Clauses (1)
2 Chr 10:10
Subordinate Clauses (4)
1 Chr 5:2, 9; 13:2, 4

Adverb (2 = 0.17%)
Narrative Main Clauses (2)
2 Chr 1:5; 33:14

Noun (5 = 0.43%)
Narrative Main Clauses (4)
1 Chr 5:17; 8:7; 9:1; 26:28
Subordinate Clauses (1)
2 Chr 22:7

Minus (35 = 3.01 %)
Narrative Main Clauses (15)
1 Chr 1:11, 13, 18 (2), 19, 20; 29:27 (2); 2 Chr 1:15; 9:27; 27:4; 27:8
(2); 28:19, 20; 35:19
Reported Speech Main Clauses (1)
1 Chr 17:22
Subordinate Clauses (18)
1 Chr 1:12, 19; 43; 16:41; 17:6, 23; 29:19, 27; 2 Chr 1:4; 7:6, 17, 21;
9:1, 10, 10:6; 22:11; 35:20; 36:14

a. Qatal > Aorist Indicative (840 = 72.23%)

The aorist indicative is the common equivalent for the translation of
qatal forms. This is the most natural equivalent for *qatal* forms as both
qatal forms and aorists express perfective aspect and occur most
frequently in past time frames. Over half (429) of the *qatal* forms
translated by aorists occur in narrative main clauses, 99 occur in
reported speech main clauses, and 312 in subordinate clauses. There
are 23 *wᵉqatal* forms (coordinated *qatal* forms as opposed to consecutive
forms) translated by aorists, which are dealt with separately in the
section on *wᵉqatal* forms.

There are a few places where the *qatal* form translated by an aorist
seems awkward.[45] Sometimes an aorist is used to translate a stative

---

[45] This is apart from cases where the tense is preserved but the verb semantics
differs. An interesting example of this, referring to men of Judah בָּעֲלוּ לְמוֹאָב "who

verb,[46] particularly to indicate the inception of an action or state (an inceptive aorist), e.g., "In those days Hezekiah *became sick*" חָלָה translated ἠρρώστησεν (2 Chr 32:24). This may reflect the trend in rabbinic Hebrew, in which stative verbs mostly have an inceptive notion. The static notion is indicated by adjectives (see note 23 above). The verb הָיָה with this notion of "become" is frequently translated by a form of ἐγένετο "become" (indicating the inception into a state of existence). An aorist is also used to view the state as a whole, especially if the state existed in a past context and does not indicate whether it continued to exist beyond that context. For example, verbs such as יָשַׁב "to dwell," are mostly translated by an aorist.[47] However, sometimes the notions of inception into a state or the lack of continued existence beyond context are not so obvious, e.g., with the verb יָדַע "to know," "*I know* (וְיָדַעְתִּי) that you search the heart" translated ἔγνων (1 Chr 29:17), and וַאֲנִי שְׂנֵאתִיהוּ "but I *hate* him" translated καὶ ἐγὼ ἐμίσησα αὐτόν (2 Chr 18:7).

b. Qatal > Imperfect Indicative (81 = 6.97%)

The translation of the *qatal* form by the imperfect is the second most common translation equivalent, occurring almost 7% of the time. However, 75% of these imperfects are due mostly to constraints or preferences of certain verbal forms in the target language for imperfective aspect in past contexts. Verbs such as εἰμί "to be" do not have an aorist form in Greek. Approximately half of the imperfects

---

married into (or ruled over) Moab," is translated κατῴκησαν ἐν Μωαβ "they dwelt in Moab" (1 Chr 4:22). Perhaps the notion of intermarrying with Gentiles was abhorrent to the translator and was changed to a less controversial verb of dwelling. In another case, an active verb הֲבִיאֹתַנִי "you have brought me" is translated as a stative ἠγάπησάς με "you have loved me" (17:16), perhaps indicating a misreading of the consonants הבא "bring" by אהב "love."

[46] Cf. Fanning, *Verbal Aspect*, 135-40, which deals with specific classes of verbs that are categorized as stative according to his criteria of no change, e.g., verbs of 'being,' existence, and location (e.g., to sit, to remain); and verbs indicating passive or inert possession (e.g., to have), perception (e.g., to see), and cognition (e.g., to know, to want, to think) requiring no effort or exertion to maintain.

[47] יָכוֹל "to be able," and אָבָה "to be willing" (usually indicating a state limited to or unspecified beyond the duration of the context), are also translated by an aorist (although יָכוֹל and אָבָה are more commonly translated by an imperfect). יָכוֹל is translated by an aorist one out of ten times (2 Chr 30:31), and אָבָה is translated by an aorist (of θέλω) twice out of 5 times (1 Chr 11:18; 19:19).

(38) are translations of הָיָה especially with the meaning "to be."[48]
Other verbs, particularly those with stative *Aktionsart* or *lexis*, naturally
having durative or imperfective force, are also more inclined to use an
imperfect form in Greek, for example, δύναμαι "to be able" (which
translates יָכוֹל 6 times, 1 Chr 21:16; 2 Chr 5:14; 7:2; 29:34; 32:13, 14;
cf. 7:7 ἐξεποίει), βούλομαι "to want" (which translates אָבָה 3 times, 1
Chr 10:4; 11:19; 2 Chr 21:7, and יָעַץ one time, 25:16), ἔχω "to have"
(occurring 2 times, 1 Chr 28:12; 2 Chr 11:21), ὑπάρχω "to exist"
(occurring 2 times, 20:33; 26:10), and φοβοῦμαι "to fear," (1 Chr
10:4). These verbs account for about half of the remaining examples.
The remaining 25% of the imperfects could be considered as being
given imperfective aspect by the translator due to a reason other than
being constrained by the verbal forms of the target language. Many of
these imperfects occur in statements summarizing the reign of a king
and are perhaps marked out with imperfective aspect to stress the
iterativity or habituality of certain actions, especially with the activities
of the kings. For example, θύω "to sacrifice" (2 Chr 28:3—with Ahaz
as subject; 33:22—with Amon as subject) and ἐκκλίνω "to turn away"
(as a negative "did not depart" 2 Chr 20:32—with Jehoshaphat as
subject; 34:2, 33—both with Josiah as subject), and four verbs in 2
Chronicles 33:6 (with Manasseh as subject) occur in the imperfect. Six
times imperfects occur with verbs of motion.[49] Sometimes they indicate
action occurring simultaneous with another action (with one of the
actions in a subordinate clause), as in 2 Chronicles 10:1 "Rehoboam
went to Shechem, for all Israel *had come*" or 12:11 "whenever the King
went, the guard *would come*," or indefinite time in a summary statement
"The Lord gave victory to David wherever *he went*" (1 Chr 18:6, 13).
Sometimes adverbs of time reinforce a habitual or iterative notion and
hence imperfective aspect, such as "so *they did* <u>day after day</u>" (2 Chr
24:11). Perhaps in some contexts the imperfect is used to indicate

---

[48] The verb εἰμί translating a *qatal* form of הָיָה occurs 22 times in narrative main
clauses (1 Chr 2:33, 34, 50; 3:1; 4:5; 9:20, 26; 11:13, 20; 23:17, 22; 24:2, 28; 2 Chr
9:9; 12:12; 13:2, 7; 15:19; 18:34; 21:20; 28:9; 29:34), one time in a reported speech
main clause (2 Chr 32:13), and 15 times in subordinate clauses (1 Chr 4:14; 14:4;
18:7, 10; 19:5; 24:5; 26:10; 2 Chr 1:3; 8:6; 10:15; 18:32; 21:6; 22:3, 4; 26:10). See
note 23 above, which mentions the diachronic development of הָיָה from an inceptive
existential, meaning "to become" more to a stative meaning "to be."

[49] Campbell also points out the common association of imperfective aspect verbs
(especially the historic present, but perhaps also the imperfect) with lexemes of "*verbs of
propulsion*" such as "coming and going, giving and taking, raising up and putting
down," indicating "some kind of propulsion form one point to another" (*Basics of
Verbal Aspect*, 43).

logical duration (due to the number of people involved) or to draw out the time taken for the action, for example "the people of Judah captured (aorist) another ten thousand, *took* (*wayyiqtol* translated as an imperfect) them to the top of Sela, and *threw them down* (*wayyiqtol* translated as an imperfect) from the top of Sela, so that all of them *were dashed to pieces* (*qatal* translated as an imperfect)" (2 Chr 25:12). So also "the servants of Huram and the servants of Solomon who *brought* gold from Ophir, brought algum wood and precious stones" (2 Chr 9:10; so also 1 Chr 22:4).

c. Qatal > Perfect Indicative (35 = 3.01%)

All the *qatal* forms translated by perfect indicatives in Greek occur in either reported speech or in subordinate clauses.[50] In these clauses, the time is relative to the time of the verb of speaking or the main verb. It seems that the translators considered them a suitable form to indicate action that transpired in the past and still has relevance up to the present (i.e., of the moment of speaking or the main verb).[51] The perfect with stative aspect particularly stresses the resultant state of an action, therefore it is quite significant which verbs the translators chose to give this aspect. Some verbs such as οἶδα "to know" are constrained by the inventory of the language to use a perfect form since they do not have a present form (οἶδα occurs twice, in 1 Chr 17:18 and 2 Chr 2:8<7>). However, with most verbs the perfect was the conscious choice of the translator.

Perfects are used to translate verbs such as נָתַן "to give" (1 Chr 21:23 (2); 29:3, 14; 2 Chr 2:10<9>; 25:16), הֲכִינוֹתִי "I provide or prepare" (1 Chr 29:2, 3, 16; 2 Chr 29:19),[52] "to send" (2 Chr

---

[50] Out of 35 perfects, 32 translate *qatal* forms in reported speech clauses, 11 of which also occur in subordinate clauses.

[51] When *qatal* occurs with הִנֵּה "behold" (2 Chr 2:10<9>; 16:3; and 29:9) and with עַתָּה "now" (2 Chr 2:13<12>; 7:16 in the second clause), the translator translated *qatal* with a Greek perfect. These particles emphasize the present moment and the perfect is appropriate in these places to indicate the action continues to the moment of speaking. In other places an aorist is used with עַתָּה (1 Chr 17:27; 29:17; 2 Chr 7:16; 10:11; 18:22; 29:31) and with הִנֵּה (1 Chr 22:14; 2 Chr 9:6; 18:22; 25:19).

[52] These examples all occur in the first person and in direct speech, and the force of the perfect seems to be that what is prepared is present before the speaker, for example, "*we have made ready* and sanctified; see, they are in front of the altar" (2 Chr 29:19). The aorist is also used to translate the same verb on a number of occasions (1 Chr 12:39<40>; 14:2; 15:3, 12 (1st person); 22:3, 14 (2) (1st person); 28:2 (1st person); 2 Chr 1:4; 2:7<6>; 3:1; 19:3; 27:6; 35:14, 15), but the sense that what has been prepared is not necessarily present.

2:12<11>), and "to sanctify" (29:19), particularly related to the building of the temple as in בָּנִיתִי "I *have built* you an exalted house" (6:2). The Greek perfect is appropriate for announcing an action which commenced prior to the time of speaking but which has relevance up to the time of speaking. Sometimes the action may even be accomplished by the speech act (i.e., a performative) "I hereby *give* oxen for the burnt offering" (1 Chr 21:23) or "I *am sending* to you silver and gold" (2 Chr 16:3). The perfect is also appropriate for actions conducted by God which have resulting or enduring relevance, such as, "to choose," e.g., "God *has chosen* Judah" (1 Chr 28:4), "*He has chosen* Solomon" (28:6, 10; 29:1) and "the Levites" (2 Chr 29:11), "God's name *has been invoked*" upon the temple (6:33) and upon His people (7:14), "God *has consecrated*" the temple (7:16), and "the wrath of the Lord *has been poured out*" (34:21). It is also appropriate for human behavior which has lasting consequences, particularly related to God and His dealings with them, e.g., ἡμάρτηκα "I *have sinned*" (1 Chr 21:8), πεποίθαμεν "we *rely, have put our trust* in God" (2 Chr 14:11<10>), "you *have acted foolishly*" (16:9), "a rage that *has reached* up to heaven" (28:9). The use of the perfect τέθνηκεν to indicate death in 2 Chronicles 22:10 is also quite striking. Athaliah not only realized that her son Ahaziah had died, she is also conscious that he is now in a state of death, there is no longer a male heir from his house to continue his line.[53] The perfect is also used in the expression "our fathers *have fallen*" (29:9) with similar force.

Perhaps the perfect could have been used more often in the translation of Chronicles. According to Evans, 288 out of 2478 (11.62%) of the *qatal* forms in the Pentateuch were translated by Greek perfects (compared to only 3% in Chronicles).[54] The fact that many of these examples are theologically motivated may indicate that their use was reserved by the translator for significant texts. The use of the perfect with God as a subject has been noted by Schehr as "especially appropriate where God addresses mortals, bestowing upon them some permanent condition."[55]

---

[53] It is interesting to note that the parallel section in 2 Kings 11:1 has an aorist form of the verb.

[54] For each of the five books respectively (Genesis through Deuteronomy) there were 86+77+19+55+51 perfects out of 868+467+190+421+532 *qatal* forms (*Verbal Syntax*, 281-93).

[55] Timothy Sche[h]r, "The Perfect Indicative in Septuagint Genesis," *BIOSCS* 24 (1991): 16, (contra Evans who considers the perfect with God appropriate, but not

d. Qatal > Present Indicative (17 = 1.46%)

Sixteen of the 17 *qatal* forms that are translated by a present indicative occur in reported speech, with 12 of them occurring in the expression כֹּה אָמַר "thus says...."[56] Twice the verb יָדַע "to know" is translated by a present γινώσκω, where the state of knowing coincides with the time of speaking (1 Chr 25:16; 2 Chr 6:30). One time הָיָה in the expression כִּי לָרֹב הָיָה "for there is so much of it" is translated, using the present ἐστίν "there is" ὅτι εἰς πλῆθός ἐστιν (1 Chr 22:14). A past time understanding of the Hebrew is awkward, as the state of the existence of so much material for the temple still exists at the time of speaking, (cf. most English translations which render the clause with a present tense). In the only example outside of reported speech, Hezekiah saw that "Sennacherib *had come* (ἥκει) to fight against Jerusalem" (2 Chr 32:2). The present of this verb ἥκω has present perfect sense which brings the action of coming up to the time of the main verb "see."

e. Qatal > Future Indicative (62 = 5.33%)

All the *qatal* forms translated by future indicative forms occur in main clauses in reported speech. All but one are translations of *wᵉqatal* (sequential) forms, which are dealt with in the section on *wᵉqatal* forms. The sole non-*wᵉqatal qatal* form translated by a future occurs in the Lord's utterance to Rehoboam "You abandoned me, so *I have*

---

specially significant. He believes what is important is that the perfect occurs in direct speech rather than "which particular speaker uses it," *Verbal Syntax*, 165-66).

[56] The translation of this expression by a present is the most common way to render it into Greek (1 Chr 17:7, 21:10, 11; 2 Chr 11:4; 18:10; 20:15; 21:12; 24:20; 32:10; 34:24, 26; 36:23). It is also translated by an aorist four times (1 Chr 17:4; 2 Chr 12:5; 18:26; 34:23). For more on the different tenses used in this oracular formula and the distinction between οὕτως and τάδε, see Pietersma and Saunders' introduction to *A New English Translation of the Septuagint* (NETS) *Ieremias*, IOSCS, 2005. Cited 30 January 2007. Online at http://ccat.sas.upenn.edu/nets/edition/ier.pdf. The aorist is used in the translation of Isaiah four times when a personal reference to the prophet himself is included (Isa 18:4; 21:6, 16; 31:4). "The oracle, received by the prophet in the past, is *now* conveyed to its intended audience, but presented simply as divine speech in the past, not as oracular utterance in the present, i.e., something transmitted by the prophet as mouthpiece of God. In other words, an oracle has become reported divine speech, even though *oratio recta* has been retained" (10) They also comment about the bi-sectioning of Ieremias: chapters 1-29 use τάδε λέγει and chapters 30 onward use οὕτως εἶπεν, for the most part, to translate כֹּה אָמַר. The former represents "a divine speech act in the present mediated by the prophet as mouthpiece of God," and the latter "a divine speech act in the past reported by the prophet" (11).

abandoned you (וְאַף־אֲנִי עֲזַבְתִּי) to the hand of Shishak" (2 Chr 12:5) where the Greek has a future ἐγκαταλείψω "I *will abandon* you." The future fits the context in the sense that Shishak's attack was future to the verb of speaking, however, a past time understanding of the *qatal* form would also be appropriate if the action of forsaking is understood as having already been determined by God.

f. Qatal > Aorist Participle (24 = 2.06%)

In 20 out of the 24 occasions an aorist participle is used to translate a *qatal* form in a relative אֲשֶׁר clause, e.g., אֲשֶׁר נוֹלַד־לוֹ "who were born to him" οἱ τεχθέντες αὐτῷ (1 Chr 3:1; so also 12:15<16>; 19:9; 21:17; 2 Chr 6:38, 39; 7:22; 8:8; 9:13; 10:8, 10 (2); 12:3, 5; 18:12; 25:10; 29:16; 34:16, 21, 23). These clauses are translated as Greek attributive participles, which are common Greek structures and are equivalent to relative clauses.[57] The four remaining examples of aorist participles translating a *qatal* form also are attributive participles.[58]

---

[57] In all of these 20 examples, the relative אֲשֶׁר is the subject of the relative clause and is immediately followed by a verb with no intervening morpheme. This makes it easier for the translator to use an attributive participle to translate the relative and the verb by an article and a participle without having to rearrange the word order. It is interesting to note that אֲשֶׁר as the subject of a relative clause followed by a *qatal* form is translated only 22 times by the formal equivalent more closely corresponding to the Hebrew, a nominative relative pronoun and an aorist indicative, e.g., אֲשֶׁר נוֹלַד־לוֹ translated οἱ ἐτέχθησαν αὐτῷ (1 Chr 2:9—the same structure in 1 Chronicles 3:1 is rendered by an aorist attributive participle). When אֲשֶׁר has a different function (e.g., as an object) the formal equivalent, a relative pronoun and an indicative is used.

[58] One asyndetic relative clause (a clause without a relative pronoun) לַצָּבָא בָּאוּ עַל־דָּוִיד is translated as an attributive participle τῆς στρατιᾶς οἱ ἐλθόντες (attributive participle) πρὸς Δαυιδ "the troops *who came* to David" (1 Chr 12:23<24>). One time a *qatal* form preceded by a definite article הַנִּמְצָאוּ־פֹה "who are present here" is translated τὸν εὑρεθέντα ὧδε an attributive participle (29:17). This is a rare structure and is equivalent to a relative clause, cf. Waltke and O'Connor, *Biblical Hebrew Syntax*, 248. In the expression וִיהוּדָה הָגְלוּ לְבָבֶל "And Judah was taken into exile in Babylon," the translators took Judah with what preceded it (i.e., "the Book of the Kings of Israel and Judah"). Then they supplied a preposition and translated the verb as an attributive participle, μετὰ τῶν ἀποικισθέντων "with *those who were taken into exile*" (1 Chr 9:1). In 2 Chronicles 20:7 a pronoun and a *qatal* form אַתָּה אֱלֹהֵינוּ הוֹרַשְׁתָּ "Did you not, O our God, drive out" are translated by a pronoun, a verb "to be," and an attributive participle, σὺ εἶ ὁ κύριος ὁ ἐξολεθρεύσας, "are not You, O Lord, the One who drove out...."

g. Qatal > Present Participle (7 = 0.6%)

Three of the present participles are attributive participles translating a
relative clause or an asyndetic relative clause. A relative אֲשֶׁר clause,
מֵאֲשֶׁר הָיָה לְפָנֶיךָ "from him who was before you," is translated ἀπὸ
τῶν ὄντων (1 Chr 17:13). One asyndetic relative clause
כָּל־לְבָבוֹ הֵכִין "all who set their hearts" is translated πάσης
καρδίας κατευθυνούσης "every heart set" (2 Chr 30:19).[59] Two
wᵉqatal forms are translated as present participles (2 Chr 12:11, see
below). Three present participles are interpreted as temporal verbal
forms. The verb מָלָךְ in יְהוָה מָלָךְ "YHWH reigns" is translated as
an omni-temporal κύριος βασιλεύων "the Lord is reigning" (1 Chr
16:31). Two *qatal* forms are translated by a periphrastic present
participle with ἦν, the past form of the verb "to be" indicating
imperfective or durative aspect. דָּשׁ is translated by ἦν ἀλοῶν
"Ornan *was threshing*" (1 Chr 21:20), perhaps indicating that the
translators understood this form as a Hebrew participle, or they
considered that it was going on simultaneously with the main verbs
"Ornan <u>turned</u> and <u>saw</u> the angel while he *was threshing.*" כִּי חָמַל
"because he had compassion" is translated by ὅτι ἦν φειδόμενος
"because he *was one who had compassion on* (or, *one who spared)* His people"
(2 Chr 36:15), perhaps to indicate customary action or one who
possesses the attribute.

h. Qatal > Perfect Participle (3 = 0.26%)

All three perfect participles are passive attributive participles. In each
case, the voice was changed from an active in Hebrew to a passive in
Greek. Twice the subject could be considered not that important. In
the section on the building of the temple which begins in 2 Chronicles
3:1, with Solomon last expressed as the subject of the verbs in 3:3, in
4:9 "He (Solomon?) *overlaid* their doors" becomes "their doors *were
overlaid*" (also perhaps preparing for the change in subject in 4:11 to
Huram). In 34:24 a third plural *qatal* form (which often functions as a
vague personal subject) "they read" in a relative clause becomes the
perfect passive "the book *that was read* (τῷ ἀνεγνωσμένῳ)." Finally, in

---

[59] One asyndetic relative *qatal* form יָשְׁבוּ (with a variant reading יֹשְׁבֵי—a Hebrew
participle) is translated by the present participle κατοικοῦντες "that lived" (1 Chr
2:55). We take the variant reading or *qere* (read) for the purpose of analysis (see *qotel*
forms, section h; cf. note 12 above).

2 Chronicles 26:22 "the first and the last acts Isaiah *wrote*" becomes "acts *written* by the prophet Isaiah" with the translators supplying the preposition ὑπό governing the agent Isaiah.

i. Qatal > Aorist Infinitive (7 = 0.6%)

Six out of the seven aorist infinitives translate *qatal* forms that follow a preposition or כִּי. They function as subordinate clauses and are translated by a Greek preposition and an articular infinitive, which is a common structure in Greek and is equivalent to a circumstantial clause. Twice ἐν τῷ and an infinitive translates a prepositional phrase (בְּעֵת—2 Chr 20:22; 29:27);[60] and one time a כִּי clause (with causal or temporal sense—24:25). One time עַל אֲשֶׁר is translated by διὰ τό and an infinitive "because" (1 Chr 13:10), אַחַר is translated by μετὰ τό and an infinitive "after" (2 Chr 35:14), עַד by ἕως "until" and an infinitive (36:21). It seems that the translator translated the preposition and a *qatal* form in the same way as an infinitive construct governed by a preposition with a preposition and an articular infinitive.[61]

j. Qatal > Present Infinitive (1 = 0.09%)

The only time a present infinitive occurs is when a relative clause with a *qatal* form מִגְּבִירָה אֲשֶׁר־עָשְׂתָה לַאֲשֵׁרָה מִפְלָצֶת "from [being] queen mother because *she had made* an abominable image for Asherah" is translated loosely "*from being* (τοῦ μὴ εἶναι) priestess to Astarte" (2 Chr 15:16).

---

[60] One time a main clause וְגַם בַּמֶּלֶךְ נְבוּכַדְנֶאצַּר מָרָד "he also rebelled against King Nebuchadnezzar" is translated ἐν τῷ τὰ πρὸς τὸν βασιλέα Ναβουχοδονοσορ ἀθετῆσαι, "when he rebelled…" (2 Chr 36:13).

[61] Twice prepositions immediately followed by *qatal* forms functioning like asyndetic relatives (cf. Joüon and Muraoka, *Grammar of Biblical Hebrew*, 594) are translated by relative clauses. The semantic notion of בַּהֵכִין "to [the place that] *he prepared*" is translated in a subordinate clause, but syntactically it is not translated. The subordinate clause syntactically translates כִּי נָטַע "for he planted" with an aorist indicative ὅτι ἡτοίμασεν "for he prepared" (2 Chr 1:4). One time אֶל־הֲכִינוֹתִי לוֹ "to [the place that] *I have prepared* for it" is translated by an aorist indicative in a relative clause οὗ ἡτοίμασα αὐτῇ (1 Chr 15:12). Prepositions followed by relative pronouns preceding *qatal* forms are mostly translated by relative pronouns and aorist indicatives, e.g., עַד אֲשֶׁר־בָּאתִי ἕως οὗ ἦλθον "until I came" (2 Chr 9:6), תַּחַת אֲשֶׁר לֹא־הָלַכְתָּ ἀνθ' ὧν οὐκ ἐπορεύθης "because you have not walked" (21:12, also 34:25) or by an attributive participle, e.g., לְפָנֶיךָ מֵאֲשֶׁר הָיָה ἀπὸ τῶν ὄντων ἔμπροσθέν σου "from him who was before you" (1 Chr 17:13).

k. Qatal > Perfect Infinitive (2 = 0.17%)

The first perfect infinitive occurs when a coordinated negative *qatal* clause (in the *niphal*) in reported speech וְלֹא נִשְׁעַנְתָּ "and did not *rely* (lit., *lean*) *on*" follows an *niphal* infinitive construct of the same root בְּהִשָּׁעֶנְךָ, and both are translated by the same Greek infinitive πεποιθέναι (2 Chr 16:7). The *niphal* is quite commonly translated into a Greek perfect emphasizing the resultant state of the action. The second perfect infinitive occurs when a *qatal* form הַהֵכִין preceded by the preposition עַל (functioning like an asyndetic relative) is translated "because of what God had prepared (διὰ τὸ ἡτοιμακέναι)" (2 Chr 29:36). Perhaps the perfect was chosen to emphasize the state resulting from the cleansing and sanctifying of the temple at the time of Hezekiah.

l. Qatal > Aorist Subjunctive (28 = 2.41%)

All the *qatal* forms translated by aorist subjunctives also occur in reported speech. All but three are translations of *wᵉqatal* (sequential) forms (dealt with in the section on *wᵉqatal* forms below). The two non-*wᵉqatal qatal* forms occur either in a subordinate clause or in a clause governed by a subordinate conjunction, and they are translated by Greek subordinating conjunctions that grammatically require a subjunctive form, for example, כִּי translated ὅταν "whenever" (1 Chr 17:11), and an asyndetic *qatal* form governed by the conditional conjunction ἐάν in the phrase וּבָא אָלָה "if someone sins… and comes [and] *swears*" is translated by an aorist subjunctive καὶ ἔλθῃ καὶ ἀράσηται (2 Chr 6:22). It is translated as if it were a *wᵉqatal* form with the conjunction καὶ supplied by the translator.

m. Qatal > Present Subjunctive (2 = 0.17%)

Both *qatal* forms translated by a present subjunctive are translations of two *wᵉqatal* forms and are dealt with in the section on *wᵉqatal* forms.

n. Qatal > Aorist Imperative (4 = 0.34%)

The four *qatal* forms translated by an aorist imperative are translations of *wᵉqatal* forms and are dealt with in the section on *wᵉqatal* forms below.

o. Qatal > Adjective (8 = 0.69%)

Most of the *qatal* forms that are translated into adjectives are Hebrew stative verbs.[62] For example, גָּבַר "to be prominent" is translated δυνατὸς (1 Chr 5:2), רָבוּ "to be many" is translated πολλὰ (5:9), טוֹב "to be good" ἀγαθὸν (13:2), יָשַׁר "to be right" εὐθὴς (13:4), וְשָׂבֵעַ זָקֵן "to be old and full [of days]" πρεσβύτης καὶ πλήρης (23:1), and עָבָה "to be thick[er]" παχύτερος (2 Chr 10:10). Finally, a *niphal* (passive) נוֹלַד "he was descended" is translated by ἦν "to be" and an adjective ἀπόγονος "descended from" (1 Chr 20:6). Apart from the verb רָבָה the other verbs occur only as *qal* forms in Chronicles on these occasions.[63]

p. Qatal > Adverb (2 = 0.17%)

Both *qatal* forms that are translated as adverbs are a little problematic. The first *qatal* perfect שָׂם "to put, place" seems to have been interpreted as the adverb שָׁם "there" (reading a שׁ for a שׂ) and translated by the Greek adverb ἐκεῖ "there" and the verb "to be" ἦν (2 Chr 1:5). The other form is a *wᵉqatal* form (see below).

q. Qatal > Noun (5 = 0.43%)

Twice הִתְיַחְשׂוּ "they were enrolled by genealogies" is translated by the nouns ὁ καταλοχισμὸς "the enumeration" (1 Chr 5:17) and ὁ συλλοχισμὸς (9:1). In the three other places that a *qatal* form is translated as a noun, there may be some differences in the *Vorlage* or at least in the way the translators read it. The verb הֶגְלָם "he carried them into exile" is interpreted as a personal name ιγλααμ "Heglam" (8:7). הִהְקְדִּישׁ "he made holy" is translated τῶν ἁγίων "the holy things" perhaps because the same verb is repeated later in the verse (26:28). A *qatal* form in a relative clause אֲשֶׁר מְשָׁחוֹ יְהֹוָה "whom YHWH had anointed" is translated χριστὸν κυρίου "the anointed of the Lord" (2 Chr 22:7).

---

[62] As was mentioned in note 23, in rabbinic Hebrew adjectives replace stative verbs. The translation of these *qatal* forms as adjectives is perhaps reinforcing this trend.

[63] טוֹב occurs one time as a *hiphil* causative (2 Chr 6:8). רָבוּ occurs in two other places in *qal* (simple) and is translated by aorist passive forms meaning, "they were multiplied" (1 Chr 5:23; 23:17). It also occurs more than 15 times in the *hiphil* causative form.

r. Qatal > Minus (35 = 3.01 %)

Finally, 35 times the translator of Chronicles does not translate the *qatal* form of the verb. In some places the entire verse or a range of verses are lacking in the Septuagint, e.g., 1 Chronicles 1:11-16, 18-23 (which includes eight *qatal* forms), and 2 Chronicles 27:8 (which includes two *qatal* forms). In other places an entire clause is lacking (with the English translation of the *qatal* form in italics), e.g., אֲשֶׁר מָלְכוּ בְּאֶרֶץ אֱדוֹם לִפְנֵי מְלָךְ־מֶלֶךְ לִבְנֵי יִשְׂרָאֵל "who *reigned* in the land of Edom before any king reigned over the Israelites" (1 Chr 1:43), אֲשֶׁר צִוִּיתִי "whom I *commanded*" (17:6—translated in some Gk. MSS), בַּהֲכִין לוֹ דָוִיד כִּי נָטָה־לוֹ "David had prepared for it; for *he had pitched* a tent for it" (2 Chr 1:4—parablepsis, omitting the clause between the two לוֹs, translated in some Gk. MSS), אֲשֶׁר עָשָׂה "that *he had made*" (7:6), וְלֹא חַזְּקוֹ "instead of *strengthening* him" (28:20), נַעֲשָׂה הַפֶּסַח הַזֶּה: אַחֲרֵי כָל־זֹאת אֲשֶׁר הֵכִין יֹאשִׁיָּהוּ אֶת־הַבַּיִת "this passover *was kept*. After all this, when Josiah *had set* the temple in order" (35:19b-20a), הִקְדִּישׁ "*he had consecrated*" (36:14). In 2 Chronicles 9:10 a relative clause which contains the first occurrence of a repeated verb אֲשֶׁר הֵבִיאוּ is omitted. There are a number of other places where a verb that is repeated is left out. For example, the second of the repeated verbs are omitted by the translator דִּבַּרְתָּ (1 Chr 17:23), נָתַן (2 Chr 1:15; 9:27), הָלַךְ (7:17), and בָּנָה (27:4). מָלַךְ which occurs in 1 Chronicles 29:26 is repeated three times in verse 27 but omitted three times by the translators. One time a verb that has a verb with similar meaning nearby in the context is omitted in translation הַבְּרוּרִים אֲשֶׁר נִקְבוּ בְּשֵׁמוֹת "chosen and *expressed* by names" ἐκλεγέντες ἐπ᾽ ὀνόματος "chosen by name" (16:41). Four times a form of הָיָה "to be, become" is not translated, resulting in a noun sentence in Greek with the verb "to be" understood (1 Chr 17:22; 2 Chr 7:21; 9:1; 10:6).

s. Summary

Most of the time the translator resorted to the common equivalent for *qatal* forms, the aorist (accounting for almost 80% of the *qatal* forms excluding *wᵉqatal* forms). The second most common form used to translate *qatal* forms was the imperfect. About 75% of these imperfect forms are constrained by the inventory of the language, e.g., there is no aorist form for verbs such as εἰμί "to be," so the writer or speaker is constrained by the language to use an imperfect in past contexts to translate הָיָה when it has this meaning. The other imperfects set off certain actions from strings of aorists, e.g., as summary or simultaneous. The third most common form was the perfect indicative. All 35 of them occur in reported speech main clauses or subordinate clauses. In reported speech, time is relative to the verb of speaking, and in subordinate clauses time is relative to the time of the main verb. The perfect conveys the notion of an action that transpired in the past with a resultant state that has relevance up to the present (either of speech or narrative), and so it is particularly suited to these clauses. Greek futures or subjunctives are mostly used to translate w^eqatal forms (dealt with in the section on w^eqatal forms). *Qatal* forms translated as adjectives occur as a translation of some stative verbs, and most of the other forms, including most minuses, are a reflection of some problem with the text, either due to an omission, a different reading of the unpointed text, or a misreading of it. Occasionally repeated verbs are left out. The translation may also reflect the diachronic development of Hebrew, for example, when *qatal* stative forms are translated as (inceptive) aorists or as adjectives, which mirror the way statives function in rabbinic Hebrew.

Occasionally the Hebrew syntax is reworked by the translator to use common Greek structures. For example, a *qatal* form in a relative clause in which the relative pronoun is the subject of the clause is translated by an attributive participle (a common Greek structure). Alternatively, a *qatal* form in a temporal clause is translated by articular infinitives following a preposition.

The fact that the translator utilized other Greek forms than the aorist to translate *qatal* forms indicates a certain amount of flexibility, recognizing that the common equivalent would not work in every context, as well as sensitivity to more standard Greek idioms (see the sections in chapter 5 particularly in the use of non-standard equivalent Greek verbs such as the imperfect and perfect).

3. *W^eqatal*

As most of the sequential *w^eqatal* forms cannot be formally distinguished from coordinated *qatal* forms, the *w^eqatal* forms are counted above with the other *qatal* forms. However, when the *w^eqatal* forms are analyzed here separately, paying attention to the text type in which they occur and the verb form preceding them, it is easier to distinguish the archaic use of sequential forms from coordinated forms. Most of the coordinated forms occur in narrative and are mostly preceded by a *qatal*, a *wayyiqtol*, or a noun sentence in past contexts. Sequential (consecutive) forms occur in reported speech and are mostly preceded by a *yiqtol*, another *wᵉqatal* sequential form, or a volitive form. (As *wᵉqatal* forms are main clause forms, none occur in subordinate clauses).

The most common forms used to translate sequential *wᵉqatal* forms are future indicatives, subjunctives, and imperatives. They mostly continue the force of the preceding verb. Most coordinated forms are translated by past tense verbs in Greek, especially the aorist.

The following table gives the breakdown on how the *wᵉqatal* forms in Chronicles were translated into Greek.

TABLE 4: THE TRANSLATION OF *Wᴱ QATAL* FORMS

Wᵉ QATAL	TOTAL	Percentage	Narrative Main Clauses (Clause %)	Reported Speech Main Clauses	Subordinate Clauses
Aorist Indicative	23	17.97	11 (57.9)	12 (11.0)	
Imperfect Indicative	5	3.91	4 (21.1)	1	
Perfect Indicative	2	1.56		2	
Present Indicative	1	0.78		1	
Future Indicative	61	47.66		61 (56.0)	
Present Participle	2	1.56	2 (10.5)		
Aorist Subjunctive	26	20.31		26 (23.9)	
Present Subjunctive	2	1.56		2	
Aorist Imperative	4	3.13		4	
Adjective	1	0.78	1		
Adverb	1	0.78	1		
Total	128	100	19	109	

Total 128
Aorist Indicative (23 = 17.97%)
Narrative Main Clauses (11)
Qatal + weqatal > Aorist Indicative (4)
1 Chr 11:22; 2 Chr 31:21; 33:19; 34:4
Wayyiqtol + weqatal > Aorist Indicative (3)
2 Chr 3:7; 12:10; 33:4
Weqatal + weqatal > Aorist Indicative (1)
2 Chr 33:6
Noun sentence + *weqatal > Aorist Indicative* (2)
1 Chr 7:21; 8:7
Infinitive construct + *weqatal > Aorist Indicative* (1)
2 Chr 24:11
Reported Speech Main Clauses (12)
Qatal + weqatal > Aorist Indicative (7)
1 Chr 17:10; 22:18; 2 Chr 1:8; 6:37; 7:12; 19:3; 29:6
Wayyiqtol + weqatal > Aorist Indicative (2)
1 Chr 17:8, 17
Noun sentence + *weqatal > Aorist Indicative* (3)
1 Chr 22:18; 28:2; 29:17
Imperfect Indicative (5 = 3.91%)
Narrative Main Clauses (4)
Qatal + weqatal > Imperfect Indicative (1)
2 Chr 33:6
Weqatal + weqatal > Imperfect Indicative (2)
2 Chr 33:6 (2)
Noun sentence + *weqatal > Imperfect Indicative* (1)
1 Chr 9:26
Reported Speech Main Clauses (1)
Noun sentence + *weqatal > Imperfect Indicative* (1)
2 Chr 13:9
Perfect Indicative (2 = 1.56%)
Reported Speech Main Clauses (2)
Qatal + weqatal > Perfect Indicative (2)
2 Chr 7:16; 29:19
Present Indicative (1 = 0.78%)
Reported Speech Main Clauses (1)
Qatal + weqatal > Present Indicative (1)
2 Chr 25:19

Future Indicative $(61 = 47.66\%)^{64}$

Reported Speech Main Clauses (61)

Yiqtol + *wᵉqatal* > *Future Indicative* (27)

1 Chr 14:10; 17:11, 12, 14; 19:12 (2); 22:9, 11; 28:7; 2 Chr 6:21, 23, 25, 26, 27, 30, 33, 36; 7:18, 21; 12:7; 18:12, 21; 19:10 (2); 23:7; 25:19; 34:28

Wᵉqatal + *wᵉqatal* > *Future Indicative* (23)

1 Chr 4:10; 17:9 (3), 11 (2); 22:11; 2 Chr 6:21, 23, 25, 26, 27, 30, 35 (2), 36 (2), 39 (3); 7:20, 22; 10:7

Imperative + *wᵉqatal* > *Future Indicative* (6)

1 Chr 14:10, 14; 15:12; 2 Chr 18:11, 26; 20:16

Noun sentence + *wᵉqatal* > *Future Indicative* (2)

1 Chr 22:10; 2 Chr 15:6

Infinitive construct + *wᵉqatal* > *Future Indicative* (3)

1 Chr 23:32; 2 Chr 6:21, 7:16

Present Participles (2 = 1.56%)

Narrative Main Clauses (2)

Qatal + *wᵉqatal* > *Present Participle* (1)

2 Chr 12:11

Wᵉqatal + *wᵉqatal* > *Present Participle* (1)

2 Chr 12:11

Aorist Subjunctive (26 = 20.31%)

Reported Speech Main Clauses (26)

Yiqtol + *wᵉqatal* > *Aorist Subjunctive* (10)

1 Chr 10:4; 28:8; 2 Chr 6:19, 22, 24, 29, 34; 7:19; 10:7; 32:4

Wᵉqatal + *wᵉqatal* > *Aorist Subjunctive* (15)

2 Chr 6:22, 24 (3), 32 (2), 37 (3), 38 (2); 7:19 (3); 10:7

Noun sentence + *wᵉqatal* > *Aorist Subjunctive* (1)

2 Chr 6:32

Present Subjunctive (2 = 1.56%)

Reported Speech Main Clauses (2)

Yiqtol + *wᵉqatal* > *Present Subjunctive* (1)

1 Chr 4:10

Wᵉqatal + *wᵉqatal* > *Present Subjunctive* (1)

1 Chr 4:10

---

[64] Including καταφυτεύσω (1 Chr 17:9), ἀναπαύσω (22:9), and ἀναστήσω (17:11; 2 Chr 7:18) all coded incorrectly by *GRAMCORD* as aorist subjunctives (see Appendix 1).

Aorist Imperative (4 = 3.13%)
Reported Speech Main Clauses (4)
Imperative + *wᵉqatal* > *Aorist Imperative* (4)
1 Chr 17:4; 19:5; 21:10; 2 Chr 18:33
Adjective (1 = 0.78%)
Narrative Main Clauses (1)
Qatal + *wᵉqatal* > *Adjective* (1)
1 Chr 23:1
Adverb (1 = 0.78%)
Narrative Main Clauses (1)
Qatal + *wᵉqatal* > *Adverb* (1)
2 Chr 33:14

a. Wᵉqatal > Aorist Indicative (23 = 17.97%)

Most of the *wᵉqatal* forms that are translated by an aorist indicative follow *qatal* or *wayyiqtol* forms, or noun sentences in past contexts. They reflect standard coordinated *wᵉqatal* forms. The breakdown is as follows:

i. Qatal + wᵉqatal > Aorist Indicative (11)

The eleven *qatal* forms that precede a *wᵉqatal* are non-sequential and are preceded by a fronted nominal (either a pronoun subject or a fronted object), or a relative pronoun, or begin a reported speech clause. Most of the *wᵉqatal* forms (with the English translation of the *qatal* form in italics) that follow the *qatal* form are also non-sequential and seem to indicate the relating of events without stressing any sequentiality, either temporal or logical. For example, "for he has delivered...*and* the land *is subdued*" (1 Chr 22:18), "You have shown great and steadfast love to my father David, *and have made* me succeed him as *king*" (2 Chr 1:8), "We have sinned; we have done wrong, and *we have acted wickedly*" (6:37), "I have heard your prayer, *and have chosen* this place" (7:12), "for *you destroyed* the sacred poles...*and have set* your heart to seek God" (19:3), "the sites on which *he built* high places *and set up* the sacred poles" (33:19; so also 29:6; 31:21).⁶⁵ All of these forms

---

⁶⁵ The expression יָרַד וְהִכָּה "he also went down *and killed*" translated κατέβη καὶ ἐπάταξεν (1 Chr 11:22) could be considered appropriate for a sequential *wayyiqtol* form but a *wᵉqatal* form occurs. This could reflect a late biblical Hebrew use in the non-synoptic sections of Chronicles in which it is possible to detect a slight trend away

are translated as coordinated aorists in Greek with no differentiation formally between them and the aorists used in the translation of *wayyiqtol* forms.[66]

ii. Wayyiqtol + wᵉqatal > Aorist Indicative (5)

Most of the *wᵉqatal* forms following *wayyiqtol* forms break the sequence, for example, "you have also spoken of your servant's house...and you regard me" (1 Chr 17:17)[67], "so he lined the house with gold...*and he carved* cherubim" (2 Chr 3:7—where carving the cherubim can be considered as out of sequence with lining the house, perhaps going on simultaneously?). A series of *wayyiqtol* forms (underlined) are broken up by a *wᵉqatal* form only to be continued by a *wayyiqtol* "he rebuilt the high places...and erected altars...made sacred poles, worshipped all the host of heaven, and served them, 4 *and he built* altars in the house of the LORD" (33:3-4; cf. v. 5 and he built (*wayyiqtol*) altars for the host of heaven).[68] Perhaps the switch to the *wᵉqatal* form by the author was to emphasize the seriousness of the action, he *even* built altars in the house of the LORD, or, it is (more likely) a separate archival source.

---

from sequential *wayyiqtol* forms toward coordinated *wᵉqatal* forms with the same past perfective force. It is interesting to note, however, in v. 23 the same verb יָרַד occurs as a *wayyiqtol* form in sequence וַיֵּרֶד...וַיִּגְזֹל "and he went down...and snatched." Also in the expression "he broke down the sacred poles...*and he made dust* of them and scattered it (*wayyiqtol*)" a *qatal* form is continued by a *wᵉqatal* form rather than a *wayyiqtol* form. However, it in turn is continued by a *wayyiqtol* (2 Chr 34:4).

[66] One time a *wᵉqatal* form is translated by an aorist in a context where a future might be more appropriate (as in most English versions). "Evildoers shall wear them down no more as they did formerly, from the time that I appointed judges over my people Israel; *and I will subdue* all your enemies." The Greek translation links the *wᵉqatal* form וְהִכְנַעְתִּי "and I will subdue" with the preceding *qatal* form צִוִּיתִי and translates them ἔταξα...καὶ ἐταπείνωσα "I appointed and subdued" (1 Chr 17:9-10).

[67] The *wᵉqatal* form is not present in the parallel passage (2 Sam 7:19). Perhaps the *wᵉqatal* form reflects a modernization of the text by the Chronicler by using a coordinated *qatal* form as opposed to a *wayyiqtol* form?

[68] In one example the actions could be considered as sequential "Rehoboam made shields of bronze...*and committed* them to the hands" (2 Chr 12:10); however, a *wᵉqatal* form is chosen instead of a *wayyiqtol* form. In 1 Chronicles 17:8-9 there is a transition from past actions accomplished by God to future promises. The transition is marked by the break in the sequence from *wayyiqtol* forms to a *wᵉqatal* form. It seems that the translator ignored the break in sequence and treated the *wᵉqatal* form וְעָשִׂיתִי, translated ἐποίησά "*and I have made*," as if it were a *wayyiqtol* form in the sequence "*and I have been* with you wherever you went, *and have cut off* all your enemies before you; *and I have made* for you a name" (v. 8). However, it seems more natural to translate the *wᵉqatal* form as a future promise "*and I will make*" as the NRSV and other English versions do. In the following verses *wᵉqatal* forms are translated by futures.

These forms are all translated the same way in Greek with no way to formally distinguish the underlying Hebrew form, whether it was a sequential *wayyiqtol* form or a non-sequential coordinated *wᵉqatal* form.

iii. W*ᵉqatal* + *wᵉqatal* > Aorist Indicative (1)

The only example of a *wᵉqatal* form following another *wᵉqatal* form translated by an aorist is the last of a four simple coordinated *wᵉqatal* forms in narrative "he <u>practiced soothsaying and augury and sorcery</u>, *and dealt* with mediums and with wizards" (2 Chr 33:6). The three preceding forms in the sequence are translated by imperfects (see below). It is probably best to understand this verb as a rare example of *wᵉqatal* sequential form in late biblical Hebrew with iterative force. It is in a context of *yiqtol* forms with past durative force.

iv. Noun sentence + *wᵉqatal* > Aorist Indicative (5)

In most examples of *wᵉqatal* forms following noun sentences, the noun sentence occurs in a past or a timeless context, for example, "Is not the LORD your God with you? *And has he* not *given* you *peace*" (1 Chr 22:18), "I had planned to build (lit., it was with my heart)...*and I made preparations*" (28:2), "all this abundance...comes from your hand and is all your own, *and you know*" (29:16–17).

v. Infinitive construct + *wᵉqatal* > Aorist Indicative (1)

In this example the infinitive construct preceding the *wᵉqatal* form functions as a temporal clause "and when they saw...*they would come*" (2 Chr 24:11). It is probably best to understand this verb as another rare example of *wᵉqatal* sequential form in late biblical Hebrew with iterative force. It is in context of *yiqtol* forms with past durative force.[69]

b. W*ᵉqatal* > Imperfect Indicative (5 = 3.91%)

Two of the imperfect forms are translations of וְהָיָה forms and follow noun sentences in past contexts. One is translated by the imperfect of εἰμί. The Hebrew is difficult, בֶּאֱמוּנָה הֵמָּה אַרְבַּעַת גִּבֹּרֵי הַשֹּׁעֲרִים

---

[69] See Jan Joosten, "Disappearance of Iterative WEQATAL," *Biblical Hebrew in Its Northwest Semitic Setting: Typological and Historical Perspectives.* (ed. S. Fassberg and A. Hurvitz; Winona Lake: Eisenbrauns, 2006), 140.

הֵם הַלְוִיִּם וְהָיוּ עַל־הַלְּשָׁכוֹת "the four chief gatekeepers, who were
faithful were Levites, and were over the chambers" translated ἐν
πίστει εἰσὶν τέσσαρες δυνατοὶ τῶν πυλῶν οἱ Λευῖται ἦσαν
ἐπὶ τῶν παστοφορίων "four strong men are in charge of the gates
[who] were Levites over the chambers" (1 Chr 9:26). The other וְהָיָה
form is translated by the imperfect of γίνομαι (2 Chr 13:9). It follows
a participle and has indefinite past sense "everyone who comes to be
consecrated...*then becomes*...." The other three imperfects are part of a
simple coordinated sequence of *wᵉqatal* verbs which follow a *wᵉ-x qatal*
clause, וְעוֹנֵן וְנִחֵשׁ וְכִשֵּׁף "he practiced soothsaying and augury and
sorcery" translated καὶ ἐκληδονίζετο καὶ οἰωνίζετο καὶ
ἐφαρμακεύετο (2 Chr 33:6).[70]

c. Wᵉqatal > Perfect Indicative (2 = 1.56%)

The two *wᵉqatal* forms translated by perfect indicative forms that follow
qatal forms are both translations of the *hiphil* of the verb "to sanctify"
וְעַתָּה בָחַרְתִּי וְהִקְדַּשְׁתִּי אֶת־הַבַּיִת הַזֶּה "And now I have chosen *and
consecrated* this house" translated ἐξελεξάμην καὶ ἡγίακα (2 Chr
7:16), and הֵכַנּוּ וְהִקְדָּשְׁנוּ וְהִנָּם לִפְנֵי מִזְבַּח "we have made ready *and
sanctified* [the vessels]; and behold they are before the altar..."
translated ἡτοιμάκαμεν καὶ ἡγνίκαμεν ἰδού ἐστιν ἐναντίον τοῦ
θυσιαστηρίου (29:19). The perfect emphasizes the resultant state of
the action of sanctification, which has relevance right up to the time of
speaking. This is reinforced by the presence of the particles וְעַתָּה
"now" (7:16) and וְהִנָּם "behold" (29:19) in these verses. Perhaps we
could also say that the perfect is used in these examples for
theologically important texts and ideas (see *Qatal* section c above and
note 55).

d. Wᵉqatal > Present Indicative (1 = 0.78%)

The present indicative form follows a *qatal* form and indicates the
inception into a state which continues to exist at the time of speaking,

---

[70] This is in contrast to the fourth *wᵉqatal* form, which is translated by an aorist, "*he
dealt* with mediums and with wizards." The first three forms come from the *piel*
(intensive/factitive) stem, and the fourth is a simple *qal* form. Perhaps the translator
considered that the force of the *piel* was iterative durative and the *qal* punctual. Most
of the time these verbs וְעוֹנֵן וְנִחֵשׁ וְכִשֵּׁף are given durative aspect by the Septuagint
translators (e.g., נִחֵשׁ in Gen 44:5, 15; Deut 18:10; 1 Kgs 20:33; 2 Kgs 17:17; 21:6).
However, these words are all denominative words with nominal force.

"You say, 'See, I have defeated Edom,' *and* your heart *has lifted* you up
(וְנָשָׂאֲךָ)" translated ἐπαίρει "*lifts*" (2 Chr 25:19). The Greek present
emphasizes that the state exists at the time of speaking, rather than the
inception into it.

e. W^eqatal > Future Indicative (61 = 47.66%)

Futures translate almost half of the *w^eqatal* forms. Most of them follow
either a *yiqtol* form in a future context or another *w^eqatal* form. A few
follow volitive forms such as imperatives or *yiqtol* jussives.

i. Yiqtol + w^eqatal > Future Indicative (27)

Nineteen of the *w^eqatal* forms that follow a *yiqtol* form and are
translated as a future function as the apodosis of a future condition
(where the conditional clause is translated by ἐάν and a subjunctive),
e.g., "If the Arameans are too strong for me, *then you shall help* me" (1
Chr 19:12 (2); so also 2 Chr 6:21 (3), 23 (2), 25 (2), 30 (2), 35 (2), 39 (3);
7:18, 20; 10:7).

Most of the rest of the *w^eqatal* forms continue the future sense of the
yiqtol, e.g., "Shall I go up against the Philistines? *And will you give* them
into my hand?" (1 Chr 14:10). A couple of the *yiqtol* forms are best
understood as jussives, so the *w^eqatal* form continues the volitive force
of the jussive or has the nuance of purpose. For example,
יְהִי יְהוָה עִמָּךְ וְהִצְלַחְתָּ "may YHWH be with you, *so that you may
succeed*" (1 Chr 22:11), and וִיהִי־נָא דְבָרְךָ...וְדִבַּרְתָּ טוֹב "let your word
be...and *may you speak* favorably" (2 Chr 18:12). However, in the
translation of these two verses the translator employs futures, which
may be considered as a confident assertion in the mouth of the
speaker: ἔσται (future) μετὰ σοῦ κύριος καὶ εὐοδώσει "the Lord
shall be with you, *and He will prosper* [you]" (1 Chr 22:11) and καὶ
ἔστωσαν (imperative) δὴ οἱ λόγοι σου...καὶ λαλήσεις ἀγαθά, "let
your words be...and *you shall speak* favorably" (2 Chr 18:12).[71]

---

[71] This is probably preferable to considering that the translator was just defaulting
to the common equivalent for the *yiqtol* forms, the future. In both of these verses, there
are short *yiqtol* (jussive) forms (which are formally distinct from the long *yiqtol*
(imperfect) forms) preceding the *weqatal* form, and these are translated by a Greek
future. This intimates that the translator made a conscious decision to reinterpret the
jussive wishes as future assertions. An alternative way of understanding these futures is
that they are the so-called jussive future, rare in Attic Greek but common in the
Septuagint, cf. Conybeare and Stock, *Grammar of Septuagint Greek*, 72.

ii. W^eqatal + w^eqatal > Future Indicative (23)

Most of the *w^eqatal* forms that follow another *w^eqatal* form translated by
a future continue on the sequence of events, e.g., God states that after
He has appointed a place for His people, *He will plant* them, and *they
will live* (1 Chr 17:9),[72] or there is a confident assertion that after God
has heard the prayer of His people, *He will forgive* (2 Chr 6:21), and
after He has forgiven, *He will bring* them again into the land (6:25), *He
will give* them rain (6:27), and *He will give* to them according to their
ways (6:30). These are also in a context where the *yiqtol* form could be
considered as a jussive wish. However, the translator made them into
confident assertions, perhaps because they were based upon promises
(cf. Deut 30:5; 28:12) in God's word being confirmed (2 Chr 6:17).

Sometimes the *w^eqatal* form translated into a Greek future functions
as an apodosis of a conditional (a third class or general condition,
following ἐάν and an aorist subjunctive). The *w^eqatal* form either *begins*
the apodosis after a coordinated protasis, e.g., if the people go out in
battle and pray, *then God will hear* (2 Chr 6:35), if they repent and pray,
then God will hear (6:39), if Solomon would be kind and would speak
kindly, *then the people will be* his servants forever (10:7); or the *w^eqatal*
form *continues* the apodosis, e.g., if the people sin then God will be
angry with His people, and *He gives* them into the hand of their
enemies, and *they will carry* them captive (6:36 (2)).

iii. Imperative + w^eqatal > Future Indicative (6)

Sometimes the *w^eqatal* form translated by a future indicative has the
force of a promise or prophecy if the imperative is fulfilled, especially if
the subject is different from the imperative, for example, "go up...*and I
will give*" (1 Chr 14:10), "go up and triumph...*and the Lord will give*" (2
Chr 18:11), "go up...*and you shall come* upon them" (1 Chr 14:14), and
"go down...*and they will come up*" (2 Chr 20:16).[73] The Greek future also
functions with strong imperatival force, continuing the imperative,
especially when the verb is in the second person, e.g., "take Micaiah,

---

[72] However, the first *w^eqatal* form in the sequence of three following a *w^eqatal* form
does not seem to follow sequentially in the way that the translator translates it. It is
translated by an aorist "I have made a name..." which is followed by "and I will
appoint a place."

[73] This *w^eqatal* form follows הִנֵּה and a participle with an immediate future sense.
However, the participle can be considered as circumstantial and the *w^eqatal* form
contingent on the preceding imperative.

carry him back...*and you shall say*" (2 Chr 18:26), and "sanctify yourselves...*and you shall bring*" (1 Chr 15:12).

iv. Noun sentence + w*qatal > Future Indicative (2)

In the first example of a noun sentence followed by a *w*qatal* form, "He shall be a son to Me, and I a Father to him, *and I will establish*" (1 Chr 22:10), the verb in the noun sentence "I a Father" is gapped and can be supplied from the previous clause, which contains a *yiqtol* form. In the second example the translation of the *w*qatal* form וְכֻתְּתוּ "They were broken in pieces" (2 Chr 15:6) by a future form is unusual, as the context is past. This verse is part of Azariah's speech to Asa, in a section which is usually considered as a historical account of Israel's past failures, "they turned to the LORD...and sought him, he was found by them...great disturbances afflicted...*they were broken in pieces*...for God troubled them" (vv. 4-6). However, the Septuagint translator considered it as a future prophecy (cf. v. 8 in which it is called the prophecy of Azariah son of Oded), translating *wayyiqtol* forms in verse 4 as futures "he shall turn them to the Lord...and He will be found," along with וְכֻתְּתוּ "and they *will fight* (πολεμήσει), nation against nation and city against city." The final (subordinate) clause, however, is translated with an aorist "for God troubled (ἐξέστησεν) them with every sort of distress." It seems as though the translator wanted to preserve the notion of prophecy and yet be faithful to preserve the tense/aspect of the verb in the subordinate clause. However, an awkward reading results.

v. Infinitive construct + w*qatal > Future Indicative (3)

In 1 Chronicles 23:32 the *w*qatal* form "*and they shall keep*" follows a noun "their duty is to..." and a series of infinitive constructs. The other two *w*qatal* forms follow infinitive construct purpose clauses. The first וְשָׁמַעְתָּ translated as a confident assertion "and *you shall hear* (ἀκούσῃ)" (2 Chr 6:21) follows two infinitive construct purpose clauses "that your eyes may be (לִהְיוֹת) open" and "that you may hear (לִשְׁמֹעַ)" (v. 20), which are dependent on a jussive "let your word be confirmed (יֵאָמֵן)" (v. 17) continued by a *w*qatal* form וּפָנִיתָ "and may you regard" (v. 19). The other example is "so that My name will be there forever; My eyes and My heart *will be* there" (7:16)

f. Wᵉqatal > Present Participle (2 = 1.56%)

The two *wᵉqatal* forms translated by present participles occur in sequence in narrative and follow a *qatal* form (2 Chr 12:11). Instead of treating the two *wᵉqatal* forms as sequential past durative forms after a *qatal* בָּאוּ הָרָצִים וּנְשָׂאוּם וֶהֱשִׁבוּם "the guards would come *and bear* them *and would then bring them back* to the guardroom" the translator interprets them as noun subjects (perhaps as substantive Hebrew participles?) of the *qatal* form εἰσεπορεύοντο οἱ φυλάσσοντες καὶ οἱ παρατρέχοντες καὶ οἱ ἐπιστρέφοντες "the guards and *the footmen* and *those who returned* to meet the footmen went in."

g. Wᵉqatal > Aorist Subjunctive (26 = 20.31%)

The translation of *wᵉqatal* forms by the aorist subjunctive is the second most common equivalent. Most of the examples are due to constraints of the grammar of the target language.

i. Yiqtol + wᵉqatal > Aorist Subjunctive (10)

The *wᵉqatal* forms translated by aorist subjunctives frequently follow a conditional clause (indicated by the conjunctions אִם or כִּי) translated by ἐάν and the subjunctive and are considered as continuing the protasis of the condition (2 Chr 6:22, 24, 34; 7:19, 10:7). The apodosis usually contains a future form (see above).[74] One *wᵉqatal* form continues פֶּן "lest" and a *yiqtol* form (1 Chr 10:4—translated by μή and the subjunctive), and one continues לְמַעַן "in order that" and a *yiqtol* form (1 Chr 28:8—translated by ἵνα and the subjunctive). Both *wᵉqatal* forms are translated by aorist subjunctives and reflect the standard Greek use following the particles μή (with the sense of *lest*) and ἵνα.

In 2 Chronicles 6:19 a *wᵉqatal* form continues a *yiqtol* jussive form (that was translated by an imperative) in verse 17 "Let your word be confirmed...and *may you regard.*" The aorist subjunctive is unusual, with an optative of wish being more standard Greek.[75]

---

[74] In 2 Chronicles 6:29 a relative אֲשֶׁר and a *yiqtol* are translated as an indefinite relative [ἣ ἐάν] and an aorist subjunctive, literally, "every prayer, every petition what [ever] shall be for any individual."

[75] The optative is only used rarely in Chronicles (seven times—1 Chr 12:17<18>; 21:3; 22:12; 2 Chr 6:41; 24:22), and all of them are optatives of wish translating jussive *yiqtols*. However, the optative is common in other books of the Bible, especially

In 2 Chronicles 32:4 a *wᵉqatal* form continues a *yiqtol* with a future sense, "Why should the Assyrian kings come *and find* water?" The translator translates the *yiqtol* form by μή and an aorist subjunctive and translates the *wᵉqatal* form with the same force, having the sense, "lest the Assyrian kings come *and find* water."

ii. Wᵉqatal + wᵉqatal > Aorist Subjunctive (15)

All of the *wᵉqatal* forms that continue another *wᵉqatal* form are part of a complex protasis of a conditional (underlined below), which begins with the particle אִם and a *yiqtol* form (and is translated by ἐάν and the subjunctive, e.g., "If someone sins against another and is required to take an oath *and comes* [and] swears" (2 Chr 6:22, so also v. 24 (3); 7:19 (3); 10:7), or the condition is implied "*when* any foreigner...*comes and prays*" (2 Chr 6:32 (2), so also vv. 37 (3), 38 (2)).

iii. Noun sentence + wᵉqatal > Aorist Subjunctive (1)

In 2 Chronicles 6:32 a *wᵉqatal* form which follows a noun sentence וְגַם אֶל־הַנָּכְרִי אֲשֶׁר לֹא מֵעַמְּךָ יִשְׂרָאֵל הוּא וּבָא can be literally translated "And also [with reference] to the foreigner, who is not of your people Israel, and he comes." It also functions as an implied conditional, "If [there is] a foreigner...and he comes." At least this seems to be the way the translator understood it, using aorist subjunctives to translate the *wᵉqatal* forms that follow.

h. Wᵉqatal > Present Subjunctive (2 = 0.17%)

The two *wᵉqatal* forms translated by a present subjunctive occur in the protasis of a conditional. The first follows אִם and a *yiqtol* form, the second, the other *wᵉqatal* form. The conditional clause is actually functioning as a wish. "Oh (אִם > ἐάν "I wish...") that you would bless me and enlarge (πληθύνῃς present subjunctive) my border, and that your hand might be (ᾖ present subjunctive) with me" (1 Chr 4:10). These occur in reported speech.

---

the poetic books of Job (120 times) and Psalms (90 times), occurring 554 times in the Septuagint according to *GRAMCORD*.

i. W^eqatal > Aorist Imperative (4 = 3.13%)

All the *w^eqatal* forms translated by aorist imperatives follow imperatives and continue the volitional force of the imperative, for example, "Go and *tell,*" (lit., "and you shall tell," 1 Chr 17:4; so also 19:5; 21:10; 2 Chr 18:33). They all occur in reported speech.

j. W^eqatal > Adjective (1 = 0.78%)

The *w^eqatal* form translated by an adjective follows a *qatal* stative form and translates a stative form, זָקֵן וְשָׂבַע "David was old *and full* of days" (1 Chr 23:1). This is another example of a stative verb form being replaced by an adjective as in rabbinic Hebrew (see note 23 above).

k. W^eqatal > Adverb (1 = 0.78%)

The *w^eqatal* form translated by an adverb follows a *qatal* form "He built the wall...and carried it around (וַיְסָבֵּב)" translated by the adverb κυκλόθεν which functions as an adjective (2 Chr 33:14). The translator had the adverb κυκλόθεν modify the noun from the previous clause rather than translate the *waw* preceding the verb which would indicate the beginning of a new clause.

l. Summary

The translator was able to successfully distinguish between sequential and coordinated *w^eqatal* forms from the environment, in particular from the verbal form that precedes them. The translator did not have any problem recognizing the two kinds of *w^eqatal* forms and was quite comfortable using a Greek future for a form that was probably only functioning as a coordinated past form at the time of translation, at least in spoken Hebrew. Future indicatives account for slightly less than half of the sequential *w^eqatal* forms. About 22% of the *w^eqatal* forms are translated by subjunctives (mostly due to the constraints of Greek grammar). A large number of futures and subjunctives continue an apodosis or a protasis in a conditional. At times the translator translated *w^eqatal* forms as futures when they continue a *yiqtol* with the force of a jussive wish. Perhaps the translator was just defaulting to the common equivalent, or perhaps this indicates that the translator considered them as confident assertions of future events. Perhaps the use of the future in these assertions indicates the confidence of the translator in God and His word (cf. 2 Chr 6:17-30, coming from the mouth of Solomon).

About a quarter of *wᵉqatal* forms are translated by past indicative forms (mostly aorists), and these mostly reflect coordinated *wᵉqatal* forms. The coordinated (non-sequential) *wᵉqatal* forms were translated by the standard equivalent for a *qatal* form, an aorist, rather than a Greek form that may be more appropriate according to the discourse, such as an imperfect, a pluperfect, or a circumstantial present participle to indicate background, antecedent, or simultaneous action. The translator used imperfects only in one place for iterative past action (2 Chr 33:6) and used perfects only twice for resultant states deriving from past actions but relevant up to the time of speaking (7:16; 29:19). One time a coordinated *wᵉqatal* form in past time is taken as a future prophecy (15:6). Perhaps the translator was defaulting to the common equivalent for this form.

4. Yiqtol

The majority of the *yiqtol* forms are found in reported speech, with about 68% in main clause reported speech and the majority of the subordinate clause *yiqtol* forms also in reported speech. The most common equivalent to the *yiqtol* is the Greek future, but, as can be seen below, less than half of the *yiqtol* forms were translated into futures by the translator of Chronicles. Since the *yiqtol* forms in classical biblical Hebrew (but not in rabbinic Hebrew) express imperfective aspect and occur in the past, present, future, omni-temporal, and timeless contexts, they correspond to Greek past forms (such as the imperfect), present, and future forms. The modal or volitive sense of the *yiqtol* corresponds more closely to the Greek non-indicative moods, the subjunctive (especially the aorist subjunctive), imperative, and optative, which account for about 37% of the translation equivalents in Chronicles.[76] Many of these, but not all, reflect the long first person

---

[76] While the *yiqtol* forms are considered to have imperfective aspect they are translated by imperfective Greek forms (present or imperfect) only in about 14% of the time. They are translated 45.87% of the time by the future indicative and 23.65% of the time by the aorist subjunctive, which, from an aspectual point of view, are considered neutral and perfective respectively. However, some also consider the

(cohortative) and short third person (jussive) modifications of the prefix form, which are included here with other *yiqtol* forms. The few aorist forms mostly reflect the archaic use of *yiqtol* as a preterite. The *yiqtol* form with past durative sense is also archaic, being replaced by a periphrastic participle with הָיָה in contemporary Hebrew.

When a *yiqtol* form is preceded by the conjunction *waw*, it usually reflects a coordinated *yiqtol* form without indicating sequentiality. Sometimes the *wᵉyiqtol* form has a purpose sense, especially following a volitive form.[77] Often the subject of the *wᵉyiqtol* form differs from the preceding verbal form, and sometimes the action or state of the *wᵉyiqtol* form is simultaneous with or even temporally preceding the verb before it. The *wᵉyiqtol* forms are mostly preceded by a *yiqtol* form, a *wᵉyiqtol* form, an imperative, or another volitive form. The few *yiqtol* forms that occur in narrative reflect its imperfective or durative past use.

The following table gives the breakdown on how the *yiqtol* forms in Chronicles were translated into Greek (with the included *wᵉyiqtol* forms given in square brackets [ ] and underlined in the verse references).

TABLE 5: THE TRANSLATION OF *YIQTOL* FORMS

YIQTOL	TOTAL	Percentage	Narrative Main Clauses (%)	Reported Speech Main Clauses	Subordinate Clauses
Aorist Indicative	13 [3]	3.7 [5.56]	9 (33.3) [2] [66.7]	1 [1]	3 (3.5)
Imperfect Indicative	15 [2]	4.27 [3.7]	10 (37.0)	3 [2]	2
Perfect Indicative	1	0.28		1	
Present Indicative	9	2.56		5	4 (4.7)
Future Indicative	161 [29]	45.87 [53.7]	4 (14.8)	134 (56.1) [29] [56.9]	23 (27.1)
Aorist Participle	1	0.29			1
Present Participle	1	0.29			1
Aorist Infinitive	4 [1]	1.14 [1.85]		3 [1]	1
Present Infinitive	1	0.29	1		

---

future as imperfective in the sense of expressing incomplete action (i.e., the action has not yet taken place).

[77] Cf. the section on *yiqtol* forms in chapter 3, note 29, and Baden's conclusion in, "The *wᵉyiqtol* and the Volitive Sequence," 150. See also note 91.

Aorist Subjunctive	83 [7]	23.65 [12.96]		36 (15.1) [7] [13.7]	47 (55.3)
Present Subjunctive	4	1.13		1	3 (3.5)
Aorist Imperative	23 [5]	6.55 [9.3]		23 (9.6) [5] [9.8]	
Present Imperative	19 [2]	5.41 [3.7]		19 (7.8) [2] [3.9]	
Aorist Optative	6 [1]	1.71 [1.85]		6 [1]	
Present Optative	1	0.29		1	
Noun	1	0.29		1	
Minus	8 [4]	2.28 [7.4]	3 (11.1) [1]	4 [3]	1
Total	351 [54]	100 [100]	27 [3]	239 [51]	85

Total 351
Aorist Indicative (13 = 3.7%) [3 = 5.56%]
Narrative Main Clauses (9) [2]
1 Chr 11:8; 20:3; 23:14; 2 Chr 4:5; 5:2; 21:10; 24:11 (2); 29:34
W^eqatal + *w^eyiqtol* 2 Chr 24:11
W^eyiqtol + *w^eyiqtol* 2 Chr 24:11
Reported Speech Main Clauses (1) [1]
2 Chr 34:25
Qatal + *w^eyiqtol* 2 Chr 34:25
Subordinate Clauses (3)
1 Chr 6:65<50>; 29:14; 2 Chr 31:18
Imperfect Indicative (15 = 4.27%)[78] [2 = 3.7%]
Narrative Main Clauses (10)
1 Chr 9:24; 2 Chr 1:16, 17; 5:9; 9:15, 16, 21; 24:11; 25:14 (2)
Reported Speech Main Clauses (3) [2]
1 Chr 17:5, 8; 2 Chr 10:14
Qatal + *w^eyiqtol* 1 Chr 17:5, 8
Subordinate Clauses (2)
1 Chr 12:22<23>; 2 Chr 9:4
Perfect Indicative (1 = 0.29%)
Reported Speech Main Clauses (1)
2 Chr 20:12

---

[78] Including one verb ἐβάρυνεν (2 Chr 10:14) with an identical aorist and imperfect form interpreted as an imperfect by *GRAMCORD* and one form ἤμην (1 Chr 17:8) incorrectly coded as an aorist.

Present Indicative (9 = 2.56%)[79]
Reported Speech Main Clauses (5)
1 Chr 21:3; 29:17; 2 Chr 18:17; 19:2; 25:19
Subordinate Clauses (4)
1 Chr 21:24; 2 Chr 2:6<5>; 6:20; 19:6

Future Indicative (161 = 45.87%)[80] [29 = 53.7%]
Narrative Main Clauses (4)
1 Chr 9:27, 28; 2 Chr 5:6; 23:19
Reported Speech Main Clauses (134) [29]
1 Chr 11:2 (2), 5, 6, 17, 19; 12:19<20>; 13:2, 12; 14:14, 15 (2); 16:10, 18, 32, 33; 17:4, 7, 9 (2), 10, 12, 13 (3), 14, 18; 19:2, 13; 21:2, 10, 13, 22 (2); 22:5, 8, 9 (2), 10 (2), 11, 13; 28:3, 6 (2), 9 (2), 20; 2 Chr 1:10 (2), 12 (2); 2:6<5>, 16<15> (3); 6:9, 16, 18, 21, 23, 25, 26, 27, 30, 33; 7:14 (1 + 2), 15, 18, 20 (2), 21; 8:11; 10:4, 9, 10 (2), 11, 14; 11:4 (2); 12:7, 8; 13:12; 15:2 (2), 13; 18:3, 5, 6, 10, 14, 19 (1 + 2), 20, 21 (3); 19:9, 10 (3), 11; 20:9 (1 + 3), 12, 20, 23:7; 24:20; 25:4 (2), 7, 8; 28:23 (2); 29:10; 30:6, 8, 9; 32:11, 12 (2), 13; 33:4, 7, 8; 34:25, 26, 28
W^eqatal + *w^eyiqtol* 1 Chr 14:15
Yiqtol + *w^eyiqtol* (8) 1 Chr 13:2; 2 Chr 2:16<15>; 7:14, 20; 12:8; 18:19; 20:9; 28:23
W^eyiqtol + *w^eyiqtol* (5) 2 Chr 1:10; 7:14; 18:19; 20:9 (2)
Imperative + *w^eyiqtol* (12) 1 Chr 21:2, 10, 22 (2); 2 Chr 1:10; 10:4; 18:5, 14; 19:11; 20:20; 30:6, 8
Qotel + *w^eyiqtol* (1) 2 Chr 10:9
Noun sentence + *w^eyiqtol* (2) 2 Chr 18:6; 29:10
Subordinate Clauses (23)
1 Chr 9:28; 17:11; 2 Chr 1:10; 2:12<11>; 5:6; 6:9, 18, 26 (2), 27 (2), 34, 36 (2); 12:8; 13:12; 18:13, 24; 23:4, 6; 25:4; 32:14, 15

Aorist Participle (1 = 0.29%)
Subordinate Clauses (1)
2 Chr 19:10

---

[79] Five forms interpreted as present indicatives by *GRAMCORD* would be better understood as second person plural present imperatives, which happen to have identical forms. For example, **Μὴ πονηρεύεσθε** "do my prophets no harm" is better taken as a present imperative (1 Chr 16:22—some MSS [e, f, p, y, and z] read a present subjunctive **πονηρεύησθε** here; so also 2 Chr 18:30; 20:15, 17; 32:15—see Appendix 1).

[80] Including **πορεύσῃ** (1 Chr 14:14) and **ποιήσω** (21:10) coded wrongly by *GRAMCORD* as aorist subjunctives (see Appendix 1).

Present Participle (1 = 0.29%)
Subordinate Clauses (1)
2 Chr 2:6<5>

Aorist Infinitive (4 = 1.14%) [1 = 1.85%]
Reported Speech Main Clauses (3) [1]
1 Chr 12:32<33>; <u>22:12</u>; 2 Chr 6:26
Yiqtol + *wᵉyiqtol* 1 Chr 22:12
Subordinate Clauses (1)
1 Chr 19:5

Present Infinitive (1 = 0.29%)
Narrative Main Clauses (1)
2 Chr 4:6

Aorist Subjunctive (83 = 23.65%) [7 = 12.96%]
Reported Speech Main Clauses (36) [7]
1 Chr 13:2 (2); <u>3</u>; 14:10; 16:22; <u>19:13</u>; 21:3, 12, 13; 22:13; 28:20 (2); 2 Chr 1:7; 6:42; 7:13, <u>14 (4)</u>, 17; 12:7; 14:7<6> (1 + <u>1</u>); 18:5, 14; 20:12, 15, 17; 25:16, 17; 28:13; 29:11; 30:8; 32:4, 7, 17
Yiqtol + *wᵉyiqtol* (2) 2 Chr 7:14; 14:7<6>
Wᵉyiqtol + *wᵉyiqtol* (4) 1 Chr 13:3; 2 Chr 7:14 (3)
Imperative + *wᵉyiqtol* 1 Chr 19:13
Subordinate Clauses (47)
1 Chr 4:10; 10:4; 19:12 (2); 21:18, 24; 22:13; 28:7, 8, 9 (2); 2 Chr 1:11; 2:14<13>; 6:16, 21, 22, 24 (2), 28 (4), 29 (2), 30, 33 (2), 34; 7:13 (3), 17, 19; 10:7; 15:2 (2), 13; 18:5, 13, 14, 15, 27; 20:9; 21:15; 30:9; 31:4; 32:18

Present Subjunctive (4 = 1.13%)
Reported Speech Main Clauses (1)
2 Chr 35:21
Subordinate Clauses (3)
2 Chr 6:31; 32:15; 33:8

Aorist Imperative (23 = 6.55%) [5 = 9.3%]
Reported Speech Main Clauses (23) [5]
1 Chr 16:30 (2), 31 (1 + <u>1</u>); 17:23; 21:17, <u>23</u>; 22:14; 2 Chr 1:9; 2:14<13>; 6:17, 41; 14:11<10>; <u>16:3</u>; 19:7; 23:3, 6, 14 (2); 24:5, <u>22</u>; 30:18; <u>36:23</u>
Yiqtol + *wᵉyiqtol* 2 Chr 24:22
Wᵉyiqtol + *wᵉyiqtol* 1 Chr 16:31
Imperative + *wᵉyiqtol* (2) 1 Chr 21:23; 2 Chr 16:3
Noun sentence + *wᵉyiqtol* 2 Chr 36:23

Present Imperative (19 = 5.41%) [2 = 3.7%]
Reported Speech Main Clauses (19) [2]
1 Chr 16:22, <u>31</u>; 22:13; 28:20; 2 Chr 6:40; 9:8; 15:7; 18:7, <u>12</u>, 16, 30;
20:15, 17; 23:6, 11; 30:7; 32:15 (3)
Weyiqtol + *weyiqtol* 1 Chr 16:31
Noun sentence + *weyiqtol* 2 Chr 18:12

Aorist Optative (6 = 1.71%) [1 = 1.85%]
Reported Speech Main Clauses (6) [1]
1 Chr 12:17<18> (1+ <u>1</u>); 21:3; 22:12; 2 Chr 6:41; 24:22
Yiqtol + *weyiqtol* 1 Chr 12:17<18>

Present Optative (1 = 0.29%)
Reported Speech Main Clauses (1)
1 Chr 12:17<18>

Noun (1 = 0.29%)
Reported Speech Main Clauses (1)
1 Chr 16:32

Minus (8 = 2.28%) [4 = 7.4%]
Narrative Main Clauses (3) [1]
2 Chr 4:2; <u>24:11</u>, 27
Weyiqtol + *weyiqtol* 2 Chr 24:11
Reported Speech Main Clauses (4) [3]
1 Chr <u>17:24 (2)</u>; <u>22:16</u>; 2 Chr 32:7
Weyiqtol + *weyiqtol* 1 Chr 17:24
Imperative + *weyiqtol* 1 Chr 17:24; 22:16
Subordinate Clauses (1)
1 Chr 22:9

a. Yiqtol > Aorist Indicative (13 = 3.7%)

Three of the *yiqtol* forms translated by aorist indicatives follow the
conjunction אָז "then Solomon *assembled*" (2 Chr 5:2; so also 21:10) or
the preposition עַד "until the other priests *had sanctified* themselves"
(29:34). These can perhaps be understood as the archaic preterite use
of the prefix form. In these cases, the aorist is the most natural Greek
tense form, having the same punctual or perfective aspect as the
preterite.[81] In 1 Chronicles 29:14 a *yiqtol* form with a modal sense

---

[81] One time a *yiqtol* form is translated by two aorists, but the text has problems. It
seems that the portion of the text that contains the *yiqtol* form
הָעִיר מִסָּבִיב מִן־הַמִּלּוֹא וְעַד־הַסָּבִיב וְיוֹאָב יְחַיֶּה אֶת־שְׁאָר הָעִיר "the city all
around, from the Millo in complete circuit; and Joab *repaired* the rest of the city" has

"who am I and who are my people that *we should be able* to offer?" is translated by an aorist, best understood as "that *we have been able*." The aorist makes sense according to the context, as David and the people had already offered material for the building of the temple.

In 2 Chronicles 34:25 a *wᵉyiqtol* form is translated by an aorist in reported speech following a purpose clause with a *qatal* form, which is also translated by an aorist. The *wᵉyiqtol* form is usually understood as a future "so that they have provoked me to anger… and My wrath *will be poured out* on this place and will not be quenched" (2 Chr 34:25) with the outpouring of wrath as an event future to the time of speaking. However, the Greek aorist has the sense of "My wrath *has been poured out* on this place and will not be quenched." Perhaps the translator took the *wᵉyiqtol* form as a *wayyiqtol* form following the *qatal* form. Both readings make sense in the context. A theological implication of the Greek reading is that God has already poured out His wrath because of the evil committed by the kings preceding Josiah. The experience of the people at the time of the narrative then was a reflection of this wrath already having been poured out rather than a future event.

The remaining *yiqtol* forms translated as aorists all occur in narrative and seem to have a past imperfective or durative force in Hebrew, but are translated as aorists with perfective or punctual aspect. For example, a *yiqtol* form, perhaps functioning as a summary statement, "thus David *did* (יַעֲשֶׂה) to all the cities of the Ammonites" is translated by an aorist (1 Chr 20:3). Customary actions represented by a *wᵉqatal* form followed by three *wᵉyiqtols* are all translated by aorists, "the king's secretary and the officer of the chief priest *would come* (וּבָא) and *empty* (וִיעָרוּ) translated ἐξεκένωσαν) the chest and *take it* (וְיִשָּׂאֻהוּ) and *return it* (וִישִׁיבֻהוּ) both translated by one Greek word κατέστησαν) to its place" (2 Chr 24:11).[82] Some of these past *yiqtols*

---

been omitted through parablepsis by homoioteleuton, and then the LXX has added a clause καὶ ἐπολέμησεν καὶ ἔλαβεν τὴν πόλιν "and he fought and took the city" (1 Chr 11:8). Some MSS agree with the MT and translate the *yiqtol* יְחַיֶּה by the aorist περιεποιήσατο "and he gained possession of."

[82] The switch to the *wᵉyiqtol* forms probably signaled a break in sequence perhaps due to an implied change in subject—the king's secretary and the officer of the chief priest came, but others emptied the chest and returned it to its place? The translator translated the *wᵉqatal* form as an aorist and followed by translating the *wᵉyiqtol* forms with two more aorists. Perhaps he understood them as *wayyiqtol* forms (since they are formally identical in unpointed text) with a past perfective sequential sense and that the king's secretary and the officer of the chief priest were the subjects of all of the verbs. The *wᵉqatal* form (וּבָא) would then be taken as a simple coordinated *qatal* form with a different subject to the verbs preceding it. However, the past durative *wᵉyiqtol*

could be interpreted as timeless, for example, the molten sea "*held* [or *could hold*] 3000 baths" (2 Chr 4:5),[83] and Moses' sons "*were to be reckoned* (יִקָּרְאוּ) among the tribe of Levi" (1 Chr 23:14; so also 6:65<50>).[84]

b. Yiqtol > Imperfect Indicative (15 = 4.27%)

The translation of *yiqtol* forms by the imperfect indicative in Greek reflects an understanding by the translator that these *yiqtol* forms have a durative past sense (in contrast to the translation of these forms by the aorist mentioned above). Sometimes temporal adverbs reinforce the durative notion. For example, "from day to day people *kept coming* (יָבֹאוּ) to David to help him" where the durative notion is strengthened by the adverbial expression "from day to day (לְעֶת־יוֹם בְּיוֹם)" (1 Chr 12:22<23>). So also "once every three years the ships of Tarshish *used to come*" (2 Chr 9:21). In 24:11 a *yiqtol* imperfect, "Whenever the chest *was brought*" is followed by three *wᵉyiqtol* forms, all having the force of habitual or customary activity. However, the translator translates only the first *yiqtol* with a Greek imperfect, two of the three *wᵉyiqtol* forms are translated by aorists, and one is not translated. In 25:14, which reads "After Amaziah came from the slaughter of the Edomites, he brought (וַיָּבֵא) the gods of the people of Seir, set them up (וַיַּעֲמִידֵם) as his gods, and *worshipped* (יִשְׁתַּחֲוֶה) them, *making offerings* (יְקַטֵּר) to them," two *yiqtol* forms are set in contrast to the preceding *wayyiqtol* forms, perhaps to stress the repeated or customary nature of the acts of worshipping and offering. The translator also captures this contrast using aorists and imperfects to translate the *wayyiqtol* and *yiqtol* forms respectively. In another example the translator translates יַעֲלֶה "went into" by two imperfects ἐπῆσαν (2 Chr 9:15) and ἀνεφέρετο (v. 16).

---

makes better sense in the context. Interestingly, the summary statement which follows uses a *qatal* form, "So *they did* (עָשׂוֹ) day after day," which is translated by an imperfect (ἐποίουν). Perhaps this indicates a contextual contrast.

[83] Cf. the translation by S. R. Driver for the parallel passage in 1 Kings 7:26 "*used to* or *would* contain" in *A Treatise on the Use of the Tenses in Hebrew and Some Other Syntactical Questions* (Grand Rapids: Eerdmans, 1998), 34.

[84] Perhaps the writer of Chronicles is contrasting between Moses' sons (who are Levites but not part of the special priestly class reserved for Aaron's sons) and Aaron's sons using different Hebrew verb tenses. Perhaps the *yiqtol* form (in v. 14) referring to Moses' sons is in contrast to the *wayyiqtol* form in v. 13 referring to the sons of Aaron "set apart (וַיִּבָּדֵל, translated by the aorist καὶ διεστάλη) to consecrate the most holy things." The translator of Chronicles levels this distinction by using aorists for both verbs.

This may be to offset a *wayyiqtol* form "he made the shields" with (background) information about how much gold *went into* the shield.

Three times a *yiqtol* form of הָיָה is translated by the past tense of εἰμί, which occurs only in the imperfect in the past time. They have habitual or customary sense, e.g., "the gate keepers *were* (i.e., *used to be*)" (1 Chr 9:24). The other two examples are translations of וָאֶהְיֶה "I have been" by the imperfect of the verb "to be" ἤμην (17:5, 8). These may have been understood as *wayyiqtol* forms, although the force of the verbs is not sequential "I have not lived in a house…but *I have been* from tent to tent…I took you…and *I have been* with you in every place."[85]

c. Yiqtol > Perfect Indicative (1 = 0.28%)

The only perfect indicative form used to translate a *yiqtol* form occurs in 2 Chronicles 20:12, "we *do not know* (לֹא נֵדַע) what to do." This is due to the constraints of the target language. The Greek verb οἶδα used is perfect in form but considered present in meaning.[86]

d. Yiqtol > Present Indicative (9 = 2.56%)

A number of the *yiqtol* forms translated by presents could be considered timeless or omni-temporal. The present indicative is

---

[85] These first person singulars are analyzed as coordinated imperfects by *GRAMCORD*. The secondary past durative sense of the imperfect certainly fits the context "I have lived in a tent—v. 5, and I have been with you v. 7). However, others interpret them as *wayyiqtol* forms (e.g., Japhet, *Chronicles*, 331, Todd S. Beale and William A. Banks, *Old Testament Parsing Guide* (Chicago: Moody Press, 1986), and John Joseph Owens, *Analytical Key to the Old Testament*. Vol. 2. (Grand Rapids: Baker, 1992). Usually the short form of הָיָה distinguishes the *wayyiqtol* form (i.e., the first person singular וָאֱהִי as in Judg 18:4; Neh 1:4; 2:11, 13, 15 (2); Job 30:9; Ps 18:23; 38:14; 69:11; 73:14; Ezek 11:16) from the coordinated *yiqtol* form (i.e., וְאֶהְיֶה as in Gen 26:3; 31:3). However, there is one shortened form that seems to have a coordinated rather than a consecutive sense (Hos 13:7), and there are a number of longer forms that seem to have consecutive sense, although most of them could also be interpreted as coordinated durative past time verbs (i.e., וָאֶהְיֶה 2 Sam 7:6, 9; 22:24; 1 Chr 17:5, 8; Job 7:20; Ps 102:7; Prov 8:30 (2); Hos 11:4). The Masoretes also considered all of these longer forms consecutive, pointing the *waw* with a *qamets*, rather than coordinated, which would be pointed with a *shewa*. Waltke and O'Connor consider these long examples in the first person examples of *waw* with the pseudo-cohortative, *Biblical Hebrew Syntax*, 544 (see especially note 2 on that page).

[86] An almost identical structure הֲלֹא תֵדְעוּ "*Do you* not *know*" is translated by a future form οὐ γνώσεσθε "*you shall* not *know*" (2 Chr 32:13—see section e. para. 6 below).

appropriate in rendering these expressions into Greek, e.g., God "you *take pleasure* (תִּרְצֶה) in uprightness" becomes, "you *love* (ἀγαπᾷς) righteousness" (1 Chr 29:17). Also "heaven and highest heaven *cannot contain* (יְכַלְכְּלֻהוּ) Him" is translated by the Greek present φέρουσιν (2 Chr 2:6<5>). One *yiqtol* form, which represents action future to the time of speaking "may you heed the prayer that your servant *prays* (יִתְפַּלֵּל) toward this place," is translated as a present προσεύχεται, with omni-temporal force (2 Chr 6:20). Other *yiqtols* with omni-temporal or customary force are also rendered by the present, "he does not prophesy" (18:17) and "you do not judge" (19:6).

Three times a *yiqtol* form is translated by a present indicative in questions, "why *do* you *seek*?" (1 Chr 21:3), "why *do* you *love* those who hate the Lord?" (2 Chr 19:2), and "why *do* you *provoke* trouble?" (2 Chr 25:19).[87] These cases could be considered as examples of present *yiqtol* forms with the action or state going on at the time of speaking.

In 1 Chronicles 21:24 a *yiqtol* form "I *will buy* them for the full price" is translated by a present. Perhaps the translator sees the action of buying initiated in the present (similar to a performative), at least in the intention or volition of the speaker, and carrying over into the future time "I am buying them."[88]

e. Yiqtol > Future Indicative (161 = 45.87%)

This is the most common Greek equivalent for the *yiqtol* forms with almost half of the *yiqtol* forms translated into Greek futures. Although the *yiqtol* form has a broader range of meanings than the Greek future, ranging from durative past to a modal volitive form, the translator occasionally employed a Greek future to translate a *yiqtol* form with one of these senses.

The future is used in standard ways in Greek to translate predictions, e.g., "*he will desert* to his master Saul" (1 Chr 12:19<20>),

---

[87] Twice לָמָּה is translated by ἵνα τί, but the verb that follows is a present indicative (ζητεῖ 1 Chr 21:3; συμβάλλεις 2 Chr 25:19) rather than a subjunctive, which is the regular form following ἵνα, which is normally used to indicate purpose. However, לָמָּה is most commonly rendered by ἵνα τί and an indicative in the Septuagint. This also occurs six times in the New Testament (three times quoting the LXX with ἵνα τί written as one word ἱνατί). According to Robertson, in the structure ἵνα τί "τί is really the subject of [the aorist subjunctive] γένηται (ellipsis)", and "it is not unknown in Attic Greek," *Grammar of the New Testament*, 739. But in Chronicles six times לָמָּה is translated by another structure (1 Chr 17:6; 21:3; 2 Chr 24:20; 25:15, 16; 32:4) rather than ἵνα τί and an indicative.

[88] Cf. "Futuristic Present," Fanning, *Verbal Aspect*, 221 ff.

promises, e.g., "*I will deal* loyally with Hanun" (19:2), questions, e.g.,
"*will you go* with me to Ramoth-gilead" (2 Chr 18:3), and in the
apodosis of future conditions, e.g., "if you seek him, *he will be found* by
you; but if you forsake him, *he will abandon* you forever" (1 Chr 28:9
(2)).[89] It is also used for commands especially in the second person
instead of the imperative, particularly in formal legal settings, e.g.,
"Before one altar *you shall worship*" (32:12), but also for forceful
commands or prohibitions with לֹא and a *yiqtol,* as opposed to אַל and
a jussive, e.g., "*You shall not go up or fight* against your kindred" (11:4).[90]
Sometimes the statement may have the force of both an injunction
and a prediction, e.g., "*You shall* not *build* me a house" (1 Chr 17:4;
22:8; 28:3; 2 Chr 6:9).

There are also a few places where a Greek future is used when
another Greek form is more usual. For example, a future is used
instead of the aorist subjunctive for prohibitions (translating אַל and a
jussive—2 Chr 13:12, translated as a rhetorical question "*will you
fight?*" and in 25:7 with οὐ "the army *will* not *go* with you"), for
emphatic negation (with οὐ μὴ—2 Chr 32:15), and for deliberative
questions (1 Chr 11:19).

The future is also used to translate jussive *yiqtol* forms and would
usually be translated by imperatives or optatives (of wish). Most of the
time the *yiqtol* indicative and jussive are not formally distinct.
However, with certain verb forms (such as *lamed-he,* middle weak and
hiphil verbs) it is possible to distinguish the *yiqtol* indicative (long form)
from a jussive (short form). There are a number of examples where a
short (jussive) form of these verbs is translated by a future, e.g.,
יְהִי יְהוָה עִמָּךְ "YHWH *be* with you" is translated as a confident
assertion ἔσται μετὰ σοῦ κύριος "the Lord *shall be* with you" (1 Chr
22:11). Most of the other examples are *wᵉyiqtol* forms indicating wishful
purpose, which are translated as a confident assertion by the
translator, e.g., וְיָשֹׁב מִמֶּנּוּ חֲרוֹן אַפּוֹ "so that his fierce anger *may turn
away* from us" translated καὶ ἀποστρέψει τὴν ὀργὴν θυμοῦ αὐτοῦ

---

[89] They occur 22 times in future conditions (1 Chr 22:13; 28:9 (2); 2 Chr 6:16, 23,
25, 27, 30, 33; 7:14 (3), 20 (2); 15:2 (2); 20:9 (4); 30:9; 33:8).

[90] The expression לֹא תַעֲלֶה "*You shall* not *go up*" which is translated οὐ πορεύσῃ
(1 Chr 14:14) is interpreted by *GRAMCORD* as a third person singular aorist
subjunctive. However, this form is better understood as a future (three forms: the
future second person singular middle voice, the aorist subjunctive second person
middle voice, and the third person singular active forms are identical).

"and *He will turn* His fierce anger" (2 Chr 29:10; so also 30:6, 8; 18:19; 19:11).

The future form is commonly used to translate *wᵉyiqtol* clauses which have some force of purpose, especially following imperatives, "bring me a report, *so I may know*" (1 Chr 21:2; so also 21:10, 22 (2); 2 Chr 1:10 (2)),[91] or a promise with God as the subject, "Go up, *and* God *will give* it" (2 Chr 18:5, so also 10:4; 18:14; 19:11; 20:20; 30:6, 8). Most of the *wᵉyiqtol* forms have different subjects from the preceding verb, and this can have the effect of breaking up the sequentiality of actions, even though they may follow temporally; for example, two *wᵉyiqtol* forms, which follow cohortative *yiqtols*, "let us send...*so that they will gather*" (1 Chr 13:2), and "I will sacrifice...*so that they will help me*" (2 Chr 28:23). Others follow imperatives (1 Chr 21:2, 10; 21:22 (2); 2 Chr 1:10; 10:4; 18:5, 14; 19:11; 30:6, 8). In other cases the grammatical subject is the same, but the actual agents of the action were quite likely to be different, e.g., "we will cut timber...*and we will bring*" (2 Chr 2:16<15>), or sequence is not important, such as, "I will hear...*and I will forgive*" (7:14), and "I will cast out...*and I will make* it a byword (7:20; so also 12:18).

One time a *yiqtol* of the verb יָדַע "to know" in the expression הֲלֹא תֵדְעוּ מֶה עָשִׂיתִי "*do you* not *know* what I have done?" is translated by a future οὐ γνώσεσθε ὅ τι ἐποίησα "*you shall* not *know* what I have done" (2 Chr 32:13) when a present would be more appropriate. The Greek translation implies that it is not possible to know all that the Assyrians have done to all the peoples of the lands. The statement in Greek lacks the force of the Hebrew rhetorical question.[92]

Six times a future occurs in narrative, which is unusual in Greek. They are as follows: "*they would spend the night* (παρεμβαλοῦσιν)" to translate יָלִינוּ (1 Chr 9:27),[93] "for they were required to count them when *they were brought in* (εἰσοίσουσιν) and *taken out* (ἐξοίσουσιν)" to

---

[91] The literal translation of the *wᵉyiqtol* clauses by futures does not really capture the force of purpose in Greek; it mainly indicates prospective action. A future indicative occasionally indicates purpose in Greek, but following ἵνα or ὅπως and not really by itself. Greek purpose clauses commonly consist of ἵνα or ὅπως and the subjunctive. Sometimes the rare future participle also carries the force of purpose. See note 77 and chapter 3, note 29.

[92] Perhaps in recognition of this awkwardness two MSS (b, e₂) read an aorist imperative καί γνῶτε "and *know* what I have done."

[93] One MSS reads a present indicative παρεμβάλλουσιν, which does not really help the reading, unless it is understood as a historic present.

translate יְבִיאוּם...יוֹצִיאוּם (9:28), "that they *could not be numbered* ἀριθμηθήσονται or *counted* (λογισθήσονται)" (2 Chr 5:6), and "so that no one *should* [Gk. *shall*] *enter* (καὶ οὐκ εἰσελεύσεται) who was in any way unclean" (2 Chr 23:19). While most examples reflect durative past use of the *yiqtol* form, the last example perhaps reflects a desire on behalf of the translator to stress the timelessness of the injunction rather than reporting it in narrative. The second and third examples could be considered as equivalent to the rare use of the future in indefinite relative clauses, although the translation lacks an indefinite relative conjunction such as ὅταν. The fourth, fifth, and sixth examples could be considered as equivalent to the rare use of the future in purpose clauses, although the translation lacks a purpose clause conjunction such as ἵνα.[94] The fact that a future was used in these examples could also indicate that the translator was "defaulting" to the common equivalent for the *yiqtol* forms rather than paying attention to the sense of the context.

f. Yiqtol > Aorist Participle (1 = 0.28%)

The aorist participle reflects the translation of a Hebrew relative clause with *yiqtol*, "every case *which will come*," by an attributive (relative) participle, κρίσιν τὴν ἐλθοῦσαν "the case *which comes*." The aorist has perfective aspect, viewing the action as a whole (2 Chr 19:10).

g. Yiqtol > Present Participle (1 = 0.28%)

The present participle also reflects the translation of a Hebrew relative clause with *yiqtol* "who am I that *I will build*?" by an attributive participle in Greek becomes "who am I, building?" (2 Chr 2:5<4>).

h. Yiqtol > Aorist Infinitive (4 = 1.14%)

Twice *yiqtol* forms in the context of a Hebrew infinitive are translated as infinitives in Greek. The first is a *wᵉyiqtol* form following a jussive *yiqtol* of wish "may the LORD grant you...*and may he give* you *charge* over Israel even to keep the law" (lit., 1 Chr 22:12). It is translated by

---

[94] Examples of futures with conjunctions that normally govern subjunctives occur rarely in the New Testament, for example, with ἵνα (Gal 2:4) and with ὃς ἄν (Mark 8:35).

an infinitive functioning as an object of the preceding verb, and the
meaning of the *wᵉyiqtol* form is changed from *give charge* to *be strong*:
"may the LORD grant you, both *to have strength* over Israel and to keep
and do the law." In the second example, the *yiqtol* form follows an
infinitive construct and functions as a negative purpose clause, "when
heaven is shut up and *there is* no rain (2 Chr 6:26). The Greek infinitive
functions as a purpose clause. The resulting translations, containing
two or more infinitives in series, fit the context.

One *yiqtol* form is translated as an aorist infinitive as the object of a
verb of knowing (1 Chr 12:32<33>). One aorist infinitive is the
translation of a subordinate עַד אֲשֶׁר "until" clause with a *yiqtol* form
עַד אֲשֶׁר־יִצְמַח זְקַנְכֶם "until your beards have grown " by ἕως and a
genitive articular infinitive ἕως τοῦ ἀνατεῖλαι (1 Chr 19:5). This is a
little unusual. The subjunctive is the usual verb following ἕως for
future events.[95]

i. *Yiqtol > Present Infinitive (1 = 0.28%)*

In the use of a present infinitive for a *yiqtol* form in 2 Chronicles 4:6,
seems to be influenced by the context, which has an infinitive of
purpose preceding it. The translator interprets the *yiqtol* form as having
the same sense of purpose.

j. *Yiqtol > Aorist Subjunctive (83 = 23.65%)*

Subjunctives in Greek can be divided into two categories, main clause
subjunctives (for first person exhortations and deliberative questions,
second person prohibitions with punctual aspect, and to indicate
emphatic negation), and subordinate clause subjunctives (usually with
a subordinate conjunction). About 35% (28) of the aorist subjunctives
in Chronicles that translate *yiqtol* forms are main clause subjunctives in
Greek, the rest occur in subordinate clauses.[96]

Both hortative and deliberative subjunctives occur in the first
person. Six hortative subjunctives translate exhortations (first person

---

[95] Cf. Acts 8:40, which has the same construction.
[96] There are 35 Hebrew main clauses in which a *yiqtol* form is translated by a
subjunctive. Some of them become subordinate clauses when translated into Greek.
For example, a coordinated *wᵉyiqtol* clause is translated into a conditional clause with
ἐάν and an aorist subjunctive (2 Chr 7:14). The three *wᵉyiqtol* clauses following it are
also translated by aorist subjunctives governed by the conditional.

cohortative *yiqtol* forms, three of them being *wᵉyiqtol* forms) "let us…" (1 Chr 13:2,[97] 3; 19:13; 2 Chr 14:7<6> (2); 25:17). Eight subjunctives translate deliberative questions "Shall I/we…?" (1 Chr 14:10; 21:12; 2 Chr 1:7; 18:5 (2), 14 (2); 20:12).[98]

Nine aorist subjunctives translate prohibitions (with אַל and a *yiqtol* jussive form) "do not…" (1 Chr 16:22; 22:13; 28:20; 2 Chr 6:42; 20:15, 17; 29:11; 30:8; 32:7). One time אַל and a *yiqtol* jussive are translated by the emphatic negative οὐ μή and a subjunctive (1 Chr 21:13). On five occasions לֹא and a *yiqtol* form are translated οὐ μή and a subjunctive (1 Chr 21:24; 28:20; 2 Chr 12:7; 28:13; 32:17).[99]

The remaining aorist subjunctives are subjunctives in subordinate clauses in Greek. They can be divided into conditional clauses, indefinite relative clauses, purpose clauses, and indefinite temporal clauses.

More than a third of the aorist subjunctives occur in conditional clauses that are rendered into Greek by ἐάν and a subjunctive.[100] This is the Greek *third class* condition used for tentative, present general or future more vivid conditions. Sometimes coordinated *yiqtol* clauses

---

[97] The Hebrew text has two cohortatives "*let us spread* נִפְרְצָה, *let us send abroad* נִשְׁלְחָה." They are translated εὐοδωθῇ ἀποστείλωμεν "*if it should be prospered, let us send* " (13:2). Perhaps the translator interprets the first cohortative as a *niphal* passive form.

[98] Two of the deliberate questions follow אִם and are translated by εἰ or ἤ and the aorist subjunctive (2 Chr 18:5, 14).

[99] The emphatic negative force is not indicated by any particular structure in Hebrew. The negative לֹא is translated both by the single negative οὐ as well as by the double or emphatic negative οὐ μή. In certain negative statements, the translator supplied this emphatic negative force, which is indicated below by the addition of the adverbial phrase [by any means]. Twice the emphatic negative statements come from the mouth of David, "*I will not* [by any means] *take* for the LORD what is yours [Ornan's]" (1 Chr 21:24), "He will not (the simple negative οὐ) fail you or [by any means οὐ μή] *forsake* you [Solomon]" (28:20), one time in God's mouth "my wrath *shall not* [by any means] *be poured* out on Jerusalem by the hand of Shishak" (2 Chr 12:7), one time in the mouth of Israelite leaders after being warned by the prophet Oded about taking Judean captives "*You shall not* [by any means] *bring* the captives in here" (28:13), and one time in the mouth of the Assyrian taunter "so the God of Hezekiah *will not* [by any means] *rescue* his people from my hand" (32:17); cf. 32:15, which has οὐ μή and a present subjunctive in the same mouth: "for *no* god of any nation or kingdom *has been able* to save" (see below).

[100] Conditionals beginning with the conjunction אִם followed by *yiqtol* are rendered into ἐάν and an aorist subjunctive 19 times (1 Chr 4:10; 19:12 (2); 22:13; 28:7, 9 (2); 2 Chr 6:16, 22, 24; 7:13, 17, 19; 10:7; 15:2 (2); 18:27; 20:9; 30:9). Six times כִּי followed by *yiqtol* is translated by ἐάν and an aorist subjunctive (2 Chr 6:24, 28 (4), 34), twice הֵן followed by *yiqtol* is translated by ἐάν and an aorist subjunctive (2 Chr 7:13), and one time ἐάν is inserted in the translation of a coordinated *yiqtol* clause, which is joined to a conditional clause.

follow the conditional particle and the conditional force carries over to the coordinated clauses (2 Chr 7:14 (4), 17). Hence, they are also translated by aorist subjunctives.

Five additional aorist subjunctives follow ἐάν in the translation of indefinite relative clauses, in which אֲשֶׁר is translated by a relative pronoun and ἐάν (2 Chr 6:29 (2), 33; 15:13; 18:13). Three times אֲשֶׁר clauses are given an indefinite relative sense by the addition of the particle ἄν to a relative pronoun (2 Chr 2:14<13>; 6:21, 30).

Four clauses contain aorist subjunctives that reflect the translation of purpose clauses in which *yiqtol* is governed by the conjunction לְמַעַן. It is translated into ἵνα (1 Chr 28:8) or ὅπως and the aorist subjunctive (2 Chr 6:33; 31:4; 32:18). One time אֲשֶׁר is translated by ὅπως "you asked for wisdom and knowledge *that you may judge*" and has the sense of purpose (2 Chr 1:11).[101] One time פֶּן and a *yiqtol* form is translated by μή and an aorist subjunctive to form a negative purpose clause (1 Chr 10:4).[102]

One time עַד and a *yiqtol* form is translated by ἕως οὗ "until" and an aorist subjunctive, "*until* your bowels *come out* (עַד־יִצְאוּ)" translated ἕως οὗ ἐξέλθῃ (2 Chr 21:15). This is a standard way in Greek to represent a temporal clause where the temporal element is in the indefinite future.

k. Yiqtol > Present Subjunctive (4 = 1.13%)

All four occurrences of *yiqtol* forms translated by present subjunctives reflect standard Greek uses. There are two main clause and two subordinate clause subjunctives. One time וְאַל and a *yiqtol* form is translated by μή and a subjunctive as a negative purpose clause "so that he will not destroy you" (2 Chr 35:21), and לֹא is translated by

---

[101] This reflects a rare and perhaps late biblical Hebrew (and especially rabbinic and Qumran Hebrew) use of the relative pronoun אֲשֶׁר. אֲשֶׁר is also translated by ἵνα as the object of a verb of swearing, "swear *to tell me* (אֲשֶׁר לֹא־תְדַבֵּר) nothing" which is translated ἵνα μὴ λαλήσῃς (2 Chr 18:15). Likewise, a כִּי clause as an object of a verb of speaking is translated ἵνα ἀναβῇ "tell David *that he should go up*" (1 Chr 21:18).

[102] Other examples of μή with an aorist subjunctive having negative purpose occur in with a וְלֹא *yiqtol* clause (2 Chr 7:13). Three times interrogative clauses with לָמָה "why?" are translated into Greek with a negative purpose. "Why should he bring sin on Israel?" becomes ἵνα μὴ γένηται "[do it not] *lest it become* a sin to Israel" (1 Chr 21:3). "Stop! Why *should you be struck?*" becomes πρόσεχε μὴ μαστιγωθῇς "take heed *lest you be scourged*" (2 Chr 25:16). "Why *should* the Assyrian kings *come?*" becomes μὴ ἔλθῃ "[we are doing this] *lest* the Assyrian kings *come*" (32:4).

the emphatic negative οὐ μή and a subjunctive (32:15). One time a conditional clause with אִם is translated by ἐάν and a subjunctive (33:8), one time a purpose clause with לְמַעַן is translated into ὅπως and a subjunctive (6:31).

l. Yiqtol > Aorist Imperative (23 = 6.55%)

Most of the aorist imperatives are third person imperatives "let him…." These are translations of *yiqtol* jussive forms. Sometimes they reflect a request from an inferior to a superior addressed in the third person, e.g., Ornan to David, "*let* my lord the king *do* what seems good to him" (1 Chr 17:23). Three times a second person *yiqtol* form (reflecting a strong or formal injunction) is translated by an imperative, twice by a second person imperative (1 Chr 22:14; 2 Chr 24:5) and one time by a third person imperative, "*you shall not* (לֹא) *slay* her in the Lord's house" becomes "*let her not die*" (23:14).[103] Twice two *yiqtol* jussive forms in the same verse are translated differently, the first by an optative (of wish) and the second by a third person imperative, e.g., "*May* your priests, O LORD God, *be clothed* with salvation, and *let* your faithful *rejoice* in your goodness" (2 Chr 6:41; so also 24:22).

m. Yiqtol > Present Imperative (19 = 5.41%)

Twelve of the present imperatives that translate *yiqtol* forms are prohibitions. Eleven are translations of אַל and a *yiqtol* jussive.[104] Many of the present imperatives are a translation of Hebrew stative verbs, such as יָרֵא translated by φοβοῦμαι "to fear" (1 Chr 22:13; 28:20; 2 Chr 20:15, 17), הָיָה (6:40; 9:8; 30:7), and רָפָה "to be weak" (15:7), which lend themselves to imperfective (durative) aspect.

---

[103] The aorist imperative is rare in prohibitions. It also occurs in the translation of the phrase וְאַל־יָבוֹא "Do not let anyone enter" which is translated by the aorist imperative μὴ εἰσελθέτω (2 Chr 23:6). Most of the time μή and an aorist subjunctive are used for perfective or punctual prohibitions. (Everywhere else in Chronicles אַל and a *yiqtol* jussive is translated this way).

[104] Found in 1 Chronicles 16:22; 22:13; 28:20; and 2 Chronicles 15:7; 18:7; 20:15, 17; 30:7; 32:15 (3). One example is an expanded translation of a *hiphil* וְאַל־יַסִּית "let him not deceive you" by μὴ πεποιθέναι ὑμᾶς ποιείτω "let him not make you to be persuaded" (2 Chr 32:15). The final prohibition is a translation of a *yiqtol* form preceded by the negative לֹא, לֹא תִלָּחֲמוּ "you shall not fight" translated μὴ πολεμεῖτε (18:20).

n. *Yiqtol > Aorist Optative (6 = 1.71%)*

The aorist optatives reflect a translation of jussives as optative of wishes (1 Chr 12:17<18> (2); 21:3; 22:12; 2 Chr 6:41; 24:22), a standard Greek use of the optative.

o. *Yiqtol > Present Optative (1 = 0.28%)*

The present optative reflects a translation of an apodosis of hypothetical condition, "if you have come to me in friendship, my heart *will be* (εἴη) knit to you" (1 Chr 12:17<18>); a standard, although rare, use of the optative.

p. *Yiqtol > Noun (1 = 0.28%)*

One time a *yiqtol* form יַעֲלֹץ "let it exult" is translated by the noun ξύλον "tree" perhaps understanding the Hebrew word עֵץ (1 Chr 16:32). Perhaps the translator was influenced by the expression הַשָּׂדֶה עֵץ "tree(s) of the field," which occurs at least ten times in the Hebrew Bible, such as, "the trees of the field shall clap their hands" (Isa 55:12; so also, Exod 9:25; Deut 20:19; Jer 7:20; Ezek 34:27). However, the translation does not preserve the parallel structure of the Hebrew text.

q. *Yiqtol > Minus (8 = 2.28%)*

The first two *yiqtol* forms that are not translated seem to be a classic case of parablepsis by homoioteleuton from the preceding verse, in which three clauses are omitted (1 Chr 17:24). Many MSS (b, e^{a2}, f, j, p, q, t, z, e₂) translate the two *yiqtol* forms by aorist subjunctives. Twice the verb *to be* is omitted in a noun sentence (1 Chr 22:9, 16). Twice only one of two verbs in close proximity is translated, וְיִשָּׂאֵהוּ וִישִׁיבֵהוּ "and take it and return it" is translated κατέστησαν "set it down" (2 Chr 24:11), and אַל־תִּירְאוּ וְאַל־תֵּחַתּוּ "do not be afraid or dismayed" is translated μὴ πτοηθῆτε "do not be alarmed" (32:7). One time an adverb and a verb from the same root יָסֹב...סָבִיב are translated by a single noun τὸ κύκλωμα (4:2). One time the Hebrew text itself is problematic and the Greek translation is quite removed from it (24:27).

r. Summary

Most of the *yiqtol* forms in the text of Chronicles function in a way similar to the way they functioned in Hebrew contemporary to the translator. They mostly occur in future contexts or have a volitive sense. Future time *yiqtols* are translated by futures, volitive *yiqtols* by imperatives, subjunctives, and optatives, and subordinate clause *yiqtols* translated by subjunctives (if the Greek subordinate clause required it) or by futures for verbs indicating events future to the time of speaking. The rare preterite *yiqtols* were mostly translated by aorists, past imperfective (durative) *yiqtol* forms were translated by imperfects (although on at least two occasions, they were rendered by aorists, both being *wᵉyiqtol* forms, perhaps interpreted as *wayyiqtol* forms, which in unpointed text are usually identical), and omni-temporal or timeless *yiqtols* were translated by presents.

Difficult readings occur when the translator rendered a *yiqtol* form by a future in narrative (instead of a durative past—e.g., 1 Chr 9:27, 28 (2)) or instead of a present (2 Chr 32:13). It seems that he was defaulting to the common equivalent, perhaps influenced by Hebrew contemporary to the translator, in which *yiqtol* was almost always a future, instead of translating according to the sense of the context.

B. Participles and Infinitives

1. Qotel (Active Participle)

As was mentioned in the previous chapter, the Hebrew participle is a verbal adjective that can function both as a verb (labeled predicative) and as an adjective or a substantive (labeled attributive). We focus more on the *qotel* form functioning as a verb used predicatively rather than on its adjectival/nominal function, except when an attributive Hebrew participle is translated as a relative clause with an indicative form.[105] We are particularly interested when the translator uses an

---

[105] An example of a relative clause translating an attributive participle is, כל הַמַּקְדִּישׁ "everyone who had dedicated" translated by an aorist indicative πᾶν ὁ ἡγίασαν (1 Chr 26:28; so also 29:8; 2 Chr 7:11; 11:16; 21:17). Hebrew participles are classified most simply into predicative (stressing the participle's function as a verb) and attributive (stressing the participle's function as an adjective or nominal), cf. Joüon and Muraoka, *Grammar of Biblical Hebrew*, 409-17. Waltke and O'Connor divide the attributive/adjectival function into three subcategories (as a substantive, adjective, or relative clause), *Biblical Hebrew Syntax*, 612-31. Participles occurring as the predicate of

indicative form to translate the Hebrew participle. Perhaps this reflects the temporal function of the participle in later biblical Hebrew, especially in the Hebrew spoken at the time of the translation.

Participles occur in all text types. The most common equivalent is the present participle, followed by present indicative, the perfect participle, and the imperfect (if we take into account only predicative participles). Present indicative forms occur mostly in reported speech and indicate an action going on simultaneously with the time of speech (present) or imminent action (present or future). Imperfect indicatives

---

a complement of a lexical (e.g., הָיָה) or non-lexical (i.e., implied) copula are considered predicative/verbal, unless they are preceded by a definite article, with a pronominal suffix, e.g., שֹׂנְאֶיךָ "those who hate you" (2 Chr 1:11), in construct state, e.g., סֹחֲרֵי הַמֶּלֶךְ "traders of the king" (1:16), or functioning as an indefinite substantive, e.g., אִישׁ־מֵבִין "a man of understanding" (1 Chr 27:32), in which case they are classified as attributive participles. Sometimes a predicative participle with or without an expressed copula functions as a substantive, e.g., with a copula הֵמָּה הָיוּ־לוֹ יוֹעֲצִים "they were his counselors" (2 Chr 22:4) or without a copula, "Jonathan...*was a counselor* (יוֹעֵץ)" (1 Chr 27:32). Cf. Joüon and Muraoka, "there is no periphrastic form if the qotel or qatal used with the verb הָיָה is used as a substantive or an adjective" (*Grammar of Biblical Hebrew*, 411). Sometimes this is difficult to determine. Most of these cases the participle is classified as functioning attributively.

When a participle functions as a substantive, it can also be difficult to categorize participles as participles or nouns. We follow the analysis of *GRAMCORD* in designating a form a participle or a noun. For example, *GRAMCORD* interprets the following as participles: אֹרְגִים "weavers" (1 Chr 11:23), וְגֵרִים "strangers" (16:19), הַמְשֹׁרְרִים "singers" (9:33), לַמַּחְצְצְרִים "trumpeters" (2 Chr 5:13), and וְהַסֹּחֲרִים הָרֹכְלִים "traders and merchants" (9:14), but interprets others such as הָרֹאֶה and הַחֹזֶה "the seer" as nouns, although historically they probably developed from a participle. The translator translates both הָרֹאֶה and הַחֹזֶה by present participles, הָרֹאֶה is translated ὁ βλέπων (1 Chr 9:22; 29:29); and הַחֹזֶה is translated ὁ βλέπων (29:29) and הַחֹזֶה ὁ ὁρῶν (21:9, 2 Chr 9:29; 12:15; 29:25; 33:18, 19).

We count as predicates only the participles in which their verbal function is predominant. For a finer distinction between the adjectival and verbal or predicate (adverbial) use of participles see Martin M. Culy, "The Clue is in the Case: Distinguishing Adjectival and Adverbial Participles," *PRSt* 30 (2003): 441-453. He argues that all oblique (non-nominative) case participles (apart from genitive absolutes) are attributive and not adverbial. We follow this distinction, for example, in 2 Chronicles 22:8, "Jehu...found the captains of Judah and the sons of Ahaziah's brothers *serving* Ahaziah; and he slew them," the participle *serving* is considered attributive since it modifies the object of the main verb and is translated by an accusative case participle in Greek (so also 1 Chr 10:8; 15:29 (2); 21:16; 2 Chr 18:16). See also John A. Cook, "The Hebrew Participle and Stative in Typological Perspective," *JNSL* 34/1 (2008): 1-19. He follows Stassen to classify intransitive predicates as a continuum in terms of "their degree of stability or permanence over time" on a time stability scale from unstable—location (John is in the kitchen.) and event (John walks.), to an intermediate—property (John is tall.), to the most stable—class (John is a carpenter.), here 6-7). He applies this approach to participles and statives, concluding that they are adjectives rather than nouns or verbs (see chapter 3, note 33).

are the most common indicative form in narrative followed by the aorist. A variety of indicative forms are used to translate participles. In addition, perfect, pluperfect, and future forms are all used. Perfect participles also occur the most in narrative. It does not come as a surprise that imperfective and stative Greek forms are preferred by the translator to translate Hebrew participles, since the Hebrew participle represents "an action as a state" and sometimes indicates ongoing action simultaneous to the event line verb.[106]

The following table gives the breakdown on how the *qotel* forms in Chronicles were translated into Greek.

TABLE 6: THE TRANSLATION OF *QOTEL* FORMS

(Predicative Forms Compared to the Total Number of *Qotel* Forms)

QOTEL	TOTAL	Percentage	Narrative Main Clauses (Clause %)	Reported Speech Main Clauses	Subordinate Clauses
Aorist Indicative	12 predicate 19 total	3.84	9 (9.2) 15 (4.4)	2 (4.4) 3 (2.7)	1 (4.8) 1 (2.2)
Imperfect Indicative	23 23	4.65	20 (20.4) 20 (5.9)		3 (14.3) 3 (6.7)
Perfect Indicative	2 2	0.40		1 1	1 (4.8) 1 (2.2)
Pluperfect Indicative	3 3	0.61	2 2	1 1	
Present Indicative	38 39	7.88	2 2	27 (60.0) 28 (25.5)	9 (42.9) 9 (20.0)
Future Indicative	3 4	0.81		2 2	1 (4.8) 2 (4.4)
Aorist Participle	0 34	6.87	0 26 (7.6)	0 7 (6.4)	0 1 (2.2)
Present Participle	43 203	41.01	36 (36.7) 161 (47.3)	5 (11.1) 32 (29.1)	2 (9.5) 10 (22.2)
Perfect Participle	24 46	9.29	20 (20.4) 35 (10.3)	2 7 (6.4)	2 (9.5) 4 (8.9)
Aorist Infinitive	1 3	0.61	1	1 2	
Present Infinitive	1 6	1.21	5		1 (4.8) 1 (2.2)
Aorist Imperative	1 2	0.4		1 2	

---

[106] Joüon and Muraoka, *Grammar of Biblical Hebrew,* 409. See chapter 3, note 33.

Present Imperative	0 1	0.02		0 1	
Adjective	6 21	4.24	3 14 (4.1)	2 5 (4.5)	1 (4.8) 2 (4.4)
Adverb	0 1	0.02		0 1	
Noun	2 79	15.96	2 52 (15.3)	16 (14.5)	11 (24.4)
Minus	5 9	1.82	4 6	1 3	
Total	164 495	100	98 340	45 110	21 45

Total 495
Aorist Indicative $(19 = 3.84\%)$
Narrative Main Clauses (15)
Attributive (6):
1 Chr 26:28; 29:8; 2 Chr 7:11; 11:16; 21:17; 31:6
Predicative (9):
1 Chr 5:8; 15:29; 2 Chr 4:4; 13:14; 22:12; 23:13; 24:14; 35:11, 24
Reported Speech Main Clauses (3)
Attributive (1):
2 Chr 31:10
Predicative (2):
1 Chr 16:19; 2 Chr 18:19
Subordinate Clauses (1)
Predicative (1):
1 Chr 16:33
Imperfect Indicative $(23 = 4.65\%)$
Narrative Main Clauses (20)
Predicative (20):
1 Chr 12:29<30>, 40<41>;13:7; 20:1; 2 Chr 7:3; 9:14 (2), 23, 24; 17:11 (2); 18:9, 11; 20:21; 24:12; 27:2; 29:28; 30:16; 32:23; 34:22
Subordinate Clauses (3)
Predicative (3):
2 Chr 9:21; 22:6; 34:10
Perfect Indicative $(2 = 0.40\%)$
Reported Speech Main Clauses (1)
Predicative (1):
2 Chr 32:10
Subordinate Clauses (1)

Predicative (1):
2 Chr 2:8<7>

Pluperfect Indicative $(3 = 0.61\%)^{107}$

Narrative Main Clauses (2)
Predicative (2):
1 Chr 11:15; 2 Chr 6:3
Reported Speech Main Clauses (1)
Predicative (1):
2 Chr 18:18

Present Indicative $(39 = 7.88\%)^{108}$

Narrative Main Clauses (2)
Predicative (2):
2 Chr 4:3 (2)
Reported Speech Main Clauses (28)
Attributive (1):
1 Chr 29:11
Predicative (27):
1 Chr 17:1; 21:10; 22:9; 28:9; 29:12, 13 (2); 2 Chr 2:4<3>; 9:7; 10:6,
9; 13:8, 10, 11; 18:15; 19:6; 20:2, 6, 11, 16; 24:20; 28:10, 13; 32:10,
11; 34:24, 28
Subordinate Clauses (9)
Predicative (9):
1 Chr 28:9; 2 Chr 2:5<4>, 9<8>; 6:19; 13:11; 16:9; 29:8; 30:7; 34:28

Future Indicative $(4 = 0.81\%)$

Reported Speech Main Clauses (2)
Predicative (2):
2 Chr 18:24; 21:14
Subordinate Clauses (2)
Attributive (1):
2 Chr 6:9

---

[107] Including παρεμβεβλήκει (1 Chr 11:15) and παρειστήκει (2 Chr 6:3), which
are incorrectly coded by *GRAMCORD* as perfect indicatives (see Appendix 1).

[108] Including τίκτεται (1 Chr 22:9) incorrectly coded by *GRAMCORD* as a perfect
indicative and ταράσσεται (29:11) incorrectly coded as a future. Excluding five
forms coded present indicative active third person plural by *GRAMCORD* better
taken as dative masculine plural present active participles (which are formally
identical). They all translate Hebrew attributive participles and are all preceded
by a dative masculine plural definite article in Greek. For example, in the clause
לַחֹטְבִים לִכְרוֹת הָעֵצִים נָתַתִּי "I will provide to your servants, *the woodsmen who cut* the
timber" the participle כֹּרְתֵי is translated by the dative participle (not present
indicative) τοῖς κόπτουσιν "to those who cut" (2 Chr 2:10<9>; so also 1 Chr 8:6,
13; 2 Chr 24:12; 31:4; 34:10—see Appendix 1).

Predicative (1):
2 Chr 28:23

Aorist Participle (34 = 6.87%)
Narrative Main Clauses (26)
Attributive (26):
1 Chr 1:46; 2:55; 4:38; 7:21; 12:1; 2 Chr 8:7; 20:22; 22:1; 24:26; 25:3, 24; 29:29; 30:21, 25 (2); 31:1; 32:31; 33:25; 34:9, 14, 30, 32, 33; 35:7, 17, 18
Reported Speech Main Clauses (7)
Attributive (7):
1 Chr 21:12; 2 Chr 20:12; 30:6, 9; 34:17, 21, 26
Subordinate Clauses (1)
Attributive (1):
2 Chr 5:11

Present Participle (203 = 41.01%)[109]
Narrative Main Clauses (161)
Attributive (125):
1 Chr 2:55; 4:23; 5:18 (3); 7:11; 8:6, 13 (2), 40; 9:2, 16, 19 (2); 10:4 (2), 5; 11:4, 5, 23, 39; 12:1, 8<9>, 32<33>, 33<34>, 35<36>, 36<37>, 38<39>; 13:6; 15:25, 26, 27 (2), 29 (2); 16:4, 5; 18:2, 6; 20:5; 21:15; 23:24; 25:1, 3, 7; 27:1 (3), 26; 28:18; 2 Chr 3:11 (2), 12; 4:4 (4); 8:10; 9:1, 4, 14; 10:17; 11:1; 12:10 (2), 11 (2); 14:8<7>; 15:3, 5 (2), 9; 16:2; 17:16, 19; 19:2; 20:18, 21, 23 (2); 21:9, 11; 22:1, 8, 11; 23:12 (2), 13; 24:12, 13; 25:5; 26:5, 7, 11 (2), 13; 28:9, 12, 15, 23; 30:6, 10, 22, 25; 31:4, 6, 16; 32:4, 22, 26, 33; 33:9, 18; 34:4, 9 (2), 10 (2), 12, 13, 22, 30, 32; 35:18, 25
Predicative (36):
1 Chr 6:32<17>, 49<34>; 8:40; 12:39<40> (2); 13:8; 15:24, 28 (2), 18:14; 2 Chr 4:5; 5:6, 12; 7:4, 6; 9:20, 21, 26; 17:12; 18:9 (2); 20:25; 22:9; 23:13; 26:21; 29:28 (2); 30:10 (3), 21, 22 (2); 36:16 (3)
Reported Speech Main Clauses (32)
Attributive (27):
1 Chr 11:2 (2), 6; 16:10; 22:15, 19; 23:5; 2 Chr 2:7<6>, 10<9> (2), 12<11>; 6:14, 16, 36; 7:18, 21; 13:9; 18:18; 20:7, 15, 20; 21:13; 23:7; 29:11 (2); 34:17, 27

---

[109] Including one present participle σαλπίζουσαι (2 Chr 29:28) analyzed by *GRAMCORD* as an aorist participle, six present participles analyzed as present indicatives (1 Chr 8:6, 13; 2 Chr 2:10<9>; 24:12; 31:4; 34:10), κατοικῶν (1 Chr 9:16) and λειτουργῶν (2 Chr 9:4) analyzed as nouns, and ποιῶν (18:14) analyzed as an adjective (see Appendix 1).

Predicative (5):
1 Chr 19:3; 21:12; 29:5; 2 Chr 6:14; 34:16
Subordinate Clauses (10)
Attributive (8):
1 Chr 4:40; 11:10; 19:3; 22:18; 2 Chr 15:5; 19:10; 23:6; 34:28
Predicative (2):
1 Chr 29:17; 2 Chr 18:7

Perfect Participle (46 = 9.29%)[110]

Narrative Main Clauses (35)
Attributive (15):
1 Chr 6:33<18>, 39<24>; 10:8; 21:5 (2), 16; 23:29; 25:7; 28:18; 2
Chr 5:6; 8:18; 9:7, 14; 26:15; 34:10
Predicative (20):
1 Chr 9:29; 12:15<16>; 15:27; 21:15, 16; 2 Chr 3:13 (2); 5:8, 12 (2);
7:6 (2); 9:18 (2), 19; 18:9, 34; 20:13, 24; 22:12
Reported Speech Main Clauses (7)
Attributive (5):
1 Chr 13:2; 2 Chr 2:13<12>, 14<13>; 18:16; 20:7
Predicative (2):
1 Chr 17:14, 24
Subordinate Clauses (4)
Attributive (2):
2 Chr 10:8; 26:18
Predicative (2):
1 Chr 19:5; 2 Chr 10:6

Aorist Infinitive (3 = 0.61%)

Narrative Main Clauses (1)
Attributive (1):
2 Chr 25:5
Reported Speech Main Clauses (2)
Attributive (1):
1 Chr 15:16
Predicative (1):
1 Chr 21:12

---

[110] Including a perfect participle εἰδότας analyzed by *GRAMCORD* as an aorist participle (2 Chr 8:18), ἀνωρθωμένος analyzed as a future participle (1 Chr 17:14) and as a present participle (1 Chr 17:24), περιεζωσμένος (15:27) and ἠτιμωμένοι (19:5) analyzed as pluperfect participles, and πεπληρωκὼς (12:15<16>) and καθεσταμένοι (2 Chr 34:10) analyzed as a perfect indicatives (see Appendix 1).

Present Infinitive (6 = 1.21%)
Narrative Main Clauses (5)
Attributive (5):
1 Chr 16:42; 26:29; 2 Chr 5:13 (2); 20:22
Subordinate Clauses (1)
Predicative (1):
1 Chr 21:12

Aorist Imperative (2 = 0.4%)
Reported Speech Main Clauses (2)
Attributive (1):
2 Chr 23:14
Predicative (1):
1 Chr 17:27

Present Imperative (1 = 0.2%)
Reported Speech Main Clauses (1)
Attributive (1):
2 Chr 23:4

Adjective (21 = 4.24%)
Narrative Main Clauses (14)
Attributive (11):
1 Chr 6:61<46>, 70<55>, 77<62>; 12:2 (2); 24:20; 25:8; 27:32; 28:18; 2 Chr 4:2; 26:13
Predicative (3):
1 Chr 4:9; 11:21, 25
Reported Speech Main Clauses (5)
Attributive (3):
1 Chr 17:21; 29:4; 2 Chr 1:11
Predicative (2):
1 Chr 16:25 (2)
Subordinate Clauses (2)
Attributive (1):
2 Chr 20:29
Predicative (1):
1 Chr 15:22

Adverb (Prepositional Phrase) (1 = 0.02%)
Narrative Main Clauses (1)
Attributive (1):
1 Chr 28:1

Noun (79 = 15.96%)

Narrative Main Clauses (52)

Attributive (50):

1 Chr 2:7; 4:23, 40; 6:33<18>; 9:30, 33; 10:3 (2); 12:24<25>, 33<34>; 15:16,[111] 19, 27; 18:15; 25:2; 26:14, 16; 27:29, 32, 33; 2 Chr 1:2, 16; 2:2<1>, 18<17>; 5:12; 8:10; 9:11; 14:8<7> (2); 16:1 (2); 17:17; 19:5; 20:21; 22:11; 23:8 (2), 20; 26:10, 20, 21 (2); 32:31; 34:8, 11, 12; 35:3, 15, 23, 25

Predicative (2):

1 Chr 21:20; 2 Chr 9:28

Reported Speech Clauses (16)

Attributive (16):

1 Chr 12:18<19>; 14:11; 16:9, 12; 17:6, 8, 10; 21:12, 22:9; 23:4; 2 Chr 6:36; 19:6; 25:8, 16; 26:23; 34:17

Subordinate Clauses (11)

Attributive (11):

1 Chr 17:10; 2 Chr 6:24, 28, 34; 16:12, 14; 18:16; 20:27; 22:3, 4; 26:10

Minus (9 = 1.82%)

Narrative Main Clauses (6)

Attributive (2):

1 Chr 12:2; 2 Chr 36:8

Predicative (4):

2 Chr 23:13; 33:17; 34:12, 13

Reported Speech Main Clauses (3)

Attributive (2):

1 Chr 16:24; 2 Chr 34:24

Predicative (1):

2 Chr 18:19

a. Qotel > Aorist Indicative (19 = 3.84%)

Seven attributive participles are translated by aorist indicatives in a relative clause in Greek. Many of these are preceded by כָּל and a definite article "all who..." (e.g., 1 Chr 26:28; 2 Chr 7:11; 11:16;

---

[111] This example is in indirect speech in Hebrew, but it is interpreted as direct speech in Greek.

21:17; cf. 1 Chr 29:8; 2 Chr 31:6, 10, which have only a definite article preceding).[112]

At least eight circumstantial participles are translated by aorist indicatives. All of them have a different subject (topic) than the verb preceding and perhaps also indicate simultaneous action in Hebrew, for example, "when their genealogy was reckoned…he *dwelt* in Aroer (1 Chr 5:8), "so they cried to the Lord, and the priests *blew trumpets* (מַחְצְרִים)" (2 Chr 13:14), "And one said this, while another *said* that" (18:19), "she looked…and the people rejoiced [adj. lit., were happy] and *blew* trumpets" (23:13), "while the priests sprinkled the blood…the Levites *skinned* [them]" (35:11), and "he died and was buried…. And all Judah and Jerusalem *mourned* for Josiah" v. 24).[113] It seems that the standard hypotactic use of the circumstantial participle in Greek (especially a genitive absolute as the subject differs from that of the main verb) would have been an appropriate way to render this structure; however, the translator did not use it in these cases. Sometimes the *qotel* form may have been interpreted (i.e., vocalized) as a *qatal* form by the translator.[114]

Three times הָיָה and a participle is rendered by an aorist in Greek, e.g., וַיִּהְיוּ מַעֲלִים עֹלוֹת בְּבֵית־יְהוָה תָּמִיד כֹּל יְמֵי יְהוֹיָדָע "and they *offered* burnt offerings (translated καὶ ἀνήνεγκαν ὁλοκαυτώσεις) in the house of the Lord continually all the days of Jehoiada" (2 Chr 24:14). According to the context with the adverbs *continually*, and *all the days* the Hebrew participle reinforces the ongoing iterative or habitual action. However, the translator did not use either the verb "to be" or a

---

[112] In addition, a relative in Greek translates one predicative participle. עוֹמֵד is translated by a relative in Greek ἣ ἐποίησαν "by which they made them" in the description of the building of the temple (2 Chr 4:4). The use of a relative to translate a Hebrew attributive participle is a little unusual. If anything, the translator preferred to translate a Hebrew relative clause with a Greek attributive participle especially if the relative was the subject of the clause (cf. note 57 above).

[113] One time a Hebrew periphrastic participle followed by a circumstantial participle is translated by a Greek periphrastic participle followed by an aorist "And *he was hidden* with them in the house of God six years while Athaliah *reigned* over the land" (2 Chr 22:12).

[114] The participle בָּא, which is formally identical to the *qatal* form, twice is translated by an aorist (1 Chr 15:29; 16:33). Perhaps the translator considered the form as a *qatal* form. In the first example the aorist fits the context (see the next footnote). However, the second example, "for He *is coming* to judge the earth כִּי־בָא לִשְׁפּוֹט אֶת־הָאָרֶץ" the translator has God *having* already *come* (ἦλθεν) to judge the earth, which seems a little awkward, unless it is referring to a past event in which God exercised His judgment (e.g., Noah's flood). The fact that there is no expressed subject with the participle (most Hebrew participles functioning as verbs have expressed subjects) perhaps compelled the translator to understand a *qatal* form here.

Greek durative form (such as an imperfect or a periphrastic participle) to indicate the iterative nature of the verb. Perhaps the translator was influenced by the *wayyiqtol* form וַיְהִי to use the common equivalent an aorist form (although the imperfect of εἰμί is mostly used to translate periphrastic structures). In the other examples the durative nature of the participle is not pronounced. In one example the participle גֵּרִים is functioning more as the substantive *strangers,* בִּהְיוֹתְכֶם...וְגֵרִים "when they were...*strangers*" which is translated καὶ παρῴκησαν "and they dwelt as strangers" with the notion of stranger contained in the prefix παρά (1 Chr 16:19).[115]

b. *Qotel > Imperfect Indicative (23 = 4.65%)*

All of the *qotel* forms translated as imperfects are predicative participles. They are either circumstantial participles or participles which the translator considered had iterative, customary, or habitual force. Most of the circumstantial participles have a different subject to the main verb and indicate action simultaneous with that of the main verb, such as: "they were there with David three days...those who were near to them, *brought* food (1 Chr 12:39<40>), "they carried the ark of God on a new cart...and Uzza and Ahio *drove* the cart" (13:7), "Joab led out the army...But David *stayed* at Jerusalem" (20:1), "the king of Israel and Jehoshaphat the king of Judah were sitting...and all the prophets *were prophesying*" (2 Chr 18:9-11), "Ahaziah...went down to see Jehoram...because *he was sick*" (22:6), "he did right in the sight of the Lord...but the people continued *acting corruptly*" (27:2), "and at the time the burnt-offering began...the whole assembly *worshipped*" (29:28), "and they stood...the priests *sprinkled* the blood" (30:16), "Hilkiah...went to Huldah (now she *lived* in Jerusalem)" (34:22). Sometimes the subject is the same but the action can be considered simultaneous, e.g., "all the sons of Israel, *seeing* the fire...bowed down" (7:3), "as they went out before the army and *said*" (20:21).

Examples of imperfects with iterative, customary, or habitual force are, "until now the greatest part of them *had kept* their allegiance" (1 Chr 12:28<29>), "for the king had ships which *went* to Tarshish; lit., the ships of the king *went*" (2 Chr 9:21), "and all the kings of the earth

---

[115] In the other example, the participle בָּא, in "and it happened when the ark of the covenant of the Lord *came,* וַיְהִי אֲרוֹן בְּרִית יְהוָה בָּא" is translated καὶ ἐγένετο...καὶ ἦλθεν (1 Chr 15:29). The verb הָיָה is really functioning as an introductory "and it came to pass" rather than a copula.

were seeking the presence of Solomon…. And *they brought*" (vv. 23-24),
"some of the Philistines *brought*…the Arabians also *brought*" (17:11),
"and many *were bringing* gifts" (32:23), "and the workmen who were
working (עֹשִׂים אֲשֶׁר translated οἱ ἐποίουν) in the house" (34:10).
One time a periphrastic Hebrew participle שֹׂכְרִים חֹצְבִים וְחָרָשִׁים
וַיִּהְיוּ "and *they hired* masons and carpenters" is translated by an
imperfect καὶ ἐμισθοῦντο (24:12) and has a similar iterative or
logical durative sense in Greek to the Hebrew. (The parallel section in
2 Kings 12:12 has a *wayyiqtol* form that is translated by an aorist).

c. *Qotel > Perfect Indicative (2 = 0.40%)*

Both perfect indicatives translate predicative participles in reported
speech. Both have present meaning. One of the perfect indicative
forms is the verb οἶδα "to know" which is perfect in form but has
present meaning, אֲנִי יָדַעְתִּי אֲשֶׁר עֲבָדֶיךָ יוֹדְעִים "I know that your
servants *are skilled* [lit., *know*]" translated ἐγὼ οἶδα ὡς οἱ δοῦλοί σου
οἴδασιν (2 Chr 2:8<7>). The other perfect indicative is the
translation of the participle בֹּטְחִים "On what *are you trusting*" by
πεποίθατε which emphasizes the resultant state "On what *have you
placed your trust*" and hence "what *do you trust*" (32:10).

d. *Qotel > Pluperfect Indicative (3 = 0.61%)*

The pluperfect forms are translations of predicative circumstantial
participles. Instead of translating them as simultaneous actions, the
translator considered them as actions that had occurred before the
time of the main verb and have a resultant state up to its time. "Now
three of the thirty chief men went down to the rock to David…while
the army of the Philistines *was encamped* (Gk. παρεμβεβλήκει, lit., had
already encamped) in the valley of Rephaim" (1 Chr 11:15). The
Hebrew text emphasizes the simultaneous action with the participle,
whereas the Greek specifies that the Philistines had *already* encamped
there prior to the action of going down. So also in the next two
examples, the pluperfect emphasizes the resultant state of the act of
standing that took place prior to the main verb, "Then the king turned
around and blessed all the assembly of Israel, while all the assembly of
Israel *stood*" (translated παρειστήκει, 2 Chr 6:3) and "I saw the Lord
sitting on His throne, with all the host of heaven *standing* (translated
εἱστήκει) on His right and on His left" (18:18).

e. Qotel > Present Indicative (39= 7.88%)

Most of the present indicatives translate predicative participles and occur in reported speech. Some reflect actions or states going on at the same time as the verb of speaking, for example, "behold, I *am dwelling* in a house of cedar" (1 Chr 17:1), "a great multitude *is coming* against you" (2 Chr 20:2, so also v. 11; 29:8; 30:7; 32:10, 11). Sometimes the present reflects the content of the verb of speaking, e.g., "we *give thanks* to you and *praise* your glorious name" (29:13), or has a performative sense, "I *offer* you three things" (1 Chr 21:10). Perhaps the translator considered these participles as present tense forms corresponding to their function in spoken Hebrew at the time of translation.

Other present forms reflect omni-temporal or timeless actions or states, especially referring to actions of God, for example, "for the Lord *searches* all hearts, and *understands* every intent of the thoughts" (1 Chr 28:9; so also 2 Chr 16:9), and מוֹשֵׁל "You are ruler" translated ἄρχεις and κυριεύεις respectively (1 Chr 29:12; 2 Chr 20:6).[116] They also may refer to general or customary human actions, "listen to the cry and to the prayer which Your servant *prays* before You" (6:19; so also 9:7—which is really an anarthrous attributive; 19:6), "we have priests *ministering* to the Lord who are descendants of Aaron" (2 Chr 13:10), and "*they offer* every morning and evening" (v. 11).

Sometimes the present has a future sense. This is also inherent in the Hebrew participle, especially with the particle הִנֵּה "behold," for example, "See, a son *shall be born* to you" translated τίκτεταί "is born" (1 Chr 22:9), so also "I now *am about to build*" (2 Chr 2:4<3>, 5<4>, 9<8>), and "behold, they *will come up* by the ascent of Ziz" (20:16; so also 34:24, 28).

Twice present indicatives occur in narrative, in the description of the calves surrounding the molten sea and the laver in the temple (4:3). Perhaps the translator used presents for the description because it still held true at his time?

---

[116] It is interesting to note that when מוֹשֵׁל is used to refer to God a present indicative verb is used. When it is used to refer to a man a present participle is used, e.g., ἡγούμενος (2 Chr 7:18 (attributive participle); 9:26). An attributive participle וְהַמִּתְנַשֵּׂא לְכֹל לְרֹאשׁ "and [You are] *one who is exalted* as head above all," is also used to refer to God. The reading is awkward and is translated into Greek "before Your face every king and nation *is troubled* ταράσσεται" (1 Chr 29:11).

f. Qotel > Future Indicative (4 = 0.81%)

The future occurs rarely and only in reported speech. The future sense is inherent in the Hebrew participle especially with the particle הִנֵּה "behold," for example, "behold, *you shall see* on that day" (2 Chr 18:24), and "behold, the Lord *is going to strike* your people" (21:14); so also an attributive participle הַיּוֹצֵא translated as a relative clause with a future ὃς ἐξελεύσεται "your son *who shall be born* to you [lit., *come out* from your loins]" (2 Chr 6:9). One time the translators used a future whereas most understand this as referring to a past event, "because the gods of the kings of Aram *helped* (מַעְזְרִים translated κατισχύσουσιν "*will strengthen*") them, I will sacrifice (אֲזַבֵּחַ) to them" (28:23). Perhaps the fact that the following verbs are future tense forms influenced the translator's decision to use a future.

g. Qotel > Aorist Participle (34 = 6.87%)

All the aorist participles are attributive participles (mostly preceded by a definite article). The participle usually refers to the agent of a punctual event. They function as equivalent to relative clauses. The translator preferred to translate certain verbs by an aorist participle. The most common are verbs of motion such as: הַבָּאִים translated by οἱ ἐλθόντες "who came" or a compound of it (1 Chr 2:55; so also 4:38; 12:1; 2 Chr 20:12, 22; 22:1; 30:25),[117] הַמּוּבָא translated by τὸ εἰσενεχθὲν "that was brought" (34:9) or τὸ εἰσοδιασθὲν "which had been brought" (34:14), שֹׁלֵחַ translated by τῷ ἀποστείλαντί "who sent" (1 Chr 21:12; so also 2 Chr 32:31; 34:26). Also common are הַנִּמְצָאִים translated by οἱ εὑρεθέντες "who were present, lit., found" (2 Chr 5:11; so also 25:24; 29:29; 30:21; 31:1; 34:17, 30, 32, 33; 35:7, 17, 18),[118] הַנּוֹתָר translated by ὁ καταλειφθεὶς "who were left" (8:7; so also 30:6; 34:21). Verbs referring to single events such as הַמִּתְקַשְּׁרִים or הַקֹּשְׁרִים translated by οἱ ἐπιθέμενοι "who conspired" (24:26; 33:25), and הַמַּכֶּה translated ὁ πατάξας "who struck" (1 Chr 1:46) and φονεύσαντας "who had murdered" (2 Chr 25:3) also occur as aorist participles.

---

[117] הַבָּאִים is translated one time οἱ εὑρεθέντες (2 Chr 30:25), four times τοῦ εἰσπορευομένου (1 Chr 27:1; so also 2 Chr 13:9; 23:7; 31:16), twice τῶν ἐρχομένων (2 Chr 28:9, so also v. 12), and one time by a relative and an aorist indicative ἠθέλησεν (7:11).

[118] הַנִּמְצָא is also translated by a relative clause and an aorist indicative twice (1 Chr 29:8; 2 Chr 21:17), and it is omitted one time (36:8).

h. Qotel > Present Participle (203 = 41.01%)

The present participle is the most common equivalent of Hebrew active participles. Certain verbs are frequently translated as present participles, especially those with durative sense, such as stative verbs, e.g., הַיֹּשְׁבִים οἱ κατοικοῦντες those "who dwelt" (1 Chr 2:55; so also 4:23, 40; 10:17; 8:6, 13 (2); 9:2, 16; 11:4, 5; 22:18; 2 Chr 10:17; 15:5; 16:2; 19:10; 20:7, 15, 18, 20, 23 (2); 21:11, 13; 22:1; 26:7; 30:25; 31:4, 6; 32:22, 26, 33; 33:9; 34:8, 27, 28, 30, 32; 35:18), καθημένου "enthroned" (1 Chr 13:6; so also 2 Chr 6:16; 18:9 (2), 18), or מַחֲזִיק χωροῦσαν "containing" (4:5). Present participles are also used for verbs referring to people who do an action habitually or customarily, e.g., נֹשְׂאֵי αἴροντες those "*who carried* (shields)" (1 Chr 5:18; so also 10:4 (2), 5; 11:39; 12:8<9>; 2 Chr 14:8<7>), דֹּרְכֵי τείνοντες those "*who drew* (the bow)" (1 Chr 5:18; so also 8:40), יֹצְאֵי ἐκπορευόμενοι those "*who went out* (to war)" (5:18; so also 7:11; 12:32<33>, 35<36>; 2 Chr 26:11), עֹשֵׂה ποιούντων those "*who make* (war)" (2 Chr 11:1; 26:11), עוֹשֵׂה those "*who do* (the work)" (1 Chr 23:24; 2 Chr 24:12; 26:13; 34:10 (2), 13; 17), עֹרְכֵי παραστασσόμενοι "equipped" (1 Chr 12:34<35>), and הַהֹלְכִים τοῖς πορευομένοις those "who walk" (2 Chr 6:14). A number of these Hebrew participles are in reality nouns, for example, הַיֹּשְׁבִים comes to mean "inhabitants." However, the Greek translator frequently used a participle to translate them. This also accounts for some periphrastic constructions. Hebrew nominal participles with הָיָה are translated into Greek periphrastics, (see 1 Chr 6:32<17> below). Perhaps this reflects the increase in periphrastic constructions in Hebrew contemporary with the translator.

The durative notion of the participle is sometimes reinforced by the verb הָיָה and translated into a Greek periphrastic tense with the verb "to be" and a participle, e.g., וַיִּהְיוּ מְשָׁרְתִים "And they *ministered*" or "and *they were ministers*," translated ἦσαν λειτουργοῦντες "*they were ministering*" (1 Chr 6:32<17>), וַיִּהְיוּ־שָׁם עִם־דָּוִיד יָמִים שְׁלוֹשָׁה אֹכְלִים וְשׁוֹתִים "they *were* there with David three days, *eating and drinking*," translated καὶ ἦσαν ἐκεῖ ἡμέρας τρεῖς ἐσθίοντες καὶ πίνοντες (12:39<40>; so also 2 Chr 20:25), וַיְהִי עֹשֶׂה מִשְׁפָּט "and he *administered* justice," translated ἦν ποιῶν κρίμα (1 Chr 18:14), and וַיְהִי יְהוֹשָׁפָט הֹלֵךְ וְגָדֵל "so Jehoshaphat grew greater," translated ἦν

Ιωσαφατ πορευόμενος μείζων (2 Chr 17:12).[119] Sometimes the durative timeless notion of the Hebrew participle is reinforced by the addition of the verb "to be" in Greek, e.g., אַתָּה בֹחֵן לֵבָב "you *try* the heart" translated σὺ εἶ ὁ ἐτάζων καρδίας (1 Chr 29:17; so also v. 15); so also אֵין כֶּסֶף נֶחְשָׁב "silver *was* not *considered* valuable" οὐκ ἦν ἀργύριον λογιζόμενον (2 Chr 9:20; so also 18:7).

Sometimes a Hebrew circumstantial participle indicating simultaneous action is translated as a Greek present circumstantial participle. For example, "when the priests came forth...and one hundred twenty priests *blowing* trumpets (מַחְצְרִים translated σαλπίζοντες)...the house was filled" (2 Chr 5:11-13) "they carried the ark...and David and all Israel *were celebrating* (מְשַׂחֲקִים translated παίζοντες)" (1 Chr 13:8). In 1 Chronicles 15:25-29 a number of participles are used to give the setting or background for the ark entering the city of Jerusalem, "David and the elders *were* (וַיְהִי) those *going* (הַהֹלְכִים οἱ πορευόμενοι) to bring up the ark...all the Levites who *were carrying* (הַנֹּשְׂאִים αἴροντες), all Israel *brought up* (מַעֲלִים ἀνάγοντες) the ark...(מַשְׁמִעִים ἀναφωνοῦντες) sounding cymbals...when the ark came...Michal looked out...and saw King David *leaping* and *making merry* (מְרַקֵּד וּמְשַׂחֵק ὀρχούμενον παίζοντα), and she despised him." Some other examples are, "the Levites brought up the ark...and King Solomon and all the congregation of Israel *were sacrificing* (מְזַבְּחִים θύοντες)" (2 Chr 5:6), "they worshipped and gave praise...then the king and all the people *offered sacrifice* (זֹבְחִים θύοντες)" (7:4), "Solomon sacrificed...while the priests...*blew* trumpets (מַחְצְרִים σαλπίζοντες)" (7:6), and they caught him while

---

[119] Sometimes, when participles associated with a durative notion are used to sum up a prolonged activity, the translator translates the participles as substantival participles, וַיִּהְיוּ הָרָצִים עֹבְרִים...וַיִּהְיוּ מַשְׂחִיקִים עֲלֵיהֶם וּמַלְעִגִים בָּם "So the couriers *passed* from city to city...but they were *scorning* them, and *mocking* them," translated καὶ ἦσαν οἱ τρέχοντες διαπορευόμενοι...καὶ ἐγένοντο ὡς καταγελῶντες αὐτῶν καὶ καταμωκώμενοι, lit., "and they became as their *scorners* and *mockers*" (30:10; so also in 36:16).

Three times the *wayyiqtol* form of הָיָה with a participle is translated by the aorist of γίνομαι. One time is in 30:10 above. Another example occurs in 20:25. However, the context suggests a durative notion, since it has the temporal adverbial *three days*, וַיִּהְיוּ יָמִים שְׁלוֹשָׁה בֹּזְזִים אֶת־הַשָּׁלָל "and they were three days *plundering* the spoil" translated καὶ ἐγένοντο ἡμέραι τρεῖς *σκυλευόντων αὐτῶν* (genitive absolute) τὰ σκῦλα, lit., "and three days came to pass *while they were plundering* the spoil." The final example in 1 Chronicles 15:29 וַיְהִי אֲרוֹן בְּרִית יְהוָה בָּא "As the ark of the covenant of the LORD came" is translated as if there were two *wayyiqtol* forms, καὶ ἐγένετο...καὶ ἦλθεν, perhaps understanding the second verb as a *qatal* form of rather than a participle, with which it is formally identical.

he *was hiding* (מִתְחַבֵּא translated ἰατρευόμενον *healing*) in Samaria (22:9), and "the sons of Israel celebrated the Feast…and the priests *praised* (וּמְהַלְלִים καθυμνοῦντες) the Lord day after day (30:21; so also v. 22).

i. Qotel > Perfect Participle (46 = 9.29%)

About 25 of the participles translated by a perfect are predicative with the other 21 being attributive participles. The predicative participles are occasionally preceded by הָיָה (as a periphrastic form), e.g., כִּי־הָיוּ הָאֲנָשִׁים נִכְלָמִים מְאֹד, "for the men *were* greatly *humiliated*," translated ὅτι ἦσαν ἠτιμωμένοι σφόδρα [120] (1 Chr 19:5; so also 17:14[121]; 2 Chr 5:8; 10:6; 18:34; 22:12; 30:10). The translator usually translates both the verb הָיָה and the participle. One time a Hebrew periphrastic participle embedded in a relative clause, אֶת־הַזְּקֵנִים אֲשֶׁר־הָיוּ עֹמְדִים "the elders who *had served* (lit., *were standing*)" is converted into an attributive participle in Greek τοὺς πρεσβυτέρους τοὺς ἑστηκότας "the elders *standing*" (2 Chr 10:6). Mostly, however, the notion of the verb "to be" has to be supplied for a grammatical reading of the predicate, as the participle occurs in a noun clause coordinated by a *waw*, e.g., וּמֵהֶם מְמֻנִּים "and some of them also *were* appointed" translated καὶ ἐξ αὐτῶν καθεσταμένοι (1 Chr 9:29; so also 15:27; 2 Chr 3:13 (2); 7:6 (2)). Sometimes the action of the participle is simultaneous with that of the main verb, e.g., "and all Judah *was standing* (עֹמְדִים ἑστηκὼς) then (וְ καὶ) the spirit of YHWH came upon Jahaziel" (2 Chr 20:13-14; so also 9:18 (2), 19; 1 Chr 21:15). There are a few examples of asyndetic circumstantial participles in Hebrew, which are translated as circumstantial participles in Greek. One example in the genitive case (the genitive

---

[120] In this example, the Hebrew structure is strictly speaking not a periphrastic, since a noun comes between הָיָה and the participle (cf. the split infinitive in English). It seems that translator understood this example as a periphrastic even to the extent that he omitted the intervening subject. There are several examples where a Hebrew participle (especially a nominal participle), in close proximity but not adjacent to הָיָה, is treated as a periphrastic by the translator (1 Chr 8:40; 12:39<40>; 19:5; 2 Chr 5:8; 17:12; 22:12; 26:21; 30:10). Greek with its more flexible word order allows intervening material between the verb "to be" and the participle.

[121] 1 Chronicles 17:14 contains a rare example of a future perfect periphrastic (future of the verb "to be" with a perfect participle) in reported speech, וְכִסְאוֹ יִהְיֶה נָכוֹן עַד־עוֹלָם "and his throne shall be established forever" translated καὶ ὁ θρόνος αὐτοῦ ἔσται ἀνωρθωμένος ἕως αἰῶνος (cf. v. 24 which has the participle without the verb "to be").

absolute) occurs in 2 Chronicles 5:12 "the priests sanctified themselves (indicative main verb)…and all the Levites…*clothed* (מְלֻבָּשִׁים αὐτῶν τῶν ἐνδεδυμένων) in fine linen…<u>were standing</u> (עֹמְדִים ἑστηκότες—so also 3:13; 18:9). Sometimes the participle modifies the object of a verb, classified as adjectival by Culy (see note 105, e.g., וַיַּרְא אֶת־מַלְאַךְ יְהוָה עֹמֵד "and [David] saw the angel of YHWH *standing*" translated καὶ εἶδεν τὸν ἄγγελον κυρίου ἑστῶτα, with the perfect participle indicating the state that the object was in when observed (1 Chr 21:16; so also 10:8 "they found Saul *fallen*;" 2 Chr 18:16, "I saw Israel *scattered*").

Some verbs are frequently translated by perfect participles; for example, הָעֹמְדִים, especially when it is used intransitively, is translated by the perfect participle οἱ ἑστηκότες (which is always intransitive) or a compound of it (1 Chr 6:33<18>; so also 6:39<24>; 21:15, 16; 2 Chr 3:13; 5:12; 7:6 (2); 9:7, 18, 19; 10:6[122], 8; 18:34 (*hiphil*); 20:13). יוֹדֵעַ is translated by εἰδότα (2 Chr 2:13<12>; so also 2:14<13>; 8:18).[123]

In addition, the perfect is frequently used for Hebrew passive forms, particularly those of the derived or augmented conjugations, such as, the *niphal*, the factitive *pual*, and the causative *hophal*. Examples of the *pual* translated by a perfect participle are: מְמֻנִּים translated καθεσταμένοι "appointed" (1 Chr 9:29), מְכֻרְבָּל περιεζωσμένος "clothed" (15:27), מְכֻסִּים περιβεβλημένοι "covered" (21:16), מְלֻמְּדֵי δεδιδαγμένοι "who were trained" (25:7), and מְלֻבָּשִׁים τῶν ἐνδεδυμένων "clothed" (2 Chr 5:12; so also 18:9). Examples of the *hophal* are: לַמֻּרְבֶּכֶת translated τὴν πεφυραμένην "what is well-mixed (1 Chr 23:29), מָאֳחָזִים ἐνδεδεμένοι "attached" (2 Chr 9:18),

---

[122] This example is one in which אֲשֶׁר is the subject of a relative clause אֲשֶׁר־הָיוּ עֹמְדִים "who *had served*, lit., *stood* before," which is translated by an attributive participle τοὺς ἑστηκότας.

[123] The use of the perfect participle of οἶδα is constrained by Greek grammar. It seems that the use of the perfect participle of ἵστημι "to set (transitive), to stand (intransitive)" may also be constrained by the grammar. The perfect and second aorist forms of ἵστημι are intransitive. It is interesting to note that in the translation of the book of Chronicles the translator used only perfect participles (14 + 4 of compounds of ἵστημι) and not second aorist participles. Conversely, the translator used only second aorist indicative forms and not perfect indicative forms of ἵστημι. Perhaps the paradigm in the mind of the translator for the intransitive use of ἵστημι consisted of perfect participles and second aorist indicatives. With other books in the Septuagint the translators were not so rigid, although there was a preference for perfect participles (64 in the canonical books) as opposed to second aorist participles (with only 7 cases).

הַמְקֻדָּשִׁים τοῖς ἡγιασμένοις "who are consecrated" (26:18), and הַמֻּפְקָדִים οἱ καθεσταμένοι "who had the oversight" (34:10). Examples of the *niphal* are: הַנִּשְׁאָרִים translated τοὺς ὑπολελειμμένους "those left" (1 Chr 13:2), נָכוֹן ἀνωρθωμένος "established" (17:14, so also 24), נִכְלָמִים ἠτιμωμένοι "humiliated" (19:5), הַנּוֹעָדִים οἱ ἐπισυνηγμένοι "those gathered" (2 Chr 5:6), and נְפוֹצִים διεσπαρμένους "scattered" (18:16).

The perfect participle is also used one time for a *hitpael* with a passive sense, מִתְחַבֵּא translated κατακεκρυμμένος "hidden" (22:12). It is used one time for a stative *piel*, מְמַלֵּא translated πεπληρωκὼς "overflowing" (1 Chr 12:15<16>) and it is even used for an active causative *hiphil* (2 Chr 18:34).

j. Qotel > Aorist Infinitive (3 = 0.61%)

An attributive participle מַשְׁמִיעִים "*loud-sounding* (cymbals)" in indirect speech (direct speech in Greek) is translated by an aorist infinitive τοῦ φωνῆσαι with a sense of purpose "in order to sound aloud" following an imperative (in Greek) (1 Chr 15:16). Two infinitives follow the verb *choose* in the preceding verse "choose...either to flee (φεύγειν present infinitive)...or...the sword to destroy (ἐξολεθρεῦσαι, Heb. overtake)" (21:12). The participle "for/as one overtaking" לְמַשֶּׂגֶת preceded by a לְ could easily be understood by the translator as the very common construction of לְ followed by an infinitive. In the third example a Hebrew indefinite attributive participle יוֹצֵא "men who go out to war" is translated by an aorist infinitive as a complement to the adjective δυνατοὺς "able" ἐξελθεῖν "to go out" (2 Chr 25:5).

k. Qotel > Present Infinitive (6 = 1.21%)

Four attributive participles preceded by a לְ are translated by present infinitives. The first, לְמַשְׁמִיעִים "for those who should sound aloud," is translated by τοῦ ἀναφωνεῖν "to sound aloud" (1 Chr 16:42). A noun לְשֹׁטְרִים and a substantive participle וְלִשְׁפְטִים in the expression "were [appointed] to outside duties for Israel, as officers and judges" are translated τοῦ γραμματεύειν "to write" and διακρίνειν "to judge" (26:29). Two substantive participles לַמַּחַצְצְרִים (לִמְחַצְרִים) וְלַמְשֹׁרֲרִים in "it was the duty of the trumpeters and the singers" are translated ἐν τῷ σαλπίζειν καὶ ἐν τῷ ψαλτῳδεῖν "there was one voice in the trumpeting and in the psalm singing" (2 Chr 5:13). Perhaps these participles are understood by the translator as infinitives following לְ (ἐν also suggests בְּ).

Another attributive participle functioning as a substantive in the clause "the Lord set ambushes; lit., gave ones who ambush" מְאָרְבִים is translated "the Lord gave to fight " (πολεμεῖν, 20:22) as an infinitive complement of the verb *give*. Finally a predicative participle נִסְפֶּה "three months *to be swept away*; lit., *being swept away*" is translated φεύγειν "to flee" (1 Chr 21:12), the infinitive following the verb "choose."

l. Qotel > Aorist Imperative (2 = 0.4%)

There are two aorist imperatives, both occur in reported speech. "And it is blessed (וּמְבֹרָךְ) forever" is translated εὐλόγησον "bless [it] for ever" (1 Chr 17:27). Perhaps this reflects the desire or wish of the translator and maybe his anxiety or uncertainty as to the assurance of the existence and sanctity of the Temple (especially after the reign of Antiochus Epiphanes 175-164 BCE). The participle has no expressed subject. Perhaps the translator considered that this was a form other than a participle. The second imperative is the translation of an attributive participle וְהַבָּא "and whoever goes after" that follows an imperative. It is translated as an imperative, lit., "enter after her" (2 Chr 23:14). Perhaps the translation was influenced by the presence of the preceding imperative.

m. Qotel > Present Imperative (1 = 0.2%)

An attributive participle בָּאֵי הַשַּׁבָּת "who come on duty on the Sabbath" is translated by a present imperative εἰσπορευέσθωσαν "let them come" (2 Chr 23:4). The imperatival force certainly fits the context. The Hebrew text follows the participial phrase with a noun sentence having the force of a jussive of the verb "to be," *"let them be for."*

n. Qotel > Adjective (21 = 4.24%)

Most of the participles translated by adjectives are classified attributive. The six predicative participles translated by adjectives either translate the Hebrew verb "to be," e.g., וַיְהִי יַעְבֵּץ נִכְבָּד "Jabez *was more honorable*" translated καὶ ἦν Ιγαβης ἔνδοξος (1 Chr

4:9); or if the Hebrew lacks a verb "to be" insert one in Greek, e.g., כִּי מֵבִין הוּא "because he *was skillful*" translated ὅτι συνετὸς ἦν (1 Chr 15:22; so also 16:25); or the verb "to be" needs to be understood for the clause to make sense, e.g., כִּי גָדוֹל יְהוָה וּמְהֻלָּל מְאֹד "For great [is] the LORD, and [He is] greatly *to be praised*" (16:25; so also 11:21, 25).

Many of the participles, translated by adjectives are participles of stative verbs in Hebrew for example, נִכְבָּד "be more honorable" is translated ἔνδοξος (1 Chr 4:9; 11:21, 25), הַנּוֹתָרִים "those who remain" is translated καταλοίποις (6:61<46>, 70<55> 77<62>; 24:20), and וְנוֹרָא is translated φοβερός (16:25) or ἐπιφανές (17:21). So also מֵבִין "skillful or understanding" is translated συνετός "skillful" (15:22; 27:32) or τελείων "perfect" (25:8), and שֹׂנְאֶיךָ "those who hate you" (2 Chr 1:11) and הָאֹיֵב "enemies" (20:29; 26:13) are both translated ὑπεναντίους "opposers." Passive participles, especially factitive pual forms which emphasize the bringing about of a state, e.g., מְהֻלָּל "praised" αἰνετός (1 Chr 16:25), מְזֻקָּק "refined" δοκίμου (28:18; 29:4), and מוּצָק "cast" χυτήν (2 Chr 4:2) are also translated as adjectives. Finally, מַיְמִינִים וּמַשְׂמְאֵלִים "using both the right hand and the left" are translated ἐκ δεξιῶν καὶ ἐξ ἀριστερῶν "on the right and the left" (1 Chr 12:2).

o. Qotel > Adverb (Prepositional Phrase) (1 = 0.02%)

One time an attributive participle הַמְשָׁרְתִים "those who served the king" is expanded in translation to περὶ τὸ σῶμα τοῦ βασιλέως "[those] around the body of the king" (1 Chr 28:1).

p. Qotel > Noun (79 = 15.96%)

Most of the participles that are translated by nouns in Greek function substantivally and have either a definite article, a suffix, or are in construct state so are not counted as predicates. For example, a participle with a suffix (preceded by the verb הָיָה, which is translated by the verb "to be" in Greek), אִמּוֹ הָיְתָה יוֹעַצְתּוֹ "his mother was his counselor" translated μήτηρ αὐτοῦ ἦν σύμβουλος (2 Chr 22:3, so also v. 4; cf. 27:32, 33; 25:16, all with the same participle without a verb "to be"), and a participle in construct אֹהֵב אֲדָמָה הָיָה "he was a lover of the ground" translated φιλογέωργος ἦν (26:10; so also 1 Chr

9:30).[124] The participle מְצֹרָע "leprous" could perhaps be included as a predicate, but it is translated by the noun λεπρός "a leper" in Greek and is analyzed as attributive (2 Chr 26:20, 21 (2), 23).

There are two examples of predicative participles that cannot really function as substantives but are translated by nouns, although the first is difficult to categorize (an adverbial accusative?), being a transliterated word. מִתְחַבְּאִים "they hid themselves" is transliterated μεθαχαβιν (1 Chr 21:20). The second, וּמוֹצִיאִים "and they were bringing" is translated ἡ ἔξοδος "the way out" (2 Chr 9:28). All the other examples given above are interpreted as nouns and are not counted as predicates.

Most of the participles that were translated as nouns function as nouns in Hebrew. Among the most common are הַמְשֹׁרְרִים "singers" translated as ψαλτῳδοί (1 Chr 6:33<18>; 9:33; 15:16, 19, 27; 2 Chr 5:12; 20:21; 35:15), הַמּוֹרִים (1 Chr 10:3), הַיֹּרִים (1 Chr 10:3; 2 Chr 35:23), וְדֹרְכֵי קֶשֶׁת (2 Chr 14:8<7>), and נֹשְׂקֵי־קֶשֶׁת (17:17) all translated οἱ τοξόται "archers". הַמּוֹשְׁלִים (2 Chr 23:20) and הַשָּׂרִים translated οἱ ἄρχοντες (2 Chr 35:25), אֹיֵב translated ἐχθρός (1 Chr 14:11; 17:8, 10; 21:12; 22:9; 2 Chr 6:24, 28, 34, 36; 20:27; 25:8), and שֹׁפְטִים translated "judges" κριταί (1 Chr 17:10; 23:4 (as a predicate); 2 Chr 1:2; 19:5, 6).

One time a participle "Asaph, who prophesied הַנִּבָּא" was translated προφήτου (1 Chr 25:2). יוֹעֵץ "counselor" is translated by a proper name Ιωας (26:14), rather than the usual σύμβουλος (as in 27:32, 33; 2 Chr 22:3, 4; 25:16).

On the one hand, we might expect a larger percentage of participles to be translated as nouns, since over time participles become nominalized and function to all intents and purposes as nouns. On the other hand, due to the increase in the use of periphrastic forms, both in Hebrew contemporary to the translator and in Hellenistic Greek, we might expect some of the nominal participles to be translated as analytic verb forms.

q. Qotel > Minus (9 = 1.82%)

Five of the minuses are predicate participles. One time the same verb

---

[124] Φιλογέωργος is a rare Greek compound noun that is attested one time or twice by other later Attic or Hellenistic Greek writers such as Xenophon and Aristotle.

repeated is omitted "And one said [saying] this while another said [lit., saying] that" (2 Chr 18:19). One time the verb from the same root as the following noun is omitted עוֹמֵד עַל־עַמּוּדוֹ "the king was *standing* by his pillar" is translated literally "the king was upon his standing (ἐπὶ τῆς στάσεως)" (23:13). One time the same verb that occurred in the preceding verse is omitted, "He *sacrificed* upon it...nevertheless the people still *sacrificed* in the high places" (33:17) although some Greek MSS (g, m, y, z) read the imperfect ἐθυσίαζε. One time a verb synonymous with a noun is omitted, "And the men *did* the *work* faithfully" (34:12). One time a participle meaning "those *who were supervising*" is omitted, perhaps because the Greek preposition ἐπὶ "over" was considered to have captured the force of the participle (34:13). [125]

r. Summary

The present participle is the common equivalent for the *qotel* form accounting for about 40% of the forms. It is used for durative habitual or customary action (sometimes reinforced by the verb "to be"). It also translates Hebrew circumstantial participles indicating simultaneous action. The perfect translates certain roots, particularly those with stative *Aktionsart*. It also is used to translate passive *niphal*, *pual*, and *hophal* participles. Aorist participles only translate attributive participles, and usually refer to the agent of a punctual event. It is quite striking that no circumstantial participles were translated by an aorist participle. Perhaps the translator felt that the aorist participle with its punctual/perfective aspect was too far removed from the sense of the Hebrew participle, especially when it functions circumstantially with durative/imperfective notion. Participles of stative verbs are often translated by adjectives, and substantive participles are frequently translated by nouns.

Indicative forms translate about 18% of participles, almost all of which reflect translations of predicative participles (except a few

---

[125] Four attributive participles are omitted. One time a whole verse is omitted (1 Chr 16:24). One time the substantive participle "those who are equipped" is omitted (1 Chr 12:2). One time "what was found against him" is omitted (2 Chr 36:8). Finally, the phrase "and on its inhabitants יֹשְׁבָיו" is omitted in the clause "I am bringing evil on this place and on its inhabitants" (34:24). The same expression occurs in vv. 27 and 28 but is not present in v. 25, which has "place" but not "inhabitants." The parallel passage in 2 Kings 22:16 has both "place" and "inhabitants."

attributive participles translated by aorists in relative clauses).[126] Most
of the past indicative forms used to translate the Hebrew participle
reflect the circumstantial use of the participle. The subject of the
participle frequently differs from the subject of the main verb. The
present tense is the most common indicative form, accounting for
more than 8% of all occurrences and 43% of all the indicative forms,
which is not surprising, since in Mishnaic or rabbinic Hebrew the
participle became equivalent to the present tense. The translator may
have been influenced by his contemporary Hebrew in the use of the
present to translate participles.

In addition, many times הָיָה and a participle (in close proximity,
but not necessarily adjacent to each other) is translated as a
periphrastic in Greek. This increase in periphrastic forms may be
influenced by the increase in periphrastic forms in the translator's
contemporary Hebrew, which was facilitated by the increase of these
forms in Hellenistic Greek.

2. Qatul (Passive Participle)

As with active participles, so with qatul forms, we emphasize the
predicative verbal function of the participles. The qatul forms occur in
all clause types. Almost half of the qatul forms are predicative
participles in which the verbal function is emphasized. These
predicative participles are either translated into Greek by indicative
forms or participles functioning circumstantially or supplementary
participles with the verb "to be" specified or implied.

Since the qatul passive participle is used either to indicate a state
resulting from a process or a completed action or a state, it is not
surprising that the Greek perfect forms are common equivalents for
these forms. Over half of the qatul forms are rendered by Greek
perfects, mostly by perfect participles but also some perfect indicative
forms. Since the qatul pattern developed from a nominal pattern for

---

[126] The few aorist indicatives in relative clauses used to translate attributive
participles is a reversal of the translation of a qatal form in a relative clause by an
attributive participle in Greek (see the Qatal section a above). This rearrangement of
syntax is perhaps a reversal of the propensity of Greek for the attributive participle,
although the relative clause is also a very common structure in Greek. At least 20
aorist, 3 perfect, and 3 present attributive participles translate qatal forms in relative
clauses (when the relative pronoun is the subject of the relative clause). Conversely, 7
attributive Hebrew participles are translated by aorist indicatives in a relative clause in
Greek.

adjectives expressing states, there are also a number of *qatul* forms translated by adjectives and nouns in Greek.

The following table gives the breakdown on how the *qatul* forms in Chronicles were translated into Greek.

TABLE 7: THE TRANSLATION OF *QATUL* FORMS

(Predicative Forms Compared to the Total Number of *Qatul* Forms)

QATUL	TOTAL	Percentage	Narrative Main Clauses (Clause %)	Reported Speech Main Clauses	Subordinate Clauses
Aorist Indicative	1 predicate 1 total	1.37	1 (4.3) 1 (1.9)		
Perfect Indicative	6 6	8.22	3 (13.0) 3 (5.6)		3 (42.9) 3 (37.5)
Present Indicative	1 1	1.37		1 (11.1) 1 (9.1)	
Aorist Participle	2	2.74	2 (3.7)		
Present Participle	1 1	1.37	1 (4.3) 1 (1.9)		
Perfect Participle	23 32	43.84	16 (69.6) 23 (42.6)	5 (55.6) 6 (54.5)	2 (28.6) 3 (37.5)
Adjective	5 20	27.4	2 (8.7) 16 (29.6)	3 (33.3) 4 (36.4)	
Noun	2 8	10.96	0 6 (11.1)		2 (28.6) 2 (37.5)
Minus	2	2.74	2 (3.7)		
Total	39 73	100	23 54	9 11	7 8

Total 73

Aorist Indicative (1 = 1.37%)

Narrative Main Clauses (1)

Predicative (1):

2 Chr 4:3

Perfect Indicative (6 = 8.22%)

Narrative Main Clauses (3)

Predicative (3):

2 Chr 32:32; 33:19; 35:25

Subordinate Clauses (3)
Predicative (3):
2 Chr 23:18; 25:4; 35:12
                    Present Indicative (1 = 1.37%)
Reported Speech Main Clauses (1)
Predicative (1):
2 Chr 1:12
                    Aorist Participle (2 = 2.74%)[127]
Narrative Main Clauses (2)
Attributive (2):
1 Chr 14:4; 16:41
                    Present Participle (1 = 1.37%)
Narrative Main Clauses (1)
Predicative (1):
1 Chr 12:1
                    Perfect Participle (32 = 43.84%)
Narrative Main Clauses (24)
Attributive (7):
1 Chr 4:41; 5:18; 9:33; 16:40; 2 Chr 9:20; 32:5; 34:31
Predicative (16):
1 Chr 6:48<33>; 9:1; 21:16 (2); 29:29; 2 Chr 9:29; 12:15; 13:22;
16:11; 20:34; 24:27; 25:26; 27:7; 28:26; 35:27; 36:8
Reported Speech Main Clauses (6)
Attributive (1):
2 Chr 34:24
Predicative (5):
1 Chr 16:36; 2 Chr 6:20, 40; 7:15; 9:8
Subordinate Clauses (3)
Attributive (1):
2 Chr 34:21
Predicative (2):
2 Chr 31:3; 35:26
                    Adjective (20 = 27.4%)
Narrative Main Clauses (16)
Attributive (14):
1 Chr 7:40; 9:22; 12:24<25>; 24:6; 2 Chr 4:16, 20; 9:15 (2), 16; 13:3
(2), 17; 17:18; 25:5

---

[127] The aorist passive participle ἐκλεγέντες (1 Chr 16:41) is incorrectly coded as a present participle by *GRAMCORD* (see Appendix 1).

Predicative (2):
1 Chr 24:6 (2)
Reported Speech Main Clauses (4)
Attributive (1):
2 Chr 6:32
Predicative (3):
1 Chr 29:10; 2 Chr 2:12<11>; 6:4
Noun (8 = 10.96%)
Narrative Main Clauses (6)
Attributive (6):
1 Chr 19:10; 23:24; 2 Chr 11:1; 20:21; 23:14; 28:14
Subordinate Clauses (2)
Attributive (2):
2 Chr 30:5, 18
Minus (2 = 2.74%)
Narrative Main Clauses (2)
Attributive (2):
1 Chr 12:23<24>; 2 Chr 4:22

a. Qatul > Aorist Indicative (1 = 1.37%)

The *qatul* form יְצוּקִים "The oxen…were cast" is translated by the
aorist indicative active ἐχώνευσαν "they cast oxen" (2 Chr 4:3).
Perhaps, because the subject הַבָּקָר "oxen" is grammatically singular,
the translator felt to change the subject of the verb by changing the
voice from passive to active.

b. Qatul > Perfect Indicative (6 = 8.22%)

All of the perfect indicative forms are translations of כַּכָּתוּב into
καθὼς γέγραπται (2 Chr 23:18; 25:4) or ὡς γέγραπται "as *it is
written*" (35:12) or of הִנָּם כְּתוּבִים translated ἰδοὺ γέγραπται
"behold, *it is written*" (32:32; 33:19; 35:25).[128]

---

[128] The more common way to render הִנָּם כְּתוּבִים is by a perfect participle (13
times). It is not clear why the translator chose a different structure (the perfect
indicative) for these three examples; perhaps it was used to distinguish different
sources. Firstly, the perfect indicative is used in reference to a record of Hezekiah
written in the vision of Isaiah the prophet (2 Chr 32:32); secondly, it is used
concerning Manasseh's prayer which is written in the records of the seers (33:19, cf.
the apocryphal *Prayer of Manasseh?*), and thirdly, concerning Jeremiah's lament for
Josiah written in the lamentations (35:25). The perfect participle is used when what is
recorded is also found in the book of Kings (of Israel and Judah) (1 Chr 9:1; 2 Chr

c. Qatul > Present Indicative (1 = 1.37%)

The *qatul* form translated by a present indicative occurs in the clause "wisdom and knowledge *have been granted* (נָתוּן) to you" (2 Chr 1:12). It is translated by a first person active form δίδωμι "I give you." The verb following is also first person active form of the same verb, so the translation in Greek fits the context. Perhaps the Greek present is to be understood as a performative, "I [hereby] give to you."

d. Qatul > Aorist Participle (2 = 2.74%)

Two attributive participles הַיְלוּדִים and הַבְּרוּרִים are translated by aorist passive participles τῶν τεχθέντων "who *were born*" (1 Chr 14:4) and ἐκλεγέντες "who *were chosen*" (16:41).

e. Qatul > Present Participle (1 = 1.37%)

A circumstantial *qatul* form עָצוּר is translated by a present middle/passive participle συνεχομένου "he *was* still *restricted*" (1 Chr 12:1). It is a genitive absolute, referring to David, who is grammatically removed from the subject of the main verb, the mighty men of David.

f. Qatul > Perfect Participle (32 = 43.84%)

A large number (20) of the perfect participles are translations of *qatul* form of כָּתַב "to write" by the perfect middle/passive participle of γράφω, γεγραμμένοι. The perfect participles are either translations of הַכְּתוּבִים "which are written" and function attributively (1 Chr 4:41; 16:40; 2 Chr 34:21, 24, 31), or are translations of כַּכָּתוּב "as it is written" (2 Chr 31:3; 35:26), or function predicatively, with הִנֵּה "behold, they are written" (1 Chr 9:1; 29:29; 2 Chr 9:29; 12:15; 13:22; 16:11; 20:34; 24:27; 25:26; 27:7; 28:26; 35:27; 36:8). Perhaps the use of the *qatul* form and its translation by the prefect emphasizes the enduring state of the written word. It invests it with some authority

---

16:11; 24:27; 25:26; 27:27; 28:26; 35:27; 36:8), or in the writings of Samuel the seer (1 Chr 29:29), the prophets Nathan (2 Chr 9:29), Shemaiah (12:15), Iddo (13:22), and Jehu son of Hanani (20:34). It is interesting to note that the most standard way of citing quotes in the New Testament is to use a perfect indicative (67 times), with the participle mostly occurring in John's Gospel (5 times out of a total of 7 in the New Testament).

and these forms are used as quotation formulae for official documents and quotes from religious texts.

The other participles are attributive (1 Chr 5:18; 9:33; 2 Chr 9:20; 32:5), or predicative, with the verb הָיָה, translated by εἰμί and the participle, e.g., פְּתֻחוֹת translated ἀνεῳγμένους "be open" (2 Chr 6:20, so also 40; 7:15), or with the verb "to be" implied, e.g., נְתוּנִים translated δεδομένοι "were appointed" (1 Chr 6:48<33>), בָּרוּךְ translated εὐλογημένος "blessed be" (16:36; cf. 2 Chr 9:8 in which the verb "to be" is present). Two function as circumstantial participles modifying the object of a verb of seeing and "David...saw the angel of the Lord standing between earth and heaven, with his *drawn* (שְׁלוּפָה) sword [or his sword *drawn*] in his hand *stretched out* (נְטוּיָה)" (1 Chr 21:16 (2)).

g. Qatul > Adjective (20 = 27.4%)

There are only three predicative participles all from the verb בָּרוּךְ which are all translated εὐλογητός "blessed" (1 Chr 29:10; 2 Chr 2:12<11>; 6:4). Most of the *qatul* forms translated as adjectives are attributive participles. They reflect an interpretation of the resultant state inherent in the *qatul* form by a Greek stative adjective (often with a verbal sense inherent in it), for example, בְּרוּרִים, which is translated ἐκλεκτοί "choice" or "chosen" (1 Chr 7:40; so also 9:22), חֲלוּצֵי "equipped" translated δυνατοί "powerful" (12:24<25>; so also 2 Chr 17:18), καθαροῦ "pure" used to translate מָרוּק "polished" סָגוּר "pure" שָׁחוּט "beaten" (4:16, 20; 9:15) respectively, שָׁחוּט is also translated ἐλατούς "beaten" (9:15, so also v. 16), הַנְּטוּיָה "outstretched" is translated ὑψηλόν "high" (6:32), and בָּחוּר "chosen" is translated δυνατῶν "powerful" (13:3 (2), so also v. 17; 25:5).

Finally, three times אָחֻז "taken" is translated εἷς "one," perhaps a misreading of the preceding numeral אֶחָד (1 Chr 24:6 (3)).

h. Qatul > Noun (8 = 10.96%)

Most of the *qatul* forms that are translated as nouns reflect the substantival use of the *qatul* form. For example, בָּחוּר "chosen" or "choice" functioning substantivally is translated νεανίου "young men" (1 Chr 19:10; so also 2 Chr 11:1), לִפְקוּדֵיהֶם "those of them who were counted" is translated κατὰ τὴν ἐπίσκεψιν "according to the numbering, lit., inspection" (1 Chr 23:24), הֶחָלוּץ "the army, lit., the equipped, armed" is translated τῆς δυνάμεως "force" (2 Chr 20:21) or οἱ πολεμισταί "warriors" (28:14), פְּקוּדֵי "appointed" is translated ἀρχηγοῖς "leaders" (23:14), and כַּכָּתוּב "as it was prescribed, or, according to what was written" is translated κατὰ τὴν γραφήν "according to the scripture" (2 Chr 30:5, so also v. 18).

i. Qatul > Minus (2 = 2.74%)

Twice a *qatul* form is omitted, and both are attributive participles. The adjectival הֶחָלוּץ translated "equipped for war" (1 Chr 12:23<24>) is omitted from the phrase "leaders of the army." סָגוּר, usually translated καθαροῦ, is omitted along with the first section of the verse (2 Chr 4:22).

j. Summary

The most common equivalents for the *qatul* passive participle are forms that carry a stative notion, either perfect forms (mostly participles) or adjectives. The two active indicative non-perfect forms result from the translator changing the passive notion of the *qatul* form to an active indicative aorist "they cast" (2 Chr 4:3) and present "I give" (1:12).

3. *Qᵉtol (Infinitive Construct)*

Infinitive constructs are all classified as subordinate clauses. They occur frequently in both narrative and subordinate clauses. They most commonly function as the object (complement) of certain verbs (such as verbs of speech) or are equivalent to subordinate clauses (such as purpose clauses preceded by the preposition לְ, or temporal or causal clauses preceded by the prepositions בְּ "in" and כְּ "as").

Infinitive construct forms are mostly translated by non-indicative forms in Greek. The common equivalent for the infinitive construct is a Greek infinitive, which is used to translate over two-thirds of all the infinitive constructs (with the aorist infinitive predominating, accounting for 50% of all forms). Participles account for about 12%, and indicative forms (especially the aorist indicative) for about 8% of the infinitives. Aorist and imperfect indicatives are used to translate infinitives in narrative, and perfect, present, and future indicatives in reported speech. In our analysis we pay most attention to the places where an infinitive equivalent to a subordinate clause is translated by a Greek indicative form or a circumstantial participle. The indicative forms may reflect the trend away from using a preposition and an infinitive construct as an equivalent to a temporal clause. At the time of translation and in later Hebrew an indicative form in temporal clauses was preferred to the infinitive.

The following table gives the breakdown on how the infinitive construct forms in Chronicles were translated into Greek.

TABLE 8: THE TRANSLATION OF $Q^E TOL$ INFINITIVE CONSTRUCT FORMS

$Q^E TOL$	TOTAL	Percentage (= Clause %)	Narrative Main Clauses	Reported Speech Main Clauses	Subordinate Clauses
Aorist Indicative	41	6.7			41
Imperfect Indicative	3	0.49			3
Perfect Indicative	1	0.16			1
Present Indicative	1	0.16			1
Future Indicative	1	0.16			1
Aorist Participle	4	0.65			4
Present Participle	72	11.77			72
Perfect Participle	1	0.16			1
Aorist Infinitive	313	51.14			313
Present Infinitive	93	15.20			93
Perfect Infinitive	3	0.49			3
Aorist Subjunctive	6	0.98			6
Aorist Imperative	1	0.16			1
Present Imperative	1	0.16			1
Adjective	5	0.82			5
Preposition	1	0.16			1
Noun	50	8.17			50
Minus	15	2.45			15
Total	612	100			612

Total 612
Aorist Indicative (41 = 6.7%)[129]
Subordinate Clause (Narrative) (39)
1 Chr 5:1; 6:32<17>; 10:13; 21:15; 2 Chr 3:3; 5:13; 7:1; 8:16; 10:2,
15; 12:1; 18:31, 32; 20:23; 21:5, 19, 20; 22:2, 8; 24:10, 11, 14; 26:3, 5;
29:24, 28, 29, 34 (2); 31:1, 5, 21; 32:17; 33:12, 19, 23; 34:19; 36:6;
36:16
Subordinate Clause (Reported Speech) (2)
2 Chr 20:37; 21:13

Imperfect Indicative (3 = 0.49%)
Subordinate Clause (Narrative) (3)
2 Chr 7:3; 11:1; 24:22

Perfect Indicative (1 = 0.16%)
Subordinate Clause (Reported Speech) (1)
2 Chr 31:10

Present Indicative (1 = 0.16%)
Subordinate Clause (Reported Speech) (1)
2 Chr 19:2

Future Indicative (1 = 0.16%)
Subordinate Clause (Reported Speech) (1)
2 Chr 30:9

Aorist Participle (4 = 0.65%)
Subordinate Clause (Narrative) (2)
2 Chr 25:14; 30:5
Subordinate Clause (Reported Speech) (2)
1 Chr 29:17; 2 Chr 20:10

Present Participle (72 = 11.77%)
Subordinate Clause (Narrative) (52)
1 Chr 4:9, 10; 5:9; 11:1; 12:19<20>, 32<33>; 13:12; 14:10; 16:2, 4;
17:3; 18:3; 21:9; 23:31; 2 Chr 2:3<2>; 7:1, 3; 10:3, 6, 7, 12, 14, 16;
11:2; 12:7; 16:2; 18:11, 12, 30, 34; 19:9; 20:2, 37; 21:12; 25:4, 7, 17,
18; 26:5; 29:29; 30:6, 18; 31:19; 32:4, 6, 9, 17; 33:14; 34:18, 20;
35:21; 36:22
Subordinate Clause (Reported Speech) (20)
1 Chr 11:2; 16:18; 17:6, 24; 21:10; 22:8; 23:26; 2 Chr 6:4, 16, 37;
7:18; 10:9, 10; 11:3; 20:8; 23:7 (2); 25:18; 32:11, 12

---

[129] Including one aorist indicative ὕψωσαν (2 Chr 5:13) analyzed by *GRAMCORD*
as an aorist participle (see Appendix 1). One time the infinitive seems to function as in
a main clause וְגַם־לִשְׁאוֹל בָּאוֹב "and moreover to ask for a medium," but it is
translated as a subordinate clause ὅτι ἐπηρώτησεν Σαουλ ἐν τῷ ἐγγαστριμύθῳ
"because Saul had asked for a ventriloquist" (1 Chr 10:13).

Perfect Participle (1 = 0.16%)
Subordinate Clause (Narrative) (1)
2 Chr 5:11

Aorist Infinitive (313 = 51.14%)
Subordinate Clause (Narrative) (199)
1 Chr 4:39; 5:1; 7:21, 22; 8:8; 9:32; 10:9, 13; 11:10, 18, 19; 12:19<20>, 20<21>, 23<24>, 31<32>, 33<34>, 36<37>, 38<39> (2); 13:4, 5, 6, 9; 14:1, 8; 15:2, 3, 14, 16, 19, 21, 25, 26; 16:43; 18:3, 5, 10 (2); 19:6, 19; 21:1, 15, 18 (2), 28, 30 (2); 22:2 (3), 6, 17; 23:13, 30; 25:5; 26:27; 27:23; 29:9; 2 Chr 2:1<1:18>; 3:2, 3; 4:11, 12, 13; 5:2, 10, 11, 14; 7:2, 7, 11; 8:6; 9:1, 23; 10:1, 18 (2); 11:1, 16 (2), 22; 12:7, 11, 12, 13 (2), 14; 13:13; 14:4<3> (2); 15:8, 9, 12; 16:1, 5; 18:2, 12; 20:3, 4 (2), 18, 20, 21, 23 (2), 25, 29, 31, 32, 35[36], 36 (2), 37; 21:7 (2); 22:6 (2), 7 (2), 9; 23:18; 24:1, 4, 9, 12 (2), 19, 25; 25:10, 13, 14, 16, 20; 26:2, 13, 15, 16 (2), 19 (2), 20; 27:1; 28:1, 6, 16, 22 (2); 29:15, 16 (2), 17, 27, 34; 30:1 (2), 2, 3, 5 (2), 12 (2), 13, 17, 23; 31:4, 7, 11, 14, 15, 19; 32:1, 3, 18 (2), 31 (2); 33:1, 6 (2), 9, 19; 34:1, 3 (2), 8 (2), 10 (2), 11 (2), 31; 35:12, 16 (2), 22; 36:13, 14, 21, 22
Subordinate Clause (Reported Speech) (114)
1 Chr 4:10; 11:19; 12:17<18>; 14:15 (2); 16:19, 21, 33, 35; 17:4, 9, 21 (3), 25 (2), 27; 19:2 (2), 3; 21:17, 24; 22:5, 7, 19 (2); 28:2, 4, 5, 7, 10, 20; 29:3, 4, 5, 12 (2), 14, 16, 19; 2 Chr 2:3<2> (2), 4<3>, 6<5>, 7<6> (2), 9<8>, 11<10>, 14<13> (2); 6:1, 2, 5, 6, 7, 8, 19, 20 (2), 22, 23 (4), 26, 33; 7:13; 9:8 (4); 10:6; 11:4; 13:5, 8, 9, 11; 16:9; 18:7, 23, 24, 26; 19:3; 20:6, 10, 11 (2), 17; 24:5, 6; 25:8 (2), 9, 16; 26:18 (2); 28:10, 13; 29:10, 11; 30:19; 32:11, 13, 14 (2), 15; 33:8 (2); 34:21, 26, 27; 35:6, 21, 23

Present Infinitive (94 = 15.2%)
Subordinate Clause (Narrative) (60)
1 Chr 1:10; 6:49<34>; 9:25; 10:8; 15:2 (2); 16:4 (2), 7, 37, 40, 41; 23:13 (3), 30 (2); 24:19; 26:12; 27:24; 2 Chr 3:1; 4:6 (2); 5:13 (3), 14; 7:6; 8:13, 14 (2); 10:6; 11:14; 13:15; 16:5; 17:7; 18:31; 20:19; 22:3, 6; 23:16; 26:15 (2); 28:25; 31:2 (3); 32:17; 33:21; 34:12, 14, 31, 33; 35:12, 14, 15, 22, 36:2, 5, 9, 11
Subordinate Clause (Reported Speech) (32)
1 Chr 16:35; 17:6, 7, 27; 22:12, 13; 23:5; 28:4; 29:19; 2 Chr 2:4<3>, 6<5>, 8<7>, 14<13>; 6:5 (2), 6, 16, 20, 33; 7:16; 13:12; 14:11<10>; 15:2; 29:11 (2), 21, 30; 30:9; 31:10; 32:8 (2); 33:16

Perfect Infinitive (3 = 0.49%)
Subordinate Clause (Narrative) (1)
2 Chr 32:31
Subordinate Clause (Reported Speech) (2)
2 Chr 16:7, 8

Aorist Subjunctive (6 = 0.98%)
Reported Speech (6)
1 Chr 17:11; 19:3; 2 Chr 7:17; 18:10; 25:9; 34:25

Aorist Imperative (1 = 0.16%)
Subordinate Clause (Reported Speech) (1)
1 Chr 15:16

Present Imperative (1 = 0.16%)
Subordinate Clause (Narrative) (1)
2 Chr 5:13

Adjective (5 = 0.82%)
Subordinate Clause (Narrative) (4)
1 Chr 12:8<9>; 19:11, 17; 2 Chr 34:7
Subordinate Clause (Reported Speech) (1)
2 Chr 25:19

Preposition (1 = 0.16%)
Subordinate Clause (Narrative) (1)
1 Chr 19:10

Noun (50 = 8.17%)
Subordinate Clause (Narrative) (40)
1 Chr 4:31, 33; 5:7, 6:15<41>; 7:5, 7, 9, 40; 9:22; 10:13; 13:5; 19:5;
20:1; 25:3 (2); 2 Chr 2:18<17>; 4:20; 7:6, 8; 12:12, 15; 16:13; 17:7;
23:13; 24:14; 26:5, 8; 28:23; 29:3; 31:1, 16, 17, 18; 32:24; 34:3, 8;
35:20; 36:19, 21 (2)
Subordinate Clause (Reported Speech) (10)
1 Chr 19:3; 22:5; 23:4; 28:2; 29:19; 2 Chr 6:21, 30, 33, 39; 32:11

Minus (15 = 2.45 %)
Subordinate Clause (Narrative) (11)
1 Chr 1:43; 12:22<23>; 32; 2 Chr 10:10; 20:27; 22:7; 27:8; 34:16, 31;
35:20; 36:20
Subordinate Clause (Reported Speech) (4)
1 Chr 12:17<18>; 17:19; 2 Chr 6:31; 15:4

a. Qǝtol > Aorist Indicative (41 = 6.7%)

Over half (21) of the infinitive constructs translated by aorist indicatives occur with the preposition כְּ and are translated by a subordinate clause in Greek with ὡς meaning *when* or *while* (1 Chr 21:15; 2 Chr 5:13; 7:1; 10:2; 12:1; 18:31, 32; 20:23, 37; 21:13, 19 (with כְּעֵת); 22:8; 24:11, 14; 29:29; 31:1, 5; 33:12, (cf. v. 19 occurring with a *waw* but not כְּ), 23; 34:19).[130]

The aorist also occurs in the translation of infinitives preceded by other prepositions into Greek subordinate clauses. For example, בְּ in the phrase בְּמָלְכוֹ is translated by an aorist and a prepositional phrase κατέστη ἐπὶ τὴν βασιλείαν "he was established in his kingdom" (2 Chr 21:5); it is translated by ὅτε and an aorist ἐβασίλευσεν (21:20) and translated ἐβασίλευσεν (in 22:2 and 26:3, both without ὅτε). The infinitive construct with עַד is translated by ἕως οὗ "until" and an aorist (1 Chr 6:32<17>; 2 Chr 8:16; 29:34) or by ἕως and an aorist (36:16). The combination of two prepositions עַד־לְ is translated by ἕως οὗ and an aorist (24:10; 29:28). לְמַעַן "in order to" and an infinitive is translated λέγων and an aorist "saying, YHWH *has confirmed* His word" (2 Chr 10:15). The translation is more forceful than the Hebrew text, emphasizing the actual fulfillment of the word as opposed to merely the purpose for the preceding clause. לִשְׁאוֹל is translated by ὅτι and an aorist "because he asked" (1 Chr 10:13). Three infinitives of purpose לְכַפֵּר "to make expiation" (2 Chr 29:24), לְהֲלִיכוֹ "to bring him" (36:6), and וְלֵאמֹר "and to speak" (32:17) are translated by an aorist in a main clause, καὶ ἐξιλάσαντο "and they made expiation," καὶ ἀπήγαγεν "and he led him," and καὶ εἶπεν "and he said" respectively. An infinitive of result וְלֹא לְהִתְיַחֵשׂ "so that he is not enrolled" is translated by the aorist καὶ οὐκ ἐγενεαλογήθη (1 Chr 5:1).[131]

---

[130] This is the most common way to render כְּ and an infinitive construct. כְּ and an infinitive construct is translated only three times by a Greek preposition and an infinitive (ἐν and τῷ and an aorist infinitive—1 Chr 14:15; 2 Chr 15:8; 16:5). Perhaps this reflects the influence of contemporary spoken Hebrew. In rabbinic Hebrew כְּ and בְּ and an infinitive construct is replaced by an indicative form, cf. Sáenz-Badillos, *History of the Hebrew Language*, 193.

[131] These last four examples (1 Chr 5:1; 2 Chr 29:24; 32:17; 36:6), as well as 2 Chronicles 7:3; 11:1 (which have imperfects), and 30:9 (which has a future) are interesting in that the translator uses a coordinated (paratactic) structure to translate a subordinate (hypotactic—purpose) structure in Hebrew, thus making the translation (into a language that prefers hypotactic structures) more paratactic than the original!

A few times a gerund of manner is translated by an aorist. For example, כִּי הַלְוִיִּם יִשְׁרֵי לֵבָב לְהִתְקַדֵּשׁ "for the Levites were more upright in heart in sanctifying" is translated ἡγνίσθησαν "for the Levites were sanctified" (2 Chr 29:34). A genitive וּבִימֵי דָּרְשׁוֹ "and in the days of his seeking" is translated by an aorist ἐν ταῖς ἡμέραις αὐτοῦ ἐζήτησεν "and in his days he sought" (26:5).

An infinitive construct as a complement of a noun clause וְאֵלֶּה הוּסַד שְׁלֹמֹה "and these are the measurements [lit., *founding*] of Solomon" is translated ἤρξατο "he began" (3:3).[132]

An infinitive complement of the verb "begin" in the expression בְּכָל־מַעֲשֶׂה אֲשֶׁר־הֵחֵל...לִדְרוֹשׁ "in every work which he began...*to seek*" is translated ἐν ᾧ ἤρξατο...ἐξεζήτησεν "in every work which he began...*he sought*" (31:21).

b. Qᵉtol > Imperfect Indicative (3 = 0.49%)

Twice infinitives are translated as main clause imperfects. In the first example, an infinitive following a main verb is translated as a main verb וַיִּשְׁתַּחֲווּ וְהוֹדוֹת "they worshipped and gave thanks" is translated προσεκύνησαν καὶ ἤνουν (2 Chr 7:3). In the second example, an infinitive of purpose עָשָׂה מִלְחָמָה לְהִלָּחֵם "he [Rehoboam] assembled...those who make war *to fight*" is translated ποιούντων πόλεμον καὶ ἐπολέμει "those who make war, and *he fought*" (11:1). One time an infinitive construct occurs with the preposition כְּ and is translated by a subordinate clause in Greek with ὡς meaning *when* or *while* and the imperfect indicating action simultaneous with the time of the main verb, וּכְמוֹתוֹ אָמַר "and as he was dying, he said" translated καὶ ὡς ἀπέθνησκεν εἶπεν (24:22).

Perhaps the imperfect (as opposed to the aorist) was chosen to emphasize the durative nature of these actions. The first imperfect follows another imperfect ἑώρων three clauses previously, which translates a Hebrew participle רֹאִים "When all the children of Israel saw [lit., *seeing*]...they worshipped, and *gave thanks*" (7:3). The translator may have understood the infinitive absolute as a Hebrew participle, although the expected participle form would be מוֹדִים rather than

---

In three of the examples, the infinitive is closely preceded by a *waw* (1 Chr 5:1; 2 Chr 7:3; 32:17).

[132] The form הוּסַד, a *hophal* infinitive construct, is difficult since there are no attested forms for this verb in either *hiphil* or *hophal*. It is generally regarded as a *qal* or *piel* active form of the verb יסד with Solomon as the subject.

הוֹרֹת. In the second example, the imperfect could have the sense of "Rehoboam *kept on fighting* against Israel," since later it mentions that "there were wars between Rehoboam and Jeroboam continually" (12:14).

c. Q*tol > Perfect Indicative (1 = 0.16%)

The only perfect indicative occurs at the beginning of a section of reported speech, מֵהָחֵל...לָבִיא "Since they began to bring [lit., from the beginning of the bringing] the offering" which is translated ἐξ οὗ ἦρκται ἡ ἀπαρχὴ φέρεσθαι "Since the offering *has begun* to be brought..." (2 Chr 31:10). The Greek perfect emphasizes the resultant state of the action of action of beginning to bring, i.e., the dedication of the offerings leading to their continued offering.

d. Q*tol > Present Indicative (1 = 0.16%)

The only present indicative used to translate an infinitive translates לַעְזֹר followed by an indicative *yiqtol* form in reported speech, הַלָרָשָׁע לַעְזֹר וּלְשֹׂנְאֵי יְהוָה תֶּאֱהָב "Should [you] help the wicked and love those who hate YHWH?" They are both translated by Greek presents, σὺ βοηθεῖς ἤ...φιλιάζεις "Should you help or...love" (2 Chr 19:2). The translation makes a difficult Hebrew reading smoother.

e. Q*tol > Future Indicative (1 = 0.16%)

The infinitive has the force of a result clause in a future context, כִּי בְשׁוּבְכֶם עַל־יְהוָה אֲחֵיכֶם וּבְנֵיכֶם לְרַחֲמִים...וְלָשׁוּב "For as you return to YHWH your kindred and your children will find compassion...and [so] *return*." It is translated by a paratactic future promise καὶ ἀποστρέψει "and *he will return [you]*" (30:9).

f. Q*tol > Aorist Participle (4 = 0.65%)

The four aorist participles function as circumstantial participles. The aorist is rarely used and reflects a punctual event preceding the time of the main verb. For example, לְהִתְנַדֶּב "offering freely" is translated προθυμηθέντα (1 Chr 29:17), בְּבֹאָם "when they came" is translated ἐξελθόντων "having come" (2 Chr 20:10), מֵהַכּוֹת "from the slaughter" is translated πατάξαντα "having slaughtered" (25:14), and finally, one of two infinitives reflecting a reported command "they decreed…that the people *should come* and keep [lit., make] the passover (לָבוֹא לַעֲשׂוֹת)" is translated *ἐλθόντας* ποιῆσαι "*having come* to keep" (30:5).

g. Q^etol > Present Participle (72 = 11.77%)

Most of the present participles (55) are translations of the infinitive complementizer לֵאמֹר "saying," used to introduce direct speech, by the participle λέγων. The Greek present participle functions as a (redundant) circumstantial participle indicating action (mostly) occurring simultaneously with a verb of speaking, for example, קָרְאָה שְׁמוֹ יַעְבֵּץ לֵאמֹר "and she called his name Jabez, *saying*" is translated ἐκάλεσεν τὸ ὄνομα αὐτοῦ Ιγαβης λέγουσα (1 Chr 4:9, so also 4:10; 11:1; 12:19<20>; 13:12; 14:10; 16:18; 17:3, 6, 24; 21:9, 10; 22:8; 2 Chr 2:3<2>; 6:4, 16, 37; 7:18; 10:3, 6, 7, 9, 10, 12, 14, 16; 11:2, 3; 12:7; 16:2; 18:11, 12, 30; 19:9; 20:2, 8, 37; 21:12; 25:4, 7, 17, 18 (2); 30:6, 18; 32:4, 6, 9, 11, 12, 17; 34:18, 20; 35:21; 36:22). Sometimes one of the verbs of speaking is omitted in translation. For example, either the main verb is omitted, e.g., וַיָּבֹא...וַיְדַבְּרוּ אֶל־רְחַבְעָם לֵאמֹר "they came…and spoke to Rehoboam, *saying*" translated καὶ ἦλθεν...πρὸς Ροβοαμ λέγοντες "they came…to Rehoboam, *saying*" (2 Chr 10:3); or the infinitive is omitted, וַיְדַבְּרוּ אִתּוֹ...לֵאמֹר "they spoke with him…*saying*" is translated ἐλάλησαν αὐτῷ "they spoke with him" (10:10; so also 34:16).

Similar to this is the use of an infinitive gerund from the same root as another verb in the context, for example, יוֹדְעֵי בִינָה לַעִתִּים לָדַעַת "<u>those who had understanding</u> of the times, *to know*" (1 Chr 12:32<33>). It is translated by a present circumstantial participle γινώσκοντες "*knowing.*"

Sometimes an infinitive with a preposition equivalent to a circumstantial clause is translated by a circumstantial participle. In all of the following examples, the subject of the circumstantial clause differs from that of the main clause. Therefore, the translator employs the genitive absolute construction, placing the circumstantial participle and its subject in the genitive case. For example, "*while* Saul *was* king (בִּהְיוֹת שָׁאוּל מֶלֶךְ)…you commanded" is translated "Saul *being* king (ὄντος Σαουλ βασιλέως)…" (1 Chr 11:2), "David also struck down King Hadadezer…*as he* [Hadadezer] *went* (בְּלֶכְתּוֹ)" is translated πορευομένου (18:3), "then *at sunset* (לְעֵת בּוֹא הַשֶּׁמֶשׁ)" he died" is translated "*while* the sun *was setting* (δύνοντος τοῦ ἡλίου)" (2 Chr 18:34), and "stay with the king in his comings and goings (בְּבֹאוֹ וּבְצֵאתוֹ)" is translated εἰσπορευομένου καὶ ἐκπορευομένου "*while* he *is coming* and *going*" (23:7). So also a genitive absolute occurs as a translation of וְלָבוֹא "*reaching* the entrance at the Fish Gate" ἐκπορευομένων "*as men go out*" (33:14), but the text is corrupted.

Three times a present participle functions as a supplementary participle to translate an infinitive complement of כָּלָה "to finish." For example, וַיְכַל דָּוִיד מֵהַעֲלוֹת "when David had finished *offering*" is translated συνετέλεσεν Δαυιδ *ἀναφέρων* (1 Chr 16:2), וּכְכַלּוֹת שְׁלֹמֹה לְהִתְפַּלֵּל "when Solomon had ended his prayer" is translated ὡς συνετέλεσεν Σαλωμων *προσευχόμενος* "when Solomon had finished *praying*" (2 Chr 7:1), and וּכְכַלּוֹת לְהַעֲלוֹת "when the offering was finished" is translated ὡς συνετέλεσαν *ἀναφέροντες* "when they had finished *offering*" (29:29).

One time an object infinitive is translated as a present participle, רֹאִים בֶּרֶדֶת הָאֵשׁ "they saw the fire come down" translated ἑώρων καταβαῖνον τὸ πῦρ (7:3).

Twice infinitives with לְכֹל are translated as attributive present participles. For example, לְכֹל הַעֲלוֹת עֹלוֹת "whenever burnt offerings are offered" is translated ἐπὶ πάντων τῶν ἀναφερομένων ὁλοκαυτωμάτων (23:31), and וּלְכָל־הִתְיַחֵשׂ בַּלְוִיִּם "everyone among the Levites who was enrolled" is translated καὶ παντὶ καταριθμουμένῳ ἐν τοῖς Λευίταις "to everyone enrolled among the Levites" (31:19).

A prepositional phrase עַד־לְבוֹא מִדְבָּרָה "as far as the beginning of the desert" is translated ἕως ἐρχομένων τῆς ἐρήμου (1 Chr 5:9), and the first infinitive in a series of infinitives of purpose וּלְהַזְכִּיר וּלְהוֹדוֹת וּלְהַלֵּל "to invoke, to thank, and to praise" is translated by a circumstantial participle ἀναφωνοῦντας "lifting up voices" (16:4).

One time an infinitive indicating obligation or necessity אֵין־לָשֵׂאת "Levites no longer need to carry" is translated by a periphrastic participle οὐκ ἦσαν αἴροντες "were not bearers" (23:26). Another infinitive וַיְהִי לִדְרֹשׁ "he set himself *to seek* God" is translated by a periphrastic participle ἦν ἐκζητῶν "he was [one] *seeking*" (2 Chr 26:5).

h. Qᵉtol > Perfect Participle (1 = 0.16%)

The sole perfect participle translates an infinitive construct with the negative אֵין as an adverbial, אֵין לִשְׁמוֹר לְמַחְלְקוֹת "without *regard* to their divisions," which is translated by a periphrastic perfect οὐκ ἦσαν διατεταγμένοι "without *having been arranged*" (2 Chr 5:11).

i. Qᵉtol > Aorist Infinitive (313 = 51.14%)

The aorist infinitive is the closest to a common equivalent to the Hebrew infinitive construct. It is particularly common for translations of infinitives of purpose, circumstantial clauses preceded by a preposition (apart from בְּ), infinitive complements, and infinitives of indirect speech.

j. Qᵉtol > Perfect Infinitive (3 = 0.49%)

Twice the perfect infinitive reflects a translation of the phrase בְּהִשָּׁעֶנְךָ "because you relied on" by ἐν τῷ πεποιθέναι (2 Chr 16:7, 8). Both occur in reported speech indicated a resultant state that holds to the time of speech. The final example is a translation of an infinitive of purpose לָדַעַת by εἰδέναι, the infinitive of οἶδα "know," which does not have a distinct present form. Both Greek verbs prefer or require perfect forms.

k. Qᵉtol > Present Infinitive (93 = 15.2%)

The present infinitive is used to translate the infinitive of הָיָה "to be, become" (13 times), stative verbs, verbs indicating habitual or customary action or ability (especially related to the worship and service of God or injunctions), the inception of action (complementing verbs such as חוּל "to begin" (10 times), simultaneous action (4 times), and logical duration with multiple subjects (3 times).

l. Qᵉtol > Aorist Subjunctive (6 = 0.98%)

The five aorist subjunctives reflect standard Greek uses in the translation and interpretation of Hebrew infinitives. The first is an infinitive indicating result "when (כִּי) your days are fulfilled to go (לָלֶכֶת)" which is translated by ὅταν and two coordinated subjunctives ὅταν πληρωθῶσιν...καὶ κοιμηθήσῃ "when your days are fulfilled and you sleep" (1 Chr 17:11). One time an infinitive preceded by לְ, indicating purpose, in the clause "come to you to search לַחְקֹר" is translated ὅπως ἐξερευνήσωσιν "so that they may search" (19:3) and an infinitive following לְמַעַן, indicating result, in לְמַעַן הַכְעִיסֵנִי "so that they have provoked me" is translated ἵνα παροργίσωσίν (2 Chr 34:25). The translators translated these infinitives by standard subordinate purpose clauses with ὅπως and ἵνα and a subjunctive. A gerund following a condition in the expression, אִם־תֵּלֵךְ...וְלַעֲשׂוֹת כְּכֹל אֲשֶׁר צִוִּיתִיךָ "if you walk...[by] *doing* according to all that I have commanded" is interpreted as a coordinated protasis in a conditional clause following ἐάν, ἐάν πορευθῇς...καὶ ποιήσῃς "if you walk...and *do*" (7:17). Finally, an infinitive following עַד, referring to time future to the time of speaking, in עַד־כַּלּוֹתָם "until they are destroyed" is translated ἕως ἂν συντελεσθῇ (18:10) using a subjunctive with ἕως to indicate a future event.

One aorist subjunctive reflects an infinitive of obligation in direct speech, "But what shall [must] we do וּמַה־לַּעֲשׂוֹת." It is translated as a main clause deliberative subjunctive, καὶ τί ποιήσω "and what *shall I do*" (2 Chr 25:9, although this is interpreted as a formally identical future indicative by *GRAMCORD*).

m. Qᵉtol > Aorist Imperative (1 = 0.16%)

The sole aorist imperative reflects a translation of indirect speech by direct speech in Greek. "David also commanded the chiefs of the Levites to appoint their brothers (לְהַעֲמִיד)" is translated by an imperative στήσατε "*set* their brothers." However, the imperative is unusual, since the object of the imperative retains the third person possessive pronoun "their" instead of the second person "your," which would be more fitting to speech (1 Chr 15:16), although a number of MSS (b, c₂, e₂, A, B) read "your."

n. Q^etol > Present Imperative (1 = 0.16%)

The only present imperative occurs after the insertion of a verb of speech in Greek and the infinitive is treated as a reported command וּבְהַלֵּל לַיהוָה "in praise to the LORD" is translated καὶ ἔλεγον ἐξομολογεῖσθε "and they said, *Praise* the Lord!" (2 Chr 5:13).

o. Q^etol > Adjective (5 = 0.82%)

Three of the infinitives translated into adjectives come from stative verbs, לְמַהֵר "who were swift" is translated τῷ τάχει "in speed" (1 Chr 12:8<9>), לְהַכְבִּיד "heart...*in boastfulness*" is translated ἡ βαρεῖα "*heavy, stout* heart," (2 Chr 25:19), and כַּתַּת לְהָדֵק "he beat into powder (lit., he beat *to cause to be fine*)" is translated κατέκοψεν λεπτά "he cut into *small* pieces" (34:7). Twice a frozen infinitive phrase which functions as a preposition לִקְרַאת is translated "against" ἐξ ἐναντίας "from [the] opposite" (1 Chr 19:11, 17).

p. Q^etol > Preposition (1 = 0.16%)

The same frozen infinitive phrase which functions as a preposition לִקְרַאת mentioned above is translated by the Greek preposition ἐναντίον "against" (1 Chr 19:10).

q. Q^etol > Noun (50 = 8.17%)

A noun is chosen by the translators for an infinitive often if there is a suitable abstract noun in Greek that corresponds to the verbal idea of the infinitive. Greek has many more abstract nouns than Hebrew, especially those which have come from verbal roots with endings such as -σις, -μος, and -μα (which correspond to the abstract nominal equivalents of the three Greek verbal aspects: nouns ending in -σις mostly indicate a process, i.e., imperfective aspect; nouns ending in -μος mostly indicate viewing the action as a whole, i.e., perfective aspect; and nouns ending in -μα mostly indicate the result of an action, i.e., stative aspect).

An infinitive following a preposition עַד־מְלָךְ דָּוִיד "until the reign of David" is translated ἕως βασιλέως Δαυιδ "until King David" (1 Chr 4:31). The infinitive construct preceded by לְ, לְמָלְכוֹ "of his reign(ing)" is translated βασιλείας "of his reign/kingdom" (2 Chr 16:13; so also 17:7; 29:3; 34:3, 8).

The expression הִתְיַחֵשׂ "enrolled/enrollment by genealogies" is mostly translated by nouns in a number of ways: καταλοχισμός "distribution" (1 Chr 4:33; 5:7; 9:22; 2 Chr 31:17, 18) ἀριθμὸς "number" (1 Chr 7:5, 7, 9, 40); πράξεις "achievements" (2 Chr 12:15) τῆς ἐπιγονῆς "increase" (31:16).[133]

Verbs of motion are translated by an abstract noun in expressions וְעַד־לְבוֹא חֲמָת "to Lebo-hamath" ἕως εἰσόδου "to the entrance" (13:5; so also 2 Chr 7:8), עַד־לְבוֹא מִצְרַיִם "even to the border of Egypt" ἕως εἰσόδου Αἰγύπτου (2 Chr 26:8); לְעֵת צֵאת "the time when kings go out to battle" ἐν τῇ ἐξόδῳ "at the time of the going forth, exit" (1 Chr 20:1). So also the expression לִ(קְרָאתָם) translated by adjectives and a preposition above, is translated by a noun εἰς ἀπάντησιν "to meet them; lit., for *meeting* them" (1 Chr 19:5) so also εἰς συνάντησιν "for *meeting* him" (2 Chr 35:20).

Verbs of building לִבְנוֹת and dwelling שִׁבְתְּךָ are translated "for building" εἰς τὴν κατασκήνωσιν (1 Chr 28:2), τὴν κατασκευήν "for preparation" (29:19), and שִׁבְתְּךָ τῆς κατοικήσεως "dwelling place" (2 Chr 6:21, 30, 33, 39).

A verb of supervising לְנַצֵּחַ "shall have charge" is translated ἐργοδιῶκται "overseers; lit., work pursuers" (1 Chr 23:4) and מְנַצְּחִים לְהַעֲבִיד is translated by the same compound noun ἐργοδιώκτας (2 Chr 2:18<17>).

Verbs of praise and worship, such as, עַל־הֹדוֹת וְהַלֵּל "in thanksgiving and praise" are translated ἐξομολόγησιν καὶ αἴνεσιν (1 Chr 25:3), לְהַלֵּל is translated αἶνον (2 Chr 23:13), and בְּהַלֵּל translated ἐν ὕμνοις "in hymns" (7:6). Verbs of service לְבַעֲרִם "to burn" τοῦ φωτός "lamps *of light*" (4:20), וְהַעֲלוֹת "and *offer up* [the burnt offerings]" ὁλοκαυτωμάτων "burnt offerings" (24:14).[134] The description of the Temple לְהַגְדִּיל "to be magnificent" is translated εἰς μεγαλωσύνην "for magnificence" (1 Chr 22:5); so also בְּרֹאת הָאֱלֹהִים "in fearing God" ἐν φόβῳ "in fear" (2 Chr 26:5).

Verbs of punishment and destruction are variously translated by abstract nouns, for example בְּהַגְלוֹת "into carrying away into

---

[133] It is translated by the present participle καταριθμουμένῳ "reckoned by number" (31:19).

[134] This example may have been interpreted by the translator as הָעֲלוֹת the plural of the noun הָעוֹלָה "burnt offering."

captivity" is translated ἐν τῇ μετοικίᾳ "in exile" (1 Chr 6:15<5:41>), לְהַשְׁחִית "to destroy" is translated εἰς καταφθοράν "to destruction" (2 Chr 12:12), לְהַכְשִׁילוֹ "were the ruin" εἰς σκῶλον "they became a stumbling block" (28:23), עַד־לְכַלֵּה "until they had destroyed them all" ἕως εἰς τέλος "unto the end" (31:1), לָמוּת "to die" εἰς θάνατον "unto death" (32:11), so also עַד־לָמוּת ἕως θανάτου (in v. 24), לְהַשְׁחִית "destroyed" εἰς ἀφανισμόν "to destruction" (36:19), and כָּל־יְמֵי הָשַׁמָּה "all the days *it lay desolate*" τὰς ἡμέρας τῆς ἐρημώσεως "the days of desolation" (36:21); so also לְמַלֹּאות "to fulfill" εἰς συμπλήρωσιν "to the fulfillment" (36:21).

The second infinitive in the expression לַחְקֹר וְלַהֲפֹךְ "to search and to overthrow" is translated τὴν πόλιν "to search *the city*" perhaps to be parallel with the following expression "to spy out the land" (19:3).

r. Qᵉtol > Minus (15 = 2.45%)

Three times an infinitive construct is omitted, when a larger section of text is lacking: one time when a whole relative clause is omitted (1 Chr 1:43), one time when a phrase is omitted (perhaps because of homoteleuton?—17:19), and one time when a whole verse is omitted (2 Chr 27:8). Four times an infinitive functioning as a purpose clause is omitted. Twice לְעָזְרֵנִי "to help me" (1 Chr 12:17<18>; so also "to help him" 22<23>) is omitted.[135] One time לְהִלָּחֵם "went up to fight" (2 Chr 35:20) is omitted.

Twice a verb of motion is omitted: לָבוֹא "*to come* and make him king" 1 Chr 12:31<32>). לְמַעַן יִרָאוּךָ לָלֶכֶת בִּדְרָכֶיךָ "Thus may they fear you *and walk* in your ways" ὅπως φοβῶνται τὰς ὁδούς σου "thus they may reverence (lit., fear) your ways" (2 Chr 6:31).

Infinitives from the same root or with a similar meaning to another word in the context are sometimes omitted. לֵאמֹר "saying" is omitted with another verb of speaking and in a context where there is another

---

[135] It is interesting that the translator omitted the verb עָזַר "to help" twice in the same chapter referring to the men of Benjamin and Judah who came to David at Ziklag when he was escaping Saul. One time the *qatal* form of עָזַר is translated by συμμαχέω "to fight together" (1 Chr 12:21<22>). Perhaps the translator considered that David did not need any help from these men, although the same verb עָזַר is translated in vv. 1, 17<18> (2), 18<19> (referring to him not helping the Philistines), and perhaps v. 33<34> (which reads עֹדֵר). Alternatively, perhaps the verb was omitted because of the large number of repetitions in Hebrew of this verb in this passage.

לֵאמֹר (indicating reported speech within reported speech—1 Chr 10:10) and with the word דָּבָר "word" translated λόγον (2 Chr 34:16). The infinitive לָשׁוּב is omitted when it follows וַיָּשֻׁבוּ "returned" (20:27). The infinitive is omitted in the phrase עַד־מְלֹךְ מַלְכוּת "until the establishment of the kingdom" translated ἕως βασιλείας "until the kingdom" (36:20). The second infinitive is omitted in the expression וְלִשְׁמוֹר...לַעֲשׂוֹת "to keep and to do" translated τοῦ φυλάσσειν "to keep" (34:31)

The infinitive בַּצַּר־לוֹ "in their distress" is omitted (2 Chr 15:4). Finally, the infinitive "to destroy," which may have been considered too strong to go with the anointing of God in the expression אֲשֶׁר מְשָׁחוֹ יְהוָה לְהַכְרִית אֶת־בֵּית אַחְאָב "whom the LORD had anointed *to destroy* the house of Ahab" is mitigated by being omitted in the translation χριστὸν κυρίου τὸν οἶκον Αχααβ "anointed of the Lord...the house of Ahab" (2 Chr 22:7), or perhaps there is a lacuna.

s. Summary

Two-thirds of the infinitive constructs are translated by Greek infinitives mirroring the Hebrew. If the infinitive is preceded by a preposition, the preposition is mostly translated and/or an article is inserted.[136] However, for the remaining one-third of the infinitive constructs, the translator was willing to vary the syntax and incorporate a different Greek form. The translator varied the syntax by three main ways: by using another subordinate clause, a circumstantial participle, or a paratactic structure. Sometimes the translator specified the subordinate relationship by using a particular Greek subordinate conjunction (e.g., ὡς "when" or ὅταν "whenever"), which governs either an indicative or subjunctive verb form (five times). Circumstantial participles are used to translate the common infinitive לֵאמֹר used to introduce reported speech (55 times).[137] In

---

[136] Most of the *qᵉtol* infinitive construct forms (about 94%) in Chronicles are preceded by a preposition, with over 75% (469 times) preceded by the preposition לְ. The article is not usually present in Hebrew, but an articular infinitive is a very common Greek structure. The genitive articular infinitive is commonly used to translate purpose clauses preceded by לְ, e.g., וַיֵּלְכוּ...לְבַקֵּשׁ "They journeyed...to seek" translated ἐπορεύθησαν...τοῦ ζητῆσαι (1 Chr 4:39).

[137] Miller classifies it as a complementizer to introduce direct speech complements. As she points out, it differs from the normal infinitive complement preceded by the preposition לְ, not having the same morphological shape, not functioning as the infinitive complement of the matrix verb, and not functioning as an embedded (or gerundive) infinitive, Cynthia L. Miller, *The Representation of Speech in Biblical Hebrew*

addition, there are a few other times a circumstantial participle is chosen to render an adverbial infinitive complement. Occasionally (at least six times) the translator even diverged from the Hebrew subordinate (hypotactic) infinitive structure and used a paratactic structure with καί and an indicative (see note 131 above), thus making the target language more paratactic than the original. Perhaps because this structure was so prevalent the translator felt comfortable to employ it a few more times!

4. Qatol (Infinitive Absolute)

Infinitive absolutes occur in all three clause types but most commonly in main clauses. Since the *qatol* infinitive absolute has no equivalent in Greek, the translator had to do the best according to his understanding of its sense in Hebrew. Most of the *qatol* infinitive absolute forms have adverbial force (especially as adverbs of manner). Six derive from the same root as the main verb (internal accusative—1 Chr 4:10; 21:17, 24; 2 Chr 18:27; 28:19;[138] 32:13), seven infinitive absolute forms function as adverbs in their own right, such as הַרְבֵּה "much, a lot" (1 Chr 20:2; 2 Chr 11:12; 14:13<12>; 16:8; 25:9; 32:27) and הַשְׁכֵּם "rising up early" (36:15).[139] Less frequently, the infinitive absolute is equivalent to another finite verb form, especially an imperative, a *yiqtol* form (especially with injunctive force), or as equivalent to a preceding verbal form. There are five examples of two infinitive absolutes occurring in sequence, and at least twice the second verb reflects quasi-simultaneous action (1 Chr 11:9; 2 Chr 2:9<8>; 18:29; 31:10; 36:15). The infinitive absolute disappears from rabbinic Hebrew and was probably absent from the spoken register of Hebrew at the time of translation.

Narrative: A Linguistic Analysis (HSM 55; Atlanta: Scholars Press, 1996), 199-200. It is interesting that the translators chose a different way to translate it, using the participle of λέγω. One time it is translated by the Greek aorist infinitive εἰπεῖν (1 Chr 21:18). However, in this passage it functions as a true infinitive of indirect speech rather than a complementizer introducing direct speech.

[138] This verse actually contains an infinitive absolute followed by a noun (rather than a verb) from the same root.

[139] For a fuller treatment of the infinitive absolute with a finite verb in the entire Septuagint, see Emanuel Tov, "Renderings of Combinations of the Infinitive Absolute and Finite Verbs in the Septuagint—Their Nature and Distribution," in *Studien zur Septuaginta—Robert Hanhart zu Ehren. Aus Anlaß seines 65 Geburtstages* (ed. Fraenkel, D., U. Quast, and J. W. Wevers; Göttingen: Vandenhoeck & Ruprecht, 1990), 64-73.

The following table gives the breakdown on how the infinitive absolute forms in Chronicles were translated into Greek.

TABLE 9: THE TRANSLATION OF *QATOL* INFINITIVE ABSOLUTE FORMS

QATOL	TOTAL	Percentage	Narrative Main Clauses (Clause %)	Reported Speech Main Clauses	Subordinate Clauses
Aorist Indicative	6	24	3 (27.3)	3 (27.3)	
Future Indicative	2	8		2 (18.2)	
Present Participle	9	36	4 (36.4)	2 (18.2)	3 (100)
Adjective	5	20	2 (18.2)	3 (27.3)	
Noun	3	12	2 (18.2)	1 (9.1)	
Total	25	100	11	11	3

Total 25
Aorist Indicative (6 = 24%)
Narrative Main Clauses (3)
1 Chr 5:20; 16:36; 2 Chr 28:19
Reported Speech Main Clauses (3)
2 Chr 31:10 (3)
Future Indicative (2 = 8%)
Reported Speech Main Clauses (2)
2 Chr 18:29 (2)
Present Participle (9 = 36%)
Narrative Main Clauses (4)
1 Chr 11:9 (2); 2 Chr 36:15 (2)
Reported Speech Main Clauses (2)
1 Chr 21:17; 2 Chr 32:13
Subordinate Clauses (3)
1 Chr 4:10; 21:24; 2 Chr 18:27
Adjective (5 = 20%)
Narrative Main Clauses (3)
1 Chr 20:2; 2 Chr 14:13<12>; 32:27
Reported Speech Main Clauses (2)
2 Chr 2:9<8>; 25:9
Noun (3 = 12%)
Narrative Main Clauses (2)
1 Chr 15:22; 2 Chr 11:12

Reported Speech Main Clauses (1)
2 Chr 16:8

a. Qatol > Aorist Indicative (6 = 24%)

Most of the infinitive absolutes that are translated by aorists follow *qatal* forms that are translated by an aorist (1 Chr 5:20; 2 Chr 28:19) or infinitives translated by a perfect or aorists (2 Chr 31:10 (3)). Perhaps some of these infinitive absolutes were interpreted as *qatal* forms if the *Vorlage* was written with defective as opposed to full or plene spelling, e.g., נעתר instead of נֶעְתּוֹר (1 Chr 5:20), or מעל instead of מָעוֹל (2 Chr 28:19). However, this use of an infinitive absolute following a finite verb and having the same sense as the finite verb occurs quite frequently in biblical Hebrew, although less frequently in late biblical Hebrew.[140]

One infinitive absolute follows a *wayyiqtol* form that is translated by a future, "'Blessed be the Lord, the God of Israel, from everlasting even to everlasting.' Then all the people said (Gk. will say), 'Amen,' and *praised* the Lord" (1 Chr 16:36). It seems that the translators took the *wayyiqtol* form as part of the song or as instruction following the song. Then the infinitive absolute translated by an aorist would continue from v. 7 "David gave orders to praise the Lord," as a summing up of the singing of the song.

b. Qatol > Future Indicative (2 = 8%)

The two infinitive absolutes translated by Greek futures occur at the beginning of reported speech, "*I will disguise myself* and *go* into battle הִתְחַפֵּשׂ וָבוֹא, but you put on your robes." The infinitive absolutes translated κατακαλύψομαι καὶ εἰσελεύσομαι (2 Chr 18:29). The context lends itself to a future interpretation of the infinitive absolutes.

c. Qatol > Present Participle (9 = 36%)

Five of the adverbial internal accusative uses of the infinitive absolute are translated by participles. These function as adverbial circumstantial participles in Greek modifying the main verb. For

---

[140] The use of the infinitive absolute decreases in late biblical Hebrew, cf. Willem T. van Peursen, "The Verbal System in the Hebrew Text of Ben Sira" (Ph.D. diss., Universiteit Leiden, 1999), 245.

example, "Oh that you would [indeed] bless me" אִם־בָּרֵךְ תְּבָרֲכֵנִי translated ἐὰν εὐλογῶν εὐλογήσῃς (lit., if blessing you will bless me) (1 Chr 4:10) and "I have done very wickedly" וְהָרֵעַ הֲרֵעוֹתִי translated κακοποιῶν ἐκακοποίησα (lit., doing wickedly I have done wickedly) (1 Chr 21:17; so also 21:24; 2 Chr 18:27; 32:13).

The other four present participles translate two pairs of infinitive absolutes, וַיֵּלֶךְ דָּוִיד הָלוֹךְ וְגָדוֹל "David became greater and greater" translated πορευόμενος καὶ μεγαλυνόμενος (lit., *going on* and *being magnified*—1 Chr 11:9) and הַשְׁכֵּם וְשָׁלוֹחַ "he sent [word] to them again and again" translated ὀρθρίζων καὶ ἀποστέλλων (lit., *rising up* and *sending*—2 Chr 36:15).

d. Qatol > Adjective (5 = 20%)

Four of the adjectives are translations of הַרְבֵּה by πολλά "much" (1 Chr 20:2; so also 2 Chr 14:13<12>; 32:27) or πλεῖστα "very much" (2 Chr 25:9). The final adjective is a translation of the stative verb "to be wonderful" וְהַפְלֵא in "the house which I am about to build [will be] great and *wonderful*" by ἔνδοξος (2 Chr 2:8<7>).

e. Qatol > Noun (3 = 12%)

Two nouns are employed in the translation of לְהַרְבֵּה by εἰς πλῆθος "for a great number" (2 Chr 11:12; 16:8). The third noun is a translation of יָסַר "*he gave instruction* in singing" by ἄρχων "leader". Preceding it שַׂר is translated ἄρχων (1 Chr 15:22). Perhaps the translator understood the Hebrew word שַׂר which is very similar in sound to the infinitive absolute יָסַר.

f. Summary

The participle is the preferred equivalent for the cognate infinitive absolutes functioning adverbially. Indicative forms are used when the infinitive functions like an indicative form with the context supplying the time frame and hence suggesting the appropriate Greek tense form. Adjectives and nouns are used to translate particular verb forms.

C. Other Forms

The other Hebrew verb form, the imperative, is not covered in this study. Since almost 90% of the imperative forms are translated by a Greek imperative (68% by the aorist and 21% by the present imperative) and there are only five imperatives translated by indicative forms, we will not include them in our data presentation and analysis. In addition, a number of non-verbal forms translated by Greek verb forms and Greek pluses occur. These are analyzed in chapter 5.

D. The Translation of Verb Forms according to Clause Types and Historical-Linguistic Changes

1. Main Clause Narrative

In narrative main clauses, *wayyiqtol* is the predominant verbal form (accounting for almost 60% of the verbal forms, see table 19 in appendix). It is the unmarked verbal form used to indicate the events of the narrative (continuing the main or story line). A number of *qatal* forms break up strings of clauses with *wayyiqtol* forms and usually indicate an interruption in the main or story line, either to topicalize or focus an element such as a new subject, or to indicate subsidiary line or off-the-line events.[141] The vast majority of *wayyiqtol* forms (91%) and *qatal* forms (83%), both perfective forms, are translated by aorists (the unmarked perfective event line form in Greek narrative).[142] There are a number of durative predicative participles and *yiqtol* forms occurring in the narrative sections of Chronicles. They mostly indicate

---

[141] Not every *qatal* form is necessarily a background (out-of-line) form. Approximately 15% of *qatal* forms are immediately preceded by a part of speech such as the negative לֹא. Rules of Hebrew syntax dictate that when a part of speech is inserted before the verb, the *wayyiqtol* chain must be broken and a non-*wayyiqtol* (most frequently a *qatal* form) take its place. A. Niccacci, review of David Allen Dawson, *Text-Linguistics and Biblical Hebrew*, *LASBF* 45 (1995): 543-80, interprets many of these forms as foreground (mainline), 551. John A. Cook also gives examples of *qatal* forms which are not background but rather continue the temporal sequence, e.g., in genealogies, such as Genesis 4:18, "Semantics of Verbal Pragmatics," 8. It is interesting that almost a third of the *qatal* forms in narrative occur in the first nine chapters of 1 Chronicles, which comprises mostly genealogical material.

[142] See table 19. In terms of Greek text linguistics, in narrative the aorist (indicative and postposed participles) is the usual verb form to indicate the event line (i.e., unmarked) and other verb forms ((preposed) participles, historic presents, imperfects, 'be' verbs, and verbless clauses) indicate markedness (e.g., background, circumstance etc.), Longacre, "Mark 5.1-43," 169-96.

circumstantial (simultaneous) action or reinforce a new topic or focus. Greek durative forms (imperfects, present participles) mostly translate them. However, a significant number are also translated by aorists.

The *yiqtol* form in narrative is particularly significant in terms of the historical development of the Hebrew language. In past contexts it can have two opposite meanings, an archaic perfective preterite (e.g., with אָז), and a past imperfective (durative).[143] Both of these senses of the *yiqtol* form become less common in late biblical Hebrew and are not that common in Chronicles. When they do occur the translator recognized both uses in his translation. He translated the *yiqtols* with a preterite sense by an aorist and some of the *yiqtols* with a past imperfective sense by imperfects. However, almost as many past imperfective *yiqtols* were translated by aorists. Did he consider these forms as an extension of the preterite use of *yiqtol,* or did he itemize the actions as part of the event line without a concern to give them an imperfective aspectual marking? Sometimes the *yiqtol* forms translated as aorists occur in parallel sections, and the translator followed the translation of Samuel-Kings (2 Sam 12:31 // 1 Chr 20:3; 1 Kgs 8:1 // 2 Chr 5:2; 2 Kgs 8:22 // 2 Chr 21:10). However, many times the parallel passage lacked the *yiqtol* verb or there was no parallel passage. A few times *yiqtol* past imperfective forms are translated by futures, perhaps indicating the translator was defaulting to the common equivalent according to Hebrew spoken at the time of translation, and the resulting reading is awkward.

Probably by the time of the writing and the time of the translation of Chronicles *wᵉqatal* forms were used more and more as the coordinated past form replacing *wayyiqtol*, especially in spoken Hebrew. The translator recognized several *wᵉqatal* forms as coordinated past time forms and translated them as καί followed by an aorist. However, these examples are not sequential (cf. note 149 below, for reported speech). Therefore, the replacement of *wayyiqtol* by *wᵉqatal* as a sequential form does not really occur in Chronicles, and it is uncertain how much it influenced the translation.

---

[143] *Yiqtol* durative forms occur more commonly in sections parallel to Samuel-Kings (corresponding to classical Hebrew text). Conversely the later alternative way to render past durative action, the periphrastic participle with הָיָה occurs more frequently in passages unique to Chronicles (28 times, or 21 times if you count only one of a number of participles following הָיָה. In parallel passages periphrastics occur 10 times). The distribution of the 38 periphrastic participles in the different text types of Chronicles is: narrative (26, 21 unique to Chronicles), reported speech (4, 1 unique), and subordinate clauses (8, 6 unique).

Another major change in narrative by the time of the writing of Chronicles and its translation is the decline in use of the form וַיְהִי "and it came to pass" to introduce temporal structures in narrative. It occurs thirty times in Chronicles (see note 24), including twenty-one times in passages *parallel* to Samuel-Kings (i.e., 70%). Temporal structures without the introductory וַיְהִי occur forty-two times; twenty-nine times in passages *unique* to Chronicles (69.1%). Most of the time the translator translated וַיְהִי καὶ ἐγένετο. One time καὶ ἐγένετο was omitted in translation (2 Chr 20:1), and three times it was added (2 Chr 20:26; 24:17; 29:3). (Perhaps these omissions or additions reflect the absence or presence of וַיְהִי in the *Vorlage*). Three times Chronicles lacks וַיְהִי when parallel passages Samuel-Kings have it (1 Kgs 8:54 // 2 Chr 7:1; 1 Kgs 9:1 // 2 Chr 7:11; 2 Kgs 22:3 // 2 Chr 34:8) also indicating the decline in the use of this form.

2. Main Clause Reported Speech

In reported speech, a greater variety of verb forms is used compared to narrative (see table 21 in appendix). This is because reported speech can involve three different time frames: past, present, and future, all relative to the moment of speaking.

In past time frames, *qatal* forms are more common than *wayyiqtol* forms. A greater ratio of *qatal* to *wayyiqtol* forms is one of the main distinctions between <u>oral narrative</u> (narrative in reported speech) and <u>historical narrative</u> (narrative related by the narrator).[144] There are two main reasons for this. First, there are fewer long sections of oral narrative where strings of *wayyiqtol* forms could occur.[145] Second, each section of oral narrative is usually introduced by a non-*wayyiqtol* form. The *wayyiqtol* forms in oral narrative mostly follow *qatal* forms, with a few preceded by noun sentences or a *qotel* form. This has the effect of

---

[144] There is some debate as to whether the discourse function of verb forms differs between oral narrative and historic narrative. Niccacci considers foregrounding is indicated by the *qatal* form (continued by *wayyiqtol*) for the past in direct speech (oral narrative). This is disputed by Dawson (who follows Longacre) and Endo who do not see a distinction between the two kinds of narrative in terms of the function of verbal forms (cf. A. Niccacci, review of Dawson, 558–559).

[145] The main sections of oral narrative where *wayyiqtol* forms occur are 1 Chronicles 17:8, 17; 28:4-6; and 2 Chronicles 6:6-11; 7:22; 13:6-7; 18:16-21; 20:7-8; 21:13; 25:18; 29:6-8; 34:17, 25-27.

increasing the number of non-*wayyiqtol* forms.[146] As in narrative, the aorist is the preferred equivalent for both *qatal* and *wayyiqtol* forms.

In present contexts, the noun sentence is the most common Hebrew structure (with or without a *qotel* participle).[147] These are frequently translated by the Greek present. It is quite striking that the majority of the *qotel* forms are rendered by a present indicative, especially compared to only a few present participles (the standard equivalent in narrative). By the time of translation the Hebrew participle was on the way to becoming a present form (especially in spoken Hebrew). This may have influenced the translator in his choice, although this use of the *qotel* form as a present is also found in classical biblical Hebrew, mostly in reported speech (see note 150 below).

In future contexts, the *yiqtol* and *weqatal* forms predominate. Similar to oral narrative, the simple (*yiqtol*) form is more common than the consecutive (*weqatal*) form. This is because there are only a few longer sections of consecutive future events, e.g., in longer speeches (e.g., YHWH's promise to David—1 Chr 17:9-12, and Solomon's prayer—2 Chr 6:21-36). Further, each section containing *weqatal* forms must begin with non-*weqatal* forms such as *yiqtol* forms or imperatives, with a few noun sentences or infinitive constructs.[148] The Greek future is the common equivalent for both *yiqtol* and *weqatal* forms.

The historical developments in verb use are more likely to manifest themselves in reported speech. The most striking is the participle in

---

[146] To confirm this, the six one-clause verbal utterances in past contexts in Chronicles all contain a *qatal* form. Interestingly, the *qatal* verb form is usually preceded by another part of speech, thus precluding a sequential form. The six verses with their word orders are: 1 Chronicles 17:7 (S-V); and 2 Chronicles 6:1 (S-V); 18:23 (Interrog.-V-S); 34:15 (O-V-Adv.) and 34:18 (O-V-IO-S). One verse (1 Chr 4:9 (V-Adv.) has the conjunction כִּי following a verb of speaking preceding the verb—perhaps a כִּי recitativum introducing direct speech (cf. Joüon and Muraoka, *Grammar of Biblical Hebrew*, 590).

[147] See chapter 5, especially the sections A.2 and A.5 on the imperfect and present tenses. Niccacci considers that foregrounding in the present is indicated by a nominal clause, and in the future by X-*yiqtol* as the initial verb form and *weqatal* as the continuation form. Backgrounding in the past, present, and future time frames is indicated by X-*qatal*, nominal clauses, and X-*yiqtol* respectively (A. Niccacci, review of Dawson, 558-559).

[148] All ten one-clause verbal utterances in future time contain a *yiqtol* form, eight are translated by a future in Greek (one *yiqtol* functions as a prohibition and is translated by an aorist imperative). In all of these clauses the verb is preceded by another element, usually a function word or a topic. The ten one clause verses in oral narrative future time with their word orders are: 1 Chronicles 11:5 (Neg.-V), 6 (S-Adv.-V), 17 (Interrog.-V); 12:19 (Adv.-V); 13:12 (Interrog.-V); 16:18 (PP-V); 17:4 (Neg.-Pron.-V); and 2 Chronicles 18:3 (Interrog.-V), 20 (Pron.-V); 32:11 (S-V).

present contexts functioning as a present tense, translated by the
Greek present indicative. In oral narrative there are no וַיְהִי forms,
and there are only two *yiqtol* forms in past context (both are stative
verbs; one has textual problems and the other also has present
relevance). Although oral narrative contains more *qatal* forms than
wayyiqtol forms, the reason is more due to the size of the narrative
sections rather than a change in use. Archaic consecutive forms still
operate in reported speech, and there is still a distinction between
them and simple coordinated forms.[149] Nevertheless, we could say that
verbs in reported speech more closely correspond to the Hebrew
spoken by the translators than in narrative. The *qatal* form is the
predominant past punctual form, the *qotel* form the predominant
present form, and the *yiqtol* form the predominant future form, as in
Mishnaic or rabbinic Hebrew.[150] It seems that the trend is reinforced

---

[149] Even though the percentage of *wᵉqatal* forms in speech is greater than those in
narrative, compared to *wayyiqtol* forms there is a paucity of *wᵉqatal* forms, none of
which seem to be used for the event line of narrative. Only one time does more than
one *wᵉqatal* form occur in close proximity (1 Chr 22:18 (2)), and these forms are not
really in sequence but rather itemize disjointed events. Only a few times *qatal* forms
are in close proximity, and they do not indicate narrative sequence, e.g., "You *have
shown* mercy, and You *have made* me *king*" (2 Chr 1:8 (2)), "We *have sinned*, and *have done
wrong*; we *have acted wickedly*" (6:37 (3)), or preceded by negatives: "They also *shut* the
doors…and *have* not *offered* incense nor *made* burnt offerings" (29:7). Although the
prevalence of *qatal* forms in oral narrative makes it closer to the speech of the writers,
at the time of Chronicles the *wayyiqtol* form was still the predominant form for
sequential narrative.
   Similar to the distinction between sequential and non-sequential forms in
narrative, there is a distinction between *wᵉqatal* and *wᵉyiqtol* forms indicating
coordinated future action. *Wᵉqatal* forms contain a notion of sequentiality, or at least
foregrounding, that is not present when *wᵉyiqtol* forms occur. Eventually *wᵉyiqtol*
replaces the future *wᵉqatal* as the standard coordinated and consecutive future form,
but at the time of Chronicles the older distinction was still preserved.
[150] Cf. Pérez Fernández, *Introductory Grammar of Rabbinic Hebrew*, 107. This tendency
for reported speech to be closer to Mishnaic Hebrew is evident not just in the late
biblical Hebrew of Chronicles, but it is also evident in reported speech in classical
Hebrew texts, but perhaps with lesser frequency. For example, participles also
function as a present form in classical Hebrew, as can be seen in the classical biblical
Hebrew passages parallel to Chronicles. Of the 27 reported speech main clause *qotel*
forms translated by present indicatives (see page 144), 8 *qotel* forms occur in parallel
passages (2 Sam 7:2 // 1 Chr 17:1; 2 Sam 24:12 // 1 Chr 21:10; 1 Kgs 10:8 // 2 Chr
9:7; 1 Kgs 12:6 // 2 Chr 10:6, 1 Kgs 12:9 // 2 Chr 10:9; 1 Kgs 22:16 // 2 Chr
18:15; 2 Kgs 22:16 // 2 Chr 34:24; 2 Kgs 22:20 // 2 Chr 34:28) and 17 are unique
to Chronicles. In one example, which perhaps illustrates further a development in late
biblical Hebrew from classical, a *qatal* form בָּטַחְתָּ in 2 Kings 18:19 (and Isa 36:4)
occurs as a *qotel* בֹּטְחִים in the parallel passage in 2 Chronicles 32:10. In another
example, an infinitive rather than a *qotel* form occurs in the parallel passage (1 Kgs
5:19 // 2 Chr 2:4<3>). Perhaps we could say that a situation of diglossia existed in
biblical Hebrew times, with an archaic literary dialect and a colloquial spoken dialect.

by the Septuagint translation, which frequently renders the participle with a present tense. The translation reflects the on-going development of the Hebrew language toward the tense verb system of Mishnaic Hebrew.

3. Subordinate Clauses

Most subordinate clauses with indicative forms are either adjectival clauses (with אֲשֶׁר), or adverbial clauses (with כִּי). Infinitive construct clauses are also counted as subordinate clauses, but they are not focused on in this chapter. Since subordinate clauses are grammatically subordinate, in terms of the discourse they can be considered background or out-of-line.

In past contexts the *qatal* form is the predominant indicative verb form in subordinate clauses.[151] It indicates action prior to the main verb or verb of speaking. The standard word order is for the subordinating conjunction to come right before the *qatal* form.[152] A new topic or focus may come between the conjunction and the *qatal* form, but it does not change the Hebrew verb form in the way a new topic breaks consecutive forms in main clauses. Aorist indicatives translate about 76% of the *qatal* forms. Imperfects, aorist participles, or perfects mostly translate the remaining 24% (see table 23).

In present time frames, *qatal* and *qotel* forms are translated as presents. In the future time *yiqtol* forms predominate, and these are translated by Greek futures and aorist subjunctives. The aorist subjunctives are due to constraints of Greek subordinate clauses, for example, purpose and certain condition clauses, which require a subjunctive.

The archaic literary dialect was eventually replaced by the spoken dialect in the literary register in Mishnaic Hebrew. See Gary A. Rendsburg, *Diglossia in Ancient Israel* (New Haven: American Oriental Society, 1990). The impact of the spoken register on literary Hebrew can be observed already in the reported speech sections of both classical and late biblical Hebrew, but more so in the latter.

[151] See tables 1 and 23. Approximately 408 of the total of 1035 *qatal* (non-*wᵉqatal*) forms in Chronicles (i.e., 40%) occur in subordinate clauses. A few *wayyiqtol* and *wᵉqatal* forms governed by the subordinate conjunction occur. We have analyzed them as main clause forms. The *yiqtol* form occurs approximately 50 times, and there are also a number of noun clauses governed by subordinate conjunctions.

[152] Especially in relative אֲשֶׁר clauses (more than כִּי clauses), cf. Creason, "Word Order in Relative Clauses," mentioned in chapter 3, note 17. Holmstead considers the subordinating conjunction or relative as a function word that triggers inversion from SV to XVS word order, "Relative Clause in Biblical Hebrew," 145-50.

There are a few archaic uses of forms in subordinate clauses. Five *yiqtol* forms are translated by past tense forms. Four of them occur in narrative subordinate clauses with durative sense; two are translated by aorists, and two by imperfects. Most of the Hebrew participles in subordinate clauses are translated by indicative forms especially the present indicative, perhaps an indicator that the translator considered them as equivalent to present tenses.

IV. CONCLUSION

In this chapter, we have analyzed the translation of four Hebrew indicative forms, two participles, and two infinitives. In it we identified the common equivalents as well as other equivalents. The translator was influenced by three main factors in his choice of equivalents. He was influenced by the Hebrew spoken at the time of the translation, a traditional understanding of the archaic use of certain forms, and by the textual-linguistic context the forms were in (i.e., clause type, *Aktionsart*, and discourse pragmatics).

For most of the Hebrew verb forms, the translator employed a common Greek equivalent. In his choice of equivalents, his contemporary spoken Hebrew mostly influenced him. The majority of *qatal* forms are translated by aorist indicatives, and the greatest number of *yiqtol* forms are translated by Greek futures. Participles are mostly translated by participles, and infinitive constructs by infinitives. (These results mostly agree with the results of previous studies, cf. chapter 1, note 24). Sometimes he chose present indicatives and periphrastic forms to translate participles. This was probably due to the change in the function of the participle to a tensed form and the increase in periphrastic forms (especially for durative past tenses) in his contemporary spoken Hebrew.[153] He chose the aorist and the future as common equivalents for the two archaic *wayyiqtol* and *wᵉqatal* consecutive forms based on a traditional understanding of their use.

---

[153] The use of participles indicating present time events can also be observed in reported speech sections of classical Hebrew. This is probably due to the fact that reported speech approximates the spoken register, which became standard Mishnaic Hebrew. For examples to indicate that the translators had knowledge of vernacular Hebrew spoken in Palestine in their time see Jan Joosten, "Biblical Hebrew as Mirrored in the Septuagint: The Question of Influence from Spoken Hebrew," *Text* 21 (2002): 1-19. He also encourages the study of the Septuagint as a source of information for the study of Hebrew in this time period (19).

Rarely *wayyiqtol* forms and *yiqtol* past durative forms are translated as futures, and *wᵉqatal* consecutive forms are translated as aorists. Occasionally *wayyiqtol* strings are also broken up, and the *wayyiqtol* form is translated by an infinitive, participle, adjective, adverb, or is not translated. The translator's contemporary spoken Hebrew probably influenced him in the way he translated these forms. Stative verb forms are frequently translated by adjectives, and הָיָה is frequently translated by the verb to "be." This is probably influenced by contemporary Hebrew, since in rabbinic Hebrew adjectives replace stative verbs and the meaning הָיָה "to be" supercedes its original meaning "to become," especially as it increasingly functions as a tense marker with periphrastic participles and adjectives.

In addition to these common equivalents, the translators also employed a variety of Greek forms (verbal and non-verbal) that do not exactly correspond to a particular Hebrew form, such as, imperfects, presents, perfects, pluperfects, and non-indicative moods. The textual-linguistic context or other constraints of the target language (e.g., Greek grammar) either determine or allow a non-standard equivalent to be used (Sailhamer's dynamic equivalents). Sometimes the theological context may have influenced the translator in his use of verb forms, e.g., the use of future forms in a past context or vice versa, the use of perfect forms in actions where God is involved. In the next chapter, we will focus more on the Greek verb forms used and their adequacy in representing the Hebrew text.

CHAPTER FIVE

THE RATIONALE FOR GREEK VERB FORMS

Chapter 2 considered the cultural context of the Greek translation of the book of Chronicles. Chapter 3 surveyed the inventory of Hebrew and Greek verb forms, introducing how they function in their text-linguistic context, in three clause types. It also mentioned the historical linguistic context, i.e., the differences between archaic verb use and verb use contemporary to the translator due to the historical developments in the Hebrew language. We also mentioned how additional factors in the linguistic context such as *Aktionsart: lexis* and discourse pragmatics influenced verb choice. Chapter 4 presented how the Hebrew verb forms were rendered into Greek with some mention of their historical linguistic and text linguistic contexts. This chapter focuses more on the Greek translation. It considers why the translator chose (or avoided) particular Greek verb forms (especially the non-standard equivalent verb forms) due to the influence of the cultural, historical, and textual-linguistic contexts and how the resulting translation reads.

The translator sometimes chose non-standard equivalent Greek forms (such as the imperfect and the perfect forms) due to the influence of the textual-linguistic context (clause types, situation aspect, and discourse pragmatics) and so help the Greek text read better (i.e., improve it).[1] In the cultural context, the desire of the translator to bring the reader as closer to the source influenced the translator to avoid non-standard Greek equivalents such as the "historic" present and circumstantial participle for paratactic *wayyiqtol*

---

[1] While these considerations are concerns of modern linguistic theory and unlikely to be those of either the authors or translators, they give us a methodological basis to compare the source text and the translation. It is interesting to note that Fanning also identifies three main linguistic features that influence the function of verbal aspect: lexical, contextual, and discourse features (*Verbal Aspect*, 194). He considers that the most important of these features appears to be the inherent lexical meaning [the verb's procedural characteristics or *Aktionsart*] carried by the verb itself (*Verbal Aspect*, 126). However, it seems that the significance of these features varies from language to language and inherent lexical meaning is more important in Greek than in Hebrew (see excursus in chapter 3).

forms in narrative (i.e., resist certain non-standard forms). In the historical linguistic context, the Hebrew current at the time of translation, i.e., the Hebrew of the Hellenistic/Roman period, influenced the use of certain forms. Some Hebrew participles were translated by present indicative forms, some *yiqtol* durative forms in the past were replaced by periphrastic participles, the introductory וַיְהִי sometimes was omitted or not translated, a few past *yiqtol/wayyiqtol* forms were considered as futures, infinitive absolutes were interpreted as other forms, and some *wᵉqatal* consecutive forms were considered as past forms (i.e., contemporize). These changes are observed more commonly in reported speech sections, which are more likely to reflect the spoken Hebrew of the time and be recognized as such by the translator.

We tabulate all of the Greek indicative forms and participles according to each text type (indicating which Hebrew forms they correspond to). This is followed by the analysis of each Greek form in detail according to the three text types, taking into account *Aktionsart*, and discourse pragmatic features in determining the choice of Greek verb form, especially the forms that are not common equivalents. We give verse references and more detail when Greek verb forms do not correspond to a Hebrew verb form (i.e., they correspond to a noun, noun sentence, or are a plus, i.e., they are not present in the Masoretic Hebrew text), since these equivalents were not covered in chapter 4. We also mention variations in word order, in syntactic structure (i.e., paratactic vs. hypotactic), in text type, and in temporal iconicity between the Hebrew text and the Greek translation, and the omission of a verb form that is present in the Masoretic Hebrew text (minus).

I. GREEK INDICATIVE FORMS AND PARTICIPLES

The following section contains tables of the Greek indicative forms and participles used to translate Hebrew forms. The comments for each Greek form are arranged according to Hebrew forms with mention of the difference between clause types when relevant. *Wᵉqatal* are itemized separately as well as included in *qatal* forms (the subtotal excludes the separate *wᵉqatal* forms). In addition, *wᵉyiqtol* forms are indicated in parentheses with the *yiqtol* forms. Percentages of the Hebrew form translated by the particular Greek form are given (taken from the tables of the Hebrew forms in chapter 4). Imperatives, non-verbal forms, and Greek pluses are indicated below the table with verse references according to clause types or genres, since this information is not specified in detail elsewhere in the book. In the appendix *GRAMCORD* adjustments are indicated to reconcile my statistics with theirs.

A. Indicative Forms

1. Aorist

The following table shows the aorist indicative forms and the Hebrew correspondences, including imperative and non-verbal forms and pluses (based upon the Hebrew MT).

TABLE 10: AORIST INDICATIVES TRANSLATED FROM HEBREW

AORIST	TOTAL	Percentage of Hebrew form (from ch. 4)	Narrative Main Clauses	Reported Speech Main Clauses	Subordinate Clauses
Wayyiqtol	1330	91.79	1261	69	
Qatal	840	72.23	429	99	312
Wᵉqatal	23	17.97	11	12	
Yiqtol (wᵉyiqtol)	13 (3)	3.7 (5.56)	9 (2)	1 (1)	3
Qotel	12 predicate 19 total	3.84	9 15	2 3	1 1
Qatul	1 predicate 1 total	1.37	1 1		
Qᵉtol Infin. Construct	41	6.7			41
Qᵃtol Infin. Absolute	6	24	3	3	
Qᵉtol Imperative	1	0.61		1	
Sub Total	2251 (-23 *wᵉqatal*)		1718	176	357
Adjective, Noun, Noun Sentence, and Plus	94		69	7	18
Total	2345		1787	183	375
Total Verbs in Text Type			2344	597	646
Percentage of Form in Text Type			76.24	30.65	58.05

Imperatives Translated by Aorists
Reported Speech Main Clauses (1)
2 Chr 35:3
Non-verbals Translated by Aorists and Aorist Pluses:
Narrative Main Clauses (69)
1 Chr 2:24; 4:22, 23; 10:13; 11:8; 12:18<19>; 13:6; 19:9; 21:26;
24:28; 26:27; 28:15, 16, 18; 2 Chr 4:16; 8:16; 10:2; 11:16; 12:16;
16:12; 20:20, 24; 21: 9; 22:9, 11; 23:3, 13 (2), 14, 18; 24:6, 9, 17, 19,
27; 26:16; 28:22; 29:3; 30:14, 26; 31:6, 13; 32:9, 25; 35:3, 8, 13, 16,
19 (5); 36:1, 2 (2), 4 (3), 5 (6), 8 (2), 17 (2)
Reported Speech Main Clauses (7)
1 Chr 16:9, 19; 17:17; 28:2; 2 Chr 18:12; 19:2; 35:19
Subordinate Clauses (18)
1 Chr 23:28; 2 Chr 12:1; 16:10; 24:11; 25:20; 29:3; 34:22; 35:19 (7);
36:2, 5 (3)

The aorist indicative is the common equivalent for both *wayyiqtol* forms
(in narrative and reported speech) and *qatal* forms (in all clause types).
One of the most striking features of the Greek translation of the Old
Testament is the predominance of this tense. It is even more
ubiquitous than the *wayyiqtol* form in Hebrew narrative. Aorists are
particularly prevalent in narrative relative to other forms, with 76% of
all the Greek indicative forms and participles in the narrative being
aorists (although 5% of the aorists translate other Hebrew forms).[2]
Maybe the aspectual force of the *wayyiqtol* and *qatal* forms constrained
the translator to use the aorist for both forms.

The presence of so many aorists in the translation could give the
reader the impression that there are many perfective, mainline,
unmarked events in the text. However, due to the translator's strict
adherence to the word order of the source language, the reader can,

---

[2] The percentage of aorists to all verb forms is much higher than in standard
Greek. Circumstantial participles and imperfect forms are much more common in
non-translated Greek, cf. Evans, *Verbal Syntax*, 198-219 (especially his table 9, 204-
205), who gives statistics for relative frequencies of imperfect and aorist indicatives. In
the translation of Chronicles 2345 out of 2592 or 90% of all aorists and imperfects are
aorists, higher than the highest percentage in non-Septuagintal Greek, cf. Evans cited by Evans,
higher than the highest percentage of all the Gospels and Acts (87% in the Gospel of
Matthew), but fairly typical of most of the other Septuagint books. There is diachronic
variation, with the aorist becoming more prevalent in later Greek literature, especially
in later papyri and in the New Testament. It is also interesting to note that the
imperfect occurs more commonly than the aorist in the classical Greek texts of
Herodotus, Thucydides, and Xenophon.

for the most part, reconstruct the underlying Hebrew verb form, i.e., distinguish a *wayyiqtol* form from a *qatal* form. Most of the time καί + aorist indicates a *wayyiqtol* form, and καί + X (X = another element) + aorist indicates a non-*wayyiqtol* (mostly a *qatal*) form.[3] However, all the *wᵉqatal* forms in narrative and twelve in reported speech are also translated by καί and an aorist. The *wᵉqatal* forms are mostly in past contexts and are not sequentially (temporally or logically) connected to what precedes. There are two *wᵉqatal* consecutive forms in reported speech understood as having a future sense that are translated as aorists (1 Chr 17:8, 10). The aorist tense in these contexts also makes sense as a past fulfillment rather than a future promise. It is not clear whether the translator's motivation was eschatological, i.e., he considered that Solomon's name had already been made great (v. 8), and the enemies had already been subdued (v. 10) by the time of David's speech in 1 Chronicles 17; or whether his motivation was linguistic, i.e., he considered these forms as coordinated past forms according to the context (they are preceded by a *wayyiqtol* and a *qatal* form respectively, both with past meaning) and this the most natural way to take them in the translator's Hebrew (where *wᵉqatal* forms are no longer "converted" from past to future but were the standard coordinated narrative form).

The aorist also translates other Hebrew verb forms *yiqtol, qotel, qatul, qatol* infinitive absolute. In addition, there are over ninety examples where the aorist is used to translate a non-verbal form or as a Greek plus.

Sometimes the use of the aorist as a translation equivalent is most logical, e.g., for the three *yiqtol* forms having preterite meaning with אָז "then" or עַד "until." (אָז and *yiqtol* occur in parallel passages, 1 Kgs 8:1 // 2 Chr 5:2; 2 Kgs 8:22 // 2 Chr 21:10). Other times the use of

---

[3] Eleven times a *wayyiqtol* form is not translated by καί immediately followed by an aorist (7 times καί is omitted, and 4 times the word order is varied and another element comes between καί and the aorist—see chapter 4, on *wayyiqtol* forms translated by aorists, section a.). Conversely, 38 times other forms are translated this way. Eleven *wᵉqatal* (1 Chr 7:21; 8:7; 11:22; 2 Chr 3:7; 12:10; 24:11; 31:21; 33:4, 6, 19; 34:4), at least 16 asyndetic *qatal* forms (1 Chr 1:32; 4:23; 26:27; 2 Chr 5:5; 12:7; 16:14; 21:9; 26:5; 28:9; 29:7; 31:21; 32:31; 34:4; 35:8, 20; 36:6), and 11 other forms in narrative are also translated this way. Six (*wᵉ*)*qotel* (1 Chr 15:29; 2 Chr 23:13; 24:14; 31:6, 10 in narrative and 1 Chr 16:19 in reported speech), 5 (*wᵉ*)*yiqtol* (1 Chr 11:8, 2 Chr 4:5; 29:11 (2) in narrative; and 2 Chr 34:25 in reported speech), and 4 infinitive absolute forms (1 Chr 5:20; 16:36 in narrative and 2 Chr 31:10 (2) in reported speech) are also translated by καί and an aorist. Two subordinate כִּי *qatal* clauses are also translated by καί and an aorist (2 Chr 28:21; 30:18).

the aorist as an equivalent is more unusual. Once an aorist is used to translate a *wᵉyiqtol* form (perhaps understood as a *wayyiqtol*) interpreting God's wrath as having already been poured out (2 Chr 34:25). A number of times the translator preferred to use an aorist to translate a *yiqtol* form with a past durative (or customary) sense, over the more appropriate Greek equivalent, the imperfect. Perhaps the translator saw from the context that these *yiqtol* forms could not be interpreted as future/modal forms, so he defaulted mechanically to the most common past form, the aorist (rather than the less common imperfect). The *qotel* forms (including a periphrastic participle) translated by aorists are circumstantial participles with different subjects to the main verb, and a number indicate simultaneous action. An appropriate way to render these into Greek would have been to use a circumstantial participle (especially a genitive absolute with a different subject to the main verb), or an imperfect. Once an imperative is translated by an aorist as the continuation of narrative, delaying the initiation of reported speech (2 Chr 35:3).

A number of aorists (41) translate infinitive construct forms. These are mostly translations of temporal infinitive constructs by a temporal clause in Greek (especially following ὡς "when") containing an indicative aorist. Most commonly, the translator used a Greek infinitive to render the infinitive construct, but he also felt comfortable using an aorist in a subordinate clause (about 6% of the time). Perhaps this reflects the trend away from the construction כְּ and בְּ and an infinitive construct, which is replaced by an indicative form in rabbinic Hebrew.

A number of non-verbal forms such as nouns, adjectives, or noun sentences are translated by aorists. For example, a place name בַּעֲלָתָה, perhaps not recognized by the translator and interpreted as a form of the verb עָלָה 'to go up,' is translated by an aorist וַיַּעַל דָּוִיד וְכָל־יִשְׂרָאֵל בַּעֲלָתָה אֶל־קִרְיַת יְעָרִים "and David and all Israel went up to Baalah, that is, to Kiriath-jearim," translated καὶ ἀνήγαγεν αὐτὴν Δαυιδ καὶ πᾶς Ισραηλ ἀνέβη εἰς πόλιν Δαυιδ "and David brought it [the ark] up, and all Israel *went up* to the city of David" (1 Chr 13:6; so also 4:22; 2 Chr 4:16). Many times a noun or adjective that corresponds to a verbal idea is translated by a verb, e.g., וְאֵת כָּל־הַמְקַטְּרוֹת "and all the incense altars" translated πάντα ἐν οἷς ἐθυμίωσαν τοῖς ψευδέσιν "and all on which *they offered* incense [to false *gods*]" (2 Chr 30:14; so also 1 Chr 16:12, 19; 17:17; 23:28; 2 Chr 8:16; 16:10; 18:12 (2); 23:13; 24:6, 9, 11; 26:16; 31:13; 35:8).

Sometimes the translator expanded the translation with the addition of an aorist.[4] Sometimes it is part of an additional phrase at the end of the verse, e.g., καὶ ἐπήκουσεν αὐτῷ ἐν πυρὶ...καὶ κατανάλωσεν τὴν ὁλοκαύτωσιν "and he answered by fire...and *it consumed* the whole burnt offering" (1 Chr 21:26; so also 2 Chr 21:9). Sometimes the meaning of one Hebrew verb is expanded by using two verbs to translate it, perhaps to clarify the meaning, e.g., וַיִּשְׁכַּב רְחַבְעָם עִם־אֲבֹתָיו "and Rehoboam slept with his ancestors" translated καὶ *ἀπέθανεν* Ροβοαμ καὶ *ἐτάφη* μετὰ τῶν πατέρων αὐτοῦ "and Rehoboam *died and was buried* with his ancestors" (12:16; so also 20:24; 21:5; 29:3<2>; 35:16; 36:1). Verbs of speaking are also added (1 Chr 12:18<19>; 2 Chr 20:20; 22:9; 23:13; 28:22; 34:22; 35:3). Sometimes a verb is supplied to help the reading, and the same verb may occur nearby in the context, e.g., ἔδωκεν αὐτῷ "and *he gave* to him" (1 Chr 28:15, 16—the same verb occurring in vv. 11 and 19 corresponding to a Hebrew form; so also 2 Chr 31:6; 32:9, 25; 36:17; 1 Chr 2:24).

It is not always clear whether the source of the expansion is the translator or the *Vorlage*. Sometimes an "expansion" may be due to a deletion in the MT, e.g., לְמַחְלִי אֶלְעָזָר ___ וְלֹא־הָיָה לוֹ בָּנִים "of Mahli: Eleazar, who had no sons," translated τῷ Μοολι Ελεαζαρ καὶ Ιθαμαρ καὶ *ἀπέθανεν* Ελεαζαρ καὶ οὐκ ἦσαν αὐτῷ υἱοί "of Mahli: Eleazar and Ithamar, and Eleazar *died*, and he had no sons" (1 Chr 24:28). Perhaps the MT scribe skipped from the first אֶלְעָזָר to the second אֶלְעָזָר omitting the intervening material including the verb (parablepsis by homoioteleuton—so also 2 Chr 23:3, 14, 18; cf. 10:2; 24:19).[5] There are a few sections where the Greek text is longer

---

[4] For a more detailed discussion and examples regarding the addition or expansion of various elements that served to improve the readability from a linguistic and contextual point of view, clarifying Hebrew or Greek words and explaining their content, see Emanuel Tov, *Text-Critical Use*, 46-47 and 127-30.

[5] Japhet sees this section of the text as a list of 'complementary notes' appended to existing records and prefers the MT over LXX, Japhet, *Chronicles*, 435. So also 2 Chronicles 23:3 and וַיָּשָׁב יָרָבְעָם מִמִּצְרָיִם "then Jeroboam returned from Egypt" is translated καὶ *κατῴκησεν* Ιεροβοαμ ἐν Αἰγύπτῳ καὶ *ἀπέστρεψεν* Ιεροβοαμ ἐξ Αἰγύπτου, with added context supplied, ["And it came to pass when Jeroboam the son of Nebat heard it, (now he was in Egypt, since he had fled there from the face of King Solomon,] and Jeroboam *dwelt* in Egypt,) that Jeroboam *returned* out of Egypt" (2 Chr 10:2; cf. parallel in 1 Kings 12:2 which has וַיֵּשֶׁב "and he *dwelt*"). Perhaps the translator or his *Vorlage* combines the two readings, "he returned and he dwelt."

and it includes a number of aorists (2 Chr 35:19 (13); 36:2 (3), 4 (3), 5 (9)). The longer text corresponds closely to 2 Kings and its Greek translation (2 Kgs 23:23-28, 31-33, 34-35, 36—24:4 respectively). It seems likely that *Paraleipomenon* had a Hebrew *Vorlage* that corresponded to the Hebrew text of 2 Kings in these places.[6]

2. Imperfect

The following table shows the imperfect indicative forms and the Hebrew correspondences, including non-verbal forms and pluses (based upon the Hebrew MT).

TABLE 11: IMPERFECT INDICATIVES TRANSLATED FROM HEBREW

IMPERFECT	TOTAL	Percentage of Hebrew form	Narrative Main Clauses	Reported Speech Main Clauses	Subordinate Clauses
Wayyiqtol	76	5.24	76		
Qatal	81	6.97	49	4	28
Wᵉqatal	5	3.91	4	1	
Yiqtol (wᵉyiqtol)	15 (2)	4.27 (3.7)	10	3 (2)	2
Qotel	23 predicate 23 total	4.65	20		3
Qᵉtol Infin. Construct	3	0.49			3
Sub Total	198 (-5 *wᵉqatal*)		155	7	36
Noun Sentence and Plus	49		31	2	16
Total	247		186	9	52

Alternatively, a scribe in the MT tradition could have read the similar clauses only once, and it was later vocalized to make sense. The LXX reading seems redundant since it previously states that Jeroboam "was in Egypt."

[6] See Steven L. McKenzie, *The Chronicler's Use of the Deuteronomistic History*, (HSM 33. Atlanta: Scholars Press, 1985) and A. Graeme Auld, *Kings without Privilege: David and Moses in the Story of the Bible's Kings* (Edinburgh: T & T Clark, 1994), who both argue that the Chronicler had an earlier version of the Deuteronomistic History than is preserved in Kings. Auld considers that the writer of Kings and the Chronicler both drew from a common source rather than Chronicles from Kings (25).

			Total Verbs in Text Type		2344	597	646
Total Verbs in Text Type			2344		597		646
Percentage of Form in Text Type			7.94		1.51		8.05

Non-verbals Translated by Imperfects and Imperfect Pluses:

Narrative Main Clauses (31)

1 Chr 2:21; 4:27; 9:30; 11:12, 20; 20:6, 8; 21:20; 22:3, 4; 2 Chr 1:5; 4:4; 5:10, 11, 13; 8:8; 9:20; 12:3, 15; 14:6<5>; 15:17; 20:24; 22:9; 30:17; 35:15, 19, 26; 36:4, 5 (2), 16

Reported Speech Main Clauses (2)

1 Chr 11:2; 23:26

Subordinate Clauses (16)

1 Chr 11:10, 18; 13:6; 15:22; 26:6; 2 Chr 11:13; 12:4; 11:22; 15:8; 20:25; 23:9; 24:7; 32:3; 34:33; 35:24; 36:15

There are far fewer imperfects to aorists in the translation of Chronicles, with the ratio of imperfects to aorists being about 1:10 (247:2345 or a relative frequency 10.49%—see note 2 above). While the paucity of imperfect forms could be part of a general trend of the declining relative frequency of imperfect to aorist forms,[7] which becomes "pronounced in the papyri (increasingly in the later papyri) and the N[ew] T[estament]," the relative frequency of imperfects to aorists in Chronicles and indeed in the rest of the Septuagint is still significantly lower than in the New Testament (e.g., Matthew-Acts ranging from 13% to 37%) and other Greek literature of roughly the same era.[8]

One of the reasons is that the imperfect is one of the Greek forms that do not have an exact correspondence in Hebrew as a common equivalent (except perhaps for the rare occurrences of *yiqtol*, *weqatal*, or *qotel* forms in past contexts, but surprisingly it is not used by the translator much to translate these forms).[9] Most (about 66% or

---

[7] There are very few imperfect verb forms in reported speech main clauses. This could be due to the lack of long sections of narrative in reported speech in which to contrast the imperfects with aorists.

[8] Evans, *Verbal Syntax*, 203, 205. For diachronic trends in the relative frequencies of imperfects to aorists see chapter 8 of *Verbal Syntax*.

[9] In narrative, the aorist translates 9 and the imperfect 10 *yiqtol* forms, and the aorist translates 9 and the imperfect 20 *qotel* forms respectively. Also noted by Evans, *Verbal Syntax*, 120-121.

125/186) of the imperfect forms in narrative are translations of either *wayyiqtol* or *qatal* forms, of which the aorist is the common equivalent.

Two other reasons (as identified by Evans and others) for the high relative frequency of aorists to imperfects are syntactic and lexical— syntactic, in that the aorist indicative is the preferred tense form for rendering the paratactic clauses that abound in Hebrew syntax (greater than 50% of the clauses); lexical, in that the literal translation technique encourages the "regular rendering of a recurring Hebrew lexical item by a single Greek equivalent."[10]

Most of the imperfects occur due to *Aktionsart* constraints of the target language (e.g., there is no aorist form for εἰμί), situation aspect (e.g., temporal adverbs indicating duration or plural arguments), or due to the desire of the translator to mark or give prominence to a particular action. [11]

About half of the imperfects are the imperfect of εἰμί (to be). They translate הָיָה approximately 83 times.[12] Approximately 40 times they translate a noun sentence (13 with the negative existential אֵין—1 Chr 4:27; 22:3, 4; 23:26; 2 Chr 5:10, 11; 9:20; 12:3; 14:6<5>; 20:24; 22:9; 35:15; 36:16—and in the others an understood verb "to be" is supplied by the translator in Greek).[13] One verb of motion οἴχομαι also occurs only with an imperfect form (3 times). Other verbs that occur only or mostly in the imperfect are verbs with stative *Aktionsart* such as βούλομαι "to want" (4 times), ὑπάρχω "to exist" (3), ἔχω "to have" (2 out of 3 total past indicative forms), δύναμαι "to be able" (6

---

[10] Evans, *Verbal Syntax*, 217. See also pages 214-219.

[11] See Voitila, *Présent et imparfait*, 112-232 in which he accounts for the use of imperfect indicative in selected portions of the Pentateuch. He identifies a number of uses, including the imperfect used for the moment of speech, translating nominal phrases (both without the verbal predicate in Hebrew and with the predicative *qotel*), translating conjugated verbal forms: the *qatal, wayyiqtol, yiqtol* and translating infinitives. He also identifies the use of the imperfect as an atemporal or timeless form. He also identifies a similar use for the imperfect in narrative.

[12] One *wᵉqatal* form of הָיָה is also translated by the imperfect of γίνομαι (2 Chr 13:9). It carries indefinite force "whoever comes ... *becomes* a priest."

[13] Some imperfects translate pronouns, for example in subordinate clauses, כִּי מֵבִין הוּא "for he understood it," which is translated ὅτι συνετὸς ἦν (1 Chr 15:22; 26:6; 2 Chr 20:25), some are used to indicate possession, in which a noun sentence and a לְ are translated by a verb "to be" and a genitive אֲשֶׁר לִיהוּדָה "which *was* Judah's" translated ἣ ἦν τοῦ Ιουδα (1 Chr 13:6; 2 Chr 23:9; 34:33) or a dative, אֲשֶׁר לְדָוִיד "which *was* David's" translated οἳ ἦσαν τῷ Δαυιδ (1 Chr 11:10; 2 Chr 35:24). All of them occur in a past context indicating a state of existence prior to the time of the main verb.

out of 8 total past indicative forms), ἐξεποίει "to be sufficient" (1), and φοβοῦμαι "to fear" (1).[14]

In a few places, the presence of adverbials indicating duration elicits the use of imperfect with iterative or habitual force. For example, with the phrase יוֹם בְּיוֹם "day by day" a *qatal* form עָשׂוּ is translated ἐποίουν "so *they did* day by day" (2 Chr 24:11; so also 1 Chr 12:22<23> a *yiqtol* form is translated by an imperfect; in contrast to 2 Chr 20:31, in which a *qotel* form is translated by a Greek participle). A noun sentence with כָּל הַיָּמִים "all the days" translates into an imperfect (2 Chr 12:15; so also 34:33 translating a *qatal* form).

Other contextual indicators are plural arguments (i.e., subjects or objects) that can give an action iterative or customary force. Frequently imperfect verbs also cluster in the same context in which the action took place over an extended time, as can be seen in the following examples. In summary statements of a king's reign, for example, "Solomon's horses were imported...the kings traders *received* (*yiqtol*) them...they *imported* (*wayyiqtol*) from Egypt, and then *exported* (*wayyiqtol*) a chariot...these were *exported* (*yiqtol*) to all the kings of the Hittites (2 Chr 1:16-17; so also the servants of Huram and Solomon *brought* (*qatal*) gold...the traders *brought* (*qotel*)...all the kings of Arabia *brought* (*qotel*)...600 shekels of gold *went into* (*yiqtol*, twice) each shield...all the kings of the earth *sought* (*qotel*) the presence of Solomon...each one *brought* (*qotel*) a present (9:10-24; so also 32:23).[15]

---

[14] In reported speech two imperfects are used to translate the *hiphil* of the stative כָּבֵד "to be heavy" translated ἐβάρυνεν (2 Chr 10:10, 14). The first translates a *qatal* form the second a *yiqtol* form. These forms are formally identical with the aorist. However, the fact that one translates a *yiqtol* form with past imperfect force probably points to an imperfect reading. The imperfect force also fits the context. Solomon did a number of actions over a period of time to make the yoke heavy.

[15] It is interesting to note that imperfect forms often cluster together in a context, even translating a variety of Hebrew forms. Approximately 139 out of 237 imperfects or 58.65% occur in the same verse or in adjacent verses. Perhaps the translator was initially prompted by the syntax or *Aktionsart* to use an imperfect, and then he decided to express the other actions in the context in the imperfect. Examples of clustered imperfects can be seen underlined among a list of all the imperfects in Chronicles: 1 Chr 1:51; 2:3; 2:21, 22; 2:25, 26, 27, 28; 2:33, 34; 2:50, 52; 3:1; 4:5; 4:9; 4:14; 4:27; 5:16; 5:19; 5:26; 6:17; 7:19; 8:3; 8:40; 9:20; 9:24; 9:26; 9:30; 10:4 (2); 11:2; 11:9, 10; 11:12, 13 (2); 11:18, 19, 20 (2), 21 (2); 11:25; 12:22, 23; 12:30; 12:40, 41; 13:6, 7; 14:4; 15:22; 15:25; 17:5; 17:8; 18:2; 18:6 (3), 7; 18:10; 18:13 (3), 14; 19:5; 20:1, 2; 20:6 (2); 20:8; 21:5; 21:20; 21:30; 22:3, 4 (2); 23:11; 23:17 (2); 23:22; 23:26; 24:2; 24:5; 24:28; 26:6; 26:10; 28:12; 2 Chr 1:3; 1:5; 1:16, 17 (3); 4:4; 5:8 (2), 9 (4), 10, 11; 5:13, 14; 7:2, 3 (2); 7:7; 8:6; 8:8; 8:17, 18; 9:4; 9:9, 10; 9:13, 14 (2), 15, 16; 9:20, 21 (2); 9:23, 24, 25, 26; 10:1; 10:15; 11:1; 11:12, 13; 11:21, 22; 12:3, 4; 12:11, 12; 12:15; 13:2; 13:7; 13:9; 14:5; 15:8; 15:17; 15:19; 16:8; 17:9 (2), 10, 11 (2), 12; 18:2; 18:9; 18:11; 18:32; 18:34;

Singular verbs are also used in summary statements. In the following examples, all the actions are habitual and disapproved by God, for example, he *sacrificed* (*qatal*) in the valley...he *made* his sons *pass through* (*wayyiqtol*) the fire…he *sacrificed* (*wayyiqtol*) on the high places (28:3-4; so also 33:6, 22-23). As can be seen from the above examples, there are a variety of Hebrew verb forms underlying the translation by an imperfect, with only the *yiqtol* and perhaps the *qotel* forms having imperfective or durative force in the past time.

There are a few examples where an imperfect may have been used to draw attention to an action, perhaps with a new topic or reflecting action simultaneous to the main verb in another main clause or both. The imperfect usually translates a Hebrew *qotel* participle, but also *qatal*, infinitive construct, and *wayyiqtol* forms (underlined verb forms in close proximity to the imperfect are translated by another verb form, mostly an aorist). For example, "Joab <u>led</u> out the army...but David *remained* (*qotel*) in Jerusalem" (1 Chr 20:1), "the king of Israel and Jehoshaphat...<u>were sitting</u> (*qotel* > participle)...and all the prophets *were prophesying* (*qotel*)" (2 Chr 18:9), "the king <u>went</u> to Huldah, now she *was living* (*qotel*)" (34:22), "whenever the king <u>would come</u> (infin. constr.), the guard *would come* (*qatal*)" (12:11) "as he *was dying* (infin. constr.), he <u>said</u>" (24:22), "he <u>prevailed</u> against them, and that year the Ammonites *gave* (*wayyiqtol*) him" (27:5).

In subordinate clauses five times an imperfect occurs with a verb of motion, sometimes indicating habitual or background action. Twice the same statement occurs with a conjunction of indefinite time in a summary statement, "The LORD <u>gave victory</u> (*wayyiqtol* > imperfect) to David wherever *he went* (*qatal*)" (1 Chr 18:6 and v. 13). Twice imperfects indicate habitual action carried out by more than one subject, "the servants of Huram and the servants of Solomon who *brought* gold (*qatal*)" (2 Chr 9:10; so also 1 Chr 22:4). Twice an imperfect indicates action occurring as a background to another action (underlined) "Rehoboam <u>went</u> to Shechem (*qatal*), for all Israel *had come*

20:21; <u>20:24, 25</u>; 20:33; <u>21:6, 7</u>; 21:9; <u>21:16, 17</u>; 21:20; <u>22:3, 4</u>; 22:6; 22:9; 22:12; 23:9; 24:7; <u>24:10 (2), 11 (2), 12, 13</u>; 24:18; 24:22; <u>25:12 (3)</u>; <u>25:14 (2)</u>; 25:16; 26:5; 26:8; <u>26:10 (2)</u>; 26:14; <u>26:21 (2)</u>; 27:2; <u>27:5 (2)</u>; <u>28:3 (2), 4</u>; 28:9; <u>29:22 (3)</u>; 29:28; 29:30; <u>29:34 (2)</u>; 30:10; <u>30:16, 17</u>; 31:9; 32:3; <u>32:13, 14</u>; 32:23; <u>33:6 (3)</u>; 33:22; 34:10; 34:22; 34:33; 35:15; 35:19; 35:24; 35:26; <u>36:4, 5 (2)</u>; <u>36:15, 16 (2)</u>; 36:20. See also Evans, *Verbal Syntax*, 216, and Aejmelaeus, *Parataxis*, 183 who also reach similar conclusions.

(*qatal*)" (2 Chr 10:1), "he <u>stretched out</u> his hand (*wayyiqtol* > aorist or imperfect), for the ox *shook* it" (1 Chr 13:9).

3. Perfect

The following table shows the perfect indicative forms and the Hebrew correspondences, including non-verbal forms and pluses (based upon the Hebrew MT).

TABLE 12: PERFECT INDICATIVES TRANSLATED FROM HEBREW

PERFECT	TOTAL	Percentage of Hebrew form	Narrative Main Clauses	Reported Speech Main Clauses	Subordinate Clauses
Qatal	35	3.01		21	14
Wᵉqatal	2	1.56		2	
Yiqtol	1	0.28		1	
Qotel	2 predicate 2 total	0.40		1 1	1 1
Qatul	6 predicate 6 total	8.22	3 3		3 3
Qᵉtol Infin. Construct	1	0.16			1
Sub Total	45 (-2 *wᵉqatal*)		3	23	19
Noun	1			1	
Total	46		3	24	19
Total Verbs in Text Type			2344	597	646
Percentage of Form in Text Type			0.13	4.02	2.94

Non-verbals Translated by Perfects and Perfect Pluses: Reported Speech Main Clauses (1)
1 Chr 29:3

Most of the perfects occur in reported speech and subordinate clauses. The Greek perfect is particularly appropriate in these clauses since it relates prior actions with a resultant state to the time of speech or to

the time of the verb of the main clause.[16] A few of the perfects occur
due to constraints of *Aktionsart*, e.g., for the verb οἶδα (4 times) which
has no distinct present form; the verb is perfect in form but present in
meaning.[17] But more commonly a perfect is the choice of the
translator.

All of three perfect indicative forms in narrative are narrative
comment clauses translating *qatul* participles in the expression
וְהִנָּם כְּתוּבִים translated ἰδοὺ γέγραπται "behold, they *have been (are)*
written" (2 Chr 32:32; 33:19; 35:25). Three *qatul* forms in the
expression כַּכָּתוּב "as it is written" are also translated by perfect
indicatives. The perfect is appropriate in such expressions. It
emphasizes the resultant state and enduring nature of what has been
recorded and can be considered relevant right up to the time of
narration.

About 80% (37/46) of the perfect forms in reported speech
(especially for reported narrative) and subordinate clauses translate
qatal forms. The perfect is sometimes used for performative action, and
its subject is frequently God, or God is involved as the direct or
indirect object, for example, God *has chosen* Judah and Solomon (1 Chr
28:4, 6, 10) and "great is the wrath of YHWH which *has been poured*
out" (2 Chr 34:21).[18]

The perfect is appropriate in subordinate clauses to indicate a
resultant state relative to the time of the main verb, for example,
following a verb of seeing, וַיַּרְא יוֹאָב כִּי־הָיְתָה פְנֵי־הַמִּלְחָמָה אֵלָיו
"Joab saw that the line of battle *was set* against him" translated καὶ

---

[16] See Evans, *Verbal Syntax*, chapter 6, who considers "the criterial value of the
form...as stative, its aspectual content as imperfective[, and] the prior-occurrence
reference of traditional definitions...ascribed to the lexical semantics of verbs which
express actions" (145). He observes similar results in the Pentateuch, including its
special affinity for direct speech (158), also its presence in parenthetic comment
clauses in narrative (162, 164).

[17] Οἶδα translates two *qatal* forms (1 Chr 17:18; 2 Chr 2:8<7>), one *yiqtol* form
(20:12), and one *qotel* form with present meaning (2:8<7>). One *qotel* form is translated
by the perfect of πείθω "I persuade" with the notion of "I have confidence, I trust"
with present force (2 Chr 32:10). In addition, three *niphal* suffix forms are translated by
the perfect πέποιθα "I have confidence, I trust, rely on" (2 Chr 14:11<10>) and
ἐπικέκλημαι "I am called" (6:33; 7:14) (see chapter 3, note 13).

[18] See chapter 4 in the section on *qatal* forms translated into perfects. Cf. Evans,
Verbal Syntax, 165-166, who contrary to Schehr, cautions against reading too much
into the association of God with the perfect tense. The main point is that the perfect
verbs occur in direct speech, and it so happens that in Genesis 1-15 God has a major
speaking part in the limited sections of direct speech.

εἶδεν Ιωαβ ὅτι γεγόνασιν ἀντιπρόσωποι τοῦ πολεμεῖν πρὸς αὐτὸν (1 Chr 19:10, so also v. 19; 2 Chr 22:10).

4. Pluperfect

The following table shows the pluperfect indicative forms and the Hebrew correspondences (based upon the Hebrew MT).

TABLE 13: PLUPERFECT INDICATIVES TRANSLATED FROM HEBREW

PLUPERFECT	TOTAL	Percentage of Hebrew form	Narrative Main Clauses	Reported Speech Main Clauses	Subordinate Clauses
Qotel	3 predicate		2	1	
	3 total	0.61	2	1	
Total	3		2	1	
Total Verbs in Text Type			2344	597	646
Percentage of Form in Text Type			0.09	0.17	

All three pluperfects translate *qotel* participles, two in narrative and one in reported speech. In narrative, the two forms have slightly different nuances. The force of the participles in Hebrew is probably best understood as simultaneous to the main verb, the pluperfect stresses the resultant state of the action relative to the action of the main verb (in the past time), e.g., "the men went down...the army *had* already *encamped*" (1 Chr 11:15; so also 2 Chr 6:3). Perhaps the pluperfect was used to emphasize the change in topic.

A pluperfect in reported speech is also used to translate a *qotel* form "standing" with present meaning (2 Chr 18:18).

5. Present

The following table shows the present indicative forms and the Hebrew correspondences, including non-verbal forms and pluses (based upon the Hebrew MT).

TABLE 14: PRESENT INDICATIVES TRANSLATED FROM HEBREW

PRESENT	TOTAL	Percentage of Hebrew form	Narrative Main Clauses	Reported Speech Main Clauses	Subordinate Clauses
Wayyiqtol	2	0.14	2		
Qatal	17	1.46		14	3
Wᵉqatal	1	0.78		1	
Yiqtol	9	2.56		5	4
Qotel	38 predicate 39 total	7.88	2 2	27 28	9 9
Qatul	1 predicate 1 total	1.37		1 1	
Qᵉtol Infin. Construct	1	0.16			1
Sub Total	69 (-1 *wᵉqatal*)		4	48	17
Adjective, Noun, and Noun Sentence	73		6	39	28
Total	142		10	87	45
Total Verbs in Text Type			2344	597	646
Percentage of Form in Text Type			0.43	14.57	6.97

Non-verbals Translated by Presents and Present Pluses:
Narrative Main Clauses (6)

1 Chr 1:31; 2:26; 8:6; 29:29; 2 Chr 20:2; 21:18

Reported Speech Main Clauses (39)

1 Chr 15:2; 16:25; 17:16, 20 (2), 21, 26; 21:17; 22:1, 14, 16; 29:3, 10, 15, 16; 2 Chr 6:14; 14:11<10>; 15:5; 18:6, 13, 16, 31; 20:2, 6 (2), 7, 17; 22:9; 23:13; 25:9; 26:23; 28:10; 29:9, 10, 19; 32:12; 34:27; 35:3, 21

Subordinate Clauses (28)

1 Chr 9:26; 12:20<21>; 21:24; 23:27; 28:3; 29:11, 14, 15, 17; 2 Chr 4:12, 13; 6:31, 32; 8:7, 11; 11:10; 13:4; 15:7; 18:7, 16; 19:7; 20:12, 15; 23:6; 25:7, 8, 21; 33:13

The present tense mostly occurs in reported speech and indicates an action or state occurring at the same time as the moment of speech.[19]

Most of the present tense forms are used to translate noun sentences (73 without a Hebrew verb and 38 with a predicate *qotel* participle). Most of the Greek present indicative forms used to translate non-*qotel* noun sentences (66) are of the verb εἰμί "to be." They are frequently used to translate particles or pronominal elements in Hebrew noun sentences, but they are also added when a pronominal element is also translated. Most of the examples occur in reported speech, but there are thirteen comment clauses in narrative (six in main clauses and seven in relative clauses).[20]

Sixteen out of 19 times the negative existential particle אֵין "there is not" is translated οὐκ ἔστιν, once in narrative (2 Chr 21:18), ten times in reported speech (1 Chr 17:20 (2); 22:14, 16; 29:15; 2 Chr 6:14; 15:5; 18:6; 20:6; 35:3),[21] and five times in subordinate clauses (2 Chr 18:7, 16; 19:7; 20:12; 25:7). Four of the five occurrences of the existential יֵשׁ "there is" are translated ἔστιν, twice in reported speech (1 Chr 29:3; 2 Chr 25:9) and twice in subordinate clauses (2 Chr 15:7; 25:8).[22]

Frequently the verb εἰμί translates a pronominal element, which is translated by the verb alone, e.g., אֵלֶּה הֵם בְּנֵי יִשְׁמָעֵאל "these *are* the sons of Ishmael" translated οὗτοί εἰσιν υἱοὶ Ισμαηλ (1 Chr 1:31; so also 8:6; and 29:29 in narrative, 1 Chr 16:25; 21:17; 22:1; 29:10, 16; 2 Chr 18:31; 20:2, 6; 22:9; 26:23; 29:10, 19 in reported speech, and 1 Chr 9:26; 23:27; 29:15; 2 Chr 8:7, 11; 23:6 in subordinate clauses).[23] A

---

[19] See Voitila, *Présent et imparfait*, 1-111 in which he accounts for the use of present indicative in selected portions of the Pentateuch. He identifies a number of uses, including the present used for the moment of speech, translating nominal phrases (both without the verbal predicate in Hebrew and with the predicative *qotel*), translating conjugated verbal forms: the *yiqtol*, *wᵉqatal*, *qatal* and translating substantives, particles, and attributive *qotels*. He also identifies the use of the present as an atemporal or timeless form and a historic present.

[20] It is interesting to note that in narrative main clauses, a noun sentence with a pronoun in Hebrew is more commonly translated as a noun sentence with a pronoun in Greek, without a supplied verb, (e.g., 1 Chr 2:42, 55; 4:11, 23; 5:6; 7:31; 8:7, 13, 32; 9:18, 22, 23, 27, 31, 38; 11:4, 5; 12:1, 16; 27:32; 2 Chr 5:2, 3; 8:9; 10:2; 26:1; 32:9; 34:3).

[21] In addition, אֵין is translated by two other present tense verbs ἀδυνατεῖ (2 Chr 14:11<10>), and אֵין־לָהֶן "lit., there is not to them" is translated οὐκ ἔχουσιν "they do not have" (18:16). Once it is translated by the imperfect of the verb "to be" (1 Chr 4:27).

[22] One time a future of the verb "to be" is used (2 Chr 16:9).

[23] In the absence of a present tense copula the Hebrew pronoun is frequently used as a copula. This may account for the frequency of this translation.

number of times the Hebrew pronoun is translated by a Greek pronoun and a verb (a Greek plus), e.g., הִיא אֵם אוֹנָם "she *was* the mother of Onam" translated αὕτη ἐστὶν μήτηρ Οζομ (1 Chr 2:26; so also 2 Chr 20:2 in narrative; 1 Chr 17:16, 26; 2 Chr 20:7; 32:12 in reported speech main clauses, and 1 Chr 28:3; 29:14, 17; 2 Chr 6:32; 33:13 in subordinate clauses). The use of the verb εἰμί for the existential particles and pronouns may be due to the desire of the translator to represent each Hebrew form by a Greek form, but this does not account for the addition of the verb with the translation of the pronoun.

A few nouns or adjectives are also translated by Greek presents where the time frame in which the noun is, is the same as the time of speaking. For example, Athaliah's abrupt utterance in Hebrew קֶשֶׁר קָשֶׁר "Treason, treason!" is translated ἐπιτιθέμενοι ἐπιτίθεσθε "You *are* surely *plotting* against [me]" (2 Chr 23:13).[24] However, this could reflect a different understanding of the vocalization by the translator (i.e., an infinitive absolute followed by a *qatal* form).

The use of the present tense sometimes seems a little awkward, especially when a present tense form is used in narrative. It works with timeless or omni-temporal expressions, for example, geographical statements where the information given still applies at the time of translation, e.g., הִיא עֵין־גְּדִי "that is, En-gedi" αὕτη ἐστὶν Ενγαδδι (20:2; so also 11:10; 13:4; 25:21) or for references to God, e.g., "he knew that the LORD indeed *was* (Gk. ἐστιν "is") God" (33:13).[25] Twice ἐστιν is used in subordinate clauses referring to the capitals that *were* on the pillars of the temple (4:12, 13). Perhaps from the perspective of the translator the capitals were still on the pillars, whereas from the perspective of modern translators the temple no longer exists, so the Hebrew noun clause is translated by a past tense in modern versions. Alternatively, the use of the present may just be

---

[24] Other examples include: נְאֻם "declaration" translated φησιν "he says" (2 Chr 34:27), לֹא־עָלֶיךָ אַתָּה הַיּוֹם "not against you, *you* today" translated οὐκ ἐπὶ σὲ ἥκω σήμερον "not against you, *I have come* today" perhaps interpreting the pronoun אַתָּה as the Aramaic verb "to come" 2 Chr 35:21), and the adjective חַי translated ζῆ κύριος "[as] the Lord *lives*" (2 Chr 18:13; so also 6:31).

[25] The use of the present tense does seem a little unusual in the genealogies, e.g., הִיא אֵם אוֹנָם "she *was* the mother of Onam" translated αὕτη ἐστὶν μήτηρ Οζομ (1 Chr 2:26). The present tense is used in classical Greek genealogies if a statement applies to the present or is timeless, for example, when reference is made to the gods, e.g., in lines 404-52 in Hesiod's *Theogony*.

defaulting to a common equivalent for noun clauses without much consideration for the context.

Similar to this and also unusual is the translation of two Hebrew participles in narrative by present indicatives. They are used to describe the calves at the base of the molten sea and the measurement of the laver, κυκλοῦσιν αὐτήν πήχεις δέκα περιέχουσιν τὸν λουτῆρα κυκλόθεν "they *encompass* it, ten cubits *surround* the laver all around" (2 Chr 4:3). Perhaps this translation reflects the most natural way to treat the participles in the grammar of the translator, rather than a timeless reference that still applies up to the time of translation. According to the context, a past form would be more appropriate (i.e., the imperfect of the verb "to be" in the following verse "their hind parts *were* inward").

There are 28 *qotel* forms translated by a Greek present indicative. The largest number of *qotel* forms translated by a present occurs in reported speech. This is perhaps understandable since the *qotel* was increasingly used as a present tense form in late biblical Hebrew. Changes in language tend to occur in speech first. It seems most likely that this use of the *qotel* was particularly common in speech. This may have influenced the translators in their handling of this form in reported speech.

Some of these *qotel* forms refer to omni-temporal or timeless actions with God as the subject (1 Chr 28:19; 29:12; 2 Chr 16:9; 20:6), or customary human actions (9:7; 13:10, 11 (2); 19:6). Others refer to actions or states going on at the same time as the verb of speaking (e.g., 1 Chr 17:1; 2 Chr 20:2, 11; 29:8; 30:7; 32:10, 11). Sometimes a *qotel* form with an imminent future sense (especially with הִנֵּה "behold") is translated by a present (1 Chr 22:9; 2 Chr 2:4<3>, 5<4>; 20:16; 34:24, 28 (2)). One *qatul* form is translated as a present with a performative sense (2 Chr 1:12).

Twelve out of fourteen *qatal* forms in reported speech translated by a present are examples of the expression כֹּה־אָמַר (cf. it is translated four times by an aorist). The use of the present captures the notion that the message uttered is the speaking of the party being quoted, especially when a prophet is quoting God, e.g., τάδε λέγει κύριος "thus says the Lord" (1 Chr 17:7). The act of speech is in fact the utterance of the quoted party; the prophet acts as the mouthpiece of God. The present of the verb of saying captures the notion that the speech act is being performed, the message is being delivered, at the time of speaking.[26]

Twice the *qatal* form of יָדַע "to know" is translated by a present. Once it is timeless referring to God (2 Chr 6:30). In the second example the state of the verb exists up to the time of speaking (1 Chr 25:16). Once נָשָׂא "to lift up" is translated ἐπαίρει "your heart has lifted you up" (2 Chr 25:19), where the action of lifting up is considered as having present relevance by the translator.

Nine *yiqtol* forms are translated by a present. Five of them are examples of omni-temporal or timeless uses of the present (especially referring to God—e.g., 1 Chr 29:17; 2 Chr 2:6<5>, or for customary human action, e.g., 18:17; 19:6) translating a *yiqtol* form with imperfective aspect. Twice they are used to translate *yiqtol* forms in questions where the action or state is considered as continuing at the time of speaking (1 Chr 21:3; 2 Chr 19:2). Two are presents with future force, one indicating the intention of the speaker or perhaps as a performative (1 Chr 21:24), and the other a future action with habitual force "the prayer which your servant *prays* toward this place" (2 Chr 6:20).

One of the striking characteristics of Chronicles is the lack of the so-called "historic present" in narrative. Comparing the translation of Samuel-Kings with Chronicles the translator consistently renders historic presents in parallel passages as aorists.[27] Perhaps the translator

---

[26] The present is preferred to the aorist for this structure elsewhere in the Septuagint. The translator of Ezekiel uses it exclusively (126 times), and the translator of Isaiah mostly (about 44 out of 48 times). On the other hand the translator(s) of Jeremiah use the present (in Jeremiah a' chs. 2—30, 61 times) and the aorist (in b' chs. 30—51, 69 times) about the same number of times, cf. Emanuel Tov, *The Septuagint Translation of Jeremiah and Baruch: A Discussion of an Early Revision of the LXX of Jeremiah 29-52 and Baruch 1:1—3:8* (HSM 8; Missoula: Scholars Press; 1975), 56-58.

[27] For example, 18 presents in 1 Samuel (1 Reigns) 31 are all rendered as aorists in the parallel passage in 1 Chronicles 10. Other examples in parallel passages in which 17 presents in Samuel-Kings (Reigns) are all rendered as aorists in Chronicles (*Paraleipomenon*) include 2 Sam 5:1, 3 (2), 18, 21 (1 Chr 11:1, 3 (2); 14:9, 12); 2 Sam 6:6, 17 (1 Chr 13:9; 16:1); 2 Sam 8:5 (1 Chr 18:5); 1 Kgs 3:15 (2 Chr 1:13); 1 Kgs 8:6 (2 Chr 5:7); 1 Kgs 12:1 (2 Chr 10:1); 1 Kgs 14:31 (2 Chr 12:16); 1 Kgs 15:8 (2), 22, 24 (2) (2 Chr 14:1 (2); 16:6, 14, 17:1). For more on the historic present in 1 Samuel see Aejmelaeus, "Septuagint of 1 Samuel," 137, 144-45; and Harold St. J. Thackeray, *The Septuagint and Jewish Worship: A Study in Origins* (London: H. Milford, 1923), 20-22. Aejmelaeus considers that the translator "gave his expression to his own understanding of the events described in the text, highlighting, describing, and showing the dramatic turns of the narration" through the use of the historic present ("Septuagint of 1 Samuel," 144). It is interesting to note however, that the two examples of historic presents in *Paraleipomenon* used to translate a *wayyiqtol* form were

avoided the historic present because he wanted to bring his translation closer to the Hebrew, and he felt that the historic present was too far removed from the underlying Hebrew. The historical present is used frequently for verbs of saying (introducing key passages of discourse) and seeing, as was noted by Evans and Voitila in the Pentateuch.[28] In Chronicles there are only two times when a present indicative (historic present) is used to translate a *wayyiqtol* form. They could be considered as dischronologizations or temporal overlay, indicating an action occurring simultaneously to another action (translated by an aorist) or to highlight a change in topic especially with verbs from the same root or with a similar semantic domain.[29] The first example is, "the Ammonites came out and *drew up in battle array* (παρατάσσονται), and the kings who had come attacked them (παρενέβαλον—a Greek plus) in the country" (1 Chr 19:9, cf. the parallel 2 Sam 10:8, which has the aorist παρετάξαντο). The second is, "And [Israel] drew up its forces (παρετάξατο—aorist of παρατάσσω) against them. When David *set the battle in array* against the Syrians (cf. Greek, "the Syrians *set the battle in array*—παρατάσσονται—against David")...they fought with him" (1 Chr 19:17; cf. the parallel 2 Sam 10:17, which also has an aorist παρετάξατο).

6. Future

The following table shows the future indicative forms and the Hebrew correspondences, including imperative and non-verbal forms and pluses (based upon the Hebrew MT).

---

translated by aorists in 2 Reigns (i.e., 2 Samuel, part of the *kaige* sections of Reigns, see this section above). See also the places where Shenkel mentions the historic present, "Comparative Study," 67-68, 72, 83-84. He states that the "elimination of the historic present is a characteristic which P[araleipomenon] shares with the Καιγε Recension" (72).

[28] See Evans, *Verbal Aspect*, 120 (note 2) and Voitila, *Présent et imparfait*, 91-106, especially 100-105. In addition to these, Campbell also notes that they occur frequently with verbs of motion or "propulsion" in Greek literature to indicate heightened transition (*Verbal Aspect*, 65-76).

[29] In many of the examples of historic presents provided by Voitila, the historic present translates a verb from the same root or a similar semantic domain (which was translated by a different tense) and frequently occurs in the same context, perhaps to contrast different subjects (*Présent et imparfait*, 96-105). In the two examples of the historical present cited here, the Greek translations both indicate a change of topic, while in the Hebrew only the first example has the different topic.

TABLE 15: FUTURE INDICATIVES TRANSLATED FROM HEBREW

FUTURE	TOTAL	Percentage of Hebrew form	Narrative Main Clauses	Reported Speech Main Clauses	Subordinate Clauses
Wayyiqtol	6	0.41	2	4	
Qatal	62	5.33		62	
Wᵉqatal	61	47.66		61	
Yiqtol (*wᵉyiqtol*)	161 (29)	45.87 (53.7)	4	134 (29)	23
Qotel	3 predicate 4 total	0.81		2 2	1 2
Qᵉtol Infin. Construct	1	0.16			1
Qᵉtol Infin. Absolute	2	8		2	
Qᵉtol Imperative	5	3.11		5	
Sub Total	241 (-61 *wᵉqatal*)		6	209	26
Noun Sentence and Plus	12			10	2
Total	253		6	219	28
Total Verbs in Text Type			2344	597	646
Percentage of Form in Text Type			0.26	36.68	4.33

Imperatives Translated by Futures
Reported Speech Main Clauses (5)
2 Chr 18:11, 14; 19:7; 20:20; 23:7
Non-verbals Translated by Futures and Future Pluses:
Reported Speech Main Clauses (10)
2 Chr 2: 9<8>; 10:11, 14; 14:6; 25:18; 26:18; 30:9; 35:19 (2); 36:23
Subordinate Clauses (2)
2 Chr 6:36; 16:9

Most of the future forms translate verbs in reported speech. The Greek future is the common equivalent for *yiqtol* forms in reported speech. It is used for predictions, promises, future questions, and the apodosis of future conditions. It is also used for commands in legal settings and for forceful prohibitions translating לא and a *yiqtol* form. The future translates *yiqtol* forms in subordinate clauses. The action or state is future to the verb of speaking, but not necessarily future to the main verb, e.g., "I will raise up your offspring after you, *who will be* one of your own sons" translated ὃς ἔσται ἐκ τῆς κοιλίας σου (1 Chr 17:11) and מֵחַטָּאתָם יְשׁוּבוּן כִּי תַעֲנֵם "they will turn from their sin, because *you will punish* them" translated ἀπὸ τῶν ἁμαρτιῶν αὐτῶν ἐπιστρέψουσιν ὅτι *ταπεινώσεις* αὐτούς (2 Chr 6:26; so also 2:11; 6:9, 18, 26; 6:34; 12:8).

The future is also a common equivalent for *wᵉqatal* forms functioning as a consecutive form following either a *yiqtol* form or another *wᵉqatal* form in a future context. Sometimes it follows an imperative, either as a promise if the imperative is fulfilled or as a future with imperatival force. The *wᵉqatal* forms are mostly (56 out of 61) translated by καί followed by a future.[30]

There are a few unusual cases of the future used to translate *wayyiqtol* forms, twice in narrative and four times in reported speech. The two *wayyiqtol* forms in narrative are translated as if they occurred in reported speech rather than narrative (1 Chr 16:36; 2 Chr 28:23). Perhaps the translator understood the *wayyiqtol* forms as *wᵉyiqtol* forms and then translated them according to the most natural way of rendering it the Hebrew of his day, or he could be influenced by other factors such as a desire to read these forms as a future promise (which sometimes fits the context).

The future translates four *yiqtol* forms in narrative. Two *yiqtol* forms are examples of past durative forms (1 Chr 9:27; 2 Chr 23:19). The translator was not accustomed to past durative *yiqtol* forms in his contemporary Hebrew (the standard past durative form was the periphrastic הָיָה and participle). Perhaps, he defaulted to the common equivalent for the *yiqtol* forms, the future indicative, influenced by contemporary understanding of these forms as futures, without paying much attention to the context.[31]

---

[30] Five times the word order is varied with the verb סָלַח preceded by a conjunction translated by καί and the adjective followed by the verb "to be," e.g., καὶ ἵλεως ἔσῃ (2 Chr 6:21, so also v. 25, 27, 39; cf. 19:10). Once a *yiqtol* form of the same verb וְאָסְלַח is translated the same way (2 Chr 7:14). Forty-four times other forms are also translated καί followed by a future. Most are *wᵉyiqtol* forms (28 out of 29 are translated this way), but there are five *wayyiqtols* (1 Chr 16:36 (in narrative); 17:10; 2 Chr 15:4 (2); 24:20), five coordinated imperatives (2 Chr 18:11, 14; 19:7; 20:20; 23:7), one coordinated infinitive absolute (2 Chr 18:29), one coordinated infinitive construct (2 Chr 30:9), and four *yiqtol* forms: two preceded by a conjunction with intervening material which is not translated (2 Chr 6:33, 18:21) and two asyndetic forms in which καί is supplied (1 Chr 11:6; 2 Chr 25:8).

[31] The translation can barely tolerate such a use of the future. As was pointed out in the previous chapter, the future sometimes occurs in subordinate clauses (such as

There are two examples of *yiqtol* futures in narrative subordinate
clauses. The futures are equivalent to subjunctives in purpose clauses,
e.g., כִּי־בְמִסְפָּר יְבִיאוּם וּבְמִסְפָּר יוֹצִיאוּם "that *they should carry* them
in by number and carry them out by number" translated ὅτι ἐν
ἀριθμῷ εἰσοίσουσιν αὐτὰ καὶ ἐν ἀριθμῷ ἐξοίσουσιν αὐτά (1
Chr 9:28) and אֲשֶׁר לֹא־יִסָּפְרוּ "that they could not be numbered"
translated οἳ οὐκ ἀριθμηθήσονται (2 Chr 5:6).

The two *qotel* participles in reported speech that are rendered as
futures are both preceded by הִנֵּה, which has the force of imminent
future. One predicative *qotel* form in a subordinate clause is
translated by a future. Perhaps the participle was understood as an
imminent future by the translator, whereas it has been considered
as a past or a customary present by many English translations:
כִּי אֱלֹהֵי מַלְכֵי־אֲרָם הֵם מַעְזְרִים אוֹתָם "because the gods of the
kings of Aram *helped* them" translated ὅτι θεοὶ βασιλέως Συρίας
αὐτοὶ *κατισχύσουσιν* αὐτούς "because the gods of the king of Syria
will strengthen them" (2 Chr 28:23).

Two infinitive absolutes are rendered by a future. This was the
most logical way to render this form into Greek in reported speech in
future context (2 Chr 18:29). One infinitive construct is translated by a
future: "and [they will be granted] *to return*" translated ἀποστρέψει
εἰς τὴν γῆν ταύτην "*He will restore* [you] to this land" (2 Chr 30:9).

There are three noun sentences in reported speech translated by a
future of the verb "to be," in which the context indicates future time (2
Chr 26:18; 30:9; 36:23). The last example may be better taken as a
wish "*may* the LORD his God *be* with him," but the translator
understood it as a promise "the LORD his God *will be* with him."
There are a couple of noun sentences in subordinate clauses that are
translated by a future of the verb "to be," which correspond to
Hebrew existential particles, e.g., כִּי אֵין אָדָם אֲשֶׁר לֹא־יֶחֱטָא "for
there is no one who does [shall] not sin" translated ὅτι οὐκ ἔσται
ἄνθρωπος ὃς οὐχ ἁμαρτήσεται "for *there shall be* no one who shall
not sin" (2 Chr 6:36) and כִּי מֵעַתָּה יֵשׁ עִמְּךָ מִלְחָמוֹת "for from now

---

indefinite relative and purpose clauses) as equivalent to a subjunctive with subordinate
conjunctions. However, in the Greek text of Chronicles these subordinate
conjunctions are lacking. Cf. Voitila, "Translation of Tenses," 188, who identifies six
cases of *w⁽e⁾qatal* in a past narrative context (perhaps indicating a description of what
usually happened), which are translated by the standard equivalent, the future
indicative, in Numbers 10:11-25. The translation reads a little abruptly, with the
futures giving the sense of what should happen.

on *you will have* wars" translated ἀπὸ τοῦ νῦν ἔσται μετὰ σοῦ πόλεμος (16:9). The adverbial מֵעַתָּה "from now on" constrains a future reading of the existential יֵשׁ.

There are also seven pluses: two in a large section of additional text (2 Chr 35:19), one in a smaller portion of additional text (25:18), two translating a gapped verb supplied by the translator (10:11, 14), and two verbs supplied to make the reading smoother (2 Chr 2:9<8>; 14:6).

Sometimes a future has a volitive sense, e.g., אֲשֶׁר יֵלְכוּ־בָהּ "in which *they should walk*" translated ἐν ᾗ πορεύσονται ἐν αὐτῇ (2 Chr 6:27; so also "this is what *you shall do*" 23:4, "the priests *shall enter*" v. 6; "all *shall be put to death*" 25:4), or carries the sense of ability, e.g., כִּי־מִי יִשְׁפֹּט "for who *can rule* [*judge*]" translated ὅτι τίς κρινεῖ (2 Chr 1:10; so also "you *will/cannot succeed*" 13:12; "*be able* to save" 32:15, cf. v. 14 with יכל).

B. Participles and Other Forms

In Greek literature participles are very common. However, they are greatly reduced in the Greek translation of Chronicles. In particular, there are very few circumstantial participles used to translate forms other than Hebrew circumstantial participles. Those that occur are usually present participles; the aorist participles are mostly attributive. Participles occur periphrastically both in Hebrew (with a form of הָיָה) and in Greek (usually with a form of εἰμί and either a present or perfect participle). Some of the periphrastic forms substitute other verbal forms, e.g., the *yiqtol* durative in past contexts in Hebrew or the imperfect or future in Greek, others are suppletive (i.e., the only form available in the language is a periphrastic form, e.g., the passive future perfect).[32]

1. Aorist Participle

The following table shows the aorist participle forms and the Hebrew correspondences, including non-verbal forms and pluses (based upon the Hebrew MT).

---

[32] See Evans, *Verbal Aspect*, 221.

TABLE 16: AORIST PARTICIPLES TRANSLATED FROM HEBREW

AORIST PARTICIPLE	TOTAL	Percentage of Hebrew form	Narrative Main Clauses	Reported Speech Main Clauses	Subordinate Clauses
Wayyiqtol	2	0.14	2		
Qatal	24	2.06	2	2	20
Yiqtol	1	0.29			1
Qotel	0 predicate 34 total	6.87	26	7	1
Qatul	0 predicate 2 total	2.74	2		
Qᵉtol Infin. Construct	4	0.65			4
Sub Total	67		32	9	26
Noun and Plus	3		2	1	
Total	70		34	10	26
Total Verbs in Text Type			2344	597	646
Percentage of Form in Text Type			1.45	1.67	4.02

Non-verbals Translated by Aorist Participles and Aorist Participle Pluses:

Narrative Main Clauses (2)
1 Chr 4:43; 2 Chr 32:21
Reported Speech Main Clauses (1)
1 Chr 28:19

About half the aorist participles translate *qotel* attributive participles (34/70 times). In addition, an aorist participle is used to translate twenty *qatal* forms and one *yiqtol* form in relative אֲשֶׁר clauses. The verbs immediately follow the relative אֲשֶׁר and are easily rendered by an attributive participle preceded by a definite article agreeing with the antecedent noun. The relative pronoun is the subject of the verb in the relative clause.[33] However, less than 10% of the time a verb immediately following אֲשֶׁר was rendered this way. The equivalent more closely reflecting the Hebrew, a relative pronoun and an indicative, was the translator's preference. In addition, two *qatal* forms

---

[33] See chapter 4, note 57.

in reported speech translate into attributive aorist participles, equivalent to relative clauses (1 Chr 29:7; 2 Chr 20:7).

Circumstantial participles are very common in Greek narrative. They function adverbially to give the circumstance of an action in the main clause.[34] However, there are only two examples of aorist circumstantial participles in narrative sections of Chronicles. They translate two *wayyiqtol* forms (1 Chr 29:20; 2 Chr 20:18). It seems the translator was reluctant to break the paratactic structure by reducing a main verb to a subordinate circumstantial participle. An attributive aorist participle also translates an asyndetic relative *qatal* form (1 Chr 12:23<24>; so also 9:1). Four infinitive constructs are translated as circumstantial participles.

2. Present Participle

The following table shows the present participle forms and the Hebrew correspondences, including non-verbal forms and pluses (based upon the Hebrew MT).

TABLE 17: PRESENT PARTICIPLES TRANSLATED FROM HEBREW

PRESENT PARTICIPLE	TOTAL	Percentage of Hebrew form	Narrative Main Clauses	Reported Speech Main Clauses	Subordinate Clauses
Wayyiqtol	3	0.21	3		
Qatal	7	0.69	3	2	2
Wᵉqatal	2	1.56	2		
Yiqtol	1	0.29			1
Qotel	43 predicate 203 total	41.01	36 161	5 32	2 10
Qatul	1 predicate 1 total	1.37	1 1		
Qᵉtol **Infin. Construct**	72	11.77			72

---

[34] In other parts of the Septuagint, *wayyiqtol* forms are more frequently translated by either καί or δέ and a circumstantial conjunctive (especially an aorist) participle. Almost 35% of participles with καί in the canonical Septuagint occur in the Pentateuch and over 50% of them with δέ occur in Genesis and Exodus. It is interesting to note that certain verbs are more frequently translated this way: e.g., verbs of motion (e.g., קום > ἀναστάς), taking (לקח > λαβών), seeing (ראה > ἰδών), and speaking (e.g., ענה > ἀποκριθείς). See chapter 4, note 35.

Q*tol* Infin. Absolute	9	36	4	2	3
Q*tol* Imperative	1	0.61		1	
Sub Total	297 (-2 *wᵉqatal*)		172	37	88
Adjective, Noun, Noun Sentence, and Plus	92		77	12	3
Total	389		249	49	91
Total Verbs in Text Type			2344	597	646
Percentage of Form in Text Type			10.62	8.21	14.09

Non-verbals Translated by Present Participles and Present Participle Pluses:

Narrative Main Clauses (77)

1 Chr 2:30, 32; 5:2; 7:40; 9:11, 20, 22; 10:8, 11; 12:15<16>, 21<22>, 27<28>, 40<41>; 13:1; 16:5 (2); 20:1; 21:9; 25:1, 2 (2), 5, 6 (2), 8; 26:8, 10, 18 (2), 24; 27:8, 16, 26, 31, 34; 28:1; 29:29 (2); 2 Chr 3:12; 5:2, 6; 7:10; 9:29; 10:15; 11:11, 22; 12:15; 15:16; 17:2, 7, 13, 15; 20:24, 27; 21:5; 22:2; 23:12; 24:1, 15; 25:1; 28:7; 29:1, 25; 30:17; 31:3, 12, 13, 19; 33:1, 18, 19, 21; 34:1; 35:24; 36:5 (2), 10

Reported Speech Main Clauses (12)

1 Chr 11:2; 17:6, 7; 21:3; 28:9; 2 Chr 6:15; 13:9; 18:16; 19:11 (2); 23:13; 32:12

Subordinate Clauses (3)

1 Chr 6:31<16>; 29:15; 2 Chr 6:5

Over 53% of the present participles translate *qotel* forms, with most of these (160/389 or about 40% of all present participles) translating attributive *qotel* forms. Most (36/43) of the predicative *qotel* forms occur in narrative and are translated by present participles in a coordinated clause that begins with a *waw* (translated by καί). Some of these *qotel* forms are periphrastic with the verb הָיָה "to be" and are mostly translated a Greek participle and εἰμί (7 times—1 Chr 6:32<17>; 12:39<40>; 18:14; 2 Chr 9:26; 17:12; 30:10; 36:16).[35] Twice a *qotel* periphrastic form following וַיְהִי is translated by the aorist of γίνομαι

---

[35] A few times participles occur in sequences linked by καί following a periphrastic participle (1 Chr 12:39<40>; 2 Chr 30:10, 22; 36:16 (2)).

and a present participle (2 Chr 20:25; 30:10).[36] Other predicative participles in coordinated clauses function as main verb equivalents or noun clauses with an expressed verbal notion (20 times), e.g., וְאַהֲרֹן וּבָנָיו מַקְטִירִים "But Aaron and his sons *made offerings*, translated καὶ Ααρων καὶ οἱ υἱοὶ αὐτοῦ θυμιῶντες (1 Chr 6:49<34>; so also 8:40; 13:8; 15:24, 28 (2), 29 (2); 2 Chr 5:6, 12; 7:4, 6; 18:9 (2); 22:8; 23:13; 29:28 (2); 30:21, 22—see examples in chapter 4, section III.B.1.h.). This could reflect the later Hebrew development of the use of the participle as a main verb but was translated literally by the translator using the standard Greek equivalent.

Eight participles do not have a conjunction associated with them, and they function circumstantially, translating a Hebrew form that also operates in the same way (1 Chr 23:24; 2 Chr 4:5; 8:10; 9:20 [with ἦν], 21; 22:9 [the Hebrew has *waw*, which is omitted in translation]; 26:21; 30:22). The participles usually indicate an action simultaneous to the time of the main verb, and they often have a different topic. One *qatul* form also functioning as circumstantial participle in Hebrew is translated by a present circumstantial participle (1 Chr 12:1).

In reported speech most present participles translate *qotel* forms functioning attributively (32), with only five functioning predicatively. Three of the predicative participles function the same way they do in Hebrew, as circumstantial participles. Two predicative participles are attributive in Greek, e.g., כֹּל אֲשֶׁר־נִתַּן בְּיַד־עֲבָדֶיךָ הֵם עֹשִׂים "Everything that was entrusted (lit., given into the hand of) to your servants they *are doing*" is translated πᾶν τὸ δοθὲν ἀργύριον ἐν χειρὶ τῶν παίδων σου *τῶν ποιούντων* τὸ ἔργον "all the silver given [is] in the hand of your servants *doing* the work" (2 Chr 34:16; so also 1 Chr 29:5). It seems from these two examples that there may be even some reluctance on behalf of the translator to translate a Hebrew circumstantial predicative participle by a Greek circumstantial participle in speech. The translator mostly preferred a present indicative (28 times, see section on the present indicative above) or reworked the structure into an attributive participle.

---

[36] These γίνομαι periphrases occur rarely in Greek. The two occurrences in Chronicles may reflect a mechanical translation of וַיְהִי forms by καί and the aorist ἐγένετο, but only a few times is the plural וַיִּהְיוּ translated καί and the aorist of γίνομαι in addition to the above examples (1 Chr 23:11 ἐγένοντο; 2 Chr 13:3 ἐγένετο). Mostly (almost 20 times) it is translated καὶ ἦσαν.

There are a number of noun sentences where an understood verb "to be" is translated by a present circumstantial participle of εἰμί. (The use of the present is constrained by verbal *Aktionsart* since there is no aorist participle of εἰμί). These are common in 2 Chronicles in statements about the age of a king when he began or ended his reign, e.g., בֶּן־שְׁלֹשִׁים וּשְׁתַּיִם שָׁנָה יְהוֹרָם בְּמָלְכוֹ "Jehoram *was* thirty-two years old when he began to reign" translated ὄντος (genitive absolute) αὐτοῦ τριάκοντα καὶ δύο ἐτῶν κατέστη Ιωραμ ἐπὶ τὴν βασιλείαν αὐτοῦ (2 Chr 21:5; so also 22:2; 24:1, 15; 25:1; 29:1; 33:1, 21; 34:1; 36:5). A couple of times the participle of ἔχω "to have" is also used circumstantially to translate noun sentences, for example, וַיָּמָת סֶלֶד לֹא בָנִים "and Seled died, no[t having] children" translated καὶ ἀπέθανεν Σαλαδ οὐκ ἔχων τέκνα (1 Chr 2:30; so also 2:32; 25:2 (2), 6; 27:34). A few other noun sentences, phrases, or nouns are also translated as circumstantial participles, for example, וְלִתְשׁוּבַת הַשָּׁנָה שָׁלַח הַמֶּלֶךְ נְבוּכַדְנֶאצַּר "in the spring (lit., *the turning*) of the year, King Nebuchadnezzar sent" translated καὶ ἐπιστρέφοντος (genitive absolute) τοῦ ἐνιαυτοῦ ἀπέστειλεν ὁ βασιλεὺς Ναβουχοδονοσορ "when the year turned, King Nebuchadnezzar sent" (2 Chr 36:10). A number of nouns are translated by attributive participles, including a rare noun, מִפְלָצֶת "a horrid thing, an object of shuddering," perhaps not known by the translator, which is translated λειτουργοῦσαν "from being *one who ministered*," the sense supplied from the context (2 Chr 15:16).

A large number of infinitive constructs in subordinate clauses are translated by present participles. Of these, most (55) are a translation of the infinitive construct לֵאמֹר "saying" by λέγων. It functions as a circumstantial participle introducing direct speech.[37] Most of the other infinitive constructs are also translated by circumstantial participles. There are also five infinitive absolutes translated by adverbial circumstantial participles cognate to the main verb.

Of the finite verb forms translated by present participles, there is only one *wayyiqtol* form "*and he said,*" which is translated as a predicative circumstantial participle, "and he blessed, *saying*" (1 Chr 29:10; cf. the common use of the present participle to translate the infinitive complementizer לֵאמֹר "saying,"—see above and chapter 4, section III.B.3.g.). One *qatal* form in narrative is translated as a periphrastic form indicating simultaneous action (1 Chr 21:20).

---

[37] See chapter 4, note 137.

Another *qatal* form in a **כִּי** clause is translated by a periphrastic form (2 Chr 36:15). Another *qatal* form functions as a predicate of a noun sentence as an omni-temporal verb in reported speech, "the LORD *reigns*" (1 Chr 16:31). Two *wayyiqtol* forms and five *qatal* forms (one in reported speech and one in a relative clause) are translated as present participles that function attributively in translation. A *yiqtol* form in a relative clause is also translated by an attributive participle.

3. Perfect Participle

The following table shows the perfect participle forms and the Hebrew correspondences, including non-verbal forms and pluses (based upon the Hebrew MT).

TABLE 18: PERFECT PARTICIPLES TRANSLATED FROM HEBREW

PERFECT PARTICIPLE	TOTAL	Percentage of Hebrew form	Narrative Main Clauses	Reported Speech Main Clauses	Subordinate Clauses
Qatal	3	0.26	2		1
Qotel	24 predicate 46 total	9.29	20 35	2 7	2 4
Qatul	23 predicate 32 total	43.84	16 23	5 6	2 3
Q^etol Infin. Construct	1	0.16			1
Sub Total	82		60	13	9
Noun Sentence and Plus	10		7	2	1
Total	92		67	15	10
Total Verbs in Text Type			2344	597	646
Percentage of Form in Text Type			2.86	2.51	1.55

Non-verbals Translated by Perfect Participles and Perfect Participle Pluses:

Narrative Main Clauses (7)
1 Chr 9:2; 26:20; 2 Chr 4:5; 21:3; 29:33; 30:6; 31:13
Reported Speech Main Clauses (2)
2 Chr 2:7<6>; 24:6

Subordinate Clauses (1)
2 Chr 35:19

About 85% (78/92) of all the perfect participles translate *qotel* or *qatul* forms, with 47 of them (60%) being predicative participles.

Most of the predicative *qotel* forms translated by perfect participles occur in a coordinated clause that begins with a *waw* (translated by καί). They function as equivalent to a main verb. A few are periphrastic participles with the verb "to be" (1 Chr 17:14; 19:5; 2 Chr 5:8; 18:34; 22:12). Most function as a main verb by themselves, e.g., וּמַלְאַךְ יְהוָה עֹמֵד "And the angel of the LORD *was standing*" translated καὶ ὁ ἄγγελος κυρίου ἑστώς (1 Chr 21:15; so also v. 16; 9:29; 12:15<16>; 15:27; 17:24; 2 Chr 3:13; 5:12; 7:6 (2); 9:18 (2), 19; 20:13, 24). Five *qotel* participles do not have a conjunction, and they function circumstantially, translating a Hebrew form that also operates in the same way (1 Chr 10:8; 21:16; 2 Chr 3:13; 5:12; 18:9). The participles usually indicate an action or state simultaneous to the time of the main verb and often have a different topic.

Both *qotel* forms translated by perfect participles in subordinate clauses are periphrastic. One in a causal clause is translated as a perfect periphrastic (1 Chr 19:5); the other in a relative אֲשֶׁר clause is translated as an attributive participle (2 Chr 10:6).

Most of the predicative *qatul* forms translated by perfect participles occur in a coordinated clause that begins with a *waw* (translated by καί) and function as a main verb by themselves. Two function circumstantially (1 Chr 21:16 (2)). In reported speech there are four periphrastic perfect participles with the verb "to be" (2 Chr 6:20, 40; 7:15; 9:8).

The two perfect participles that translate a *qatal* form can be understood as functioning as either predicative adjectives in nominal periphrastic structures with the verb "to be" supplied, e.g., "and the rest of the acts...*were written*" (2 Chr 26:22; so also 4:9), or as circumstantial participles modifying the main verb in a preceding or following clause, e.g., "Jotham was over the royal palace...and the rest of the acts...*being written* by Isaiah." The former seems more likely, especially as the clauses with participles are preceded by a coordinated conjunction, while the latter is better Greek style. Once an attributive perfect participle translates a *qatal* form in a relative אֲשֶׁר clause.

4. Other Verb Forms

A few infinitives in narrative are used to translate indicative forms. This has the affect of making the translation a little more hypotactic than the original. However, this was not common. Perhaps, because of the desire to follow the Hebrew as literally as possible by preserving the closest Greek equivalents, the translator of Chronicles resisted the temptation to "modernize" the text to correspond to his own Hebrew, which was less paratactic than the text he was translating.

In reported speech main clauses the translators also used other non-indicative Greek verb forms to translate Hebrew verbs, especially subjunctive and imperative forms. The subjunctives were used in a volitive sense, e.g., for prohibitions (with μή and an aorist subjunctive), for hortative commands, but also for deliberation and emphatic negation (οὐ μή translating לֹא).

In subordinate clauses the translators also used other non-indicative Greek verb forms to translate Hebrew indicative verbs, especially subjunctive forms and infinitives. The subjunctives were used particularly to translate conditional clauses (with ἐάν translating אִם or כִּי),[38] but also to translate temporal clauses (once with ὅταν translating כִּי), indefinite relative clauses (three times with ἄν translating אֲשֶׁר and four times with ἐάν translating אֲשֶׁר), and purpose clauses (eleven times with ἵνα or ὅπως).[39] They mostly translated *yiqtol* forms. The translators were constrained by Greek grammar to use these non-indicative forms. Greek infinitives were the most common form used to translate 409 infinitive constructs. We will not do an in-depth study of these forms as we are focusing on indicative forms, and we have covered these forms in chapter 4.

II. ANOMALIES IN THE TRANSLATION OF VERBS

In chapter 2, section II.C, we mentioned the method of translation of the book of Chronicles and most of the Septuagint as being basically literal with features such as the close following of Hebrew word order and translating one Hebrew morpheme with an equivalent Greek one.

---

[38] An ἐάν with conditional force is mostly used to translate אִם, but it is also used to translate כִּי (2 Chr 6:24, 28 (4), 34), הֵן (2 Chr 7:13 (2), and אֲשֶׁר (2 Chr 6:29).

[39] An ἵνα (followed by a subjunctive) translates לְמַעַן (1 Chr 28:8; 2 Chr 34:25), כִּי (1 Chr 21:18), לָמָּה (21:3), אֲשֶׁר (2 Chr 18:15) and a ὅπως (followed by a subjunctive) translates בַּעֲבוּר (1 Chr 19:3), אֲשֶׁר (2 Chr 1:11), and לְמַעַן (6:31, 33; 31:4; 32:18).

This approach was driven by the cultural context in which it was desired to bring the readers to the source. This led the translators to avoid certain Greek verbal forms such as the historic present and the circumstantial participle. However, there are some anomalies in this approach, which can be observed in the translation of the verbs of Chronicles. These may have been driven by a desire to improve the reading of the target text (with occasional literary flourishes, according to the linguistic context) or to modernize the text according to the Hebrew spoken at the time of the translator.

Sometimes the Greek translation lacks a verb form where the Hebrew has one (minus). Sometimes the Greek translation adds a verb form where the Hebrew lacks one (plus). Sometimes the word order varies. In addition, the translator occasionally alters the Hebrew structure from paratactic to hypotactic or vice versa or changes the clause type from narrative to reported speech or vice versa. Sometimes these adjustments affect the verb tense. In the section below, we summarize the anomalies in the translation of the verbs in terms of minuses and pluses, and variations in word order, structure, clause type, and tense, accounting for these anomalies according to the philosophy of translation outlined in chapter 2.

A. Minuses and Pluses

There is some amount of uncertainty in considering the question of minuses and pluses as to how much can be attributed to the translator and how much to his *Vorlage*. Some of the differences may also occur in the transmission of the texts, e.g., scribal errors, such as parablepsis. Taking these into consideration, it seems that at least some of the anomalies can be attributed to the translator (see chapter 4, note 39 and note 5 in this chapter).

Some omissions may reflect a modernizing of the language, e.g., the omission of וַיְהִי (or the conjunction preceding the verb following it), the omission of a subject between הָיָה and a participle to produce a periphrastic structure, or the omission of *wayyiqtol* forms in strings of close proximity. Others may reflect an attempt to make the text more lucid or readable, e.g., omitting repeated verbs, or verbs of speaking. Of course, some of these omissions may also be attributed to the editor or scribe responsible for the transmission of the translator's *Vorlage*.

The pluses sometimes reflect an attempt by the translator (or his *Vorlage*) to making the text easier to read, e.g., using verbs to replace nouns with a verbal notion, or to substitute for unfamiliar nouns or place names. Sometimes the translator uses so-called doublets (alternate translations/glosses), or he (or his *Vorlage*) harmonizes the text.

In addition to these pluses, a non-verbal element in Hebrew is sometimes translated by a verb in Greek. Included in this category are the translation of the existential particles יֵשׁ and אַיִן by a tense of the verb "to be," 13 times by an imperfect, 20 times by a present, and twice by a future. Pronominal elements are sometimes translated by a copula "to be" verb in Greek. The mechanical rendering of existential particles and pronominal elements sometimes produces an awkward reading in the Greek text, e.g., a present tense form in past narrative, unless it is interpreted as a timeless or historic present. Sometimes noun sentences in Hebrew are translated with the insertion of a verb "to be." This may reflect the preference in Greek for the verb copula compared to the Hebrew preference for the verbless noun sentence.

B. Word Order Variation

Due to the dominance of the paratactic Hebrew conjunction and verb in main clauses, the Greek translation of Chronicles contains many indicative verb forms preceded by the conjunction καί. The most common is καί followed by an aorist, translating the ubiquitous *wayyiqtol* in narrative.[40] While these coordinated structures occur in classical and Hellenistic Greek, they do not occur with as nearly the same frequency as in the Greek translation of the Hebrew Bible. We noted previously the occasional word order variations, such as the subject (e.g., 2 Chr 26:21) or object (e.g., 2 Chr 36:13) preceding the verb. In the former example, the fronting of King Uzziah in the Greek text emphasizes that <u>the King</u> was a leper. In the latter example, the Greek text has a poetic chiastic (VO-OV) word order "and he hardened his neck and his heart he strengthened" compared to the Hebrew VO-VO sequence. Sometimes the addition or omission of a

---

[40] Occasionally a καί is omitted, for example, in reported speech (1 Chr 16:17; 28:5), or καί is inserted in an asyndetic clause. See note 3 above, for examples of *wayyiqtol* forms not translated by καί and an aorist and other forms translated by καί and an aorist.

noun subject or a conjunction also affects the resulting word order.
Sometimes the subject and verb word order is reversed, e.g., in
subordinate clauses (1 Chr 27:23; 2 Chr 6:33; cf. 30:5), or the subject
is deleted (1 Chr 19:5) or inserted (29:11).

The variation in word order may be influenced in part by late
biblical Hebrew where the word order is more varied than in classical
Hebrew. This is due to the breakdown in the use of וַיְהִי introducing
temporal clauses, participles functioning as present tenses, and the
influence of Aramaic word order (see chapter 3, section E).

C. Structure and Clause Type Variation

The most common alteration in syntactic structure occurred in
subordinate clauses when relative clauses (only when the relative was
the subject) were translated by attributive participles (see chapter 4,
note 57).

Occasionally the translator varied the syntactic structure from
paratactic to hypotactic (or vice versa), by translating a coordinated
verb form by a circumstantial participle (e.g., 1 Chr 29:20; 2 Chr
20:18) or an infinitive (e.g., 1 Chr 14:12; 2 Chr 22:9, in which the
infinitive becomes the object of a verb of speaking). In the translation
of Chronicles, this was rare, especially compared to the Pentateuch
(see chapter 4, note 35).

A few infinitive constructs are translated by coordinated indicative
forms, e.g., καί and an aorist (e.g., 1 Chr 5:1; see chapter 4, note 131
for more examples), καί and a future (2 Chr 30:9), or even by an
imperative (e.g., 1 Chr 15:16), thus rearranging the syntax from
hypotactic to paratactic. Perhaps this reflects the trend away from
using infinitive constructs in Hebrew temporal clauses. Other
subordinate clauses were translated by a coordinate structure, for
example, "they laid him on a bier *which was filled* with spices," which
becomes "...*and they filled [it]* with spices" (2 Chr 16:14), or they were
translated as asyndetic clauses (32:14, 17 in which the relative אֲשֶׁר is
not translated and 16:9; 22:6 in which כִּי is not translated). A
subordinate clause is translated as a main clause when a repeated verb
in a relative אֲשֶׁר clause is deleted, "the servants *who brought* gold from
Ophir *brought* algum" translated "the servants *brought* gold and algum"
(2 Chr 9:10). We could say that these changes help the reading,
although sometimes they make the translation more paratactic than

the Hebrew! Sometimes relative clauses are translated by using attributive participles, which are very common and indeed preferred Greek structures (see chapter 4, notes 57, 126, 105, 112, and 118).

A few times the translator altered the text type from narrative to reported speech or vice versa (or perhaps it was in his *Vorlage*). Narrative is changed to reported speech by inserting a verb of speech (2 Chr 22:9 [indirect]; 28:22-23 [direct]) or incorporating narrative into preceding speech (1 Chr 14:12; 2 Chr 14:7<6>; 24:8-9 (3)). This frequently affected the paratactic-hypotactic structure and the tense or mood of the verb form. For example, a paratactic *wayyiqtol* form "and David said, *and they burned*" is translated by an infinitive of indirect speech "and David said *to burn*" (1 Chr 14:12; cf. 2 Chr 22:9). An example of the change in tense occurs when a verb of speech is inserted to make the narrated actions of King Ahaz into reported intent, "*I will sacrifice* to the gods of Damascus," making his intention more vivid (28:23). An example of the change in mood occurs when three *wayyiqtol* forms in narrative following a verb of speech, "the king said, *and they made...and they put...and they proclaimed*," are translated as imperatives in reported speech, "Let a box be made, and let it be put...let men proclaim" (24:8-9). Putting the report in speech makes it more vivid.

At least twice reported speech is changed to narrative, also changing the mood and tense of verb forms. Once speech "*put* the ark" is incorporated into narrative "and *he put* the ark," and a verb of speaking is inserted later (2 Chr 35:3; cf. 1 Chr 16:36).

D. Tense Variation

As was mentioned above, the reinterpretation of clause types sometimes affected the verb tenses. Other anomalies in the translator's use of tenses occurred when he mechanically used a common equivalent without paying attention to the context, especially when his knowledge of his own contemporary Hebrew overruled his understanding of the archaic use of certain forms. Consequently, a few future and present tenses in narrative read awkwardly. Sometimes, especially in theologically charged passages, the translator utilizes a tense that is not expected, e.g., an aorist in a section of future promise or threat, or a future in a section related to past events. Since the subject is frequently God, the resulting translation for the most part makes sense.

A couple of times a *yiqtol* durative past form is translated by a future with awkward results (see the section on the future above). Four *wayyiqtol* forms are translated as futures and are interpreted as future promises, and one *w^eyiqtol* form is translated as an aorist and is viewed as a past event. All of them involve God. Since God transcends time, it is easier to adjust the tenses in actions involving Him and still have them make sense. Perhaps these are all examples of a different reading tradition, or a graphic confusion or misreading of consecutive and coordinated forms, reinterpreting the unpointed text.[41]

For the nonstandard or marked Greek forms the text-linguistic context, *Aktionsart: lexis*, discourse, and clause type influenced their use. In terms of clause type, the imperfect occurs mostly in narrative and subordinate clauses, and the perfect occurs mostly in reported speech and in subordinate clauses.[42] Presents and futures occur in reported speech, with historic presents in narrative almost non-existent (being consistently replaced by aorists when *Paraleipomenon* is compared to parallel sections of Reigns (Samuel-Kings)—especially 1 Chronicles 10 // 1 Samuel 31; see note 27).

Imperfects are frequently constrained by *Aktionsart* (or *lexis* especially the verb εἰμί, translating הָיָה and noun sentences, which accounts for almost half of the imperfect forms). They also occur influenced by the presence of temporal adverbials or plural arguments in the context. A few reinforce changes in topic, indicate simultaneous action, or are used for summary statements. One-sixth (30) of the imperfects and present participles in narrative indicate a Hebrew durative past form (*yiqtol* or *qotel*), but almost as frequently the durative notion was ignored and an aorist was used.

Greek perfects frequently translate *qatul* passive forms or verbs with stative *Aktionsart*. They occur most frequently in reported speech and subordinate clauses. They indicate the resultant state from an action

---

[41] This is similar to the ambiguity of tenses in prophetic texts, where the nature of the literature allows more than one reading. Perhaps the special nature of texts regarding God allows the translator's vernacular to show through (i.e., understanding *wyqtl* as a future as opposed to a *wayyiqtol* past).

[42] It is interesting to note that 25 of 26 *qatal* forms in subordinate clauses translated into imperfects occur in narrative subordinate clauses and 10 of 13 *qatal* forms in subordinate clauses translated into perfects occur in reported speech subordinate clauses. Perhaps the reason for the greater number of imperfects in narrative is the greater propensity for verbless clauses in direct speech in Hebrew.

that took place in the past but has relevance to the time of speaking or the time of the main verb. The perfect draws attention to the enduring results of certain acts, especially those related to God. Sometimes a perfect, and rarely a pluperfect, is used to translate a verb that has a different topic than the preceding verb(s), thus drawing additional attention to the topic.

The present indicative, rather than the present participle, is the equivalent for *qotel* participles in reported speech. Perhaps this translation equivalent reflects the use of the participle as a present in speech current with the time of the translation.

Hebrew durative forms indicating simultaneous action are often, but not always, translated by Greek durative forms. In narrative, Hebrew circumstantial participles are mostly translated by Greek participles. In reported speech, participles are most frequently translated by present indicative forms. Sometimes *yiqtol* durative past forms are translated by Greek durative forms, but they are almost as frequently translated by aorists. Present participles are sometimes governed by *Aktionsart* (e.g., the participle of εἰμί does not have an aorist form). Rarely, circumstantial participles translated coordinated indicative forms, indicating that the translator was reluctant to alter the paratactic structure (e.g., only four times a circumstantial participle translates *wayyiqtol*).

III. Conclusion

In narrative, the aorist is the unmarked common equivalent for both *wayyiqtol* and *qatal* forms. In reported speech and in subordinate clauses in past, present, and future contexts respectively, the aorist, the present, and the future are the common equivalents for the predominant Hebrew forms: *qatal*, noun sentences (including predicate participles), and *yiqtol* forms. In reported speech, the aorist is the common equivalent for *wayyiqtol* forms, and the future is the common equivalent for *wᵉqatal* forms. In infinitival subordinate clauses, Greek infinitives are the common equivalent for Hebrew infinitives. In his choice of common equivalents, the translator was probably influenced by two different registers of Hebrew: spoken Hebrew and written Hebrew. Spoken Hebrew contains verb forms that function in a way close to Mishnaic or rabbinic Hebrew, where the *qatal* form is a past tense, the participle is a present, and the *yiqtol* form a future. Written

Hebrew contains archaic verb forms that did not correspond to current Hebrew use, such as the consecutive *wayyiqtol* and *wᵉqatal* forms. In terms of Greek equivalents, the aorist corresponds most closely to a past and sequential narrative form, the future corresponds to a future and sequential form, and the present indicative corresponds to verbs and verb equivalents indicating an action or state in the present time. Apart from the exception mentioned above (in the section on the present tense), participles are mostly translated by participles and infinitives by infinitives.

In summary, the translation of the Hebrew verbs into Greek was well handled. The translation makes sense but does not read like standard Greek. The relative frequency of certain forms, such as the aorist, is increased to the detriment of other forms such as imperfects, circumstantial participles, and historic presents. On the one hand, the reader would realize that this is translation Greek, the translation of a sacred text endeavoring to capture the original language as closely as possible in Greek. On the other hand, it appears that the translator was not reluctant to add or subtract to make sense of a difficult reading to improve his source text (or perhaps his *Vorlage* had the improvements). The syntax is peculiar, with the propensity of the structure καί + aorist. In using it the translator was mostly concerned with the ongoing movement of the actions of the event line. Most of the actions in the Hebrew text are related in temporally iconic order; therefore, the translator can use coordinated aorists to indicate the advancement of action. Occasionally, the translator will draw attention to an action by using an imperfective form. The verb forms in the Hebrew text do not always prompt him to do this. Sometimes context alone guided him (such as temporal adverbs of duration or plural subjects). Other times imperfective forms may highlight a participant or offset one action against the other. In this respect, we can say the translator used a little artistic license.

In the final chapter, we consider how the translation reflects the influence of three contexts, historical, textual linguistic, and cultural, on the verb choice and what it tells us about the translator's understanding of the Hebrew verb system.

CHAPTER SIX

CONCLUSION

In this book, we first looked at the cultural context, the "philosophy" of translation or the translation principles behind the translation of the book of Chronicles, especially in terms of the background and translation precedents of the Jewish community in Alexandria. Then we considered the similarities and differences between Hebrew and Greek verbal systems. Following this, we analyzed the translation of the book of Chronicles in terms of the equivalents chosen for each indicative Hebrew verb form, participle, and infinitive in their textual-linguistic and historical-linguistic contexts. The next chapter dealt with the choice of the Greek verb forms used in the translation and their adequacy. In this final chapter, we consider how the translation reflects the influence of these three contexts—historical, textual-linguistic, and cultural—on the verb choice and what it tells us about the translator's understanding of the Hebrew verb system. We also consider the translation of the book of Chronicles as sectional view in the diachronic continuum of the development of both the Hebrew verbal system and the translation of the Bible into Greek.

I. How the Translation of the Verbs Reflects the Translator's Understanding of the Hebrew Verbal System

A. Historical Linguistic Context: Two Registers

According to the philosophy of translation, to bring the readers to the source text, the translator selected the most appropriate common equivalent for each verbal form, according to his understanding of the Hebrew and Greek verbal systems. His choice of common equivalents was influenced by two different registers of Hebrew: primarily, by the use of verbs in the spoken Hebrew contemporary to the translator, and secondarily, by archaic written Hebrew, informed by the study of the text and the reading tradition.

1. Influenced by Post-Classical (Contemporary) Hebrew

The use of verb forms in Hebrew contemporary with the translator, especially in spoken Hebrew, primarily influenced the translator in his choice of common equivalents. For some forms, the meaning and function remained the same in both classical and late biblical Hebrew, e.g., *qatal* and *yiqtol* forms in past and future contexts respectively. For *qatal* forms, he chose aorists as common equivalents. For *yiqtol* forms, he chose futures or aorist subjunctives (especially in subordinate clauses). Attributive participles, object infinitives, and imperatives also functioned in the same way, and they were translated mostly as participles, infinitives, and imperatives respectively.

Some forms acquired new meanings or underwent changes in use. Coordinated *qatal* and *yiqtol* forms have only past and future (or modal) meaning respectively. Circumstantial *qotel* participles function as present tense forms. הָיָה functions more commonly as the verb "to be," rather than "to become." Periphrastic participles (formed from הָיָה and a participle) function as past and future durative forms (replacing *yiqtol* forms and bare *qotel* circumstantial participles in narrative with past durative meaning). Stative verbs are replaced by adjectives (with or without הָיָה). Particles and conjunctions introduce temporal clauses with indicative verb forms (as opposed to וַיְהִי and/or infinitive constructs with prepositions). These all reflect the Hebrew of the Hellenistic period rather than the classical dialect of biblical Hebrew.

2. Influenced by Classical (Archaic) Hebrew

The translator was informed by his study of the text as to the meaning and function of certain archaic verb forms. The most striking examples of these archaic forms are *wayyiqtol* and *weqatal* consecutive forms, *yiqtol* (preterite and durative) forms (mostly in narrative), the use of וַיְהִי and/or an infinitive construct with a preposition to introduce a temporal clause, the use of stative verb forms (as opposed to adjectives) to indicate states, the use of infinitive absolutes, and the use of *qotel* participles as durative circumstantial forms (especially in narrative).

For these archaic forms, he chose common Greek equivalents that corresponded to his understanding of these forms. For the *wayyiqtol* forms, he chose καί followed immediately by an aorist. This was the dominant form in narrative. Since the aorist was also the common equivalent for the *qatal* form, only through the translator's close adherence to Hebrew word order, can the underlying *wayyiqtol* and *qatal* forms be distinguished, for the most part. For *wᵉqatal* consecutive forms, he chose either a future or an aorist subjunctive (when the *wᵉqatal* form followed a subordinate clause translated by a Greek subjunctive). For *yiqtol* preterite and durative forms, he sometimes employed aorist and imperfect forms respectively. However, we cannot really call these common equivalents since they are rare, and other forms are also employed (e.g., aorists are almost as frequent as imperfects for *yiqtol* duratives, see chapter 4, sections 4.a and 4.b). For וַיְהִי "and it came to pass," he chose καί followed immediately by the aorist of γίνομαι as a common equivalent. For temporal clauses with infinitive constructs (preceded by a preposition), he chose Greek infinitives. Infinitive absolutes were rendered in a variety of ways, as there was no appropriate common equivalent. For stative verbs, he chose verbal forms. For circumstantial participles, he chose Greek participles.

However, the changes in verb use in Hebrew contemporary to the translator sometimes influenced his choice in the way these archaic forms were translated. Occasionally archaic consecutive forms are treated like coordinated forms (producing a future in a past context and vice versa). *Qotel* participles are translated as present tenses, particularly in reported speech. Nominal or circumstantial participles are sometimes translated as a periphrastic form in Greek. וַיְהִי is sometimes omitted in translation. Infinitive constructs introducing temporal clauses are translated by indicative forms (especially aorists). Stative verbs are translated as adjectives. *Wayyiqtol* strings are broken up with some forms translated by non-indicative participles or infinitives. Sometimes one of the *wayyiqtol* forms is even omitted. In these cases, where the translator employed a contemporary equivalent for an archaic form, we could say that the translator was "modernizing" his text according to the developments of the biblical Hebrew verbal system.

B. *Textual Linguistic Context: Clause Types,* Aktionsart, *Discourse Pragmatics, and Divine Agency*

In addition to historical linguistic influences on the translation, the textual linguistic context also influenced the choice of Greek verb forms, particularly in the use of non-standard Greek verb forms that do not correspond neatly to a particular Hebrew verb form, for example, imperfects, perfects, pluperfects, historic presents, and circumstantial participles. The textual linguistic context includes situation aspect or *Aktionsart*: verbal aspect, lexical semantics of the verb and its arguments, and the context, including clause types and discourse pragmatics (sentence topic and focus, foreground and background). In addition, the theological context of the translator and text may also have influenced the choice of the verb form.

The lexical meaning (*lexis*) of the verb influences a number of imperfects and perfects in Greek, especially for verb forms that lack another tense form (e.g., εἰμί "to be" without an aorist form or the perfect οἶδα "to know," lacking a present form) or prefer one over another (e.g., πείθω "to trust," preferring a perfect to an aorist form).

Clause types play a role in the choice of verb forms. Clauses have different temporal frames. Narrative main clauses are set in the past time, reported speech main clauses are set in the time of the moment of speech, subordinate clauses have a temporal frame relative to the time of the main clause. This influences verb forms. For example, in Greek aorists and imperfects predominate in narrative, presents mostly occur in direct speech, and perfect forms mostly occur in direct speech and in subordinate clauses. Hebrew consecutive forms do not occur in subordinate clauses.

Sentence topic and focus play a significant role in the choice of Hebrew verb form, in that the fronting of an argument for topicalization or focus constrains the author to break a string of consecutive forms and use a non-consecutive form. The translator, for the most part, did not indicate the change in Hebrew tense with a change in Greek tense (for example, *wayyiqtol* and X-*qatal* forms are both translated by aorists). However, by closely following Hebrew word order, the change in topic or focus in the Hebrew text can also be recognized in translation. Occasionally, the translator varied the tense forms to reinforce a change in topic or focus.

The discourse structure plays a lesser role in the choice of verb form. Sometimes an out-of-line form may indicate backgrounding or may be used in summary statements. Sometimes the context of what the translator had already translated may have influenced the translator. For example, a number of imperfect forms occur in close proximity to one another.

Sometimes the translator uses a particular form in theologically significant contexts. For example, perfect forms are frequently used when God is involved in an action. The perfects with stative aspect (emphasizing resultant state) are appropriate for the enduring nature of God's actions. Sometimes the tenses used are not the expected tense, for example a past tense is used in the context of prediction, or a present tense is used to indicate omni-temporal or timeless actions, especially when God is the agent.

C. Cultural Context: Philosophy and Antecedents of Translation

As was mentioned above, the translator endeavored according to his "philosophy" of translation to bring the reader to the source text by choosing the most appropriate common Greek equivalent for each Hebrew form. In his cultural context, the translator was influenced by the way the translators of two preceding books, the Pentateuch and Samuel-Kings, handled Hebrew verb forms. The most striking difference between the translation of the verbs of the Pentateuch and Samuel-Kings, compared to Chronicles is in the way the translators used circumstantial participles and historic presents to translate coordinated indicative forms (especially *wayyiqtol*). Circumstantial participles were more common in the Pentateuch and historic presents more common in Samuel-Kings. Circumstantial participles were used in the translation of the Pentateuch to subordinate one action (in close proximity) to another. They occur profusely in classical Greek, which is sometimes labeled a 'participle-loving' language. Historic presents are much rarer in classical Greek and are a marked verb form, giving actions vividness. Although both verb forms were not abundant in the Pentateuch and Samuel-Kings, they are notably absent from the translation of Chronicles. This could indicate that the translator felt that these forms were too far removed from the underlying Hebrew verb forms. By avoiding using them, perhaps he was trying to demonstrate that the translation of Chronicles was more literal than these prior translations. Rather than use circumstantial participles and historic presents, the translator used imperfects in narrative and perfects in reported speech and subordinate clauses to mark out-of-line, simultaneous actions or states.

The occasional anomalies in the translation of verbs: so-called minuses and pluses, variations in word order, changes in the structure of the text (e.g., from paratactic to hypotactic), switches in genre (e.g., from narrative to reported speech), and variations in tenses also inform us regarding the translation philosophy. The fact that they are rare indicates that the translator was mostly concerned with representing the Hebrew text as closely as possible in Greek. However, the fact that there are a few anomalies also indicates that the translator was flexible and even had occasional "literary flourishes." He wanted his translation to make sense. Occasionally, he adjusts the syntax or word choice to clarify difficulties in the text or to give prominence to a particular feature. However, when his translation is compared with antecedent translations, particularly the Pentateuch and Samuel-Kings, we can see an increasing literalizing tendency, especially in his avoidance of circumstantial participles and historic presents.

II. SUMMARY

The Septuagint's translation of the verbs of Chronicles slices through two diachronic developments: the development of the Hebrew verbal system and the trend toward a more literal translation of the Bible. Firstly, the way the translator of Chronicles handled the Hebrew verbs is part of the continuum in the development of the Hebrew verbal system from classical biblical Hebrew to rabbinic or Mishnaic Hebrew. By looking at the way Hebrew verbal forms were translated, we can get some insight into the Hebrew of the time of the translator, which was the primary influence on his understanding of the Hebrew verbs. In addition to this, he recognized, through the reading tradition and his study, archaic meanings to certain verb forms. He also realized that the context dictated, or strongly suggested, the use of certain Greek verb forms that did not correspond to a particular Hebrew form. We can see by his translation of some of these archaic forms that he updated the translation to conform it more closely to contemporary Hebrew.

Secondly, the translation of the book of Chronicles is part of a trend in the process of the translation of the Bible from the freer (but still literal) translation of the Pentateuch and Samuel-Kings to the slavishly literal translation of Aquila. This trend was motivated by the desire to bring the reader to the source text and an increasing reverence for the holy writings. In the translation of the verbs, one gets the impression that the translator was striving to be more literal than his predecessors (avoiding the use of the circumstantial participles and historic presents for consecutive forms that were employed in the translation of the Pentateuch and Samuel-Kings) without going to the extreme of using the same common equivalent for each distinct Hebrew verb form, which would have resulted in a nonsensical translation (which even Aquila avoided doing). He was sensitive enough to use non-standard Greek forms where the context dictated or suggested them and minor anomalies (minuses, pluses, and changes in word order, genre, and structure) reflect minor improvements or variations within a basically literal approach.

APPENDIX 1—*GRAMCORD* ADJUSTMENTS

AORIST INDICATIVES
(2329 + 26 –10 = 2345)

Aorist participle to aorist indicative: ἐνίσχυσαν (1 Chr 4:23—a Greek plus); κατίσχυσαν (5:20; 2 Chr 11:17 (2); ἐνίσχυσαν (24:13); ἐσκύλευσαν (25:13); συνεπίσχυσαν (32:3—all translate *wayyiqtol* forms); εὐλόγησας (1 Chr 17:27—translates a *qatal* form); ὕψωσαν (2 Chr 5:13—translates an infinitive construct);
Present participle to aorist indicative: ὕψωσάς (1 Chr 17:17—translates a noun).
Imperfect to aorist indicative: ἀνήγαγον (2 Chr 6:5—translates a *qatal* form); ἐξέχεεν (36:5—a Greek plus).
Aorist optative to aorist indicative: καθεῖλαν (30:14—translates a *wayyiqtol* form).
Aorist indicatives in additional Greek text not counted by *GRAMCORD*: ἀνέστη, ἀπεστράφη, ὠργίσθη, παρώργισεν, εἶπεν, ἀπέστησα, ἀπωσάμην, ἐξελεξάμην, εἶπα (2 Chr 35:19); ἀπέστησαν, ἐποίησεν, ἔπλησεν, ἠθέλησεν (36:5[9]).

Aorist indicative to imperfect: ἤμην (1 Chr 17:8—translates a *wᵉyiqtol* form); ἐφέροσαν (22:4—translates a *qatal* form); κατεκρήμνιζον and διερρήγνυντο (2 Chr 25:12 (2)—translate *wayyiqtol forms*).
Aorist indicative to imperative: διηγήσασθε (1 Chr 16:9—translates an imperative); εἰπὸν (17:4—translates a *wᵉqatal* form); εἰσέλθατε (2 Chr 23:14—translates a *qotel* form).
Aorist indicative to perfect: ἡρέτικεν (2 Chr 29:11—translates a *qatal* form).
Aorist indicative to noun: ἐγγραφὴ (2 Chr 21:12—translates a noun).
Aorist indicative to transliteration (noun): ιγλααμ (1 Chr 8:7—translates a *qatal* form).

IMPERFECT INDICATIVES
(243 + 6 − 2 = 247)

Aorist indicative to imperfect: ἤμην (1 Chr 17:8—translates a *wᵉyiqtol* form); ἐφέροσαν (22:4—translates a *qatal* form); κατεκρήμνιζον and διερρήγνυντο (2 Chr 25:12 (2)—translate *wayyiqtol forms*).
Present indicative to imperfect: ὕμνουν (2 Chr 29:30—translates a *wayyiqtol* form)
Imperfect indicative in additional Greek text not counted by *GRAMCORD*: ἐξέχεεν (36:5).

Imperfect to aorist indicative: ἀνήγαγον (2 Chr 6:5—translates a *qatal* form); ἐξέχεεν (36:5—a Greek plus).

PERFECT INDICATIVES
(51 + 3 − 8 = 46)

Aorist indicative to perfect: ἠρέτικεν (2 Chr 29:11—translates a *qatal* form).
Present indicative to perfect: ἤκατε (1 Chr 12:17<18>—translates a *qatal* form).
Pluperfect indicative to perfect: ᾠκοδομήκατέ (1 Chr 17:6—translates a *qatal* form).

Perfect indicative to present indicative: τίκτεταί (1 Chr 22:9—translates a *qotel* form).
Perfect indicative to aorist infinitive: εὐλογῆσαι (1 Chr 16:43; 17:27; 18:10—all translate infinitive constructs).
Perfect indicative to perfect participle: πεπληρωκὼς (1 Chr 12:15<16>); καθεσταμένοι (2 Chr 34:10—both translate *qotel* forms).
Perfect indicative to pluperfect indicative: παρεμβεβλήκει (1 Chr 11:15); παρειστήκει (2 Chr 6:3; cf. 2 Chr 18:18—both translate *qotel* forms).

PLUPERFECT INDICATIVES
(2 + 2 − 1 = 3)

Perfect indicative to pluperfect indicative: παρεμβεβλήκει (1 Chr 11:15); παρειστήκει (2 Chr 6:3; cf. 2 Chr 18:18—both translate *qotel* forms).

Pluperfect indicative to perfect: ᾠκοδομήκατέ (1 Chr 17:6—translates a *qatal* form).

PRESENT INDICATIVES
(161 + 3 − 22 = 142)

Future indicative to present indicative: ταράσσεται (1 Chr 29:11— translates a *qotel* form).
Perfect indicative to present indicative: τίκτεται (1 Chr 22:9— translates a *qotel* form).
Present subjunctive to present indicative: ζῶσιν (2 Chr 6:31— translates an adjective).

Present indicative to imperative: ἐξομολογεῖσθε (1 Chr 16:8, 34; 2 Chr 20:21); ἐπικαλεῖσθε (1 Chr 16:8); αἰνεῖτε (16:10); ἔρχεσθε (2 Chr 10:5); φυλάσσετε (19:7—all translate imperative forms); πονηρεύεσθε (1 Chr 16:22); πολεμεῖτε (2 Chr 18:30); φοβεῖσθε (20:15, 17); πιστεύετε (32:15—all translate *yiqtol* forms).
Present indicative to imperfect: ὕμνουν (2 Chr 29:30—translates a *wayyiqtol* form).
Present indicative to perfect: ἥκατε (1 Chr 12:17<18>—translates a *qatal* form).
Present indicative to present participle: κατοικοῦσιν (1 Chr 8:6, 13; 2 Chr 31:4); κόπτουσιν (2:10<9>); ποιοῦσιν (24:12; 34:10—all translate *qotel* forms); ἱερατεύουσιν (31:19—translates a noun); κατοικοῦσιν (32:12—a Greek plus).

FUTURE INDICATIVES
(253 + 8 – 8 = 253)

Aorist subjunctive to future indicative: πορεύσῃ (1 Chr 14:14—translates a *yiqtol* form); καταφυτεύσω (17:9); ἀναστήσω (17:11; 2 Chr 7:18); ἀναπαύσω (1 Chr 22:9—all translate *weqatal* forms); αὐξήσω (17:10—translates a *wayyiqtol* form); ποιήσω (21:10—translates a *weyiqtol* form); ἀποστήσω (2 Chr 35:19—a Greek plus).

Future indicative to present indicative: ταράσσεται (1 Chr 29:11—translates a *qotel* form).

Future indicative to aorist subjunctive: κοιμηθήσῃ (1 Chr 17:11—translates an infinitive construct); κρατήσῃ (19:12); ἐμπέσω (21:13); θλίψῃ (2 Chr 6:28); φυλάξῃ (7:17—all translate *yiqtol* forms); ποιήσω (25:9—translates an infinitive construct).

Future indicative to noun: γεννήσεις (1 Chr 4:8—translates a noun).[1]

AORIST PARTICIPLES
(81 + 1 – 12 = 70)

Present participle to aorist passive participle: ἐκλεγέντες (1 Chr 16:41—translates a *qatul* form).

Aorist participle to aorist indicative: ἐνίσχυσαν (1 Chr 4:23—a Greek plus); κατίσχυσαν (5:20; 2 Chr 11:17 (2); ἐνίσχυσαν (2 Chr 24:13); ἐσκύλευσαν (25:13); συνεπίσχυσαν (32:3—all translate *wayyiqtol* forms); εὐλόγησας (1 Chr 17:27—translates a *qatal* form); ὕψωσαν (2 Chr 5:13—translates an infinitive construct).

Aorist participle to perfect participle: εἰδότας (2 Chr 8:18—translates a *qotel* form).

Aorist participle to present participle: σαλπίζουσαι (2 Chr 29:28—translates a *qotel* form); κατευθυνούσης (30:19—translates a *qatal* form).

---

[1] In addition, three aorist infinitives of ἐκβαλεῖν are incorrectly coded as future infinitives (1 Chr 17:21; 2 Chr 20:11; 29:16).

PRESENT PARTICIPLES
(383 + 14 − 8 = 389)

<u>Aorist participle to present participle:</u> σαλπίζουσαι (2 Chr 29:28—translates a *qotel* form); κατευθυνούσης (30:19—translates a *qatal* form).

<u>Aorist infinitive to present participle:</u> αἴρουσαι (2 Chr 9:1—translates a *qotel* form).

<u>Present indicative to present participle:</u> κατοικοῦσιν (1 Chr 8:6, 13; 2 Chr 31:4); κόπτουσιν (2:10<9>); ποιοῦσιν (24:12; 34:10—all translate *qotel* forms); ἱερατεύουσιν (31:19—translates a noun); κατοικοῦσιν (32:12—a Greek plus).

<u>Noun to present participle:</u> κατοικῶν (1 Chr 9:16); λειτουργῶν[2] (2 Chr 9:4—both translate *qotel* forms).

<u>Adjective to present participle:</u> ποιῶν (1 Chr 18:14—translates a *qotel* form).

<u>Present participle to aorist indicative:</u> ὕψωσάς (1 Chr 17:17—translates a noun).

<u>Present participle to perfect participle:</u> ἀνωρθωμένος (1 Chr 17:24—translates a *qotel* form).

<u>Present participle to aorist passive participle:</u> ἐκλεγέντες (1 Chr 16:41—translates a *qatul* form).

<u>Present participle to transliteration (noun):</u> μεθαχαβιν (1 Chr 21:20—translates a *qotel* form).

<u>Present participle to noun:</u> ἄρχων (1 Chr 5:6, 7, 15; 11:20—all translate nouns)[3]

---

[2] *BibleWorks*, Copyright © 1992-2001 BibleWorks, L.L.C. also codes this as a noun, but in nine other places they code this part of speech as a participle (1 Chr 6:32<17>; 16:4; 27:1; 2 Chr 9:4; 13:10; 17:19; 22:8; 23:6; 29:11).

[3] This form (the nominative masculine singular form) is analyzed as a noun (1 Chr 15:27), and other cases are always analyzed as nouns, e.g., ἄρχοντες (19:3; 23:24; 25:1; 26:10; 27:1).

PERFECT PARTICIPLES
(85 + 7 = 92)

<u>Aorist participle to perfect participle:</u> εἰδότας (2 Chr 8:18—translates a *qotel* form).

<u>Present participle to perfect participle:</u> ἀνωρθωμένος (1 Chr 17:24—translates a *qotel* form).

<u>Perfect indicative to perfect participle:</u> πεπληρωκὼς (1 Chr 12:15<16>); καθεσταμένοι (2 Chr 34:10—both translate *qotel* forms).

<u>Pluperfect participle to perfect participle:</u> περιεζωσμένος (1 Chr 15:27); ἠτιμωμένοι (19:5—both translate *qotel* forms).

<u>Future participle to perfect participle:</u> ἀνωρθωμένος (1 Chr 17:14—translates a *qotel* form).

APPENDIX 2—HEBREW AND GREEK VERB FORMS ACCORDING TO CLAUSE TYPES

The following tables give the breakdown of the narrative verb forms in Hebrew and Greek and their corresponding forms in the other language.[4]

TABLE 19: HEBREW VERB FORMS IN NARRATIVE MAIN CLAUSES

Narrative Main Clauses	TOTAL	Percentage of Total	Translation Equivalent	TOTAL	Percentage of Form
Wayyiqtol	1375	59.22 (1375/2322)	**Aorist Indicative**	1261	91.71 (1261/1375)
			Imperfect Indicative	76	5.53
			Present Indicative	2	
			Future Indicative	2	
			Aorist Participle	2	
			Present Participle	3	
			Aorist Infinitive	4	
Qatal	515 (+ *wᵉqatal*)	22.18	**Aorist Indicative**	429	83.3
			Imperfect Indicative	49	9.52
			Aorist Participle	2	
			Present Participle	3	
			Perfect Participle	2	
Wᵉqatal	19	0.82	**Aorist Indicative**	11	57.89
			Imperfect Indicative	4	
			Present Participle	2	
Yiqtol	27	1.16	**Aorist Indicative**	9 (2 *wᵉyiqtol*)	33.33
			Imperfect Indicative	10	37.04
			Future Indicative	4	
Qotel	98 predicate	4.2	**Aorist Indicative**	9	

[4] In the tables that follow, the totals do not always add up. In the presentation non-indicative forms are often omitted, especially when they are not significant. Complete tables indicating how Hebrew verb forms were rendered into Greek are given in chapter 4. When two figures are given for *qatal* forms, the top figure indicates *wᵉqatal* forms are excluded, and the bottom figure gives a total of all *qatal* forms. When two figures are given *qotel* and *qatul* participial forms, the top figures indicate predicate forms and the bottom figure gives a total of all forms. Percentages are only given when significant.

	340 total	14.64		15	
			Imperfect Indicative	20 / 20	20.20 (20/99)
			Pluperfect Indicative	2 / 2	
			Present Indicative	2 / 2	
			Present Participle	36 / 161	36.36 (36/99)
			Perfect Participle	20 / 35	20.20 (20/99)
Qatul	23 predicate / 54 total	0.99 / 2.33	Aorist Indicative	1 / 1	
			Perfect Indicative	3 / 3	
			Present Participle	1 / 1	
			Perfect Participle	16 / 23	69.57 (16/23)
Infinitive Absolute	11	0.47	Aorist Indicative	3	27.27
			Present Participle	4	36.36
Total	2322	100			

TABLE 20: GREEK VERB FORMS IN NARRATIVE MAIN CLAUSES

Narrative Main Clauses	TOTAL	Percentage of Total	Translation Equivalent	TOTAL	Percentage of form
Aorist	1787	76.24	*Wayyiqtol*	1261	70.57 (1261/1787)
			Qatal	418 (- w^{e}qatal) / 429	24.01
			W^{e}qatal	11	
			Yiqtol	9	
			W^{e}yiqtol	2	
			Qotel	9 / 15	
			Qatul	1 / 1	
			Qatol Infin. Absolute	3	
			Noun, Noun Sentence and Plus	69	3.86

Imperfect	186	7.95	*Wayyiqtol*	76	40.86
			Qatal	45 (- *wᵉqatal*) 49	26.34
			Wᵉqatal	4	
			Yiqtol	10	
			Qotel	20 20	10.87
			Noun Sentence and Plus	31	16.85
Perfect	3	0.13	*Qatul*	3 3	100
Pluperfect	2	0.09	*Qotel*	2 2	100
Present	10	0.43	*Wayyiqtol*	2	20
			Qotel	2 2	20
			Noun, Noun Sentence	6	60
Future	6	0.26	*Wayyiqtol*	2	33.33
			Yiqtol	4	66.67
Aorist Participle	34	1.45	*Wayyiqtol*	2	
			Qatal	2 (- *wᵉqatal*) 2	
			Qotel	0 predicate 26 total	76.47
			Qatul	0 predicate 2 total	
			Noun	2	
Present Participle	249	10.62	*Wayyiqtol*	3	
			Qatal	1 (- *wᵉqatal*) 3	
			Wᵉqatal	2	
			Qotel	36 predicate 161 total	14.45 65.66
			Qatul	1 predicate 1 total	
			Qᵃtol **Infin. Absolute**	4	
			Noun, Noun Sentence, and Plus	77	30.92
Perfect Participle	67	2.86	*Qatal*	2 (- *wᵉqatal*) 2	

			Qotel	20 predicate 35 total	29.85 52.24
			Qatul	16 predicate 23 total	23.88 34.33
			Noun Sentence	7	
Total	2344				

The following tables give the breakdown of the reported speech main clause verb forms in Hebrew and Greek and their corresponding forms in the other language.

TABLE 21: HEBREW VERB FORMS IN REPORTED SPEECH MAIN CLAUSES

Reported Speech Main Clauses	TOTAL	Percentage of Total	Translation Equivalent	TOTAL	Percentage of form
Wayyiqtol	74	8.74	**Aorist Indicative**	69	93.24
			Future Indicative	4	
Qatal	131 (- *wᵉqatal*) 240 total	15.47 28.34	**Aorist Indicative**	87 99	66.41 41.25
			Imperfect Indicative	3 4	
			Perfect Indicative	19 21	14.5
			Present Indicative	13 14	9.92
			Future Indicative	1 62	25.83
			Aorist Participle	2 2	
			Present Participle	2 2	
Wᵉqatal	109	12.87	**Aorist Indicative**	12	11.01
			Imperfect Indicative	1	
			Perfect Indicative	2	
			Present Indicative	1	
			Future Indicative	61	55.96
Yiqtol	239	28.21	**Aorist Indicative**	1 (*wᵉyiqtol*)	
			Imperfect Indicative	3	
			Perfect Indicative	1	

			Present Indicative	5	
			Future Indicative	134	56.07
Wᵉyiqtol	51	6.02	Aorist Indicative	1	
			Imperfect Indicative	2	
			Future Indicative	29	56.86
Qotel	45 predicate 110 total	5.31 12.99	Aorist Indicative	2 3	
			Perfect Indicative	1 1	
			Pluperfect Indicative	1 1	
			Present Indicative	27 28	55.1 25.45
			Future Indicative	2 2	
			Aorist Participle	0 7	
			Present Participle	5 32	9.8 29.09
			Perfect Participle	2 7	
Qatul	9 predicate 11 total	1.06 1.3	Present Indicative	1 1	
			Perfect Participle	5 6	55.56 54.55
Infinitive Absolute	11	1.3	Aorist Indicative	3	
			Future Indicative	2	
			Present Participle	2	
Qᵉtol Imperative	162	19.13	Aorist Indicative	1	
			Future Indicative	5	
Total	847	100			

Table 22: Greek Verb Forms in Reported Speech Main Clauses

Reported Speech Main Clauses	TOTAL	Percentage of Total	Translation Equivalent	TOTAL	Percentage of form
Aorist	183	30.65	*Wayyiqtol*	69	37.71
			Qatal	87 (- *wᵉqatal*) 99	47.5 54.1
			Wᵉqatal	12	
			Yiqtol	1 (*wᵉyiqtol*)	
			Wᵉyiqtol	1	
			Qotel	2 predicate 3 total	
			Qatol **Infinitive Absolute**	3	
			Qᵉtol **Imperative**	1	
			Noun Sentence and Plus	7	
Imperfect	9	1.51	*Qatal*	3 (- *wᵉqatal*) 4	33.33 44.44
			Wᵉqatal	1	
			Yiqtol	3	33.33
			Wᵉyiqtol	2	
			Noun Sentence	2	
Perfect	24	4.02	*Qatal*	19 (- *wᵉqatal*) 21	79.17 87.5
			Wᵉqatal	2	
			Yiqtol	1	
			Qotel	1 predicate 1 total	
			Noun	1	
Pluperfect	1	0.17	*Qotel*	1 predicate 1 total	
Present	87	14.57	*Qatal*	13 (- *wᵉqatal*) 14	14.94 16.09
			Wᵉqatal	1	
			Yiqtol	5	
			Qotel	27 predicate	31.03

				28 total	32.18
			Qatul	1	
			Noun, Noun Sentence, and Plus	39	44.83
Future	219	36.68	*Wayyiqtol*	4	
			Qatal	1 (- *wᵉqatal*) 62	28.31
			Wᵉqatal	61	27.85
			Yiqtol	134	61.19
			Wᵉyiqtol	29	13.24
			Qotel	2 predicate 2 total	
			Qatol **Infinitive Absolute**	2	
			Qᵉtol **Imperative**	5	
			Noun Sentence and Plus	10	
Aorist Participle	10	1.67	*Qatal*	2 (- *wᵉqatal*) 2	
			Qotel	0 predicate 7 total	70
			Plus	1	
Present Participle	49	8.21	*Qatal*	2 (- *wᵉqatal*) 2	
			Qotel	5 predicate 32 total	65.31
			Qatol **Infin. Absolute**	2	
			Qᵉtol **Imperative**	1	
			Noun, Noun Sentence, and Plus	12	24.49
Perfect Participle	15	2.51	*Qotel*	2 predicate 7 total	46.66
			Qatul	5 predicate 6 total	40
			Noun Sentence and Plus	2	
Total	597	100			

The following tables give the breakdown of the subordinate clause verb forms in Hebrew and Greek and their corresponding forms in the other language.

TABLE 23: HEBREW VERB FORMS IN SUBORDINATE CLAUSES

Subordinate Clauses	TOTAL	Percentage of Total	Translation Equivalent	TOTAL	Percentage of form
Qatal	408	35.11	Aorist Indicative	312	76.47
			Imperfect Indicative	28	6.86
			Perfect Indicative	14	3.43
			Present Indicative	3	
			Aorist Participle	20	4.9
			Present Participle	2	
			Perfect Participle	1	
			Aorist Infinitive	2	
			Present Infinitive	1	
			Aorist Subjunctive	1	
Yiqtol	85	7.31	Aorist Indicative	3	
			Imperfect Indicative	2	
			Present Indicative	4	
			Future Indicative	23	27.05
			Aorist Participle	1	
			Present Participle	1	
			Aorist Infinitive	1	
			Aorist Subjunctive	47	55.29
			Present Subjunctive	3	
Qotel	21 predicate 45 total	1.81 3.88	Aorist Indicative	1 1	
			Imperfect Indicative	3 3	13.04 6.67
			Perfect Indicative	1 1	
			Present Indicative	9 9	39.13 20
			Future Indicative	1 2	
			Aorist Participle	1	

			Present Participle	2 10	8.7 22.22
			Perfect Participle	2 4	
			Present Infinitive	1 1	
Qatul	7 predicate 8 total	0.6 0.69	Perfect Indicative	3 3	42.86 37.5
			Perfect Participle	2 3	28.57 37.5
Infinitive Construct	612	52.7	Aorist Indicative	41	6.7
			Imperfect Indicative	3	
			Perfect Indicative	1	
			Present Indicative	1	
			Future Indicative	1	
			Aorist Participle	4	
			Present Participle	72	11.77
			Perfect Participle	1	
			Aorist Infinitive	313	51.14
			Present Infinitive	93	15.19
			Perfect Infinitive	3	
			Aorist Subjunctive	6	
Infinitive Absolute	3	0.26	Present Participle	3	
Q^etol Imperative	1	0.09	Aorist Subjunctive	1	
Total	1162	100			

TABLE 24: GREEK VERB FORMS IN SUBORDINATE CLAUSES

Subordinate Clauses	TOTAL	Percentage of Total	Translation Equivalent	TOTAL	Percentage of form
Aorist	375	58.05	Qatal	312	83.2
			Yiqtol	3	
			Qotel	1 predicate 1 total	
			Infinitive Construct	41	10.93
			Noun Sentence and Plus	18	4.8
Imperfect	52	8.05	Qatal	28	53.85

			Yiqtol	2	
			Qotel	3 predicate 3 total	
			Infinitive Construct	3	
			Noun Sentence and Plus	16	30.77
Perfect	19	2.94	*Qatal*	14	73.68
			Qotel	1 predicate 1 total	
			Qatul	3 predicate 3 total	
			Infinitive Construct	1	
Present	45	6.97	*Qatal*	3	
			Yiqtol	4	
			Qotel	9 predicate 9 total	20
			Infinitive Construct	1	
			Noun, Noun Sentence, and Plus	28	62.22
Future	28	4.33	*Yiqtol*	23	82.14
			Qotel	1 predicate 2 total	
			Infinitive Construct	1	
			Noun Sentence and Plus	2	
Aorist Participle	26	4.02	*Qatal*	20	76.92
			Yiqtol	1	
			Qotel	0 predicate 1 total	
			Infinitive Construct	4	
Present Participle	91	14.09	*Qatal*	2	
			Yiqtol	1	
			Qotel	2 predicate 10 total	
			Infinitive Construct	72	79.12
			Qᵉtol **Infin. Absolute**	3	
			Noun	3	

Perfect Participle	10	1.55	*Qatal*	1	
			Qotel	2 predicate 4 total	
			Qatul	2 predicate 3 total	
			Infinitive Construct	1	
			Plus	1	
Total	646	100			

BIBLIOGRAPHY

Aejmelaeus, Anneli. *Parataxis in the Septuagint: A Study of the Renderings of the Hebrew Coordinate Clauses in the Greek Pentateuch.* Helsinki: Suomalainen Tiedeakatemia, 1982.

———. "*Participium Coniunctum* as a Criterion of Translation Technique." Pages 7-16 in *On the Trail of the Septuagint Translators: Collected Essays.* Kampen: Kok Pharos Publishing House, 1993.

———. "The Septuagint of 1 Samuel." Pages 131-149 in *On the Trail of the Septuagint Translators: Collected Essays.* Kampen: Kok Pharos Publishing House, 1993.

———. "What We Talk about When We Talk about Translation Technique." Pages 531-552 in *X Congress of the International Organization for Septuagint and Cognate Studies, Oslo 1998.* Edited by Bernard A. Taylor. Septuagint and Cognate Studies 51. Atlanta: Society of Biblical Literature Publications, 2001.

Aitken, James K. "Rhetoric and Poetry in Greek Ecclesiastes." *Bulletin of the International Organization for Septuagint and Cognate Studies* 38 (2005): 55-77.

Allen, Leslie C. *The Greek Chronicles: The Relation of the Septuagint of I and II Chronicles to the Massoretic Text.* Vetus Testamentum Supplements 25, 27. 2 vols. Leiden: Brill, 1974.

Andersen, Francis I. *The Sentence in Biblical Hebrew.* The Hague: Mouton, 1974.

Aristeas. *Letter of Aristeas.* Translated by H. St. J. Thackeray in *An Introduction to the Old Testament in Greek,* by Henry B. Swete. Cambridge: Cambridge University Press, 1902.

Auld, A. Graeme. *Kings without Privilege: David and Moses in the Story of the Bible's Kings.* Edinburgh: T & T Clark, 1994.

Baden, Joel S. "The *wᵉyiqtol* and the Volitive Sequence." *Vetus Testamentum* 58 (2008): 147-158.

Bakker, Egbert J. "Foregrounding and Indirect Discourse: Temporal Subclauses in a Herodotean Short Story." *Journal of Pragmatics* 16 (1991): 225-47.

———. "Verbal Aspect and Mimetic Description in Thucydides." Pages 7-34 in *Grammar as Interpretation: Greek Literature in Its Linguistic Contexts.* Edited by Egbert J. Bakker. Leiden: Brill, 1997.

Bandstra, Barry L. "Word Order and Emphasis in Biblical Hebrew Narrative." Pages 109-123 in *Linguistics and Biblical Hebrew.* Edited by Walter Bodine. Winona Lake: Eisenbrauns, 1992.

Barclay, John. *Jews in the Mediterranean Diaspora.* Edinburgh: T & T Clark, 1996.

Barr, James. *The Typology of Literalism in Ancient Bible Translations.* Mitteilungen des Septuaginta-Unternehmens 15. Göttingen: Vandenhoeck & Ruprecht, 1979.

———. "Translators' Handling of Verb Tense in Semantically Ambiguous Contexts." Pages 381-403 in *LXX VI Congress of the International Organization for Septuagint and Cognate Studies, Jerusalem 1986.* Edited by Claude Cox. Septuagint and Cognate Studies 23. Atlanta: Scholars Press, 1986.

———. Review of Karen H. Jobes and Moisés Silva, *Invitation to the Septuagint. Review of Biblical Literature* (10/2002): online at http://www.bookreviews.org/bookdetail.asp?TitleID=1341 (5 Nov. 2002).

———. "Did the Greek Pentateuch Really Serve as a Dictionary for the Translators of the Later Books?" Pages 523-543 in *Hamlet on a Hill: Semitic and Greek Studies Presented to Professor T. Muraoka on the Occasion of His Sixty-Fifth Birthday.* Edited by M. F. J. Baasten and W. Th. van Peursen. Orientalia Lovaniensia Analecta 118. Louvain: Peeters, 2003.

Barthélemy, Dominique. *Les Devanciers d'Aquila.* Vetus Testamentum Supplements 10.

Leiden: Brill, 1963.

———. "Pourquoi la Torah a-t-elle été traduite en grec?" Pages 23-41 in *On Language, Culture, and Religion: In Honor of Eugene A. Nida.* Edited by M. Black and W. A. Smalley. The Hague: Mouton, 1974.

Beale, Todd S., and William A. Banks. *Old Testament Parsing Guide.* Chicago: Moody Press, 1986.

Beck, John A. *Translators as Storytellers: A Study in Septuagint Translation Technique.* New York: Peter Lang, 2000.

Bickerman, Elias J. "The Septuagint as a Translation." Pages 167-200 in *Studies in Jewish and Christian History.* Vol. 1. Edited by Elias J. Bickerman. Leiden: Brill, 1976.

Binnick, Robert I. *Time and the Verb: A Guide to Tense and Aspect.* Oxford: Oxford University Press, 1991.

Blass, Friedrich, and Albert Debrunner. *A Greek Grammar of the New Testament and Other Early Christian Literature.* Translated by R. W. Funk. Chicago: University of Chicago Press, 1961.

Brock, Sebastian P. "The Phenomenon of the Septuagint." *Oudtestamentische Studiën* 17 (1972): 11-36.

———. "The Phenomenon of Biblical Translation in Antiquity." Pages 541-571 in *Studies in the Septuagint: Origins, Recensions, and Interpretations: Selected Essays.* Edited by Sidney Jellicoe. New York: Ktav, 1974.

———. "Aspects of Translation Technique in Antiquity." *Greek, Roman, and Byzantine Studies* 20 (1979): 69-87.

———. "Translating the Old Testament." Pages 87-98 in *It is Written: Scripture Citing Scripture: Essays in Honour of Barnabas Lindars.* Edited by D. A. Carson and Hugh G. M. Williamson. Cambridge: Cambridge University Press, 1988.

———. "To Revise or Not to Revise: Attitudes to Jewish Biblical Translation." Pages in 301-338 in *Septuagint, Scrolls, and Cognate Writings.* Edited by George J. Brooke and Barnabas Lindars. Septuagint and Cognate Studies 33. Atlanta: Society of Biblical Literature, 1992.

Brooke, Alan England, and Norman McLean, editors. *The Old Testament in Greek, according to the Text of Codex Vaticanus, Supplemented from Other Uncial Manuscripts, with a Critical Apparatus Containing the Variants of the Chief Ancient Authorities for the Text of the Septuagint.* Cambridge: Cambridge University Press, 1906-1940.

Brown, John Pairman. "The Septuagint as a Source of the Greek Loan-Words in the Targums." *Biblica* 70 (1989): 194-216.

Browning, Robert. *Medieval and Modern Greek.* Cambridge: Cambridge University Press, 1983.

Busto Sáiz, José Ramón. *La traducción de Símaco en el libro de los Salmos.* Madrid: CSIC, 1978.

Buth, Randall. "Hebrew Poetic Tenses and the Magnificat." *Journal for the Study of the New Testament* 21 (1984): 67-83.

———. "Methodological Collision between Source Criticism and Discourse Analysis: The Problem of 'Unmarked Temporal Overlay' and the Pluperfect/Nonsequential *Wayyiqtol.*" Pages 138-54 in *Biblical Hebrew and Discourse Linguistics.* Edited by R. D. Bergen. Dallas: Summer School of Lingusitics, 1994.

———. "Functional Grammar, Hebrew and Aramaic: An Integrated Textlinguistic Approach to Syntax." Pages 77-102 in *Discourse Analysis of Biblical Literature: What It Is and What It Offers.* Edited by Walter R. Bodine. Society of Biblical Literature Semeia Series. Atlanta: Scholars Press, 1995.

Campbell, Constantine C. *Verbal Aspect, the Indicative Mood, and Narrative: Soundings in the*

Greek of the New Testament. Studies in Biblical Greek 13. New York: Peter Lang, 2007.

——. *Verbal Aspect and Non-Indicative Verbs: Further Soundings in the Greek of the New Testament.* Studies in Biblical Greek 15. New York: Peter Lang, 2008.

——. *Basics of Verbal Aspect in Biblical Greek.* Grand Rapids: Zondervan, 2008.

Charles, Robert Henry. *The Apocrypha and Pseudepigrapha of the Old Testament in English.* Oxford: Clarendon Press, 1913.

Collins, C. John. "The *Wayyiqtol* As 'Pluperfect': When and Why." *Tyndale Bulletin* 46 (1995): 117-40.

Collins, Nina L. *The Library in Alexandria and the Bible in Greek.* Vetus Testamentum Supplements 82. Leiden: Brill, 2000.

Comrie, Bernard. *Tense.* Cambridge: Cambridge University Press, 1985.

Conybeare, F. C. and St. George Stock. *A Grammar of Septuagint Greek: with Selected Readings from the Septuagint according to the Text of Swete.* Peabody: Hendrickson, 1988.

Cook, Johann. "The Septuagint as Contextual Bible Translation—Alexandria or Jerusalem as Context for Proverbs?" *Journal of Northwest Semitic Languages* XIX (1993): 25-39.

Cook, John A. "The Hebrew Verb: A Grammaticalization Approach." *Zeitschrift für Althebräistik* 14 (2001): 117-143.

——. "The Semantics of Verbal Pragmatics." Paper presented at the annual meeting of the SBL. Toronto, Canada, November 25, 2002.

——. "The Hebrew Participle and Stative in Typological Perspective." *Journal of Northwest Semitic Languages* 34/1 (2008): 1-19.

Corwin, Rebecca. *The Verb and the Sentence in Chronicles, Ezra, and Nehemiah.* Borna, near Leipzig: The Dissertations Printer Robert Noske, 1909.

Cowe, S. Peter. "To the Reader of 1 and 2 Supplements." Pages 342-348 in *A New English Translation of the Septuagint.* Edited by Albert Pietersma and Benjamin G. Wright. New York: Oxford University Press, 2007.

Creason, Stuart Alan. "Word Order in Relative Clauses." Paper presented at the annual meeting of the SBL. Washington, D.C., November, 1993.

——. "Semantic Classes of Hebrew Verbs: A Study of Aktionsart in the Hebrew Verbal System." Ph.D. diss., University of Chicago, 1996.

Culy, Martin M. "The Clue is in the Case: Distinguishing Adjectival and Adverbial Participles." *Perspectives in Religious Studies* 30 (2003): 441-453.

Dawson, David Allen. *Text-Linguistics and Biblical Hebrew.* Sheffield: Sheffield Academic Press, 1994.

Dik, Helma. *Word Order in Ancient Greek: A Pragmatic Account of Word Order Variation in Herodotus.* Amsterdam: J. C. Gieben, 1995.

——. "Interpreting Adjective Position in Herodotus." Pages 55-76 in *Grammar as Interpretation: Greek Literature in Its Linguistic Contexts.* Edited by Egbert J. Bakker. Leiden: Brill, 1997.

Dines, Jennifer M. *The Septuagint.* London: T&T Clark, 2004.

Dobbs-Allsopp, F. W. "Biblical Hebrew Statives and Situation Aspect." *Journal of Semitic Studies* 45 (2000): 21-53.

Driver, Godfrey R. *Problems of the Hebrew Verbal System.* Edinburgh: T & T Clark, 1936.

Driver, Samuel R. *A Treatise on the Use of Tenses in Hebrew and Some Other Syntactical Questions.* Grand Rapids: Eerdmans, 1998.

Endo, Yoshinobu. *The Verbal System of Classical Hebrew in the Joseph Story: An Approach from Discourse Analysis.* Studia Semitica Neerlandica 37. Assen: Van Gorcum, 1996.

Eskhult, Mats. *Studies in Verbal Aspect and Narrative Technique in Biblical Hebrew Prose.*

Studia Semitica Upsaliensis 12. Uppsala: Acta Universitatis Upsaliensis, 1990.

Eupolemus. Pages 225-228 in *Fragmenta Historicorum Graecorum*. Vol. 3. Edited by Carolus Müller. Frankfurt/Main: Minerva, 1975.

Eusebius. *Praeparatio Evangelica*. English Title: *Preparation for the Gospel*. Translated by Edwin Hamilton Gifford. Grand Rapids: Baker, 1981.

Evans, Trevor Vivian. *Verbal Syntax in the Greek Pentateuch: Natural Greek Usage and Hebrew Interference*. Oxford: Oxford University Press, 2001.

——. "Some Alleged Confusions in Translation from Hebrew to Greek." *Biblica* 83 (2002): 238-248.

Ewald, G. Heinrich A. von. *Kritische Grammatik der Hebräischen Sprache des Alten Testaments*. Leipzig: Hahn, 1827.

Fallon, F. "Eupolemus." Pages 861-72 in *The Old Testament Pseudepigrapha*. Vol. 2. Edited by James H. Charlesworth. Garden City: Doubleday, 1983.

Fanning, Buist M. *Verbal Aspect in New Testament Greek*. Oxford: Clarendon Press, 1990.

——. "Approaches to Verbal Aspect in New Testament Greek: Issues in Definition and Method." Pages 46-62 in *Biblical Greek Language and Linguistics: Open Questions in Current Research*. Sheffield: Sheffield Academic Press, 1993.

Fernández Marcos, Natalio. *The Septuagint in Context: Introduction to the Greek Version of the Bible*. Translated by Wilfred G. E. Watson. Leiden: Brill, 2000.

Finley, Thomas J. "The *Waw*-Consecutive with 'Imperfect' in Biblical Hebrew: Theoretical Studies and Its Use in Amos." Pages 241-262 in *Essays in Honor of Charles Lee Feinberg*. Edited by John S. Feinberg and Paul D. Feinberg. Chicago: Moody Press, 1981.

Freedman, David Noel. "The Chronicler's Purpose." *Catholic Biblical Quarterly* 23 (1961): 436-442.

Garr, Randall. "Affectedness, Aspect, and Biblical Hebrew *'et*." *Zeitschrift für Althebräistik* 2 (1991): 119-134.

Gentry, Peter. *The Asterisked Materials in the Greek Job*. Society of Biblical Literature Septuagint and Cognate Studies 38. Atlanta: Scholars Press, 1995.

——. "The System of the Finite Verb in Classical Biblical Hebrew." *Hebrew Studies* 39 (1998): 7-39.

Gerleman, Gillis. *Studies in the Septuagint II. Chronicles*. Lunds Universitets Arsskrift 43/3. Lund: Gleerup, 1946.

Gesenius, W., E. Kautzsch and E. A. Cowley. *Gesenius' Hebrew Grammar*. Oxford: Clarendon Press, 1910.

Goldfajn, Tal. *Word Order and Time in Biblical Hebrew Narrative*. Oxford: Clarendon Press, 1998.

Greenberg, Joseph. "Some Universals of Grammar with Particular Reference to the Order of Meaningful Elements." Pages 73-113 in *Universals of Language*. Edited by J. Greenberg. Cambridge: MIT Press, 1966. Cited 23 January 2008. Online: http://angli02.kgw.tu-berlin.de/Korean/Artikel02/.

Gundry, Robert H. "The Language Milieu of First-Century Palestine: Its Bearing on the Authenticity of the Gospel Tradition." *Journal of Biblical Literature* 83:4 (1964): 404-408.

Hanhart, Robert. "Earlier Tradition and Subsequent Influences." Pages 339-379 in *Septuagint, Scrolls, and Cognate Writings*. Edited by George J. Brooke and Barnabas Lindars. Septuagint and Cognate Studies 33. Atlanta: Society of Biblical Literature, 1992.

Harl, Marguerite, Gilles Dorival, and Olivier Munnich. *La Bible grecque des Septante: Du judaïsme hellénistique au christianisme ancien*. Paris: Cerf, 1988.

Hatav, Galia. *The Semantics of Aspect and Modality*. Amsterdam: John Benjamins, 1997.

Heimerdinger, Jean-Marc. *Topic, Focus, and Foreground in Ancient Hebrew Narratives.* Journal for the Study of the Old Testament: Supplement Series 295. Sheffield: Sheffield Academic Press, 1999.

Hody, Humphrey. "Contra Historiam Aristeae de LXX Interpretibus Dissertatio." Pages 1-89 in *De Bibliorum Textibus.* Oxford: Oxford University Press, 1705.

Holmstedt, Robert. "The Relative Clause in Biblical Hebrew: A Linguistic Analysis." Ph.D. diss., University of Wisconsin, Madison, 2002.

Honigman, Sylvie. *The Septuagint and Homeric Scholarship in Alexandria: A Study in the Narrative of the Letter of Aristeas.* New York: Routledge, 2003.

Hopper, Paul J. "Aspect and Foregrounding in Discourse." Pages 213-242 in *Syntax and Semantics: Discourse and Syntax* 12. Edited by Talmy Givon. New York: Academic Press, 1979.

Howard, George. "The Septuagint: A Review of Recent Studies." *Restoration Quarterly* 13 (1970): 154-164.

Hurvitz, Avi. *Bein Lashon Lelashon.* English Title: *Biblical Hebrew in Transition—A Study in Post-Exilic Hebrew and its Implications for the Dating of the Psalms.* Jerusalem: Bialik Institute, 1972.

Janowitz, Naomi. "The Rhetoric of Translation: Three Early Perspectives on Translating Torah." *Harvard Theological Review* 84 (1991): 129-140.

Japhet, Sara. *I & II Chronicles: A Commentary.* Old Testament Library. Louisville: Westminster, John Knox Press, 1993.

Jellicoe, Sydney. *The Septuagint and Modern Study.* Oxford: Oxford University Press, 1968.

———. "Some Reflections on the **KAIΓE** Recension." *Vetus Testamentum* 23 (1973): 15-24

Jobes, Karen H., and Moisés Silva. *Invitation to the Septuagint.* Grand Rapids: Baker, 2000.

Joosten, Jan. "Pseudo-Classicisms in Late Biblical Hebrew, in Ben Sira, and in Qumran Hebrew." Pages 146-159 in *Sirach, Scrolls, and Sages.* Edited by T. Muraoka and J. F. Elwolde. Studies on the Texts of the Desert of Judah 33. Leiden: Brill, 1999.

———. "Biblical Hebrew as Mirrored in the Septuagint: The Question of Influence from Spoken Hebrew." *Textus* 21 (2002): 1-19.

———. "Disappearance of Iterative WEQATAL." Pages 135-147 in *Biblical Hebrew in Its Northwest Semitic Setting: Typological and Historical Perspectives.* Edited by S. Fassberg and A. Hurvitz. Winona Lake: Eisenbrauns, 2006.

———. "Reflections on the 'Interlinear Paradigm' in Septuagintal Studies." Pages 163-178 in *Scripture in Transition: Essays on Septuagint, Hebrew Bible, and Dead Sea Scrolls in Honour of Raija Sollamo.* Edited by Anssi Voitila and Jutta Jokiranta. Supplements to the Journal for the Study of Judaism 126. Leiden: Brill, 2008.

Joüon, Paul, and Takamitsu Muruoka. *A Grammar of Biblical Hebrew.* 2 Vols. Rome: Pontifical Biblical Institute, 1991.

Klein, Ralph. "Chronicles, Book of 1-2." Pages 992-1002 in vol. 1 of *The Anchor Bible Dictionary.* Edited by David Noel Freedman. 6 vols. New York: Doubleday, 1992.

Knoppers, Gary N. and Paul B. Harvey. "Omitted and Remaining Matters: On the Names Given to the Book of Chronicles in Antiquity." *Journal of Biblical Literature* 121 (2002): 227-243.

Kropat, A. *Die Syntax des Autors der Chronik verglichen mit der seiner Quellen.* Beihefte zur Zeitschrift für die alttestamentliche Wissenschaft 16. Gießen: Verlag von Alfred Töpelmann, 1909.

Lange, Armin. "'Considerable Proficiency' (*Letter of Aristeas* 121): The Relationship of the *Letter of Aristeas* to the Prologue of Ecclesiasticus." Paper presented at the annual meeting of the SBL. San Diego, Ca., November 19, 2007.

Levin, Yigal. "Who Was the Chronicler's Audience? A Hint from His Genealogies," *Journal of Biblical Literature* 122 (2003): 229-245.

Levine, Lee I. *Judaism and Hellenism in Antiquity: Conflict or Confluence?* Peabody: Hendrickson, 1999.

Long, Gary. "The Written Story: Toward Understanding Text as Representation and Function." *Vetus Testamentum* 49 (1999): 165-185.

Longacre, Robert E. *Joseph, a Story of Divine Providence. A Text Theoretical and Textlinguistic Analysis of Genesis 37 and 39-48.* Winona Lake: Eisenbrauns, 1985.

———. "Discourse Perspective on the Hebrew Verb: Affirmation and Restatement." Pages 177-89 in *Linguistics and Biblical Hebrew.* Edited by Walter Bodine. Winona Lake: Eisenbrauns, 1992.

———. "*Weqatal* Forms in Biblical Hebrew Prose." Pages 50-98 in *Biblical Hebrew and Discourse Linguistics.* Edited by Robert D. Bergen. Dallas: Summer Institute of Linguistics, 1994.

———. "Mark 5.1-43: Generating the Complexity of a Narrative from Its Most Basic Elements." Pages 169-96 in *Discourse Analysis and the New Testament: Approaches and Results.* Edited by Stanley Porter and Jeffrey T. Reed. Journal for the Study of the New Testament: Supplement Series 170. Sheffield: Sheffield Academic Press, 1999.

Mandilaras, Basil G. *The Verb in the Greek Non-Literary Papyri.* Athens: Hellenic Ministry of Culture and Sciences, 1973.

Marquis, Galen. "Word Order As a Criterion for the Evaluation of Translation Technique in the LXX and the Evaluation of Word Order Variants As Exemplified in LXX-Ezekiel." *Textus* 13 (1986): 59-84.

Martin, W. J. "'Dischronologized' Narrative in the Old Testament." Pages 179-186 in *Congress Volume: Rome 1968.* Supplements to Vetus Testamentum 17. Leiden: Brill, 1969.

McFall, Leslie. *The Enigma of the Hebrew Verbal System.* Sheffield: Almond Press, 1982.

McKay, Kenneth L. *A New Syntax of the Verb in New Testament Greek: An Aspectual Approach.* Studies in Biblical Greek 5. New York: Peter Lang, 1994.

McKenzie, Steven L. *The Chronicler's Use of the Deuteronomistic History.* Atlanta: Scholars Press, 1985.

Mélèze-Modrzejewski, Joseph. "How to Be a Greek and Yet a Jew in Hellenistic Alexandria." Pages 65-91 in *Diasporas in Antiquity.* Edited by Shaye J. D. Cohen and Ernest S. Frerichs. Brown Judaic Studies 288. Atlanta: Scholars Press, 1993.

Miller, Cynthia L. *The Representation of Speech in Biblical Hebrew Narrative: A Linguistic Analysis.* Harvard Semitic Monographs 55. Atlanta: Scholars Press, 1996.

Moulton, James Hope. *A Grammar of New Testament Greek I. Prolegomena.* Edinburgh: T & T Clark, 1908.

Nash, Peter Theodore. "The Hebrew Qal Active Participle: A Non-Aspectual Narrative Backgrounding Element." Ph.D. diss., University of Chicago, 1992.

Niccacci, Alviero. "On the Hebrew Verbal System." Pages 117-137 in *Biblical Hebrew and Discourse Linguistics.* Edited by Robert D. Bergen. Dallas: Summer Institute of Linguistics, 1994.

———. "Analysis of Biblical Narrative." Pages 175-98 in *Biblical Hebrew and Discourse Linguistics.* Edited by Robert D. Bergen. Dallas: Summer Institute of Linguistics, 1994.

———. Review of David Allen Dawson, *Text-Linguistics and Biblical Hebrew. Liber annuus Studii biblici franciscani* 45 (1995): 543-80.

———. "Basic Facts and the Theory of the Biblical Hebrew Verb System in Prose." Pages 167-202 in *Narrative Syntax and the Hebrew Bible: Papers of the Tilburg Conference 1996*. Edited by Ellen van Wolde. Leiden: Brill, 1997.

Nickelsburg, George W. E., with Robert A. Kraft. "Introduction: The Modern Study of Early Judaism." Pages 1-30 in *Early Judaism and Its Modern Interpreters*. Edited by Robert A. Kraft and George W. E. Nickelsburg. Vol. 2 of *The Bible and Its Modern Interpreters*. Edited by Douglas A. Knight. Atlanta: Scholars Press, 1986.

Nickelsburg, George W. E. *Jewish Literature between the Bible and the Mishnah*. Minneapolis: Fortress Press, 2005.

Nida, Eugene A. *Towards a Science of Translating*. Leiden: Brill, 1964.

Notley, R. Steven. "Non-Septuagintal Hebraisms in the Third Gospel." Paper presented at the annual meeting of the SBL. Boston, Mass., November 22, 2008.

Olofsson, Staffan. *The LXX Version: A Guide to the Translation Technique of the Septuagint*. Coniectanea Biblica: Old Testament Series 30. Stockholm: Almqvist & Wiksell, 1990.

Owens, John Joseph. *Analytical Key to the Old Testament*. Vol. 2. Grand Rapids: Baker, 1992.

Pearce, Sarah. "Contextualising Greek Chronicles." Pages 22-27 in *Zutot* 2001; Edited by S. Berger, M. Brocke, and I. Zwiep. Dordrecht/Boston: Kluwer Academic Publishers, 2002.

———. "Hairy Feet or Just Plane Hares: Monarchy in the Greek Pentateuch." Paper presented at an International Colloquium of the AHRB Greek Bible Project. Oxford, March 24, 2003.

Pérez Fernández, Miguel. *An Introductory Grammar of Rabbinic Hebrew*. Translated by John Elwolde. Leiden: Brill, 1997.

Philo. *De Vita Mosis*. Philo Vol. 7. Translated by F. H. Colson. Cambridge: Harvard University Press, 1950.

Pietersma, Albert. "The Place of Origin of the Old Greek Psalter." Pages 252-274 in *The World of the Aramaeans I. Biblical Studies in Honour of Paul-Eugène Dion*. Edited by P. M. Michèle Daviau, John Wevers and Michael Weigl. Journal for the Study of the Old Testament. Supplement Series 324. Sheffield: Sheffield Academic Press, 2001.

———. "A New Paradigm for Addressing Old Questions: The Relevance of the Interlinear Model for the Study of the Septuagint." Pages 337-64 in *Bible and Computer: The Stellenbosch AIBI-6 Conference. Proceedings of the Association Internationale Bible et Informatique "From Alpha to Byte". University of Stellenbosch 17-21 July, 2000*. Edited by Johann Cook. Leiden: Brill, 2002.

———. "LXX and DTS: A New Archimedean Point for Septuagint Studies?" *Bulletin of the International Organization for Septuagint and Cognate Studies* 39 (2006): 1-11.

———. "Beyond Literalism: Interlinearity Revisited." Paper presented at the annual meeting of the SBL. Boston, Mass., November 24, 2008.

Pietersma, Albert and Marc Saunders. "Introduction to *A New English Translation of the Septuagint* (NETS Provisional Edition) *Ieremias*, IOSCS, 2005. Cited 30 January 2007. Online at http://ccat.sas.upenn.edu/nets/edition/ier.pdf.

Polak, Frank H. "Context Sensitive Translation and Parataxis in Biblical Narrative." Pages 525-539 in *Emanuel: Studies in Hebrew Bible, Septuagint, and Dead Sea Scrolls in Honor of Emanuel Tov*. Edited by Shalom M. Paul, Robert A. Kraft, Weston W. Fields. Supplements to Vetus Testamentum 94. Leiden, Brill, 2003.

Polzin, Robert. *Late Biblical Hebrew Toward an Historical Typology of Biblical Hebrew Prose*. Harvard Semitic Monographs 12. Missoula: Scholars Press, 1976.

Porter, Stanley E. *Verbal Aspect in the Greek of the New Testament, with Reference to Tense and*

Mood. Studies in Biblical Greek 1. New York: Peter Lang, 1993.

———. *Idioms of the Greek New Testament.* Biblical Languages: Greek 2. Sheffield: Sheffield Academic Press, 1999.

Rabin, Chaim. "The Translation Process and the Character of the Septuagint." *Textus* 6 (1968): 1-26.

Rehm, Martin. *Textkritische Untersuchungen zu den Parallelstellen der Samuel-Königsbücher und der Chronik.* Altestamentliche Abhandlungen 13/3. Münster: Aschendorff, 1937.

Reichenbach, Hans. *Elements of Symbolic Logic.* New York: Macmillan Co. 1947.

Rendsburg, Gary. *Diglossia in Ancient Israel.* New Haven: American Oriental Society, 1990.

Revell, Ernest John. "Stress and the *Waw* 'Consecutive' in Biblical Hebrew." *Journal of the American Oriental Society* 104 (1984): 437-44.

———. "The Conditioning of Stress Position in *Waw* Consecutive Perfect Forms in Biblical Hebrew." *Hebrew Annual Review* 9 (1985): 277-300.

Rife, J. Merle. "The Mechanics of Translation Greek." *Journal of Biblical Literature* 52 (1933): 244-252.

Rijksbaron, Albert. *The Syntax and Semantics of the Verb in Classical Greek: An Introduction.* Amsterdam: J. C. Gieben, 1994.

Robertson, Archibald Thomas. *A Grammar of the Greek New Testament in the Light of Historical Research.* Nashville: Broadman Press, 1934.

Rogers, V. M. "The Old Greek Version of Chronicles: A Comparative Study of the LXX with the Hebrew Text from a Theological Approach." Ph.D. diss., Princeton Theological Seminary, 1954.

Rosenbaum, Michael. *Word-Order Variation in Isaiah 40-55: A Functional Perspective.* Assen: Van Gorcum, 1997.

Rundgren, Fritz. *Das Althebräische Verbum. Abriss Der Aspektlehre.* Uppsala: Almqvist and Wiksell, 1961.

Sáenz-Badillos, Angel. *A History of the Hebrew Language.* Cambridge: Cambridge University Press, 1993.

Sailhamer, John H. *The Translation Technique of the Greek Septuagint for the Hebrew Verbs and Participles in Psalms 3-41.* New York: Peter Lang, 1991.

Salvesen, Alison. Review of Claude Cox, ed., *LXX VI Congress of the International Organization for Septuagint and Cognate Studies, Jerusalem 1986. Journal of Semitic Studies* 34 (1989): 203-205.

———. *Symmachus in the Pentateuch.* Manchester: University of Manchester, 1991.

Schattner-Rieser, Ursula. "L'hébreu post-exilique." Pages 189-224 in *La Palestine à l'époque perse.* Edited by E.-M. Laperrousaz and A. Lemaire. Paris: Cerf, 1994.

Schehr, Timothy P. "Syntax of the Moods and Tenses of the Greek Verb in Septuagint Genesis 1-15." Ph.D. diss., Hebrew Union College, 1990.

———. "The Perfect Indicative in Septuagint Genesis." *Bulletin of the International Organization for Septuagint and Cognate Studies* 24 (1991): 14-24.

Schmidt, Daryl D. "Verbal Aspect in Greek: Two Approaches." Pages 63-73 in *Biblical Greek Language and Linguistics: Open Questions in Current Research.* Sheffield: Sheffield Academic Press, 1993.

Schneider, Wolfgang. *Grammatik des biblischen Hebräisch: ein Lehrbuch.* Munich: Claudius Verlag, 1974.

Schniedewind, William M. *The Word of God in Transition: From Prophet to Exegete in the Second Temple Period.* Journal for the Study of the Old Testament. Supplement Series 197. Sheffield: Sheffield Academic Press, 1995.

———. "Qumran Hebrew as an Antilanguage." *Journal of Biblical Literature* 118 (1999): 235-252.

——. *Society and the Promise to David: The Reception History of 2 Samuel 7:1-17.* Oxford: Oxford University Press, 1999.

——. Review of Ziony Zevit, *The Anterior Construction in Classical Hebrew. Bulletin of the American Schools of Oriental Research* 318 (2000): 79-81.

Shenkel, James Donald. "A Comparative Study of the Synoptic Parallels in I Paraleipomena and I-II Reigns." *Harvard Theological Review* 62 (1969): 63-85.

Smith, Mark. *The Origins and Development of the Waw-Consecutive: Northwest Semitic Evidence from Ugarit to Qumran.* Atlanta: Scholars Press, 1991.

Soisalon-Soininen, Ilmari. *Die Infinitive in der Septuaginta.* Annales Academiae Scientiarum Fennicae. Helsinki: Suomalainen Tiedeakatemia, 1965.

Sollamo, Raija. *Renderings of Hebrew Semiprepositions in the Septuagint.* Annales Academiae Scientiarum Fennicae, Dissertationes Humanarum. Litterarum 19. Helsinki, Suomalainen Tiedeakatemia, 1979.

——. "The Letter of Aristeas and the Origin of the Septuagint." Pages in 329-342 in *X Congress of the International Organization for Septuagint and Cognate Studies, Oslo 1998.* Edited by Bernard A. Taylor. Septuagint and Cognate Studies 51. Atlanta: Society of Biblical Literature Publications, 2001.

Sternberg, Meir. "Temporal Discontinuity, Narrative Interest, and the Emergence of Meaning." Pages 264-320 in *The Poetics of Biblical Narrative: Ideological Literature and the Drama of Reading.* Edited by Meir Sternberg. Bloomington: Indiana University Press, 1985.

Talmud. Minor tractates. Soferim. *Massekhet Soferim.* Edited by Michael Higger. New York: Debe Rabanan, 1937.

Talstra, Eep, and Arian J. C. Verheij. "Comparing Samuel/Kings and Chronicles: The Computer Assisted Production of an Analytical Synoptic Database." *Textus* 14 (1988): 41-60.

Thacker, Thomas William. *The Relationship of the Semitic and Egyptian Verbal System.* Oxford: Oxford University Press, 1954.

Thackeray, Harold St. J. *The Septuagint and Jewish Worship: A Study in Origins.* London: H. Milford, 1923.

Toury, Gideon. "A Handful of Methodological Issues in DTS: Are They Applicable to the Study of the Septuagint as an Assumed Translation? *Bulletin of the International Organization for Septuagint and Cognate Studies* 39 (2006): 13-25.

Tov, Emanuel. *The Septuagint Translation of Jeremiah and Baruch: A Discussion of an Early Revision of the LXX of Jeremiah 29-52 and Baruch 1:1—3:8.* Missoula: Scholars Press, 1975.

——. "The Impact of the LXX Translation of the Pentateuch on the Translation of Other Books." Pages 577-592 in *Mélanges Dominique Barthélemy: Études bibliques offertes à l'occasion de son 60e anniversaire.* Edited by P. Casetti, O. Keel, A. Schenker. Göttingen: Vandenhoeck & Ruprecht, 1981.

——. "The Representation of the Causative Aspects of the *Hiph'il* in the Septuagint—A Study in Translation Technique." *Biblica* 63 (1982): 417-424.

——. "The Septuagint." Pages 161-188 in *Mikra: Text, Translation, Reading and Interpretation of the Hebrew Bible in Ancient Judaism and Early Christianity.* Edited by Martin Jan Mulder and Harry Sysling. Philadelphia: Fortress, 1988.

——. "Renderings of Combinations of the Infinitive Absolute and Finite Verbs in the Septuagint—Their Nature and Distribution." Pages 64-73 in *Studien zur Septuaginta—Robert Hanhart zu Ehren. Aus Anlaß seines 65 Geburtstages.* Edited by D. Fraenkel, U. Quast, and J. W. Wevers. Göttingen: Vandenhoeck & Ruprecht, 1990.

——. *Textual Criticism of the Hebrew Bible.* Minneapolis: Fortress, 1992.

——. *The Text-Critical Use of the Septuagint in Biblical Research*. Jerusalem Biblical Studies 3. Jerusalem: Simor, 1997.

Trebolle Barrera, Julio. "Édition préliminaire de 4QChroniques." *Revue de Qumran* 15 (1992): 523-28.

Turner, Nigel. "Biblical Greek—the Peculiar Language of a Peculiar People." Pages 505-512 in *Studia Evangelica Vol. 7. International Congress on Biblical Studies Papers 1973*. Edited by Elizabeth A. Livingstone. Berlin: Akademie Verlag, 1982.

van der Kooij, Arie. "Perspectives on the Study of the Septuagint: Who Are the Translators?" Pages 214-229 in *Perspectives in the Study of the Old Testament and Early Judaism: A Symposium in Honour of Adam S. Van Der Woude on the Occasion of His 70th Birthday*. Edited by Florentino Garcia Martinez and Ed Noort. Vetus Testamentum Supplements 73. Leiden: Brill, 1998.

van der Merwe, Christo H. J. "Discourse Linguistics and Biblical Hebrew Grammar." Pages 13-49 in *Biblical Hebrew and Discourse Linguistics*. Edited by Robert D. Bergen. Dallas: Summer Institute of Linguistics, 1994.

——. "An Overview of Hebrew Narrative Syntax." Pages 1-20 in *Narrative Syntax and the Hebrew Bible: Papers of the Tilburg Conference 1996*. Edited by Ellen van Wolde. Leiden: Brill, 1997.

van Peursen, Willem T. "The Verbal System in the Hebrew Text of Ben Sira." Ph.D. diss., Universiteit Leiden, 1999.

Vannutelli, Primus, ed. *Libri Synoptici Veteris Testamenti: Seu Librorum Regum Et Chronicorum Loci Paralleli Quos Hebraice, Graece Et Latine Critice*. Romae: Pontificio Instituto Biblico, 1931-1934.

Vendler, Zeno. "Verbs and Times." *Philosophical Review* 66 (1957): 43-60.

Verheij, Arian J. C. *Verbs and Numbers: A Study of the Frequencies of the Hebrew Verbal Tense Forms in the Books of Samuel, Kings, and Chronicles*. Studia Semitica Neerlandica 28. Assen/Maastricht: Van Gorcum, 1990.

Vermes, Geza. Review of Dominique Barthélemy, *Les Devanciers d'Aquila*. *Journal of Semitic Studies* 11 (1966): 264.

Voitila, Anssi. "La technique de traduction du *yiqtol* (l'imparfait hébreu) dans l'histoire du Joseph grecque (Gen 37, 39-50)." Pages 223-237 in *LXX VII Congress of the International Organization for Septuagint and Cognate Studies, Leuven 1989*. Edited by Claude Cox. Septuagint and Cognate Studies 31. Atlanta: Scholars Press, 1989.

——. "What the Translation of Tenses Tells about the Septuagint Translators." *Scandinavian Journal of the Old Testament* 10 (1996): 183-96.

——. *Présent et imparfait de l'indicatif dans le Pentateuque grec: une étude sur la syntaxe de traduction*. Göttingen: Vandenhoeck & Ruprecht, 2001.

Wade, Martha L. "Which Is More Literal? A Comparative Analysis of Translation Techniques and Discourse Features of 1 Kgs 11:43-12:24 and 2 Chr 9:31-11:4 in the Old Greek." Paper presented at the annual meeting of the SBL. Boston, Mass., November 24, 2008.

Wallace, Daniel B. *Greek Grammar beyond the Basics: An Exegetical Syntax of the New Testament with Scripture, Subject, and Greek Word Indexes*. Grand Rapids: Zondervan, 1996.

Waltke, Bruce K. and Michael O' Connor. *An Introduction to Biblical Hebrew Syntax*. Winona Lake: Eisenbrauns, 1990.

Wasserstein, David J. Review of Nina Collins, *The Library in Alexandria and the Bible in Greek*. *Scripta Classica Israelica* 22 (2003): 318-20.

Weitzman, Steve. "Why Did the Qumran Community Write in Hebrew?" *Journal of the American Oriental Society* 119 (1999): 35-45.

Wevers, John William. "The Use of Versions for Text Criticism The Septuagint."

Pages 15-24 in *La Septuaginta en la Investigación Contemporánea: 5th Congress of the International Organization for Septuagint and Cognate Studies 1983: Salamanca, Spain.* Edited by Natalio Fernández Marcos. Madrid: Instituto "Arias Montano," C.S.I.C., 1985.

———. *Notes on the Greek Text of Exodus.* Society of Biblical Literature Septuagint and Cognate Studies 30. Atlanta: Scholars Press, 1990.

Wikgren, Allen. *Hellenistic Greek Texts.* Chicago: University of Chicago Press, 1947.

Williamson, Hugh G. M. *New Century Bible Commentary: 1 and 2 Chronicles.* Grand Rapids: Eerdmans, 1982.

Woo, Sang-Hyuk. "Etudes sur le système verbal dans la Septante de Job." Ph.D. diss., Universite Strasbourg II—Marc Bloch Faculte de Theologie Protestante, 2006.

Wright, Benjamin G. "The Letter of Aristeas and the Reception History of the Septuagint." *Bulletin of the International Organization for Septuagint and Cognate Studies* 39 (2006): 47-67.

Zevit, Ziony. *The Anterior Construction in Classical Hebrew.* Society of Biblical Literature Monograph Series 50. Atlanta: Scholars Press, 1998.

Zuber, Beat. *Das Tempussystem des biblischen Hebräisch. Eine Untersuchung am Text.* Beiheft zur Zeitschrift für die alttestamentliche Wissenschaft 164. Berlin: Walter de Gruyter, 1986.

SUBJECT INDEX

or additions affecting word order, 237
or additions of וַיְהִי, 196
omni-temporal or timeless
  aorist, 64
  perfect (Greek), 64
  present, 53, 65, 157, 221, 222, 247
  qatal, 52, 233
  qotel, 221
  yiqtol, 53, 127, 135–36, 222
one-clause verbal utterances, 197
Onkelos, 31
opos ὅπως
  followed by a subjunctive in
    translation, 235
optative of wish, 124, 144
oral narrative, 196, 197, 198
oral translation, 30, 32

P. inv. Fouad 266, 27
P.Ryl. III 458, 27
Palestine
  Greek recensions, 27
  Greek used in, 25
  Hebrew spoken, 29, 200
  Jewish community, 2
  origin of Pentateuch translators?, 25
  Septuagint abandoned in, 40
  trilingual, 20
Palestinian halakah, 40
Palestinian text
  of Samuel-Kings, 74
papyri, 20, 27, 206, 211
parablepsis, 112, 236
  by homoioteleuton, 94, 133, 144, 209
Paraleipomenon
  agreeing with Samuel-Kings rather
    than MT, 74
  meaning, 73
parallel passages. See Samuel-Kings
  parallels
  'az אָז and yiqtol, 207
  aorist to present, 223
  historic present to aorist, 222
  periphrastic, 86
  qotel, 198
  wayyiqtol to infinitive, 92
  without וַיְהִי, 85, 94, 196
  yiqtol in past context, 195
  yiqtol in past context to periphrastic,
    195

paratactic clauses, 11. See hypotactic
  clauses
  abundant in Hebrew, 212
  by participles and δέ, 91
  changed to hypotactic, 4, 76, 238
  defined, 69
  in place of hypotactic, 154, 179, 189,
    190
  instead of infinitive, 181
  replaced by subordinate clauses, 61
paratactic string
  broken, 12, 90, 95
  broken rarely, 95, 229, 241
participle (Greek), 65–66. See aorist,
  perfect, present, attributive, and
  circumstantial participle(s)
  classification, 146
participle (Hebrew), 55–56. See qotel, qatul
  classification, 55, 145–46
peitho πείθω, 46, 216, 246
Pentateuch translation
  compared to Chronicles, 27, 39, 249
  compromise of literal and free
    translation, 33
  date, 23, 27
  earlier translation?, 32
  Greek circumstantial participle, 17,
    39, 90, 91, 229, 238, 247, 249
  Greek imperfect, 212
  Greek perfect, 216
  Greek perfects for qatal, 105
  Greek present, 219
  influence later books, 28, 32, 41
  less literal than following books, 39,
    40
  of verbs, 223, 247
  origin, 25, 26
  preceded by other books?, 32
  preceding Chronicles, 247, 248
  reason for, 22, 24
  reception of, 25, 40
  revised, 23, 27, 39
  translators, 23
  verbs, 9–11, 38
  with idiomatic Greek structures, 37
perfect indicative (Greek)
  aspect, 64
  for Hebrew passives, 162
  for qatal, 105, 113
  for qatul, 171
  God as subject, 105, 201, 216, 247

AUTHOR INDEX

INDEX OF CITATIONS OF BIBLICAL AND OTHER
ANCIENT WRITINGS

Hebrew Bible

Other Writings